C# GAME PROGRAMMING COOKBOOK for UNITY 3D

C# GAME PROGRAMMING COOKBOOK for UNITY 3D

Jeff W. Murray

CRC Press
Taylor & Francis Group
Boca Raton London New York

CRC Press is an imprint of the
Taylor & Francis Group, an **informa** business

AN A K PETERS BOOK

CRC Press
Taylor & Francis Group
6000 Broken Sound Parkway NW, Suite 300
Boca Raton, FL 33487-2742

© 2014 by Taylor & Francis Group, LLC
CRC Press is an imprint of Taylor & Francis Group, an Informa business

No claim to original U.S. Government works

Printed on acid-free paper
Version Date: 20140213

International Standard Book Number-13: 978-1-4665-8140-1 (Paperback)

Library of Congress Cataloging-in-Publication Data

Murray, Jeff W.
   C# game programming cookbook for Unity 3D / Jeff W. Murray.
    pages cm
   Includes index.
   ISBN 978-1-4665-8140-1 (paperback)
    1. Computer games--Programming. 2. C# (Computer program language) 3. Unity (Electronic resource) 4. Three-dimensional display systems. I. Title.

   QA76.76.C672M8868 2014
   794.8'1526--dc23   2013048921

Visit the Taylor & Francis Web site at
http://www.taylorandfrancis.com

and the CRC Press Web site at
http://www.crcpress.com

This book is dedicated to my boys,
Ethan and William.
Be nice to the cat.

Contents

Acknowledgments

I would like to thank my wife for all the encouragement, support, and nice cups of tea. I would also like to thank my mum and dad, my brother Steve, and everyone else who knows me. Sophie cat, be nice to the boys.

Sincere thanks go to the many people who positively influence my life directly or indirectly: Michelle Ashton, Brian Robbins, George Bray, Nadeem Rasool, Christian Boutin, James and Anna, Rich and Sharon, Liz and Peter, Rob Fearon (the curator of all things shiny), everyone on Twitter who RTs my babble (you know who you are, guys!), Matthew Smith (the creator of Manic Miner), David Braben, Tōru Iwatani, and anyone who made Atari games in the 1980s.

I would like to thank everyone at AK Peters/CRC Press for the help and support and for publishing my work.

Finally, a massive thank you goes out to you for buying this book and for wanting to do something as cool as to make games. I sincerely hope this book helps your game-making adventures—feel free to tell me about them on Twitter @psychicparrot or drop by my website at http://www.psychicparrot.com.

Introduction

As I was starting out as a game developer, as a self-taught programmer my skills took a while to reach a level where I could achieve what I wanted. Sometimes I wanted to do things that I just didn't have yet the technical skills to achieve. Now and again, software packages came along that could either help me in my quest to make games or even make full games for me; complete game systems such as the Shoot 'Em-Up Construction Kit (aka SEUCK) from Sensible Software, Gary Kitchen's GameMaker, or The Quill Adventure System could bring to life the kinds of games that went way beyond anything that my limited programming skills could ever dream of building.

The downside to using game creation software was that it was tailored to create games within their chosen specific genre. If I wanted to do something outside of the limitations of the software, the source code was inaccessible and there was no way to extend or modify it. When that happened, I longed for a modular code-based system that I could plug together to create different types of games but modify parts of it without having to spend a lot of time learning how the entire system internals work—building block game development that I could actually script and modify if I needed to.

After completing my first book, *Game Development for iOS with Unity3D*, I wanted to follow up by applying a modular style of game building to Unity3D that would provide readers with a highly flexible framework to create just about any kind of game by "plugging in" the different script components. My intention was to make a more technical second book, based on C# programming, that would offer extensibility in any direction a developer might require. In essence, what you are holding in your hands right now is a cookbook for game development that has a highly flexible core framework for just about any type of game.

A lot of the work I put in at the start of writing this book was in designing a framework that not only made sense in the context of Unity but also could easily cope with the demands of different genres.

Prerequisites

You can get up and running with the required software for the grand total of zero dollars. Everything you need can be downloaded free of charge with no catches. You may want to consider an upgrade to Unity Pro at some point in the future, to take advantage of some of its advanced features, but to get started all you need to do is grab the free version from the Unity website.

Unity Free or Unity Pro (available from the Unity store at http://www.unity3d.com)

Unity Free is completely free for anyone or any company making less than $100,000 per year—it may be downloaded for no charge at all, and you don't even need a credit card. It's a really sweet deal! We are talking about a fully functional game engine, ready to make 3D or 2D games that may be sold commercially or otherwise. There are no royalties to pay, either.

Unity Pro adds a whole host of professional functionality to the engine, such as render culling and profiling. If you are a company with more than $100,000 per year of turnover, you will need a Pro license, but if you find that Unity Free doesn't pack quite enough power, you may also want to consider going Pro. You can arrange a free trial of the Pro version right from the Unity website to try before you buy. If the trial licence runs out before you feel you know enough to make a purchase, contact Unity about extending it and they are usually very friendly and helpful about it (just don't try using a trial license for 6 months at a time, as they may just figure it out!).

C# programming knowledge

Again, to reiterate this very important point, this is *not* a book about learning how to program. You will need to know some C#, and there are a number of other books out there for that purpose, even if I have tried to make the examples as simple as possible! This book is about making games, not about learning to program.

What This Book Doesn't Cover

This is not a book about programming and it is not a book about the right or wrong way to do things. We assume that the reader has some experience with the C# programming language. I am a self-taught programmer, and I understand that there may well be better ways to do things.

This is a book about concepts, and it is inevitable that there will be better methods for achieving some of the same goals. The techniques and concepts offered in this book are meant to provide solid foundation, not to be the final word on any subject. It is the author's intention that, as you gain your own experiences in game development, you make your own rules and draw your own conclusions.

Additional material is available from the CRC Press Web site: http://www.crcpress.com/product/isbn/9781466581401.

1 Making Games the Modular Way

When I first started making games, I would approach development on a project-to-project basis, recoding and rebuilding everything from scratch each time. As I became a professional developer, landing a job at a game development studio making browser-based games, I was lucky enough to work with a guy who was innovating the scene. He was a master at turning out great games (both visually and gameplay-wise) very quickly. One secret to his success lay in the development of a reusable framework that could easily be refactored to use on all of his projects. His framework was set up to deal with server communication, input handling, browser communication, and UI among other things, saving an incredible amount of time in putting together all of the essentials. By reusing the framework, it allowed more time for him and his team to concentrate on great gameplay and graphics optimization, resulting in games that, at the time, blew the competition away. Of course, the structure was tailored to how he worked (he did build it, after all), and it took me a while to get to grips with his style of development; but once I did, it really opened my eyes. From then on, I used the framework for every project and even taught other programmers how to go about using it. Development time was substantially reduced, which left more time to concentrate on making better games.

This book is based on a similar concept of a game-centric framework for use with many different types of games, rather than a set of different games in different styles. The overall goal of this book is to provide script-based components that you can use within that framework to make a head start with your own projects in a way that reduces recoding, repurposing, or adaptation time.

In terms of this book as a cookbook, think of the framework as a base soup and the scripting components as ingredients. We can mix and match script components from different games that use the same framework to make new games, and we can share several of the same core scripts in many different games. The framework takes care of the essentials, and we add a little "glue" code to pull everything together the way we want it all to work.

This framework is, of course, optional, but you should spend some time familiarizing yourself with it to help understand the book. If you intend to use the components in this book for your own games, the framework may serve either as a base to build your games on or simply as a tutorial test bed for you to rip apart and see how things work. Perhaps you can develop a better framework or maybe you already have a solid framework in place. If you do, find a way to develop a cleaner, more efficient framework or even a framework that isn't quite so efficient but works better with your own code, and do it.

In this chapter, we start by examining some of the major programming concepts used in this book and look at how they affect the design decisions of the framework.

■ 1.1 Important Programming Concepts

I had been programming in C# for a fairly long time before I actually sat down and figured out some of the concepts covered in this chapter. It was not because of any particular problem or difficulty with the concepts themselves but more because I had solved the problems in a different way that meant I had no real requirement to learn anything new. For most programmers, these concepts will be second nature and perhaps something taught in school, but I did not know how important they could be. I had heard about things like inheritance, and it was something I put in the to-do list, buried somewhere under "finish the project." Once I took the time to figure them out, they saved me a lot of time and led to much cleaner code than I would have previously pulled together. If there's something you are unsure about, give this chapter a read-through and see whether you can work through the ideas. Hopefully, they may save some of you some time in the long run.

1.1.1 Manager and Controller Scripts

I am a strong believer in manager and controller scripts. I like to try and split things out into separate areas; for example, in the *Metal Vehicle Doom* game, I have race controller scripts and a global race controller script. The race controller scripts are attached to the players and track their positions on the track, waypoints, and other relevant player-specific race information. The global race controller script talks to all the race controller scripts attached to the players to determine who is winning and when the race starts or finishes. By keeping this logic separate from the other game scripts and contained in their own controller scripts, it makes it easier to migrate them from project to project. Essentially, I can take the race controller and global race controller scripts out of the game and apply them to another game, perhaps one that features a completely different type of gameplay—for example, alien characters running around a track instead of cars. As long as I apply the correct control scripts, the race logic is in place, and I can access it in the new game.

In the framework that this book contains, there are individual manager and controller scripts dealing with user data, input, game functions, and user interface. We look at those in detail in Chapter 2, but as you read this chapter, you should keep in mind the idea of separated scripts dedicated to managing particular parts of the game structure. It was important to me to design scripts as standalone so that they may be used in more than one situation. For example, our weapon slot manager will not care what kind of weapon is in any of the slots. The weapon slot manager is merely an interface between the player and the weapon, taking a call to "fire" and responding to it by telling the weapon in the currently selected weapon slot to fire. What happens on the player end will not affect the slot manager just as anything that happens with the weapon itself will not affect the slot manager. It just doesn't care as long as your code talks to it in the proper way and as long as your weapons receive commands in the proper way. It doesn't even matter what type of object the slot manager is attached to. If you decide to attach the weapon slot manager to a car, a boat, a telegraph pole, etc., it doesn't really matter just as long as when you want them to fire, you use the correct function in the slot manager to get it to tell a weapon to fire.

Since our core game logic is controlled by manager and controller scripts, we need to be a little smart about how we piece everything together. Some manager scripts may benefit from being static and available globally (for all other scripts to access), whereas others may be better attached to other scripts. We deal with these on a case-by-case basis. To get things started, we will be looking at some of the ways that these manager scripts can communicate with each other.

As a final note for the topic in this section, you may be wondering what the difference is between managers and controllers. There really isn't all that much, and I have only chosen to differentiate for my own sanity. I see controllers as scripts that are larger global systems, such as game state control, and managers as smaller scripts applied to gameObjects, such as weapon slot management or physics control. The terms are applied loosely, so don't worry if there appear to be inconsistencies in the application of the term in one case versus another. I'll try my best to keep things logical, but that doesn't mean it'll always make sense to everyone else!

1.1.2 Script Communication

An important part of our manager- and component-based structures is how our scripts are going to communicate with each other. It is inevitable that we will need to access our scripts from a multitude of other areas of the game, which means we should try to provide interfaces that make the most sense. There are several different ways of communicating between scripts and objects in Unity:

1. **Direct referencing manager scripts via variables set in the editor by the Inspector window.**

   The easiest way to have your scripts talk to each other is to have direct references to them in the form of public variables within a class. They are populated in the Unity editor with a direct link to another script.

   Here is an example of direct referencing:

```
public void aScript otherScript;
```

   In the editor window, the Inspector shows the otherScript field. We drag and drop an object containing the script component that we want to talk to. Within the class, function calls are made directly on the variable, such as

```
otherScript.DoSomething();
```

2. **GameObject referencing using SendMessage.**
SendMessage is a great way to send a message to a gameObject and call a function in one of its attached scripts or components when we do not need any kind of return result. For example,

```
SomeGameObject.SendMessage("DoSomething");
```

SendMessage may also take several parameters, such as setting whether or not the engine should throw an error when there is no receiver, that is, no function in any script attached to the gameObject with a name matching the one in the SendMessage call. (SendMessageOptions). You can also pass one parameter into the chosen function just as if you were passing it via a regular function call such as

```
SomeGameObject.SendMessage("AddScore",2);
SomeGameObject.SendMessage("AddScore",
SendMessageOptions.RequireReceiver);
SomeGameObject.SendMessage("AddScore",
SendMessageOptions.DontRequireReceiver);
```

3. **Static variables.**
The static variable type is useful in that it extends across the entire system; it will be accessible in every other script. This is a particularly useful behavior for a game control script, where several different scripts may want to communicate with it to do things such as add to the player's score, lose a life, or perhaps change a level.
An example declaration of a static variable might be

```
private static GameController aController;
```

Although static variables extend across the entire program, you can have private and public static variables. Things get a little tricky when you try to understand the differences between public and private static types—I was glad to have friends on Twitter that could explain it all to me, so let me pass on what I was told:

Public static
A public static variable exists everywhere in the system and may be accessed from other classes and other types of script.
Imagine a situation where a player control script needs to tell the game controller script whenever a player picks up a banana. We could deal with it like this:

1. In our gamecontroller.cs game controller script, we set up a public static:

```
public static GameController gateway;
```

2. When the game controller (gamecontroller.cs) runs its Start() function, it stores a reference to itself in a public static variable like this:

```
gateway = this;
```

3. In any other class, we can now access the game controller by referring to its type followed by that static variable (GameController.gateway) such as

```
GameController.gateway.GotBanana();
```

Private static

A private static variable exists within the class it was declared and in any other instances *of the same class*. Other classes/types of script will not be able to access it.

As a working example, try to imagine that a script named player.cs directly controls player objects in your game. They all need to tell a player manager script when something happens, so we declare the player manager as a static variable in our player.cs script like this:

```
private static PlayerManager playerManager;
```

The playerManager object only needs to be set up once, by a single instance of the player class, to be ready to use for all the other instances of the same class. All player.cs scripts will be able to access the same instance of the PlayerManager.

4. **The singleton design pattern.**

In the previous part of this section, we looked at using a static variable to share a manager script across the entire game code. The biggest danger with this method is that it is possible to create multiple instances of the same script. If this happens, you may find that your player code is talking to the wrong instance of the game controller.

A *singleton* is a commonly used design pattern that allows for only one instance of a particular class to be instantiated at a time. This pattern is ideal for our game scripts that may need to communicate (or be communicated with) across the entire game code. Note that we will be providing a static reference to the script, exactly as we did in the "Static Variables" method earlier in this section, but in implementing a singleton class, we will be adding some extra code to make sure that only one instance of our script is ever created.

1.1.3 Using the Singleton Pattern in Unity

It is not too difficult to see how useful static variables can be in communication between different script objects. In the public static example cited earlier, the idea was that we had a game controller object that needed to be accessed from one or more other scripts in our game.

The method shown here was demonstrated on the Unity public wiki* by a user named Emil Johansen (AngryAnt). It uses a private static variable in conjunction with a public static function. Other scripts access the public function to gain access to the private static instance of this script, which is returned via the public function so that only one instance of the object will ever exist in a scene regardless of how many components it is attached to and regardless of how many times it is instantiated.

A simple singleton structure:

```
public class MySingleton
{
    private static MySingleton instance;

    public MySingleton ()
```

---

* http://wiki.unity3d.com/index.php/Singleton.

```
        {
                if (instance != null)
                {
                        Debug.LogError ("Cannot have two instances of singleton.");
                        return;
                }

                instance = this;
        }
        public static MySingleton Instance
          {
                get
                {
                        if (instance == null)
                        {
                                new MySingleton ();
                        }

                        return instance;
                }
          }
}
```

The singleton instance of our script may be accessed anywhere, by any script, simply with the following syntax:

```
MySingleton.Instance.MySingletonMember;
```

1.1.4 Inheritance

Inheritance is a complex concept, which demands some explanation here because of its key role within the scripts provided in this book. Have a read through this section, but don't worry if you don't pick up inheritance right away. Once we get to the programming, it will most likely become clear.

The bottom line is that inheritance is used in programming to describe a method of providing template scripts that may be overridden, or added to, by other scripts. As a metaphor, imagine a car. All cars have four wheels and an engine. The types of wheels may vary from car to car, as will the engine, so when we say "this is a car" and try to describe how our car behaves, we may also describe the engine and wheels.

These relationships may be shown in a hierarchical order:

Car

   -Wheels
   -Engine

Now try to picture this as a C# script:

Car class

   Wheels function
   Engine function

If we were building a game with lots of cars in it, having to rewrite the car class for each type of car would be silly. A far more efficient method might be to write a base class and populate it with virtual functions. When we need to create a car, rather than use this base class, we build a new class, which inherits the base class. Because our new class is inherited, it is optional whether or not we choose to override the Wheels or Engine function to make them behave in ways specific to our new class. That is, we can build "default" functions into the base class, and if we only need to use a default behavior for an engine, our new class doesn't need to override the engine function.

The base class might look something like this:

```
public class BaseCar : MonoBehavior {

        public virtual void Engine () {
            Debug.Log("Vroom");
        }

        public virtual void Wheels () {
            Debug.Log("Four wheels");
        }
}
```

There are two key things to notice in the above script. One is the class declaration itself and the fact that this class *derives* from MonoBehavior. MonoBehavior is itself a class—the Unity documentation describes it as "the base class every script derives from"—this MonoBehavior class contains many engine-specific functions and methods such as Start(), Update(), FixedUpdate(), and more. If our script didn't derive from MonoBehavior, it would not inherit those functions, and the engine wouldn't automatically call functions like Update() for us to be able to work with. Another point to note is that MonoBehavior is a class that is built in to the engine and not something we can access to edit or change.

The second point to note is that our functions are both declared as *virtual* functions. Both are public and virtual. Making virtual functions means that the behavior in our base class may be overridden by any scripts that derive from it. The behavior we define in this base class could be thought of as its default behavior. We will cover overriding in full a little further on in this section.

Let's take a look at what this script actually does: If we were to call the Engine() function of our BaseCar class, it would write to the console "Vroom." If we called Wheels, the console would read "Four wheels."

Now that we have our BaseCar class, we can use this as a template and make new versions of it like this:

```
public class OctoCar : BaseCar {
        public override void Wheels () {
            Debug.Log("Eight wheels");
        }
}
```

The first thing you may notice is that the OctoCar class derives from BaseCar rather than from MonoBehavior. This means that OctoCar inherits the functions and methods belonging to our BaseCar script. As the functions described by BaseCar were virtual, they may be overridden. For OctoCar, we override Wheels with the line:

```
public override void Wheels () {
```

Let's take a look at what this script actually does: In this case, if we were to call the Engine() function on OctoCar, it would do the same as the BaseCar class; that is, it would write "Vroom" to the console. It would do this because we have inherited the function but have not overridden it, which means we keep that default behavior. In OctoCar, however, we have overridden the Wheels() function. The BaseCar behavior of Wheels would print "Four wheels" to the console, but if we call Wheels() on OctoCar, the overridden behavior will write "Eight wheels" instead.

Inheritance plays a huge part in how our core game framework is structured. The idea is that we have basic object types and specific elaborated versions of these objects inheriting the base methods, properties, and functions. By building our games in this manner, the communication between the different game components (such as game control scripts, weapon scripts, projectile controllers, etc.) becomes universal without having to write out the same function declarations over and over again for different variations of the script. For the core framework, our main goal is to make it as flexible and extensible as possible, and this would be much more difficult if we were unable to use inheritance.

The subject doesn't stop here, but that is as far as we will be going here. Each method will be useful in different areas of game development. For example, in cases where a component requires a reference to another object such as a material or a texture, it makes sense to set this via the Unity editor. In cases where we are developing classes that are not applied to gameObjects, we may use a static variable to make it accessible to all other scripts. For the sake of sanity, it is probably likely that we will never use a static object reference without using it as a singleton.

1.1.5 Where to Now?

Think about how your objects work together in the game world and how their scripts need to communicate with each other. I find that it helps to make flow diagrams or to use mind-mapping software to work things out beforehand. A little planning early on can reduce a whole lot of code revisions later on, so try to plan ahead. That said, it is perfectly okay for your structure to grow and evolve as you develop it further. The framework shown in this book ended up going through many revisions along the way before reaching its final form.

Try to break up your scripts into smaller components to help with debugging and for flexibility. Also, try to design for reusability; hard-coding references to other scripts reduces the portability of the script and increases the amount of work you will need to do in the future when you want to carry it over into another project.

2 Building the Core Game Framework

In this chapter, we look at the structure of the base project, to which we will be adding all of the game script components, and the thinking behind it. This chapter will give context to the design decisions made in the core framework as well as provide a good base for understanding how the individual code recipes work together and why they may sometimes have dependencies on other components.

The framework for this book (as seen in Figure 2.1) features six main areas:

1. Game Controller

   The game controller acts like a central communication script for all of the different parts of the game. In a way, it is the main glue that holds together the various components that make up the game.

2. Scene Manager

   This script deals with the loading and saving of scenes. Scenes are what Unity calls its level files.

3. UI Manager

   The UI manager draws all of the main in-game user interface elements, such as score display and lives.

4. Sound Manager

   The sound manager handles sound playback. The manager holds an array containing the AudioClips of possible sounds to play. When the game first begins, the

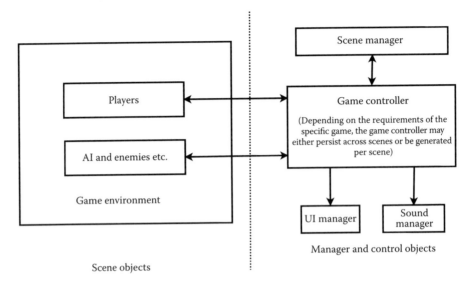

Figure 2.1 Diagram of the game framework.

sound manager creates one individual AudioSource per sound in the array. When we need to play a sound, the index number referring to a sound's place in the array is passed to the manager. It uses the sound's individual AudioSource to play the source, which helps to alleviate problems that may be caused by playing too many sound files from a single source.

5. Players
   Players may already be present in the game scene or may be instantiated by the game controller. The players have a relatively complex structure that will be explored later in Chapter 3.

6. AI and Enemies
   As with players, AI-controlled characters or enemies may already be present in the scene at load time or they may be created at runtime by the game controller or other script.

Although you may choose to work with your own framework, understanding the one used in this book will help in seeing how the components work alongside each other and how they work together. To maximize flexibility, the base classes need to be able to accommodate a host of different configurations. For example, a player control script should allow for input to be passed in from another script so that control systems may easily be switched out. The main player script does not need to know where the input is coming from, but it needs to provide a common interface for an input script to communicate with. The input script may take its input from the keyboard, mouse, artificial intelligence, networked input, etc., and just as long as a common interface is used to communicate with the player controller; it doesn't matter to the player controller as to where the input actually comes from.

▐ 2.1 Controllers and Managers

By specializing tasks to particular managers, it is possible to swap out other components without affecting core functions, which, in turn, makes it easy to carry the same code from game to game without having to rewrite it; from a first-person shooter to a racing game, the same code may be used to store user session data, load levels, or control weapons. In this book, I use two terms to specify the type of class: *controllers* and *managers*.

2.1.1 Controllers

Controllers specialize in specific tasks such as helping scripts communicate with each other, holding game-specific player information, or dealing with session data. For example, at the center of all of the example games in this book is a game controller script that acts as a central location for game scripts to communicate. Each game has its own game controller script acting like glue between the different components that otherwise have no built-in method for communicating.

2.1.2 Managers

Managers are used in this book as a term to represent a script that manages objects or data specifically (dealing with players, audio, or other game elements in a similar way to how a manager might manage staff in a company). For example, the GlobalBattleManager.cs script is used to manage RaceController.cs instances to keep track of a deathmatch battle in the example game *Tank Battle*. The manager script takes care of calculating the position of the players on the scoreboard as well as informing players as to the game's current running state.

▐ 2.2 Building the Core Framework Scripts

There are several scripts in the Scripts/BASE folder that are intended to act as templates for your own versions, or as classes to derive from, in your own games. In this section, we will be looking at the scripts that make up the main framework.

Those core framework scripts in the BASE folder that will be covered in this chapter are as follows:

- 2.2.1. BaseGameController.cs

- 2.2.2. SceneManager.cs

- 2.2.3. ExtendedCustomMonoBehavior.cs

- 2.2.4. BaseUserManager.cs

- 2.2.5. BasePlayerManager.cs

- 2.2.6. BaseInputController.cs

There are several more scripts in the BASE folder of the example games than those above; those scripts falling outside of the basic core framework will be dealt with on a case-by-case basis throughout this book, such as the AI scripts being dealt with in Chapter 9, where our AI system is covered in full, or in Chapter 8, where audio is explored.

2.2.1 BaseGameController.cs

The game controller acts as a hub for active game activity and a place where scripts that may not be directly connected can send messages to each other. By routing scripts through the game controller, they remain independent, and changing their behavior is a straightforward process of changing how messages are dealt with here rather than across multiple scripts.

The core functions of the game controller are as follows:

1. Tracking game state

    a. Storing the game state

    b. Providing functions for changing the game state

    c. Changing the game state based on calls to functions such as EndGame(), StartGame(), or PauseGame()

2. Creating any player object(s)

3. Setting up the camera (any specifics such as telling the camera which player to follow, etc.)

4. Communicating between session manager, user manager, and game actions (such as score, etc.)

5. Handling any communications between scripts that we would like to keep as standalone and not have to recode to talk directly to each other

Game controller is the core of gameplay, where overall game functions are defined and dealt with and where the current game state is held. Keeping track of the game state is important, as some elements will need to change their behavior based on this. If the game is paused, for example, we may want to suspend all input, freeze game time, and show a pop-up. When the game ends, we will need to disable player input and so on. Tracking game states is the job of the game controller script.

A typical game may have several different core states, such as

1. Game running

2. Game paused

3. Loading

4. Game ended

There may also be several custom states that are applicable to particular types of games, such as a state for showing a cutscene or perhaps a state for playing a special audio clip. I recommend creating a new state for any game action that affects how one or more of your scripts work. That way, you can always have the scripts rely on the game controller to know how to behave.

The base game controller script, found in Scripts/BASE, looks like this:

```
public class BaseGameController : MonoBehavior
{
    bool paused;
    public GameObject explosionPrefab;

    public virtual void PlayerLostLife ()
    {
        // deal with player life lost (update U.I. etc.)
    }

    public virtual void SpawnPlayer ()
    {
        // the player needs to be spawned
    }

    public virtual void Respawn ()
    {
        // the player is respawning
    }
    public virtual void StartGame()
    {
        // do start game functions
    }

    public void Explode ( Vector3 aPosition )
    {
        // instantiate an explosion at the position passed into this function
        Instantiate( explosionPrefab,aPosition, Quaternion.identity );
    }

    public virtual void EnemyDestroyed( Vector3 aPosition, int pointsValue,
    int hitByID )
    {
        // deal with enemy destroyed
    }

    public virtual void BossDestroyed()
    {
        // deal with the end of a boss battle
    }

    public virtual void RestartGameButtonPressed()
    {
        // deal with restart button (default behavior re-loads the
        // currently loaded scene)
        Application.LoadLevel(Application.loadedLevelName);
    }

    public bool Paused
    {
```

```
        get
        {
            // get paused
            return paused;
        }
        set
        {
            // set paused
            paused = value;

                    if (paused)
                    {
                    // pause time
                    Time.timeScale= 0f;
                    } else {
                    // unpause Unity
                        Time.timeScale = 1f;
                }
            }
        }
    }
}
```

2.2.1.1 Script Breakdown

Many of the key functions in BaseGameController.cs are virtual, included to serve as an established protocol for dealing with different types of game activity. That is, they contain no code in this particular file, but the intention is that you override them in your own derived versions of a game controller later on.

The BaseGameController class derives from MonoBehavior so that it can tap into automatically called system functions such as Awake(), Start(), Update(), and FixedUpdate():

```
public class BaseGameController : MonoBehavior
{
```

The functions are here as placeholders. The intention is that game controller scripts for use in actual game projects will derive from this class and populate these interface functions with functionality:

```
        bool paused;
        public GameObject explosionPrefab;

        public virtual void PlayerLostLife ()
        {
                // deal with player life lost (update U.I. etc.)
        }

        public virtual void SpawnPlayer ()
        {
                // the player needs to be spawned
        }

        public virtual void Respawn ()
```

```
{
        // the player is respawning
}

public virtual void StartGame()
{
        // do start game functions
}
```

Other functions in BaseGameController are there to help turn games around quickly. If there are things that you use in many different games, it may save time to include them all in a script like this from which you can derive all other game controllers. It saves having to rewrite the same code over and over again across multiple projects. One such example is the Explode() function, which does just that:

```
public void Explode ( Vector3 aPosition )
{
        // instantiate an explosion at the position passed into this
        // function
        Instantiate( explosionPrefab,aPosition, Quaternion.identity );
}
```

All Explode() does is instantiate a gameObject at a position passed in by the function caller. Later versions of game controller scripts will use a separate spawn manager to deal with instantiation, although at this stage, it is there simply to be as generic as possible by not being reliant on any other scripts.

After Explode, we see two more of those empty functions, used to tell the game controller when regular enemies are destroyed and when a boss is destroyed:

```
public virtual void EnemyDestroyed( Vector3 aPosition, int
pointsValue, int hitByID )
{
        // deal with enemy destroyed
}

public virtual void BossDestroyed()
{
        // deal with the end of a boss battle
}
```

All games will need some functions, such as a restart button and pause functions. In their simplest form:

```
public virtual void RestartGameButtonPressed()
{
        // deal with restart button (default behavior re-loads the
        // currently loaded scene)
        Application.LoadLevel(Application.loadedLevelName);
}
```

RestartGameButtonPressed() uses Unity's Application.LoadLevel function to reload the current scene. Application.loadedLevelName returns a string referring to the name of the scene the game currently has loaded in memory. You can also get an index number referring to the scene with Application.levelName. This index number ties up to how scenes are organized in the Build Settings (File → Build Settings), meaning that moving things around in build settings can affect how your game works if you choose to use index numbers to refer to specific scenes later on. To avoid any confusion, I prefer to stick to names whenever I deal with level loading.

The final part of the BaseGameController deals with the mechanics of pausing and unpausing a game:

```
public bool Paused
{
    get
    {
        // get paused
        return paused;
    }
    set
    {
        // set paused
        paused = value;

            if (paused)
            {
            // pause time
            Time.timeScale= 0f;
            } else {
            // unpause Unity
                Time.timeScale = 1f;
        }
    }
}
```

A Boolean variable named paused holds the game pause state internally. Rather than provide direct access to this, a getter–setter function is used so that we can act whenever the state of paused changes without having to monitor it.

The Get part simply returns the Boolean variable paused.

The Set part sets the Boolean variable paused and goes on to set Time.timeScale to either 0 (paused) or 1 (unpaused). Setting Time.timeScale affects how time passes. For example, setting timescale to 0.5 would mean that time passes 2× slower than real time. The Unity documentation states:

> Except for realtimeSinceStartup, timeScale affects all the time and delta time measuring variables of the Time class.
> If you lower timeScale it is recommended to also lower Time.fixedDeltaTime by the same amount.
> FixedUpdate functions will not be called when timeScale is set to zero.

A regular videogame would display some sort of message to tell players whenever the game is paused, but at this stage, the script is purely providing the mechanics of pausing, and we will save concerning ourselves too much with user interface until Chapter 14.

2.2.2 Scene Manager

A manager script controls the game flow between physical scenes. Buttons from the menu interface do not load scenes directly; it falls upon the scene manager script below to load them:

```
public class SceneManager : MonoBehavior
{
        public string[] levelNames;
        public int gameLevelNum;

        public void Start ()
        {
                // keep this object alive
                DontDestroyOnLoad (this.gameObject);
        }

        public void LoadLevel( string sceneName )
        {
                Application.LoadLevel( sceneName );
        }

        public void GoNextLevel()
        {
                // if our index goes over the total number of levels in the
                // array, we reset it
                if( gameLevelNum >= levelNames.Length )
                    gameLevelNum = 0;

                // load the level (the array index starts at 0, but we start
                // counting game levels at 1 for clarity's sake)
                LoadLevel( gameLevelNum );

                // increase our game level index counter
                gameLevelNum++;
        }

        private void LoadLevel( int indexNum )
        {
                // load the game level
                LoadLevel( levelNames[indexNum] );
        }

        public void ResetGame()
        {
                // reset the level index counter
                gameLevelNum = 0;
        }
}
```

2.2.2.1 Script Breakdown

Any script may call for a scene change, and menus, game controllers, or tutorial controllers may easily move between sections of the game without having to have filenames hard-coded into them.

The level manager may also be a good place to call to show loading screens, implement scene transitions (such as fade ins/outs or animations), or start downloading scenes from a remote location.

Note that in the Start() function of the class (shown below), we use DontDestroyOnLoad to keep this script and its gameObject alive even when new scenes are loaded. This means we need to prevent duplicate scene managers being instanced, but we can easily use GameObject.Find to have a look for a scene manager gameObject before instantiating a new one.

```
public class SceneManager : MonoBehavior
{
    public string[] levelNames;
    public int gameLevelNum;

    public void Start ()
    {
        // keep this object alive
        DontDestroyOnLoad (this.gameObject);
    }
```

The SceneManager.cs script provides a scene-loading function in its simplest form. Here Application.LoadLevel is used to load a scene:

```
    public void LoadLevel ( string sceneName )
    {
            Application.LoadLevel ( sceneName );
    }
```

On top of simple scene loading, the class has support for a basic progressive level loading game format. An array named levelNames holds strings referring to the names of each of the levels in a game. We use an integer variable named gameLevelNum to refer to which level the player is in. When GoNextLevel() is called, we do a quick check to make sure that gameLevelNum is within range:

```
    public void GoNextLevel()
    {
        // if our index goes over the total number of levels in the
        // array, we reset it
        if( gameLevelNum >= levelNames.Length )
            gameLevelNum = 0;
```

Then, another version of the LoadLevel function (declared after this part) is called to start loading the next scene based on the index number. Finally, gameLevelNum is incremented, ready for next time. Note that the increment happens after the load and not before. We could have done this either way, but this way, we have the minor inconvenience of gameLevelNum always being one step ahead, which we need to be aware of if we ever try to access its value from other classes. On the other hand, by incrementing it after the load, we use GoNextLevel right from the start of the game to load the first level in the array, keeping the code consistent in level loading:

```
        // load the level (the array index starts at 0, but we start
        // counting game levels at 1 for clarity's sake)
        LoadLevel ( gameLevelNum );

        // increase our game level index counter
        gameLevelNum++;
    }
```

This alternative version of the LoadLevel function shown below uses an index to get a level name from the levelNames array. It then uses the original LoadLevel function declared earlier to handle loading. Again, keeping the focus on using a single function for all loadings rather than duplicating the code or having loading happen in more than one place:

```
private void LoadLevel( int indexNum )
{
        // load the game level
        LoadLevel( levelNames[indexNum] );
}
```

The final function in the scene manager class is used to reset gameLevelNum whenever we start a new game. It is assumed that the script restarting the game will call this function before calling GoNextLevel() again.

```
public void ResetGame()
{
        // reset the level index counter
        gameLevelNum = 0;
}
}
```

2.2.3 ExtendedCustomMonoBehavior.cs

Extending MonoBehavior is a useful way to avoid repeating common functions or variable declarations. Many classes share functions and/or variables. For example, most of the scripts in this book use a variable named myTransform to refer to a cached version of their transforms to save having to look up the transform every time we need to access it. As MonoBehavior provides a host of system functions and calls, making a new class that extends, it can be a useful tool to have in the kit. Whereas a new class would use MonoBehavior, we just derive from the new ExtendedCustomMonoBehavior script instead.

For the scripts in this book, the ExtendedCustomMonoBehavior.cs script extends MonoBehavior to include

1. a myTransform variable to hold a cached reference to a transform

2. a myGO variable to hold a cached reference to a gameObject

3. a myBody variable for a cached reference to a rigidBody

4. a didInit Boolean variable to determine whether or not the script has been initialized

5. an integer variable called id to hold an id number

6. a Vector3 type variable called tempVEC to use for temporary vector actions

7. a Transform variable called tempTR used for any temporary references to transforms

8. a function called SetID(integer) so that other classes can set the variable id

The scripting for this class is straightforward and contains mostly variable declarations:

```
public class ExtendedCustomMonoBehavior : MonoBehavior
{
        // This class is used to add some common variables to
        // MonoBehavior, rather than constantly repeating
        // the same declarations in every class.

        public Transform myTransform;
        public GameObject myGO;
        public Rigidbody myBody;

        public bool didInit;
        public bool canControl;

        public int id;

        [System.NonSerialized]
        public Vector3 tempVEC;

        [System.NonSerialized]
        public Transform tempTR;

        public virtual void SetID( int anID )
        {
                id= anID;
        }
}
```

2.2.4   BaseUserManager.cs

The user manager is a script object made by the player manager to store player properties such as

- Player name

- Current score

- Highest score

- Level

- Health

- Whether or not this player has finished the game

The user manager also contains functions to manipulate its data
    Below is the BaseUserManager.cs script in full:

```
public class BaseUserManager : MonoBehavior
{
        // gameplay specific data
        // we keep these private and provide methods to modify them
        // instead, just to prevent any accidental corruption
        // or invalid data coming in
```

```csharp
        private int score;
        private int highScore;
        private int level;
        private int health;
        private bool isFinished;

        // this is the display name of the player
        public string playerName ="Anon";

        public virtual void GetDefaultData()
        {
                playerName="Anon";
                score=0;
                level=1;
                health=3;
                highScore=0;
                isFinished=false;
        }

        public string GetName()
        {
                return playerName;
        }

        public void SetName(string aName)
        {
                playerName=aName;
        }

        public int GetLevel()
        {
                return level;
        }

        public void SetLevel(int num)
        {
                level=num;
        }

        public int GetHighScore()
        {
                return highScore;
        }

        public int GetScore()
        {
                return score;
        }

        public virtual void AddScore(int anAmount)
        {
                score+=anAmount;
        }

        public void LostScore(int num)
        {
                score-=num;
        }
```

```
        public void SetScore(int num)
        {
                score=num;
        }

        public int GetHealth()
        {
                return health;
        }

        public void AddHealth(int num)
        {
                health+=num;
        }

        public void ReduceHealth(int num)
        {
                health-=num;
        }

        public void SetHealth(int num)
        {
                health=num;
        }

        public bool GetIsFinished()
        {
                return isFinished;
        }

        public void SetIsFinished(bool aVal)
        {
                isFinished=aVal;
        }
}
```

2.2.4.1 Script Breakdown

BaseUserManager.cs contains just variable declarations and functions to get or set those variables.

2.2.5 BasePlayerManager.cs

The player manager acts like glue among the input manager, the user manager, and the game-specific player controllers. It is intended to be a central point where managers are tied to game-specific player scripts.

Below is the BasePlayerManager.cs in full:

```
public class BasePlayerManager : MonoBehavior
{
        public bool didInit;

        // the user manager and AI controllers are publically accessible so that
        // our individual control scripts can access them easily
        public BaseUserManager DataManager;
```

```
// note that we initialize on Awake in this class so that it is
// ready for other classes to access our details when
// they initialize on Start
public virtual void Awake ()
{
        didInit=false;

        // rather than clutter up the start() func, we call Init to
        // do any startup specifics
        Init();
}

public virtual void Init ()
{
        // cache ref to our user manager
        DataManager= gameObject.GetComponent<BaseUserManager>();

        if(DataManager==null)
            DataManager= gameObject.AddComponent<BaseUserManager>();

        // do play init things in this function
        didInit= true;
}

  public virtual void GameFinished()
{
        DataManager.SetIsFinished(true);
}

public virtual void GameStart()
{
        DataManager.SetIsFinished(false);
}
}
```

2.2.5.1 Script Breakdown

BasePlayerManager.cs derives from MonoBehavior so that it can use the system function
Awake() to call its Init() initialization:

```
public class BasePlayerManager : MonoBehavior
{
```

The Awake() function is based on the assumption that it may be reused, so it starts
out by setting the Boolean variable didInit to false. This variable can then be used to tell
whether or not the Init() function has been called and completed execution:

```
public virtual void Awake ()
{
        didInit=false;

        // rather than clutter up the start() func, we call Init to do any
        // startup specifics
        Init();
}
```

Init() starts out by looking to find a reference to a DataManager script component (BaseUserManager as explained earlier in this chapter). gameObject.GetComponent() will return a reference to BaseUserManager if it has been added to the gameObject that this script is attached to:

```
public virtual void Init ()
{
    // cache ref to our user manager
    DataManager= gameObject.GetComponent<BaseUserManager>();
```

At this point, if the DataManager variable is null, we know that the component has not been added to this gameObject, and this code goes on to use gameObject.AddComponent() to add a BaseUserManager component through the code

```
if(DataManager==null)
    DataManager= gameObject.AddComponent<BaseUserManager>();
```

Now that the Init() function is done, didInit can be set to true:

```
    // do play init things in this function
    didInit= true;
}
```

GameFinished() will be called from an outside script (possibly the game controller script or similar game-state management script) to tell this player when the game is over:

```
public virtual void GameFinished()
{
    DataManager.SetIsFinished(true);
}
```

Just like GameFinished(), GameStart() will be called from an outside script when it is time to start the game. DataManager.SetIsFinished() is called to set the isFinished variable of this player's data manager to false:

```
public virtual void GameStart()
{
    DataManager.SetIsFinished(false);
}
}
```

2.2.6 BaseInputController.cs

The input controllers provide input for use by the player controller. The BaseInputController. cs looks like this:

```
public class BaseInputController : MonoBehavior
{
    // directional buttons
    public bool Up;
    public bool Down;
    public bool Left;
    public bool Right;
```

```
// fire / action buttons
public bool Fire1;

// weapon slots
public bool Slot1;
public bool Slot2;
public bool Slot3;
public bool Slot4;
public bool Slot5;
public bool Slot6;
public bool Slot7;
public bool Slot8;
public bool Slot9;

public float vert;
public float horz;
public bool shouldRespawn;

public Vector3 TEMPVec3;
private Vector3 zeroVector = new Vector3(0,0,0);

public virtual void CheckInput ()
{
        // override with your own code to deal with input
        horz=Input.GetAxis ("Horizontal");
        vert=Input.GetAxis ("Vertical");
}

public virtual float GetHorizontal()
{
        // returns our cached horizontal input axis value
        return horz;
}

public virtual float GetVertical()
{
        // returns our cached vertical input axis value
        return vert;
}

public virtual bool GetFire()
{
        return Fire1;
}

public bool GetRespawn()
{
        return shouldRespawn;
}

public virtual Vector3 GetMovementDirectionVector()
{
        // temp vector for movement dir gets set to the value of an
        // otherwise unused vector that always has the value of 0,0,0
        TEMPVec3=zeroVector;
        // if we're going left or right, set the velocity vector's X
        // to our horizontal input value
        if(Left || Right)
```

```
    {
            TEMPVec3.x=horz;
    }

    // if we're going up or down, set the velocity vector's X to
    // our vertical input value
    if(Up || Down)
    {
            TEMPVec3.y=vert;
    }
    // return the movement vector
    return TEMPVec3;
    }
}
```

2.2.6.1 Script Breakdown

BaseInputController.cs derives from `MonoBehavior`:

```
public class BaseInputController : MonoBehavior
{
```

The input scripts use CheckInput() as their default main update function, which is intended to be called from the player class. This CheckInput() only contains the very least amount required for input. It just takes the axis input from the Input class:

```
public virtual void CheckInput ()
{
```

The Input class provides an interface to Unity's input systems. It may be used for everything from gyrometer input on mobile devices to keyboard presses. Unity's input system has a virtual axis setup, where developers can name an axis in the Input Manager section of the Unity editor. The Input Manager is available in Unity via the menus Edit –> Project Settings –> Input.

By default, Unity has inputs already set up for horizontal and vertical virtual axis. Their names are Horizontal and Vertical, and they are accessible via Input.GetAxis(), passing in the name of the virtual axis as a parameter and receiving the return value of a float between –1 and 1. The float variable horz and vert hold the return values:

```
    // override with your own code to deal with input
    horz=Input.GetAxis ("Horizontal");
    vert=Input.GetAxis ("Vertical");
    }
```

A function is provided to return the value of horz, the horizontal axis provided by the virtual axis named Horizontal:

```
public virtual float GetHorizontal()
{
    // returns our cached horizontal input axis value
    return horz;
}
```

A function is provided to return the value of vert, the vertical axis provided by the virtual axis named Vertical:

```
public virtual float GetVertical()
{
        // returns our cached vertical input axis value
        return vert;
}
```

GetFire() returns the value of the Boolean variable Fire1. GetRespawn() returns the value of the Boolean variable shouldRespawn. At this stage, you may notice that there is no actual code to set either Fire1 or shouldRespawn in this default input script. They are both provided as a guide and with the intention of being built upon on a case-by-case basis depending on what the game requires:

```
public virtual bool GetFire()
{
        return Fire1;
}

public bool GetRespawn()
{
        return shouldRespawn;
}
```

It may be useful in some circumstances to have a movement vector rather than having to process the numbers from horz and vert. GetMovementDirectionVector() will return a Vector3 type vector based on the current state of input. Here, TEMPVec3 receives input values and gets returned by the function

```
public virtual Vector3 GetMovementDirectionVector()
{
        // temp vector for movement dir gets set to the value of an
        // otherwise unused vector that always has the value of 0,0,0
        TEMPVec3=zeroVector;
```

The vector starts out at 0,0,0, but its x and y values will be set to the values of horz and vert, respectively. Finally, the vector in TEMPVec3 is returned:

```
        TEMPVec3.x=horz;
        TEMPVec3.y=vert;

        // return the movement vector
        return TEMPVec3;
}
}
```

3 Player Structure

A player can take just about any form—humans, aliens, animals, vehicles; designing a structure that can deal with all of them is a challenge in itself. The way that players store data, the data they need to store, the various types of movement codes and their control systems make for hundreds of different possible combinations. Dealing with a player structure in a modular way requires a little careful consideration not just for how to deal with all these different scenarios but also for how our components will need to communicate with each other and communicate with the rest of the game—for example, player objects often need to communicate with the game controller, the game controller often needs to communicate with players (to relay game states, etc.), and players may also need to interact with the environment and other objects within it.

The overall player structure for this book may be broken down into several main components, as shown in Figure 3.1.

1. *Game-specific player controller*. This is a script to deal with game-specific player actions. For example, some games may require a vehicle that requires weapons, whereas some games may not. The game-specific control script will "add on" the specific extra functionality and tie together the main components to work together or communicate with other game-specific elements.

2. *Movement controller*. The movement controller takes the job of moving the player around and defines the type of player we are using. For example, a vehicle-based player would have a vehicle-based movement control script that would drive the

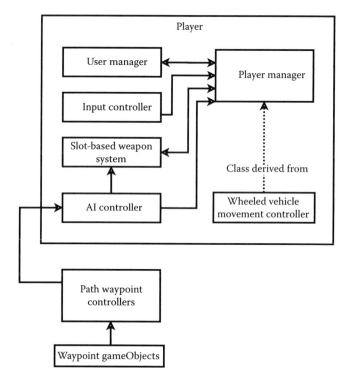

Figure 3.1 Player structure.

wheels, turn them, or operate extra vehicle-specific functions like a horn, head-lights, etc. A human would require a code to drive a character controller. A space-ship might use physics forces to drive a spaceship.

3. *Player manager.* This script is intended to be a bridge between the player control-ler and the user data manager. The user data manager takes care of storing player stats, such as score, lives, level, etc.

4. *Data manager.* The data manager takes care of the manipulation of player data and how the data are stored and retrieved. Score and health values would be stored here, and the data manager would also provide functions for saving and loading its data.

Along with these main components, we can add some extra components to mix and match player types into different forms. A weapon control script may be attached to a human to create the player in a first-person shooter, or the same weapon control script could be added to a vehicle-type player to help turn it into a tank. An AI control script may be added to drive the player or to operate the weapons and so on.

In this chapter, we will be going through some of the main components that will be used later in the book to create a user-controlled player.

3.1 Game-Specific Player Controller

The player controller derives from a movement controller (which specializes in nothing more than movement of a particular player type) and builds on its movement functionality to provide full player logic.

The movement controllers are explained later in this book. Chapter 5 outlines three different movement controllers for three different player types: a spaceship, a humanoid player, and a wheeled vehicle.

What logic goes into the player controllers depends on the game; the example games in this book use the movement controllers from Chapter 5 and add extra functionality to them, such as combining the movement controller with the weapon controllers to make armed players or combining the AI controller to have computer controller players.

For real examples of player controllers, take a look at the example games in Chapters 10 to 13.

In this section, we build a simple player controller to move a spaceship. It derives from BaseTopDownSpaceShip.cs, which can be found in full in Chapter 5. This script also includes a player manager.

```
using UnityEngine;
using System.Collections;

public class SimplePlayerController : BaseTopDownSpaceShip
{
        public BasePlayerManager myPlayerManager;
        public BaseUserManager myDataManager;

        public override void Start()
        {
                // tell our base class to initialize
                base.Init ();

                // now do our own init
                this.Init();
        }

        public override void Init ()
        {
                // if a player manager is not set in the editor, let's try
                // to find one
                if(myPlayerManager==null)
                    myPlayerManager= myGO.GetComponent<BasePlayerManager>();

                myDataManager= myPlayerManager.DataManager;
                myDataManager.SetName("Player");
                myDataManager.SetHealth(3);

                didInit=true;
        }
        public override void Update ()
        {
                // do the update in our base
                UpdateShip ();

                // don't do anything until Init() has been run
```

```
                if(!didInit)
                        return;

                // check to see if we're supposed to be controlling the
                // player before checking for firing
                if(!canControl)
                        return;
        }

        public override void GetInput ()
        {
                // we're overriding the default input function to add in the
                // ability to fire
                horizontal_input= default_input.GetHorizontal();
                vertical_input= default_input.GetVertical();
        }

        void OnCollisionEnter(Collision collider)
        {
                // React to collisions here
        }

        void OnTriggerEnter(Collider other)
        {
                // React to triggers here
        }

        public void PlayerFinished()
        {
                // Deal with the end of the game for this player
        }

        public void ScoredPoints(int howMany)
        {
                myDataManager.AddScore( howMany );
        }
}
```

▋ 3.2 Dealing with Input

Separate scripts provide input for the movement controllers to react to. This is so they may be switched out for whatever input is required, without having to change anything within the movement control script. The movement controller remains intact, regardless of what you "feed" into it, which means you could use the exact same movement control script for the main player, for AI players, and perhaps even for remote players connected over a network—just using different inputs.

BaseInputController.cs provides a collection of common variables and functions. Other input scripts will derive from it:

```
public class BaseInputController : MonoBehavior
{
        // directional buttons
        public bool Up;
        public bool Down;
```

```
public bool Left;
public bool Right;

// fire/action buttons
public bool Fire1;
```

The slot-based weapon system uses the keyboard buttons from 1 to 9 to directly select which weapon slot to use. For that reason, the input system has nine Boolean variables to take input from the number keys:

```
// weapon slots
public bool Slot1;
public bool Slot2;
public bool Slot3;
public bool Slot4;
public bool Slot5;
public bool Slot6;
public bool Slot7;
public bool Slot8;
public bool Slot9;

public float vert;
public float horz;
public bool shouldRespawn;

public Vector3 TEMPVec3;
private Vector3 zeroVector = new Vector3(0,0,0);
```

Input provides an interface to Unity's input systems. It is used for everything from gyrometer input on mobile devices to keyboard presses. According to the Unity documentation, Input.GetAxis returns the value of the virtual axis identified by axisName. The axis names are set in Unity's Input Manager (Edit → Project Settings → Input), although Horizontal and Vertical should already be set up by default:

```
public virtual void CheckInput ()
{
        // override with your own code to deal with input
        horz=Input.GetAxis ("Horizontal");
        vert=Input.GetAxis ("Vertical");
}

public virtual float GetHorizontal()
{
        // returns our cached horizontal input axis value
        return horz;
}

public virtual float GetVertical()
{
        // returns our cached vertical input axis value
        return vert;
}
```

Although the script includes a function called GetFire(), returning the value of the Boolean variable Fire1, the script does not include any code to set it. It's just there for consistency.

```
public virtual bool GetFire()
{
        return Fire1;
}
```

Again, the script contains GetRespawn() purely for protocol, with no actual functionality.

```
public bool GetRespawn()
{
        return shouldRespawn;
}
```

For convenience, BaseInputController.cs includes a simple system for returning a direction vector. The function will return a Vector3 with its x and y axes representing the levels of input:

```
public virtual Vector3 GetMovementDirectionVector()
{
        // temp vector for movement dir gets set to the value of an
        // otherwise unused vector that always has the value of 0,0,0
        TEMPVec3=zeroVector;

        // if we're going left or right, set the velocity vector's X
        // to our horizontal input value
        if(Left || Right)
        {
                TEMPVec3.x=horz;
        }

        // if we're going up or down, set the velocity vector's X to
        // our vertical input value
        if(Up || Down)
        {
                TEMPVec3.y=vert;
        }
        // return the movement vector
        return TEMPVec3;
}

}
```

The default script for input is a basic keyboard setup script named Keyboard_Input.cs. It derives from BaseInputController.cs and overrides the CheckInput() and LateUpdate() functions to add a vertical axis, checking for the fire button and a respawn button set up as Fire3 in Unity's Input Manager:

```
public class Keyboard_Input : BaseInputController
{
        public override void CheckInput ()
        {
                // get input data from vertical and horizontal axis and
```

```
                 // store them internally in vert and horz so we don't have to
                 // access them every time we need to relay input data out
                 vert= Input.GetAxis( "Vertical" );
                 horz= Input.GetAxis( "Horizontal" );

                 // set up some Boolean values for up, down, left and right
                 Up     = ( vert>0 );
                 Down   = ( vert<0 );
                 Left   = ( horz<0 );
                 Right  = ( horz>0 );

                 // get fire/action buttons
                 Fire1= Input.GetButton( "Fire1" );
                 shouldRespawn= Input.GetButton( "Fire3" );
         }

         public void LateUpdate()
         {
                 // check inputs each LateUpdate() ready for the next tick
                 CheckInput();
         }
}
```

■ 3.3 Player Manager

The player manager script acts as a simple bridge between the player controller and the user data manager. It also creates the user data manager if one is not already attached to the player prefab.

```
using UnityEngine;
using System.Collections;

public class BasePlayerManager : MonoBehavior
{
         public bool didInit;

         // the user manager and AI controllers are publically accessible so
         // that our individual control scripts can access them easily
         public BaseUserManager DataManager;

         // note that we initialize on Awake in this class so that it is
         // ready for other classes to access our details when they
         // initialize on Start
         public virtual void Awake ()
         {
                 didInit=false;
                 Init();
         }

         public virtual void Init ()
         {
                 // cache ref to our user manager
                 DataManager= gameObject.GetComponent<BaseUserManager>();

                 if(DataManager==null)
                     DataManager= gameObject.AddComponent<BaseUserManager>();
```

```
                // do play init things in this function
                didInit= true;
        }

        public virtual void GameFinished()
        {
                DataManager.SetIsFinished(true);
        }

        public virtual void GameStart()
        {
                DataManager.SetIsFinished(false);
        }
}
```

3.3.1 Script Breakdown

There is nothing particularly outstanding about the start of the script—the Awake() function calls Init() after setting the didInit Boolean to false:

```
public class BasePlayerManager : MonoBehavior
{
        public bool didInit;

        // the user manager and AI controllers are publically accessible so
        // that our individual control scripts can access them easily
        public BaseUserManager DataManager;

        // note that we initialize on Awake in this class so that it is
        // ready for other classes to access our details when they
        // initialize on Start
        public virtual void Awake ()
        {
                didInit=false;
                Init();
        }
```

The Init() function does a quick check to see whether there is already an instance of BaseUserManager attached to the player gameObject using gameObject.GetComponent. If its result is null, the script uses AddComponent to attach a new instance to it. Finally, didInit is set to true:

```
        public virtual void Init ()
        {
                // cache ref to our user manager
                DataManager= gameObject.GetComponent<BaseUserManager>();

                if(DataManager==null)
                    DataManager= gameObject.AddComponent<BaseUserManager>();

                // do play init things in this function
                didInit= true;
        }
```

The GameFinished() and GameStart() functions are there to pass a message to the user data manager. One good use for these might be a script that knows of the player's gameObject and wants to tell about the state of the game. Rather than having to use a call to GetComponent to find this script, it may use gameObject.SendMessage to call a function instead. This would be slightly more efficient than having to use GetComponent and access the function directly:

```
public virtual void GameFinished()
{
        DataManager.SetIsFinished(true);
}

public virtual void GameStart()
{
        DataManager.SetIsFinished(false);
}
}
```

■ 3.4 User Data Manager (Dealing with Player Stats Such as Health, Lives, etc.)

It is not uncommon to store player information in a game controller or similar script removed from individual player objects. This approach may be well suited to single-player games, but moving to games that have more than one player may prove to be problematic. One solution may be for the game controller to have an array of classes containing player stats, manipulating them when other functions tell it to; but why not attach the player stats to each player and make it self-sufficient?

The framework for this book uses a data manager class for each player, consisting of everything we need to store for a single player:

1. Score

2. High score

3. Level

4. Health

5. Whether or not the player is finished (no longer active)

6. Name of the player

Each player has the BaseUserManager.cs script attached to its gameObject, giving each player its own set of stats. The game controller or other script elsewhere in the game structure can easily search for and access a player's information.

The user manager script looks like this:

```
public class BaseUserManager : MonoBehavior
{
        // gameplay specific data
        // we keep these private and provide methods to modify them
        // instead, just to prevent any accidental corruption or invalid
        // data coming in
```

3.4 User Data Manager (Dealing with Player Stats Such as Health, Lives, etc.)

37

```csharp
private int score;
private int highScore;
private int level;
private int health;
private bool isFinished;

// this is the display name of the player
public string playerName ="Anon";

public virtual void GetDefaultData()
{
        playerName="Anon";
        score=0;
        level=1;
        health=3;
        highScore=0;
        isFinished=false;
}

public string GetName()
{
        return playerName;
}

public void SetName(string aName)
{
        playerName=aName;
}

public int GetLevel()
{
        return level;
}

public void SetLevel(int num)
{
        level=num;
}

public int GetHighScore()
{
        return highScore;
}

public int GetScore()
{
        return score;
}

public virtual void AddScore(int anAmount)
{
        score+=anAmount;
}

public void LostScore(int num)
{
        score-=num;
}
```

```
public void SetScore(int num)
{
        score=num;
}

public int GetHealth()
{
        return health;
}

public void AddHealth(int num)
{
        health+=num;
}

public void ReduceHealth(int num)
{
        health-=num;
}

public void SetHealth(int num)
{
        health=num;
}

public bool GetIsFinished()
{
        return isFinished;
}

public void SetIsFinished(bool aVal)
{
        isFinished=aVal;
}
}
```

3.4.1   Script Breakdown

After the variable declarations, the first thing BaseUserManager.cs contains is a function to populate the player stats with some default values, just to avoid any trouble when trying to access them.

```
public virtual void GetDefaultData()
{
        playerName="Anon";
        score=0;
        level=1;
        health=3;
        highScore=0;
        isFinished=false;
}
```

The rest of the class deals with getting and setting the player data. The logic is literally just getting or setting variables, so if you need to look at it in detail, refer back to the full script at the start of this section. For clarity, here is a list of the rest of the functions:

```
public string GetName()
public void SetName(string aName)
public int GetLevel()
public void SetLevel(int num)
public int GetHighScore()
public int GetScore()
public virtual void AddScore(int anAmount)
public void LostScore(int num)
public void SetScore(int num)
public int GetHealth()
public void AddHealth(int num)
public void ReduceHealth(int num)
public void SetHealth(int num)
public bool GetIsFinished()
public void SetIsFinished(bool aVal)
```

4 Recipes: Common Components

⬛ 4.1 Introduction

Many of the scripts in this book are in some way linked to the base framework or parts of larger systems, but there are some that we will use that could fit into a whole number of positions in a whole number of different game types. Utility scripts or commonly used systems are also going to come in really handy for the game projects. This chapter is all about those, an eclectic bunch of reusable scripts such as timers or utilities.

In the example source files, the COMMON folder can be found within the Scripts folder. This is where we store all of the scripts that may crop up now and again that are not part of the base framework. Within the COMMON folder, there are a number of subfolders. Those are

BOTS OR PLAYER CONTROL

> Contains scripts related to player or automatic control, such as a script to talk to the BaseAIController.cs script and act as a simple, functional bot moving around in a game environment.

CAMERA

> Scripts related to the camera should go in here, such as third-person or top-down camera code.

GAME CONTROL

The scripts in this folder are about overall game state control. In the example files, you will find

BattleController and GlobalBattleManager—This script is used for deathmatch-style scoring and game state logic.

RaceController and GlobalRaceManager—This script contains the base logic for racing games, such as lap counting and position tracking.

SceneManager—This script deals with the loading of scenes as well as with incremental game scene management (as used in the *Interstellar Paranoids* example game of this book).

INPUT

Different player and game types require different control systems or input methods. Any common scripts dealing with input go in this folder.

SPAWNING

Scripts related to spawning may be found here, which includes code to spawn objects when triggers are fired or to spawn paths for dynamic waypoint following objects.

UTILITY

The Utility folder is home to small helper scripts, such as the timer class or a script to automatically spin a gameObject.

WEAPONS

Any weapons-related scripts outside of the base framework may be found here.

The scripts in this chapter will be used in various places later on in the example games parts of this book.

This chapter will look in detail at the following:

- 4.2 The timer class

- 4.3 Scripts used for spawning

- 4.4 A script to set gravity

- 4.5 A script that simulates friction

- 4.6 Cameras

- 4.7 Input scripts

4.2 The Timer Class

Our timer system will be named TimerClass.cs and the full script looks like this:

```
public class TimerClass
{
        public bool isTimerRunning= false;
        private float timeElapsed= 0.0f;
        private float currentTime= 0.0f;
        private float lastTime= 0.0f;
        private float timeScaleFactor= 1.1f; // <-- If you need to scale
                                             // time, change this!


        private string timeString;
        private string hour;
        private string minutes;
        private string seconds;
        private string mills;


        private int aHour;
        private int aMinute;
        private int aSecond;
        private int aMillis;
        private int tmp;
        private int aTime;


        private GameObject callback;


        public void UpdateTimer ()
        {
                // calculate the time elapsed since the last Update()
                timeElapsed=Mathf.Abs(Time.realtimeSinceStartup-lastTime);


                // if the timer is running, we add the time elapsed to the
                // current time (advancing the timer)
                if(isTimerRunning)
                {
                        currentTime+=timeElapsed*timeScaleFactor;
                }


                // store the current time so that we can use it on the next
                // update
                lastTime=Time.realtimeSinceStartup;
        }
```

```
public void StartTimer ()
{
        // set up initial variables to start the timer
        isTimerRunning=true;
    lastTime=Time.realtimeSinceStartup;
}


public void StopTimer ()
{
        // stop the timer
        isTimerRunning=false;
}


public void ResetTimer ()
{
        // resetTimer will set the timer back to zero
    timeElapsed=0.0f;
    currentTime=0.0f;
    lastTime=Time.realtimeSinceStartup;
}


public string GetFormattedTime ()
{
        // carry out an update to the timer so it is 'up to date'
        UpdateTimer();


        // grab minutes
    aMinute=(int)currentTime/60;
        aMinute=aMinute%60;


    // grab seconds
    aSecond=(int)currentTime%60;


    // grab milliseconds
    aMillis=(int)(currentTime*100)%100;


    // format strings for individual mm/ss/mills
        tmp=(int)aSecond;
    seconds=tmp.ToString();
    if(seconds.Length<2)
            seconds="0"+seconds;


        tmp=(int)aMinute;
    minutes=tmp.ToString();
    if(minutes.Length<2)
            minutes="0"+minutes;


        tmp=(int)aMillis;
    mills=tmp.ToString();
    if(mills.Length<2)
            mills="0"+mills;
```

```
        // pull together a formatted string to return
        timeString=minutes+":"+seconds+":"+mills;


    return timeString;
}


public int GetTime ()
{
        // remember to call UpdateTimer() before trying to use this
        // function, otherwise the time value will not be up to date
    return (int)(currentTime);
}
}
```

4.2.1 Script Breakdown

In this script, we will only update time whenever the time is requested. Although there may be cases where the timer would need to be updated constantly, in the projects for this book we only need to do it on demand. So, after the variable declarations, the TimerClass. cs script begins with an update function called UpdateTimer(). Note that if you wanted the timer to update constantly, you would derive the class from MonoBehavior (instead of from ScriptableObject as it currently does) and add a call to UpdateTimer in your main Update function.

The timer works by having a variable called currentTime that stores the amount of time elapsed since the timer started. currentTime starts at zero, then UpdateTimer() calculates how much time goes by between updates and adds it to currentTime. The value of currentTime is then parsed into minutes, seconds, and milliseconds, and returned as a nice, tidy formatted string in the GetFormattedTime() function of the same class.

UpdateTimer() will be the only function that updates the timer's time system:

```
public void UpdateTimer ()
    {
            // calculate the time elapsed since the last Update()
            timeElapsed=Mathf.Abs(Time.realtimeSinceStartup-lastTime);
```

A variable called timeElapsed tracks how much time has gone by between updates. Time.realtimeSinceStartup is used for good reason. By using realtimeSinceStartup, the game can do whatever it likes to the Time.timeScale value (speeding up or slowing down Unity physics updates), and realtimeSinceStartup will still provide usable values. If Time. time were used, it would be affected by the timeScale and would fail to provide real-time values if its value were set to anything other than 1.

```
                // if the timer is running, we add the time elapsed to the
                // current time (advancing the timer)
                if(isTimerRunning)
                {
                        currentTime+=timeElapsed*timeScaleFactor;
                }
```

```
                    // store the current time so that we can use it on the next
                    // update
                    lastTime=Time.realtimeSinceStartup;
        }
```

The rest of the function checks to see whether isTimerRunning is true before updating currentTime. isTimerRunning is a Boolean that we can use to start or stop the timer without affecting anything else.

Note that one commonly used method of pausing Unity games is to set Time.timeScale to 0, which would stop a timer that didn't use Time.realtimeSinceStartup. In this case, we will be unaffected by timescale, so this alternative system will need to be used to start and stop the timer during a game pause.

The final part of the UpdateTimer() function grabs the current Time.realtimeSinceStartup and stores it in the variable lastTime, so that we can use its value to calculate the time elapsed between this and the next call to UpdateTimer.

A StartTimer() function is used to start the timer:

```
public void StartTimer ()
        {
                // set up initial variables to start the timer
                isTimerRunning=true;
                lastTime=Time.realtimeSinceStartup;
        }
```

isTimerRunning tells us whether or not to update currentTime in the UpdateTimer() function shown earlier. When the timer starts, we need to ensure that its value is true.

lastTime needs to be reset when we start the timer so that time will not be counted that occurred 'in between' the timer being stopped and the timer starting up again.

```
        public void StopTimer ()
        {
                // stop the timer
                isTimerRunning=false;
        }
```

isTimerRunning is set to false, which stops UpdateTimer() from adding any extra time to the currentTime variable.

If there is ever a need to reset the timer, we need to refresh some of the main variables to their default states. In the ResetTimer() function, timeElapsed, lastTime, and currentTime are reset:

```
public void ResetTimer ()
        {
                // resetTimer will set the timer back to zero
                timeElapsed=0.0f;
                currentTime=0.0f;
                lastTime=Time.realtimeSinceStartup;
        }
```

4. Recipes: Common Components

We reset lastTime to the current time taken from Time.realtimeSinceStartup, which effectively removes the time counted between now and the last update and starts counting from now instead. Finally, we make a quick call to UpdateTimer() to start the timer process again.

Whenever we need to display the time on the screen, it is most likely that we will need it to be formatted in an established format such as minutes:seconds:milliseconds. To do this, a little work is required to calculate the required units from our currentTime variable, as currentTime is simply a float value containing a number that bears no resemblance to what we need. Time.realtimeSinceStartup returns time as reported by a system timer in seconds. The GetFormattedTime function takes this value and breaks it up into the units we need, then puts together a nicely formatted string and returns it.

```
public string GetFormattedTime ()
    {
            // carry out an update to the timer so it is 'up to date'
            UpdateTimer();
```

Note that when GetFormattedTime() is called, we first make an UpdateTimer call to update the currentTime value. As mentioned earlier, the timer does not update itself—it is a lazy updater in that it only updates when we ask it to do something. In this case, we ask it for a formatted time string.

From there on, we are simply doing the math to get the minutes, seconds and milliseconds values from currentTime:

```
// grab minutes
aMinute=(int)currentTime/60;
aMinute=aMinute%60;

// grab seconds
aSecond=(int)currentTime%60;

// grab milliseconds
aMillis=(int)(currentTime*100)%100;
```

After minutes, seconds, and milliseconds values have been calculated and stored into the integer variables aMinute, aSecond, and aMillis, three new strings called seconds, minutes, and mills are built from them:

```
// format strings for individual mm/ss/mills
tmp=(int)aSecond;
seconds=tmp.ToString();
if(seconds.Length<2)
seconds="0"+seconds;

            tmp=(int)aMinute;
            minutes=tmp.ToString();
if(minutes.Length<2)
minutes="0"+minutes;

            tmp=(int)aHour;
            hour=tmp.ToString();
            if(hour.Length<2)
hour="0"+hour;
```

```
                  tmp=(int)aMillis;
mills=tmp.ToString();
if(mills.Length<2)
mills="0"+mills;
```

The function uses the .Length of each string to discover whether or not an extra '0' should be prefixed to the time value. This is purely for aesthetics, making the time strings consistently have two numbers even when its value is less than 10.

The final string is composed of a colon separator between each time value and then returned like this:

```
        // pull together a formatted string to return
        timeString=minutes+":"+seconds+":"+mills;


    return timeString;
}
```

At the very end of TimerClass.cs, a GetTime() function provides a way for other scripts to process the value of currentTime:

```
public int GetTime ()
    {
        // remember to call UpdateTimer() before trying to use this
        // function, otherwise the time value will not be up to date
    return (int)(currentTime);
    }
```

An example of how GetTime() may be used can be found in the *Tank Battle* game source code provided with this book (http://www.crcpress.com/product/isbn/9781466581401), where a game controller script takes the return value from a timer's GetTime() function and checks it to see whether the game has been running long enough to end.

■ 4.3 Spawn Scripts

In many cases, using Unity's built-in Instantiate function would be enough for creating objects for a desktop computer-based game, but instantiating gameObjects in Unity can be an expensive process, particularly noticeable on mobile devices. One common method of getting around the processor hit is to use pooling. Pooling is where you have a group of objects that you use and reuse without destroying them. Instead, pooled objects are hidden rather than entirely removed from memory. With this method, the memory is already allocated and the objects already exist but you are enabling and disabling them rather than having the performance hit of creating new ones and deleting unused ones.

Building a pool management system is beyond the scope of this book, although centralizing the spawning system will make it easy to switch out spawning for a better solution in the future. There are a couple of pool managers available to buy from the Unity Asset Store, or you may want to take a look at some free code to handle pooling from an awesome website called Unity Patterns (http://unitypatterns.com/new-tool-objectpool/).

4.3.1 A Simple Spawn Controller

The reason we use a spawn controller is so that we can track what has been added to the game world, if required, or switch out the spawning system for something more robust (such as a third-party library from the Unity Asset Store like PoolManager).

The spawn controller we will build in this chapter will have a few extra functions that may be useful to game development such as SetUpPlayers, which is a function that takes a list of prefabs to instantiate, a list of start positions, start rotations, and the total number of players. The function will instantiate all of the players at the correct positions and rotations:

```
public void SetUpPlayers (GameObject[] playerPrefabs, Vector3[]
playerStartPositions, Quaternion[] playerStartRotations, Transform
theParentObj, int totalPlayers)
```

An array of player prefabs can easily be set up and passed into the spawn controller to instantiate, letting the spawn controller take care of building them rather than having to write instantiation functions for each game. For example, the racing game example *Motor Vehicle Doom* will have an array of vehicles that may be set up in the Inspector window of the Unity editor. This array gets passed to the spawn controller and instantiated. By dealing with players in this way, we can easily switch out player types between levels or even build the list dynamically if required.

Below is the SpawnController.cs script:

```
using UnityEngine;
using System.Collections;


public class SpawnController : ScriptableObject
{
        private ArrayList playerTransforms;
        private ArrayList playerGameObjects;


        private Transform tempTrans;
        private GameObject tempGO;


        private GameObject[] playerPrefabList;
        private Vector3[] startPositions;
        private Quaternion[] startRotations;


        // singleton structure based on AngryAnt's fantastic wiki entry
        // over at http://wiki.unity3d.com/index.php/Singleton


        private static SpawnController instance;


        public SpawnController ()
        {
```

```
                    // this function will be called whenever an instance of the
                    // SpawnController class is made
                    // first, we check that an instance does not already exist
                    // (this is a singleton, after all!)
                    if (instance != null)
                    {
                            // drop out if instance exists, to avoid generating
                            // duplicates
                            Debug.LogWarning("Tried to generate more than one
                            instance of singleton SpawnController.");
                            return;
                    }


                    // as no instance already exists, we can safely set instance
                    // to this one
                    instance = this;
            }


            public static SpawnController Instance
            {
                    // to every other script, this getter setter is the way they
                    // get access to the singleton instance of this script
                    get
                    {
                            // the other script is trying to access an instance
                            // of this script, so we need to see if an instance
                            // already exists
                            if (instance == null)
                            {
                                    // no instance exists yet, so we go ahead and
                                    // create one
ScriptableObject.CreateInstance<SpawnController>(); // new SpawnController ();
                            }
                            // now we pass the reference to this instance back
                            // to the other script so it can communicate with it
                            return instance;
                    }
            }


            public void Restart ()
            {
                    playerTransforms=new ArrayList();
                    playerGameObjects=new ArrayList();
            }


            public void SetUpPlayers (GameObject[] playerPrefabs, Vector3[]
playerStartPositions, Quaternion[] playerStartRotations, Transform
theParentObj, int totalPlayers)
            {
                    // we pass in everything needed to spawn players and take
                    // care of spawning players in this class so that we don't
                    // have to replicate this code in every game controller
                    playerPrefabList= playerPrefabs;
                    startPositions= playerStartPositions;
                    startRotations= playerStartRotations;
```

```
        // call the function to take care of spawning all the
        // players and putting them in the right places
        CreatePlayers( theParentObj, totalPlayers );
}


public void CreatePlayers ( Transform theParent, int totalPlayers )
{
        playerTransforms=new ArrayList();
        playerGameObjects=new ArrayList();


        for(int i=0; i<totalPlayers;i++)
        {
                // spawn a player
                tempTrans= Spawn ( playerPrefabList[i],
                startPositions[i], startRotations[i] );

                // if we have passed in an object to parent the
                // players to, set the parent
                if(theParent!=null)
                {
                        tempTrans.parent= theParent;
                        // as we are parented, let's set the local
                        // position
                        tempTrans.localPosition= startPositions[i];
                }

                // add this transform into our list of player
                // transforms
                playerTransforms.Add(tempTrans);


                // add its gameobject into our list of player
                // gameobjects (we cache them separately)
                playerGameObjects.Add (tempTrans.gameObject);
        }
}


public GameObject GetPlayerGO (int indexNum)
{
        return (GameObject)playerGameObjects[indexNum];
}


public Transform GetPlayerTransform (int indexNum)
{
        return (Transform)playerTransforms[indexNum];
}


public Transform Spawn(GameObject anObject, Vector3 aPosition,
Quaternion aRotation)
{
        // instantiate the object
```

```
        tempGO=(GameObject)Instantiate(anObject, aPosition,
        aRotation);
        tempTrans= tempGO.transform;


        // return the object to whatever was calling
        return tempTrans;
    }


    // here we just provide a convenient function to return the spawned
    // objects gameobject rather than its transform
    public GameObject SpawnGO(GameObject anObject, Vector3 aPosition,
    Quaternion aRotation)
    {
        // instantiate the object
        tempGO=(GameObject)Instantiate(anObject, aPosition,
        aRotation);
        tempTrans= tempGO.transform;


        // return the object to whatever was calling
        return tempGO;
    }


    public ArrayList GetAllSpawnedPlayers()
    {
        return playerTransforms;
    }
}
```

4.3.1.1 Script Breakdown

The SpawnController class derives from ScriptableObject:

```
public class SpawnController : ScriptableObject
{
```

After the variable declarations, SpawnController.cs sets up as a singleton. As it says in the comments, this code is based on the work of AngryAnt (published on the Unity wiki site http://wiki.unity3d.com/index.php?title=Singleton). Recall that the singleton pattern was discussed earlier in Chapter 2. If you missed it, this just takes care of only ever having one instance of the script in existence at any time so that we always use the same instance regardless of where or how it is accessed by other scripts.

```
    private static SpawnController instance;

    public SpawnController ()
    {
        // this function will be called whenever an instance of the
        // SpawnController class is made
        // first, we check that an instance does not already exist
        // (this is a singleton, after all!)
        if (instance != null)
```

```
        {
                // drop out if instance exists, to avoid generating
                // duplicates
                Debug.LogWarning("Tried to generate more than one
                instance of singleton SpawnController.");
                return;
        }


        // as no instance already exists, we can safely set instance
        // to this one
        instance = this;
}


public static SpawnController Instance
{
        // to every other script, this getter setter is the way they
        // get access to the singleton instance of this script
        get
        {
                // the other script is trying to access an instance
                // of this script, so we need to see if an instance
                // already exists
                if (instance == null)
                {
                        // no instance exists yet, so we go ahead and
                        // create one
ScriptableObject.CreateInstance<SpawnController>(); // new SpawnController ();
                }
                // now we pass the reference to this instance back
                // to the other script so it can communicate with it
                return instance;
        }
    }
}
```

After the setup functions, the script moves on to a simple Restart() function that clears out all of the ArrayLists used later on by the script.

```
public void Restart ()
{
        playerTransforms=new ArrayList();
        playerGameObjects=new ArrayList();
        objectList=new ArrayList();
}
```

The SetUpPlayers function is a very specific function designed for a specific purpose. That is, it functions to pass in information about the players in the game represented by a series of arrays and an integer to say how many players are in the game in total. This information is not used immediately and will be used later on in the script by the CreatePlayers() function.

```
    public void SetUpPlayers (GameObject[] playerPrefabs, Vector3[]
playerStartPositions, Quaternion[] playerStartRotations, Transform
theParentObj, int totalPlayers)
        {
```

```
        // we pass in everything needed to spawn players and take
        // care of spawning players in this class so that we don't
        // have to replicate this code in every game controller
        playerPrefabList= playerPrefabs;
        startPositions= playerStartPositions;
        startRotations= playerStartRotations;


        // call the function to take care of spawning all the
        // players and putting them in the right places
        CreatePlayers( theParentObj, totalPlayers );
    }
```

CreatePlayers() takes all of the information passed into the SetUpPlayers() function and deals with the actual instantiation of the player objects into the game scene:

```
    public void CreatePlayers ( Transform theParent, int totalPlayers )
    {

        playerTransforms=new ArrayList();
        playerGameObjects=new ArrayList();

        for(int i=0; i<totalPlayers;i++)
        {
            // spawn a player
            tempTrans= Spawn ( playerPrefabList[i],
            startPositions[i], startRotations[i] );


            // if we have passed in an object to parent the
            // players to, set the parent
            if(theParent!=null)
            {
                tempTrans.parent= theParent;
                // as we are parented, let's set the local
                // position
                tempTrans.localPosition= startPositions[i];
            }

            // add this transform into our list of player
            // transforms
            playerTransforms.Add(tempTrans);


            // add its gameobject into our list of player
            // gameobjects (we cache them separately)
            playerGameObjects.Add (tempTrans.gameObject);
        }
    }
```

The GetPlayerGO(indexNum) function allows us to get back some information about the players spawned by the CreatePlayers() function. It simply grabs an entry from the playerGameObjects array and returns it, so that we can always get access to players via a simple integer index number.

```
    public GameObject GetPlayerGO (int indexNum)
    {
```

```
                return (GameObject)playerGameObjects[indexNum];
    }
```

As with GetPlayerGO(), the GetPlayerTransform() function allows us to quickly access the transform of a particular player indexed via an integer.

```
    public Transform GetPlayerTransform (int indexNum)
    {
                return (Transform)playerTransforms[indexNum];
    }
```

For incidental spawning, such as particle effects, the SpawnController.cs script provides a Spawn() method.

At this stage, you need to understand what prefabs are, and in turn, how they can be dynamically added to the scene. To quote the Unity documentation:

> [Prefabs are] … a collection of predefined GameObjects & Components that are re-usable throughout your game.

They are saved into the project, available in the same way regular assets are, and may be dragged into a scene or added dynamically through code with the Instantiate keyword. Instantiate makes a clone of an object you pass in as a parameter and returns a reference to the clone.

Instantiate takes three parameters:

object   An existing object (such as a prefab or gameObject) to make a copy of

position   A Vector3 position for the new object

rotation   A Quaternion rotation for the new object

One important consideration to keep in mind is that there is a CPU hit for object instantiation as memory is freed and allocated for it. This is much more noticeable on mobile platforms, particularly those lower performing systems such as older (3–4-year-old) devices. In situations where performance is an issue, it is advisable to use an object pooling system. Test early, test often, and keep an eye out for performance hits like this.

By passing in a prefab (gameObject), a 3D position vector, and a Quaternion rotation value, the Spawn function will instantiate (make an instance of) an object in the correct place with the correct rotation and return the transform of the newly instantiated object:

```
    public Transform Spawn(GameObject anObject, Vector3 aPosition,
    Quaternion aRotation)
    {
                if(objectList==null)
                        objectList=new ArrayList();


                // instantiate the object
                tempGO=(GameObject)Instantiate(anObject, aPosition,
                aRotation);
                tempTrans= tempGO.transform;
```

```
                // store this object in our list of objects
                objectList.Add(tempTrans);

                // return the object to whatever was calling
                return tempTrans;
        }
```

For occasions where it is preferable to return a newly instantiated object's gameObject rather than the transform, the SpawnGO (GO being short for GameObject) function is available. It works exactly the same as the Spawn function, but instead of returning the newly instantiated object's transform, it returns its gameObject.

```
        // here we just provide a convenient function to return the spawned
        // objects gameobject rather than its transform
        public GameObject SpawnGO(GameObject anObject, Vector3 aPosition,
        Quaternion aRotation)
        {
                if(objectList==null)
                        objectList=new ArrayList();

                // instantiate the object
                tempGO=(GameObject)Instantiate(anObject, aPosition,
                aRotation);
                tempTrans= tempGO.transform;


                // store this object in our list of objects
                objectList.Add(tempTrans);


                // return the object to whatever was calling
                return tempGO;
        }
```

The SpawnController.cs script track every object that it has created. Each one is stored in the array (an ArrayList type variable) named objectList. To have SpawnController.cs return the whole list, the function GetAllSpawnedTransforms() is provided.

```
        public ArrayList GetAllSpawnedTransforms()
        {
                return objectList;
        }
}
```

4.3.2 Trigger Spawner

The TriggerSpawner.cs script instantiates an object when another object enters the trigger to which the script is attached. One such use for this script would be to spawn an enemy when the player reaches a particular area in a level:

```
public class TriggerSpawner : MonoBehavior
{
```

```
public GameObject ObjectToSpawnOnTrigger;
public Vector3 offsetPosition;
public bool onlySpawnOnce;
public int layerToCauseTriggerHit= 13; // this should be set to the
                                       // number of the camera layer


private Transform myTransform;


void Start ()
{
        Vector3 tempPos=transform.position;
        tempPos.y=Camera.main.transform.position.y;
        transform.position=tempPos;


        // cache transform
        myTransform=transform;
}


void OnTriggerEnter(Collider other)
{
        // make sure that the layer of the object entering our
        // trigger is the one to cause the boss to spawn
        if(other.gameObject.layer!=layerToCauseTriggerHit)
                return;

        // instantiate the object to spawn on trigger enter

        Instantiate(ObjectToSpawnOnTrigger,myTransform.position+
        offsetPosition,Quaternion.identity);


        // if we are to only spawn once, destroy this gameobject
        // after spawn occurs
        if(onlySpawnOnce)
                Destroy (gameObject);
}
}
```

4.3.3 Path Spawner

This script fulfills quite a specific need, albeit one that may crop up frequently in game development. The path spawner makes a new object appear in the game and tells its waypoint-following code which path to follow (which waypoint controller script to use for finding waypoints).

In the example game *Interstellar Paranoids* from Chapter 14, it is used for the path-following enemies in each level. Waypoint paths are stored in prefabs, which may be dragged into each scene to build levels with. The Path_Spawner.cs script component is attached to the parent gameObject in the path prefabs, identifying which enemies to spawn, and then as they are spawned, telling them to use the waypoint path from the prefab.

With a path spawner system, the enemies never need to have any path names or way-point objects hard-coded to them—it can create and guide any enemy capable of following a path.

The prefabs/objects to spawn are stored in an array called spawnObjectPrefabs. This array can be as small or large as you like—if there is more than one, use timeBetweenSpawns to schedule each object one after the other.

There are two ways this script will begin to spawn objects from the spawnObjectPrefabs list. One is to set the shouldAutoStartSpawningOnLoad variable to true, and the other is to use a trigger system based on the position of the camera. In the example game *Interstellar Paranoids*, the trigger system is used so that enemies do not appear until the camera (and along with it the player) are within range.

Below is the Path_Spawner.cs script in full:

```
public class Path_Spawner : MonoBehavior
{
        public Waypoints_Controller waypointControl;


        // should we start spawning based on distance from the camera?
        // if distanceBased is false, we will need to call this class from
        // elsewhere, to spawn
        public bool distanceBasedSpawnStart;
        // if we're using distance based spawning, at what distance should
        // we start?
        public float distanceFromCameraToSpawnAt = 35f;


        // if the distanceBasedSpawnStart is false, we can have the path
        // spawner just start spawning automatically
        public bool shouldAutoStartSpawningOnLoad;


        public float timeBetweenSpawns=1;
        public int totalAmountToSpawn=10;
        public bool shouldReversePath;


        public GameObject[] spawnObjectPrefabs;


        private int totalSpawnObjects;


        private Transform myTransform;
        private GameObject tempObj;


        private int spawnCounter=0;
        private int currentObjectNum;
        private Transform cameraTransform;
        private bool spawning;


        public bool shouldSetSpeed;
        public float speedToSet;
```

```
public bool shouldSetSmoothing;
public float smoothingToSet;


public bool shouldSetRotateSpeed;
public float rotateToSet;


private bool didInit;


void Start ()
{
        Init();
}


void Init ()
{
        // cache ref to our transform
        myTransform = transform;


        // cache ref to the camera
        Camera mainCam = Camera.main;


        if( mainCam==null )
                return;


        cameraTransform = mainCam.transform;


        // tell waypoint controller if we want to reverse the path
        // or not
        waypointControl.SetReverseMode(shouldReversePath);


        totalSpawnObjects= spawnObjectPrefabs.Length;

        if(shouldAutoStartSpawningOnLoad)
                StartWave(totalAmountToSpawn,timeBetweenSpawns);
}


public void OnDrawGizmosSelected()
{
        Gizmos.color = new Color(0,0,1,0.5f);
        Gizmos.DrawCube(transform.position,new Vector3(200,0,distance
        FromCameraToSpawnAt));
}


public void Update()
{
        float aDist=Mathf.Abs(myTransform.position.z-cameraTransform.
        position.z);
```

```
                    if( distanceBasedSpawnStart && !spawning && aDist<distance
                    FromCameraToSpawnAt)
                    {
                            StartWave(totalAmountToSpawn,timeBetweenSpawns);
                            spawning=true;
                    }
            }


            public void StartWave(int HowMany, float timeBetweenSpawns)
            {
                    spawnCounter=0;
                    totalAmountToSpawn=HowMany;


                    // reset
                    currentObjectNum=0;


                    CancelInvoke("doSpawn");
                    InvokeRepeating("doSpawn",timeBetweenSpawns,timeBetweenSpawns);
            }


            void doSpawn()
            {
                    SpawnObject();
            }


            public void SpawnObject()
            {
                    if(spawnCounter>=totalAmountToSpawn)
                    {
                            // tell your script that the wave is finished here
                            CancelInvoke("doSpawn");
                            this.enabled=false;
                            return;
                    }


                    // create an object

                    tempObj=SpawnController.Instance.SpawnGO(spawnObjectPrefabs
                    [currentObjectNum],myTransform.position,Quaternion.
                    identity);


                    // tell object to reverse its pathfinding, if required
                    tempObj.SendMessage("SetReversePath", shouldReversePath,
                    SendMessageOptions.DontRequireReceiver);


                    // tell spawned object to use this waypoint controller

                    tempObj.SendMessage("SetWayController",waypointControl,Send
                    MessageOptions.DontRequireReceiver);
```

```
                // tell object to use this speed (again with no required
                // receiver just in case)
                if(shouldSetSpeed)

                tempObj.SendMessage("SetSpeed",speedToSet,SendMessage
                Options.DontRequireReceiver);

                // tell object to use this speed (again with no required
                // receiver just in case)
                if(shouldSetSmoothing)

                tempObj.SendMessage("SetPathSmoothingRate",smoothingToSet,
                SendMessageOptions.DontRequireReceiver);

                // tell object to use this speed (again with no required
                // receiver just in case)
                if(shouldSetRotateSpeed)

                tempObj.SendMessage("SetRotateSpeed",rotateToSet,SendMessage
                Options.DontRequireReceiver);

                // increase the 'how many objects we have spawned' counter
                spawnCounter++;

                // increase the 'which object to spawn' counter
                currentObjectNum++;

                // check to see if we've reached the end of the spawn
                // objects array
                if(currentObjectNum> totalSpawnObjects-1 )
                        currentObjectNum=0;
        }
}
```

4.3.3.1 Script Breakdown

This script derives from MonoBehavior:

```
public class Path_Spawner : MonoBehavior
{
```

The Path_Spawner class assumes that you will be able to set a reference to a waypoint controller in the Unity editor Inspector window (there is currently no interface to do this through code). If no waypoint controller is referenced, the script will do nothing:

```
        public Waypoints_Controller waypointControl;
```

After the rest of the variable declarations, the Start() function kicks things off with a call to Init():

```
        void Start ()
        {
                Init();
        }
```

Init() is responsible for setting up the references required to make the core of this class work. Those are the transform of the gameObject this script is attached to and the transform belonging to the main camera in the scene (found by using Unity's Camera.main):

```
void Init ()
{
        // cache ref to our transform
        myTransform = transform;


        // cache ref to the camera
        Camera mainCam = Camera.main;
```

Camera.main finds the first camera tagged with the MainCamera tag (see the tag dropdown in the Unity editor Inspector window). If there are no cameras in the scene tagged with this, the main part of this function will not work. For that reason, when mainCam is null, it drops out of Init() early:

```
if( mainCam==null )
        return;
```

The camera transform is stored in cameraTransform, which will be used to trigger spawning when distanceBasedSpawnStart is true:

```
cameraTransform = mainCam.transform;
```

This script has its own shouldReversePath Boolean variable, as well as the waypoint controller having one. This line takes the value of the Boolean variable shouldReversePath and uses it to override the existing reverse mode value held by the waypoint controller any spawned objects will use. It does this by calling waypointControl.SetReverseMode():

```
// tell waypoint controller if we want to reverse the path
// or not
waypointControl.SetReverseMode(shouldReversePath);
```

To keep a total on how many objects are in the spawnObjectPrefabs array:

```
totalSpawnObjects= spawnObjectPrefabs.Length;
```

If shouldAutoStartSpawningOnLoad is set to true, the first spawning kicks off right away. The StartWave() function takes two parameters: how many enemies it should spawn and what the time between spawns should be from here on. StartWave() will schedule future enemy spawning:

```
if(shouldAutoStartSpawningOnLoad)
        StartWave(totalAmountToSpawn,timeBetweenSpawns);
}
```

The OnDrawGizmosSelected() function draws helper graphics in the Unity editor whenever this gameObject is selected:

```
public void OnDrawGizmosSelected()
{
```

Once the color has been set by Gizmos.color, everything drawn after this point will adopt the set color:

```
Gizmos.color = new Color(0,0,1,0.5f);
```

Gizmos.DrawCube() is used here to display a cube to show how close the camera will need to be in order to trigger the spawning. This is based on the value of distanceFromCameraToSpawnAt:

```
Gizmos.DrawCube(transform.position,new Vector3(200,0,distance
FromCameraToSpawnAt));
}
```

The main reason that this script derives from MonoBehavior is so that it can use the system functions such as Update(). The Update() function is called every frame:

```
public void Update()
{
```

aDist is a temporary float variable used to figure out the difference between this transform's *z* position and the position of the camera. It uses the *z* position (and not the other axis) because of the way that the camera moves through the level. The camera progresses through the level along the world *z*-axis, so for the type of game this system is designed for it makes sense to use only the *z*-axis:

```
float aDist= Mathf.Abs(myTransform.position.z-camera
Transform.position.z);
```

If the component is set to use distanceBasedSpawnStart, there is no spawning currently happening and the distance is less than distanceFromCameraToSpawnAt, the next wave can be spawned:

```
if( distanceBasedSpawnStart && !spawning && aDist<distance
FromCameraToSpawnAt)
{
        StartWave(totalAmountToSpawn,timeBetweenSpawns);
        spawning=true;
}
}
```

StartWave() begins by resetting a few variables that will be used during the spawn cycle. A counter is used to track of the number of enemies spawned (spawnCounter), and the parameter named HowMany is copied into another variable, totalAmountToSpawn, to track how many this wave should contain:

```
public void StartWave(int HowMany, float timeBetweenSpawns)
{
        spawnCounter=0;
        totalAmountToSpawn=HowMany;


        // reset
        currentObjectNum=0;
```

A repeating call to the function doSpawn() will be made with Unity's InvokeRepeating() function. InvokeRepeating will keep on calling doSpawn() until a CancelInvoke() tells it to stop or the scene is removed from memory. Before scheduling a new repeat call, this code uses CancelInvoke() to make sure that any previous call is well and truly stopped:

```
        CancelInvoke("doSpawn");
        InvokeRepeating("doSpawn",timeBetweenSpawns,timeBetweenSpa
wns);
    }
```

doSpawn() is the function that is repeatedly called automatically by InvokeRepeating() calls. It calls SpawnObject() to add the enemy to the scene:

```
    void doSpawn()
    {
        SpawnObject();
    }
```

SpawnObject() checks the spawn counter first to see whether the wave has finished or not. When the variable spawnCounter is greater than totalAmountToSpawn, the repeating Invoke call needs to be cancelled by a CancelInvoke():

```
    public void SpawnObject()
    {
        if(spawnCounter>=totalAmountToSpawn)
        {
            // tell your script that the wave is finished here
            CancelInvoke("doSpawn");
```

When this wave has finished, this script disables itself and drops out to avoid using any unnecessary CPU cycles:

```
            this.enabled=false;
            return;
        }
```

The object (enemy) is created by the singleton-type instance of the SpawnController. Its SpawnGO() creates the object and returns a reference to the new object's gameObject:

```
        // create an object

        tempObj=SpawnController.Instance.SpawnGO(spawnObjectPrefabs
        [currentObjectNum],myTransform.position,Quaternion.identity);

        // tell object to reverse its pathfinding, if required

        tempObj.SendMessage('SetReversePath', shouldReversePath,
        SendMessageOptions.DontRequireReceiver);
```

The newly spawned object needs to know which waypoint controller to use. Rather than go through and try to find its control script, we use gameObject.SendMessage() to send a message and a single parameter to the object. Any script component attached to the gameObject that has a function named SetWayController() will be able to receive it. Just in case there are no scripts with this function name in, a final (optional) parameter in the

SendMessage() call is SendMessageOptions.DontRequireReceiver, which stops any warnings if the message is not received:

```
// tell spawned object to use this waypoint controller

tempObj.SendMessage("SetWayController",waypointControl,Send
MessageOptions.DontRequireReceiver);
```

If shouldSetSpeed is set to true, this function will attempt to set the speed of the new object based on the value of speedToSet. As with setting the waypoint controller, gameObject.SendMessage() is used to tell the object about the speed rather than having to find a specific script and call a function on it:

```
// tell object to use this speed (again with no required
// receiver just in case)
if(shouldSetSpeed)

tempObj.SendMessage("SetSpeed",speedToSet,SendMessage
Options.DontRequireReceiver);
```

When shouldSetSmoothing is true, gameObject.SendMessage() is used to send a smoothing rate to a function named SetPathSmoothingRate. This will affect how quickly the objects/enemies turn on the path:

```
// tell object to use this speed (again with no required
// receiver just in case)
if(shouldSetSmoothing)

tempObj.SendMessage("SetPathSmoothingRate",smoothingToSet,
SendMessageOptions.DontRequireReceiver);
```

If shouldSetRotateSpeed is true, gameObject.SendMessage() attempts to send the rotate speed value (from the variable rotateToSet) to a function called SetRotateSpeed():

```
// tell object to use this speed (again with no required
// receiver just in case)
if(shouldSetRotateSpeed)

tempObj.SendMessage("SetRotateSpeed",rotateToSet,SendMessage
Options.DontRequireReceiver);
```

Now that spawning and setup have finished, we increase the spawnCounter and currentObjectNum counters:

```
// increase the 'how many objects we have spawned' counter
spawnCounter++;

// increase the 'which object to spawn' counter
currentObjectNum++;
```

The variable currentObjectNum is used to point which object to spawn next in the array of objects to be spawned. When it reaches the value of totalSpawnObjects–1, that's the top end of the array and it needs to be reset back to zero:

```
// check to see if we've reached the end of the spawn
// objects array
```

```
                if(currentObjectNum> totalSpawnObjects-1 )
                        currentObjectNum=0;
        }
}
```

■ 4.4 Set Gravity

Changing gravity is often frowned upon by developers because doing so changes the way objects behave in the physics simulation. It is highly recommended that your game physics values, game world scale, and speeds are as close to real-life numbers as possible. Making a game with an environment scaled too high or too low can cause problems with the collisions system as well as make your coordinate system difficult to manage. Altering gravity to extremely high values may cause objects to behave strangely or even push down through collision meshes. Dealing with strange physics values needs to be handled with a little care and awareness of "entering the twilight zone" in physics behavior terms.

The reality is that having realistic gravity with realistically scaled 3D models and realistic physics behavior may not always be either possible or, in fact, necessary. Perhaps the effect you are going for is something outside of realistic, in which case it may become necessary to modify physics values such as gravity. Games based on another planet would likely be the most obvious use for changing these values. In the example games in this book, when gravity is altered it is purely on a personal preference of how I like game physics to feel.

The SetGravity.cs script sets gravity once in the Start() function and disables itself to save any unnecessary overhead. Its logic is extremely simple, being a single call to set Physics.gravity to a 3D vector and then disabling itself by setting this.enabled to false. The variable this is simply a reference to itself, a way of telling the script to refer to itself:

```
public class SetGravity : MonoBehavior {


        public Vector3 gravityValue = new Vector3(0,-12.81f,0);


        void Start () {
                Physics.gravity=gravityValue;
                this.enabled=false;
        }
}
```

■ 4.5 Pretend Friction—Friction Simulation to Prevent Slipping Around

The easiest way to move objects around in Unity is to simply apply forces to your rigid-bodies. By using Rigidbody.AddForce and perhaps a multiplier based on Input.GetAxis or something similar, it is quite easy to get objects moving around, but the only way to have them come to a stop is either to have them make friction against something else in the game world or to change drag values on the rigidbody. This may not always be an ideal solution and can present challenges when trying to control the turning behavior of objects floating in space or perhaps even character controllers.

To help out with controlling sideways slip, this simple PretendFriction.cs script can help:

```
using UnityEngine;
using System.Collections;

public class PretendFriction : MonoBehavior
{
        private Rigidbody myBody;
        private Transform myTransform;
        private float myMass;
        private float slideSpeed;
        private Vector3 velo;
        private Vector3 flatVelo;
        private Vector3 myRight;
        private Vector3 TEMPvec3;


        public float theGrip=100f;


        void Start ()
        {
                // cache some references to our rigidbody, mass and
                // transform
                myBody=rigidbody;
                myMass=myBody.mass;
                myTransform=transform;
        }


        void FixedUpdate ()
        {
                // grab the values we need to calculate grip
                myRight=myTransform.right;


                // calculate flat velocity
                velo=myBody.velocity;
                flatVelo.x=velo.x;
                flatVelo.y=0;
                flatVelo.z=velo.z;


                // calculate how much we are sliding
                slideSpeed=Vector3.Dot(myRight,flatVelo);


                // build a new vector to compensate for the sliding
                TEMPvec3= myRight * (-slideSpeed * myMass * theGrip);


                // apply the correctional force to the rigidbody
                myBody.AddForce(TEMPvec3 * Time.deltaTime);
        }
}
```

4.5.1 Script Breakdown

The script derives from MonoBehavior to tap into the Start() and FixedUpdate() system calls:

```
public class PretendFriction : MonoBehavior
{
```

The Start() function caches the rigidbody, the amount of mass on the rigidbody and the transform:

```
void Start ()
{
        // cache some references to our rigidbody, mass and
        // transform
        myBody=rigidbody;
        myMass=myBody.mass;
        myTransform=transform;
}
```

The FixedUpdate() function will calculate how much an object is sliding—to do this, it finds how much sideways movement the object is making (to the right relative to the transform's rotation)—to find out how much slip is happening:

```
void FixedUpdate ()
{
        // grab the values we need to calculate grip
        myRight=myTransform.right;

        // calculate flat velocity
        velo=myBody.velocity;
        flatVelo.x=velo.x;
        flatVelo.y=0;
        flatVelo.z=velo.z;

        // calculate how much we are sliding
        slideSpeed=Vector3.Dot(myRight,flatVelo);

        // build a new vector to compensate for the sliding
        TEMPvec3= myRight * (-slideSpeed * myMass * theGrip);

        // apply the correctional force to the rigidbody
        myBody.AddForce(TEMPvec3 * Time.deltaTime);
}
}
```

▌█ 4.6 Cameras

There are just two camera scripts for the example games in this book. Those are a third-person camera (a camera that sits behind and orbits around the player) and a top-down camera (a camera that sits up above the player, looking down). They use a similar interface for other scripts to be able to communicate with them, and both cameras should provide a good starting point for camera systems in your own games.

4.6.1 Third-Person Camera

A third-person camera sits behind the player. It is not quite the same as a follow camera; a third-person camera usually orbits around the player rather than simply following it around. To visualize this, imagine that the camera is tied to a pole attached to the target player. As the player moves around, the camera remains to be the length of the pole away from it but the camera is free to move around the player in a circle (see Figure 4.1).

The position of the camera is usually somewhere behind the player, with a little damping on its horizontal movement applied to it, to allow for a good sense of movement when the player turns. In some third-person camera setups, the camera may be allowed to move in or out from the target player some. In some setups, the camera may also be offset from the player a little (e.g., in the Microsoft Studios game *Gears of War*, the camera is positioned over the right shoulder of the player rather than directly behind).

Below is the Camera_Third_Person.cs script:

```
public class Camera_Third_Person : BaseCameraController
{
        public Transform myTransform;
        public Transform target;
        public float distance = 20.0f;
        public float height = 5.0f;
        public float heightDamping = 2.0f;


        public float lookAtHeight = 0.0f;


        public float rotationSnapTime = 0.3F;


        public float distanceSnapTime;


        public Vector3 lookAtAdjustVector;


        private float usedDistance;


        float wantedRotationAngle;
        float wantedHeight;
```

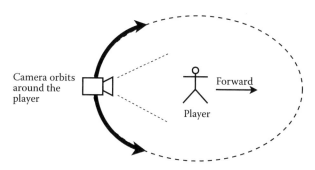

Figure 4.1 Behavior of a third-person camera.

```csharp
        float currentRotationAngle;
        float currentHeight;


        Quaternion currentRotation;
        Vector3 wantedPosition;


        private float yVelocity = 0.0F;
        private float zVelocity = 0.0F;


        public override void SetTarget( Transform aTarget )
        {
                target= aTarget;
        }


        void LateUpdate ()
{

    if ( target == null )

        return;

            if ( myTransform==null )
            {
                    myTransform=Transform;
            }


            wantedHeight = target.position.y + height;
            currentHeight = myTransform.position.y;


            wantedRotationAngle = target.eulerAngles.y;
            currentRotationAngle = myTransform.eulerAngles.y;


            currentRotationAngle = Mathf.SmoothDampAngle(currentRotation
            Angle, wantedRotationAngle, ref yVelocity, rotationSnapTime);


            currentHeight = Mathf.Lerp(currentHeight, wantedHeight,
            heightDamping * Time.deltaTime);


            wantedPosition = target.position;
            wantedPosition.y = currentHeight;


            usedDistance = Mathf.SmoothDampAngle(usedDistance, distance,
            ref zVelocity, distanceSnapTime);


            wantedPosition += Quaternion.Euler(0, currentRotationAngle,
0) * new Vector3(0, 0, -usedDistance);
```

```
              myTransform.position = wantedPosition;


              myTransform.LookAt( target.position + lookAtAdjustVector );
       }
}
```

4.6.1.1 Script Breakdown

All camera scripts used with the framework should implement a SetTarget function.
SetTarget takes a single parameter of type Transform to put into the variable named target:

```
public override void SetTarget( Transform aTarget )
      {
              target= aTarget;
      }
```

It may come as a surprise that the main update to the camera happens within
LateUpdate() and not within the Update or FixedUpdate function. The reason for this is
that we prefer everything physics-wise to have been updated before moving the camera—
which should have happened by LateUpdate()—and in doing so, there should be no dis-
crepancies between the positions of our target objects between the end of the camera
update and the drawing of the next frame. Drawing at the wrong time could cause a jitter-
ing effect as the objects we are following are updated after the camera positioning.

At the start of LateUpdate(), there are the usual null checks to make sure that we have
both a target and a cached version of the camera's transform:

```
      void LateUpdate ()
  {

      if ( target == null )

          return;

      if ( myTransform==null )
      {
              myTransform=Transform;
      }
```

The script interpolates heights and rotation values. Before the interpolation can happen, we need to find out what the target height and rotations are as well as what the current
height and rotations are. The wantedHeight variable is a float. We add the value of the public
variable height to it, allowing target height adjustment to happen by setting it in the editor:

```
              wantedHeight = target.position.y + height;
              currentHeight = myTransform.position.y;


              wantedRotationAngle = target.eulerAngles.y;
              currentRotationAngle = myTransform.eulerAngles.y;
```

currentRotationAngle is a float representing the angle, in degrees, that we need to turn the camera at to try to reach the target rotation in wantedRotationAngle. It's an interpolation carried out by Mathf.SmoothDampAngle.

Mathf.SmoothDampAngle is an interpolation function designed specifically for easing between two angles. It will automatically cap the return value between 0 and 360 as well as choose the correct way around (if your value is at 181°, it would interpolate up rather than down so that the rotation has a natural flow and doesn't go back on itself).

The Unity documentation tells us that SmoothDampAngle takes the following parameters (in order of how they should be passed in):

current	The current position.
target	The position we are trying to reach.
currentVelocity	The current velocity; this value is modified by the function every time you call it.
smoothTime	Approximately the time it will take to reach the target. A smaller value will reach the target faster.
maxSpeed	Optionally allows you to clamp the maximum speed.
deltaTime	The time since the last call to this function. By default Time.deltaTime.

In this part of the code, the yVelocity variable holds the current velocity of the interpolated move, but it is not actually used anywhere else in the script. It's a required field for SmoothDampAngle, so we just provide it for the function to work right and forget about it. Note that one possible use for getting the velocity may be speed limiting the move, but SmoothDampAngle can actually take care of this with no extra code by providing a maxSpeed parameter. This is useful for limiting interpolation speeds without having to do it yourself with velocity.

The currentRotationAngle is, in effect, the rotation amount required around the *y*-axis (hence using the name yVelocity to describe its speed). The variable rotationSnapTime decides how much time it should take for the rotation to happen, which is public and designed to be set in the Unity editor Inspector window on whichever gameObject the script is attached to:

```
currentRotationAngle = Mathf.SmoothDampAngle(currentRotation
Angle, wantedRotationAngle, ref yVelocity, rotationSnapTime);
```

The height movement is interpolated using Mathf.Lerp, which takes three parameters: the start amount, the target amount, and a time value clamped between 0 and 1.

We use the float heightDamping, multiplied by Time.deltaTime, to make the transition time based. Are you wondering why do we need to make the time parameter time based? Good question! How the time parameter of Mathf.Lerp works has been a very popular question on various forums and help pages. The time value represents how much of a portion, of the difference between two values, that should be applied each time this line of code is executed. If the time value is 0, the return value will be the start amount. If time is 1, the return value will be the target amount.

By calculating the portion with Time.deltaTime, the transition from start value to target value is smoothed out over a repeatable, fixed amount of time rather than it being frame-rate dependent and based on how many times the Mathf.Lerp calculation line is called:

```
currentHeight = Mathf.Lerp(currentHeight, wantedHeight,
heightDamping * Time.deltaTime);
```

Now that the script has calculated how much to rotate the camera and how high it should be on the *y*-axis, the script goes on to calculate where the camera is going to go position-wise.

wantedPosition is a Vector3 variable that will hold the target position. The first target position is the target transform's position and an adjustment for height using the currentHeight variable calculated above:

```
wantedPosition = target.position;
wantedPosition.y = currentHeight;
```

The next part of the code calculates how far behind the player we need to move the camera. For this, the script uses Mathf.SmoothDampAngle. zVelocity represents the speed of movement of the camera along its *z*-axis, but again it is purely a formality to use with SmoothDampAngle and does not get used anywhere else in the script:

```
usedDistance = Mathf.SmoothDampAngle(usedDistance, distance,
ref zVelocity, distanceSnapTime);
```

To place the camera at the correct position around the target using only a rotation angle, the solution lies within Quaternion.Euler. This rather frightening sounding function converts Euler angle Vector3-based rotations into a vector. That is, you pass in rotation values and you get back a direction vector instead. Multiply this by how far back we want the camera from the player, then add that to the player's current position, and we have the correct rotation, position, and offset for the camera:

```
wantedPosition += Quaternion.Euler(0, currentRotationAngle,
0) * new Vector3(0, 0, -usedDistance);


myTransform.position = wantedPosition;
```

The final part of the function causes the camera to look at the target (player). It does this by using Unity's built-in transform.LookAt() function. We pass in the position of the target object (as a Vector3) and add an extra offset to where the camera is going to look, via the lookAtAdjustVector variable. Note that you can also add an up vector to the LookAt() function, but in this case we don't need to.

Aiming the camera directly at the player from behind the player may obscure the path ahead and could make the game difficult to navigate. Instead, we add a small height adjustment to the target position, so that the camera aims above the player as if it were looking ahead, rather than right at it. With a simple target height adjustment, we can help the camera to stay parallel to the ground level and keep good visibility, making the game easier to play:

```
myTransform.LookAt( target.position + lookAtAdjustVector );
```

4.6.2 Top-Down Camera

The TopDown_Camera.cs script is a basic target-following system from a top-down perspective:

```
public class TopDown_Camera : MonoBehavior
{
        public Transform followTarget;
        public Vector3 targetOffset;
        public float moveSpeed= 2f;

        private Transform myTransform;

        void Start ()
        {
                myTransform= transform;
        }


        public void SetTarget( Transform aTransform )
        {
                followTarget= aTransform;
        }


        void LateUpdate ()
        {
                if(followTarget!=null)
                        myTransform.position= Vector3.Lerp( myTransform.
                        position, followTarget.position + targetOffset,
                        moveSpeed * Time.deltaTime );
        }
}
```

4.6.2.1 Script Breakdown

After the variable declarations, the Start() function takes care of caching a reference to the object's transform. The next function is extremely important:

```
public void SetTarget( Transform aTransform )
        {
                followTarget= aTransform;
        }
```

The SetTarget() function is used by all of the example games to tell the camera which object to follow during the game. The LateUpdate() function checks to make sure that we have a target before it tries to position the camera:

```
myTransform.position= Vector3.Lerp( myTransform.position, followTarget.
position + targetOffset, moveSpeed * Time.deltaTime );
```

The single line controlling our camera uses the Vector3.Lerp function to interpolate the camera's transform's position to that of the target stored in followTarget. We add an offset to the position (so that we end up above the target rather than inside it) and use the moveSpeed multiplied by Time.deltaTime to interpolate independent of frame rate.

It is a very simple camera but one that works really well for basic top-down games.

Note that in the *Lazer Blast Survival* example game for this book, an empty gameObject named CamTarget is used as the camera target. It is positioned in front of the player, parented to the player, so that it inherits the player's rotation. By positioning a target object in front of the player for use with a top-down camera like this, it can help gameplay by providing a better view ahead of the player rather than centering it on the screen.

■ 4.7 Input Scripts

In Chapter 3, we saw that the main player structure contained a single input script designed to take keyboard input. Adding input systems is a case of building custom input scripts that follow a similar format, so that the existing player code need not be changed to accommodate different controls.

It may be required to take input from other methods than the keyboard, such as a mouse or a joystick. You can easily set up alternate controls in the Unity editor via the Edit –> Project Settings –> Input menu.

4.7.1 Mouse Input

The Mouse_Input.cs script calculates the movement of the mouse between each frame and uses it for input.

Below is the script:

```
public class Mouse_Input : BaseInputController
{
        private Vector2 prevMousePos;
        private Vector2 mouseDelta;


        private float speedX = 0.05f;
        private float speedY = 0.1f;

        public void Start ()
        {
                prevMousePos= Input.mousePosition;
        }


        public override void CheckInput ()
        {
                // get input data from vertical and horizontal axis and
                // store them internally in vert and horz so we don't
```

```
            // have to access them every time we need to relay input
            // data out


            // calculate a percentage amount to use per pixel
            float scalerX = 100f / Screen.width;
            float scalerY = 100f / Screen.height;


            // calculate and use deltas
            float mouseDeltaY =  Input.mousePosition.y - prevMousePos.y;
            float mouseDeltaX =  Input.mousePosition.x - prevMousePos.x;


            // scale based on screen size
            vert += ( mouseDeltaY * speedY ) * scalerY;
            horz += ( mouseDeltaX * speedX ) * scalerX;


            // store this mouse position for the next time we're here
            prevMousePos= Input.mousePosition;


            // set up some Boolean values for up, down, left and right
            Up      = ( vert>0 );
            Down    = ( vert<0 );
            Left    = ( horz<0 );
            Right   = ( horz>0 );


            // get fire / action buttons
            Fire1= Input.GetButton( "Fire1" );
    }


    public void LateUpdate()
    {
            // check inputs each LateUpdate() ready for the next tick
            CheckInput();
    }
}
```

4.7.1.1 Script Breakdown

The Start() function adds a default value to prevMousePos, which will be used to calculate the movement between each update. If prevMousePos was left at zero (its default), then the first time CheckInput() happens, the script will incorrectly assume that the mouse has moved from 0,0 to the current mouse position.

Input provides an interface to Unity's input systems. It is used for everything from gyrometer input on mobile devices to keyboard presses. Input.mousePosition delivers the current position of the mouse in pixel coordinates as a 2D vector, with the bottom left of the screen at 0,0 and the top right at Screen.width, Screen.height.

```
public void Start ()
    {
```

```
                prevMousePos= Input.mousePosition;
    }
```

The input scripts use CheckInput() as their default main update function, which is intended to be called from the player class.

The mouse input system uses mouse delta movement (the amount of movement since the last update) instead of mouse position. The delta amount is converted into a percentage value (a percentage of the screen width or height), and the resulting percentage value is used as input.

CheckInput() starts by calculating a scale to work at. The floats scalerX and scalerY hold the equivalent of 1% of the screen's width and height, respectively:

```
public override void CheckInput ()
{
        // get input data from vertical and horizontal axis and
        // store them internally in vert and horz so we don't
        // have to access them every time we need to relay input
        // data out

        // calculate a percentage amount to use per pixel
        float scalerX = 100f / Screen.width;
        float scalerY = 100f / Screen.height;
```

The delta amount of mouse movement is calculated in the code by taking the current mouse position and subtracting it from the position that the mouse was at at the end of the last update.

```
                // calculate and use deltas
                float mouseDeltaY =  Input.mousePosition.y - prevMousePos.y;
                float mouseDeltaX =  Input.mousePosition.x - prevMousePos.x;
```

When the mouse position is multiplied by the scale variables (scalerX and scalerY), we end up with a percentage amount. We say that the mouse is at a percentage amount across the screen and use that percentage amount as input:

```
                // scale based on screen size
                vert += ( mouseDeltaY * speedY ) * scalerY;
                horz += ( mouseDeltaX * speedX ) * scalerX;


                // store this mouse position for the next time we're here
                prevMousePos= Input.mousePosition;
```

The mouse-based input scripts also populate Boolean variables for directional movement, if required:

```
                // set up some Boolean values for up, down, left and right
                Up      = ( vert>0 );
                Down    = ( vert<0 );
                Left    = ( horz<0 );
                Right   = ( horz>0 );
```

To make the fire button work properly, mouse button input must be set up correctly in the input settings of the Unity editor, under the Fire1 entry:

```
                // get fire / action buttons
                Fire1= Input.GetButton("Fire1");
        }
```

The script calls its own update function from LateUpdate(), which is where Unity recommends all input checking happen:

```
        public void LateUpdate()
        {
                // check inputs each LateUpdate() ready for the next tick
                CheckInput();
        }
}
```

Note that if firing does not work after applying this script, check that Unity is set up correctly to receive mouse button input as Fire1. To do this, open up Unity's Input menu (Edit → Project Settings → Input) and check that the Axes entry for Fire1 contains an entry for mouse 0 either in the negative, positive, or alt buttons.

4.7.2 Single Axis Keyboard Input

The single axis keyboard input script takes away the vertical axis and only takes input from horizontal and fire inputs. It follows the same format as the other input scripts and the input script from Chapter 3 (Player Structure), except the vertical axis is excluded:

```
public class Single_Axis_Keyboard_Input: BaseInputController
{
        public override void CheckInput ()
        {
                // get input data from vertical and horizontal axis and
                // store them internally in vert and horz so we don't
                // have to access them every time we need to relay input
                // data out
                horz=Input.GetAxis("Horizontal");


                // set up some Boolean values for up, down, left and right
                Left    =(horz<0);
                Right   =(horz>0);


                // get fire / action buttons
                Fire1=Input.GetButton("Fire1");
        }

        public void LateUpdate()
        {
                // check inputs each LateUpdate() ready for the next tick
                CheckInput();
        }
}
```

■ 4.8 Automatic Self-Destruction Script

The main use for a script that automatically destroys its gameObject will be for special effects. Particle effects such as explosions will be instantiated, their effect will play out, and then they need to be destroyed.

In the example games, a short and simple class called AutomaticDestroyObject is attached to a gameObject. After a set amount of time, set in the Unity editor Inspector window, the gameObject is destroyed along with any associated child objects attached to it.

Below is the full script:

```
public class AutomaticDestroyObject : MonoBehavior
{
        public float timeBeforeObjectDestroys;


        void Start () {
                // the function destroyGO() will be called in
                // timeBeforeObjectDestroys seconds
                Invoke("DestroyGO",timeBeforeObjectDestroys);
        }


        void DestroyGO () {
                // destroy this gameObject
                Destroy(gameObject);
        }
}
```

4.8.1 Script Breakdown

The class, which derives from MonoBehavior, is very simple. It uses Invoke to schedule a call to the DestroyGO() function at a time set by the public variable timeBeforeObjectDestroys. It probably goes without saying that DestroyGO() takes care of destroying itself, with Destroy(gameObject).

■ 4.9 Automatic Object Spinner

One common action you may need to do is spin an object. This may be for a number of reasons, the most obvious (in this book, at least) being to draw attention to power-ups in the *Interstellar Paranoids* game. By spinning the power-ups, they are more obvious to the player as something that may be interacted with, whereas static power-ups may be easily missed or ignored.

Making an object spin in Unity may be very simple, but having a script to take care of this is a useful little tool to keep in the toolkit.

Below is the script in full:

```
using UnityEngine;
using System.Collections;
```

```
public class AutoSpinObject : MonoBehavior
{
        public Vector3 spinVector = new Vector3(1,0,0);
        private Transform myTransform;


        void Start ()
        {
                myTransform=transform;
        }


        void Update () {
                myTransform.Rotate (spinVector*Time.deltaTime);
        }
}
```

4.9.1 Script Breakdown

AutoSpinObject.cs derives from MonoBehavior so that it can use Unity's automatic calls to the Start() and Update() functions:

```
public class AutoSpinObject : MonoBehavior
{
```

The function is derived from MonoBehavior so that we can update the object rotation in an Update() function.

```
        public Vector3 spinVector = new Vector3(1,0,0);
        private Transform myTransform;
```

The spinVector variable is a 3D vector that we will use to spin the object with. By using a vector, we can spin the object in any direction in the 3D space simply by changing the values this script component uses in the Inspector window of the Unity editor. Select the gameObject that has this script attached and change the value in the Inspector to change its behavior.

```
        void Start ()
        {
                myTransform=transform;
        }
```

As per every other script, we cache a reference to this object's transform in the Start() function. Caching this reference will save a lot of valuable processor time throughout the game.

The Update() function simply rotates the transform, multiplying the spinVector variable by Time.deltaTime to ensure that the rotation is frame rate independent and time based:

```
        void Update () {
                myTransform.Rotate (spinVector*Time.deltaTime);
        }
}
```

▌ 4.10 Scene Manager

The scene manager deals with loading and saving different scenes. It is intended to be used for loading different levels in a game, but also it may easily be used for loading the menu if required.

The example game *Interstellar Paranoids* uses it to load game levels. It is attached to an empty gameObject in the menu scene, and thanks to its call to DontDestroyOnLoad() in the Start() function, it will persist across scenes so that it is always available.

Additionally, this class provides some very basic functionality for game level management in linearly progressive games; that is, games that progress through the same levels each time.

The script is designed to use an array of scenes set in the Unity editor Inspector window. The script retrieves a scene reference from the array as required. It has an integer variable named gameLevelNum, which is used as an index for the array. To advance to the next level, gameLevelNum is incremented.

Below are the level management functions:

- GoNextLevel()—Increments gameLevelNum and loads the next scene in the array. If gameLevelNum is higher than the array length, it loops back to zero.

- ResetGame()—Resets gameLevelNum back to zero, as though the game were restarting.

Below is the script in full:

```
using UnityEngine;
using System.Collections;


public class SceneManager : MonoBehavior
{
        public string[] levelNames;
        public int gameLevelNum;


        public void Start ()
        {
                // keep this object alive
                DontDestroyOnLoad (this.gameObject);
        }


        public void LoadLevel( string sceneName )
        {
                Application.LoadLevel( sceneName );
        }


        public void ResetGame()
        {
                // reset the level index counter
                gameLevelNum = 0;
        }
```

```
public void GoNextLevel()
{
        // if our index goes over the total number of levels in the
        // array, we reset it
        if( gameLevelNum >= levelNames.Length )
                gameLevelNum = 0;


        // load the level (the array index starts at 0, but we start
        // counting game levels at 1 for clarity's sake)
        LoadLevel( gameLevelNum );


        // increase our game level index counter
        gameLevelNum++;
}


private void LoadLevel( int indexNum )
{
        // load the game level
        LoadLevel( levelNames[indexNum] );
}
}
```

4.10.1 Script Breakdown

The script derives from MonoBehavior and should be attached to an empty gameObject:

```
using UnityEngine;
using System.Collections;


public class SceneManager : MonoBehavior
{
```

The Start() function calls DontDestroyOnLoad() and passes in a reference to this instance's gameObject. What this does is tell the game engine not to remove the gameObject from the game when a new one is loaded. The new scene will load as expected and this gameObject will still exist in the new scene:

```
public void Start ()
{
        // keep this object alive
        DontDestroyOnLoad (this.gameObject);
}
```

LoadLevel() may be used to load a new scene directly, passing in the name of the scene as a string. Application.LoadLevel loads the specified scene:

```
public void LoadLevel( string sceneName )
{
        Application.LoadLevel( sceneName );
}
```

gameLevelNum is used to tell the scene manager which scene to load when using the automated loading in GoNextLevel() or when LoadLevel() is called without a string parameter. When a new game starts, gameLevelNum needs to be reset for the scene loading to start at the beginning again:

```
public void ResetGame()
{
        // reset the level index counter
        gameLevelNum = 0;
}
```

At the end of a game level, calling GoNextLevel() will load the next scene automatically and increment gameLevelNum:

```
public void GoNextLevel()
{
        // if our index goes over the total number of levels in the
        // array, we reset it
        if( gameLevelNum >= levelNames.Length )
                gameLevelNum = 0;


        // load the level (the array index starts at 0, but we start
        // counting game levels at 1 for clarity's sake)
        LoadLevel( gameLevelNum );

        // increase our game level index counter
        gameLevelNum++;
}
```

LoadLevel() is used by the GoNextLevel() function to load a scene from the levelNames array based on the index pass in as a parameter via indexNum:

```
private void LoadLevel( int indexNum )
{
        // load the game level
        LoadLevel( levelNames[indexNum] );
}
}
```

5 Building Player Movement Controllers

As discussed in Chapter 3, what we called a player controller is focused on movement; it is the script that determines the way that a player moves and behaves in the physics world. It is entirely focused on movement—making a ship fly, a human move along the ground, or a car to drive.

The example games call for three different vehicle types:

1. Shoot 'em up spaceship—A spaceship that moves up, down, left, and right. Its movement need not be physics based.

2. Humanoid character—This control script is capable of general human things, such as running forward, backward, and turning around.

3. Wheeled vehicle—The vehicle controller utilizes Unity's wheel colliders to work toward a more realistic physics simulation. There will be no gearing, but the vehicle will be able to accelerate, brake, or steer left and right.

5.1 Shoot 'Em Up Spaceship

This script moves the player transform left, right, up, or down on the screen. It does not use any physics forces, but instead Transform.Translate manipulates the gameObject's transform position directly.

```
public class BaseTopDownSpaceShip : ExtendedCustomMonoBehavior
{
        private Quaternion targetRotation;

        private float thePos;
        private float moveXAmount;
        private float moveZAmount;

        public float moveXSpeed=40f;
        public float moveZSpeed=15f;

        public float limitX=15f;
        public float limitZ=15f;

        private float originZ;

        [System.NonSerialized]
        public Keyboard_Input default_input;

        public float horizontal_input;
        public float vertical_input;

        public virtual void Start()
        {
            // we are overriding Start() so as not to call Init, as we
            // want the game controller to do this in this game.
            didInit=false;

            this.Init();
        }

        public virtual void Init ()
        {
            // cache refs to our transform and gameObject
            myTransform= transform;
            myGO= gameObject;
            myBody= rigidbody;

            // add default keyboard input
            default_input= myGO.AddComponent<Keyboard_Input>();

            // grab the starting Z position to use as a baseline for Z
            // position limiting
            originZ=myTransform.localPosition.z;

            // set a flag so that our Update function knows when we are OK
            // to use
            didInit=true;
        }

        public virtual void GameStart ()
        {
            // we are good to go, so let's get moving!
            canControl=true;
        }

        public virtual void GetInput ()
        {
```

```
        // this is just a 'default' function that (if needs be) should
        // be overridden in the glue code
        horizontal_input= default_input.GetHorizontal();
        vertical_input= default_input.GetVertical();
    }

    public virtual void Update ()
    {
        UpdateShip ();
    }

    public virtual void UpdateShip ()
    {
        // don't do anything until Init() has been run
        if(!didInit)
            return;

        // check to see if we're supposed to be controlling the player
        // before moving it
        if(!canControl)
            return;

GetInput();

        // calculate movement amounts for X and Z axis
        moveXAmount = horizontal_input * Time.deltaTime * moveXSpeed;
        moveZAmount = vertical_input * Time.deltaTime * moveZSpeed;

        Vector3 tempRotation= myTransform.eulerAngles;
        tempRotation.z= horizontal_input * -30f;
        myTransform.eulerAngles=tempRotation;

        // move our transform to its updated position
        myTransform.localPosition += new Vector3(moveXAmount, 0,
        moveZAmount);

        // check the position to make sure that it is within boundaries
        if (myTransform.localPosition.x <= -limitX || myTransform.
        localPosition.x >= limitX)
    {
        thePos = Mathf.Clamp( myTransform.localPosition.x, -limitX,
        limitX);
        myTransform.localPosition = new Vector3(thePos, myTransform.
        localPosition.y, myTransform.localPosition.z);
    }

        // we also check the Z position to make sure that it is within
        // boundaries
        if (myTransform.localPosition.z <= originZ || myTransform.
        localPosition.z >= limitZ)
    {
        thePos = Mathf.Clamp( myTransform.localPosition.z, originZ,
        limitZ);
        myTransform.localPosition = new Vector3(myTransform.
        localPosition.x, myTransform.localPosition.y, thePos);
    }
    }
}
}
```

Just like many of the other scripts in this book, after the variable declarations, the Start() function uses a Boolean called didInit to track whether or not the script has been initialized.

```
public virtual void Start()
        {
            // we are overriding Start() so as not to call Init, as we want
            // the game controller to do this in this game.
            didInit=false;

        this.Init();
        }
```

Rather than having all of the initialization in the Start() function, it has its own function called Init() to keep things tidy. Init() begins by caching references to the transform, gameObject, and rigidbody.

```
        public virtual void Init ()
        {
            // cache refs to our transform and gameObject
            myTransform= transform;
            myGO= gameObject;
            myBody= rigidbody;
```

Input comes from an instance of Keyboard_Controller.cs held in a variable called default_input, which we will look into in detail later in this chapter.

```
            // add default keyboard input
            default_input= myGO.AddComponent<Keyboard_Input>();
```

To keep the player within a certain space in the play area, this script uses the z position it starts at to work out how to limit movement. A float named originZ is set:

```
            // grab the starting Z position to use as a baseline for Z
            // position limiting
            originZ=myTransform.localPosition.z;
```

Once the Init() function has finished, didInit is set to true.

```
            // set a flag so that our Update function knows when we are OK to use
            didInit=true;
        }
```

For the script to function correctly within the framework, all player scripts use a Boolean variable named canControl to decide whether or not the object should be controlled by a third party such as AI or input. Note that this is not the same as enabling or disabling player movement—it just decides whether or not to allow control of the player. The function called GameStart() is called by the game controller script when the time is right to allow control to begin.

```
        public virtual void GameStart ()
        {
            // we are good to go, so let's get moving!
            canControl=true;
        }
```

The GetInput() function is virtual and is designed to be overridden if needed. This makes it easier to switch out control systems if you derive a new class from this one for other games. The variables horizontal_input and vertical_input are float values populated by the input controller in this GetInput() function and used to control the player later in the script:

```
public virtual void GetInput ()
{
    // this is just a 'default' function that (if needs be) should
    // be overridden in the glue code
    horizontal_input= default_input.GetHorizontal();
    vertical_input= default_input.GetVertical();
}
```

The Update() function calls UpdateShip():

```
public virtual void Update ()
{
    UpdateShip ();
}

public virtual void UpdateShip ()
{
    // don't do anything until Init() has been run
    if(!didInit)
        return;

    // check to see if we're supposed to be controlling the player
    // before moving it
    if(!canControl)
return;

    GetInput();
```

When the amount to move is calculated (using the input values as a multiplier), we use Time.deltaTime to make movement framerate independent. By multiplying the movement amount by deltaTime (the time since the last update), the amount we move adapts to the amount of time in between updates rather than only updating when the engine has time to do so:

```
// calculate movement amounts for X and Z axis
moveXAmount = horizontal_input * Time.deltaTime * moveXSpeed;
moveZAmount = vertical_input * Time.deltaTime * moveZSpeed;
```

Quaternion rotations are the underlying form that angles take in the Unity engine. You can use quaternions in your games, but they are notoriously difficult to get to grips with. Thankfully, for the rest of us, there is an alternative in Euler angles. Euler angles are a representation of a rotation in a three-dimensional vector, and it is much easier to define or manipulate a rotation by x, y, and z values.

Unlike UnityScript, in C#, you cannot individually alter the values of each axis in the rotation value of a transform. It has to be copied out into another variable and that variable's values change before being copied back into the transform. In the code below, the vector from eulerAngles is copied into a variable called tempRotation, and then its z rotation value is altered to an arbitrary multiplier of the horizontal input. This is purely a visual rotation to show that the ship is turning left or right—it makes the spaceship tilt nicely when the left or right keys are held down:

```
Vector3 tempRotation= myTransform.eulerAngles;
tempRotation.z= horizontal_input * -30f;
myTransform.eulerAngles=tempRotation;
```

The movement of the spaceship is applied to its transform.localPosition. The reason for this is that, in *Interstellar Paranoids*, the player is parented to the camera as it makes its way through the level. We do not want to affect the global position of the ship; it needs to stay within the coordinate space of the camera to stay on screen, and only its local position is changed when we move it around:

```
// move our transform to its updated position
myTransform.localPosition += new Vector3(moveXAmount, 0,
moveZAmount);
```

Limit checking is very basic for this script, with arbitrary values for the left and right and an amount added to the original local *z* position of the ship. The center of the screen is at 0 (we start the camera at zero on the *x*-axis) to keep things clear, using the variable limitX and a negative –limitX to stop the ship leaving the screen.

```
// check the position to make sure that it is within boundaries
if (myTransform.localPosition.x <= -limitX ||
myTransform.localPosition.x >= limitX)
{
```

Mathf.Clamp is a useful built-in utility function to take a value and clamp it between a minimum and a maximum value. When you pass a value into Mathf.Clamp, if it is more than the maximum value, then the return value will be the maximum value. If the value passed in is less than the minimum value, it will return the minimum.

In this function, Mathf.Clamp is used to populate the float variable thePos with a value (to use for the *z* position value) within both horizontal and, later in the code, vertical position limits (limitX and –limitX or limitZ and originZ) from the localPosition of the player transform:

```
thePos = Mathf.Clamp( myTransform.localPosition.x, -limitX, limitX);
```

Once the variable thePos contains a clamped (limited) value for positioning, the transform position is set:

```
myTransform.localPosition = new Vector3(thePos,
myTransform.localPosition.y, myTransform.localPosition.z);
}
```

The final part of this function deals with the clamping of the *z* position in the same way that the *x* was clamped:

```
// we also check the Z position to make sure that it is within
// boundaries
if (myTransform.localPosition.z <= originZ ||
myTransform.localPosition.z >= limitZ)
{
    thePos = Mathf.Clamp( myTransform.localPosition.z, originZ,
limitZ);
```

```
            myTransform.localPosition = new Vector3
            (myTransform.localPosition.x,
            myTransform.localPosition.y, thePos);
        }
    }
}
```

■ 5.2 Humanoid Character

The human control script uses Unity's character controller and is based on the third-person character controller provided by Unity (which is provided free, as part of the included assets with the Unity game engine).

The complete BaseTopDown.cs script looks like this:

```
using UnityEngine;
using System.Collections;

public class BaseTopDown : ExtendedCustomMonoBehavior
{
        public AnimationClip idleAnimation;
        public AnimationClip walkAnimation;

        public float walkMaxAnimationSpeed = 0.75f;
        public float runMaxAnimationSpeed = 1.0f;

        // When did the user start walking (Used for going into run after a
        // while)
        private float walkTimeStart= 0.0f;

        // we've made the following variable public so that we can use an
        // animation on a different gameObject if needed
        public Animation _animation;

        enum CharacterState {
            Idle = 0,
            Walking = 1,
            Running = 2,
        }

        private CharacterState _characterState;

        // The speed when walking
        public float walkSpeed= 2.0f;

        // after runAfterSeconds of walking we run with runSpeed
        public float runSpeed= 4.0f;

        public float speedSmoothing= 10.0f;
        public float rotateSpeed= 500.0f;
        public float runAfterSeconds= 3.0f;

        // The current move direction in x-z
        private Vector3 moveDirection= Vector3.zero;

        // The current vertical speed
        private float verticalSpeed= 0.0f;
```

```
// The current x-z move speed
public float moveSpeed= 0.0f;

// The last collision flags returned from controller.Move
private CollisionFlags;

public BasePlayerManager myPlayerController;

[System.NonSerialized]
public Keyboard_Input default_input;

public float horz;
public float vert;

private CharacterController controller;

// ----------------------------------------------------------------

void Awake ()
{
        // we need to do this before anything happens to the script
        // or object, so it happens in Awake.
        // if you need to add specific set-up, consider adding it to
        // the Init() function instead to keep this function
        // limited only to things we need to do before
        // anything else happens.

        moveDirection = transform.TransformDirection(Vector3.forward);

        // if _animation has not been set up in the inspector, we'll
        // try to find it on the current gameobject
        if(_animation==null)
            _animation = GetComponent<Animation>();

        if(!_animation)
            Debug.Log("The character you would like to control
            doesn't have animations. Moving her might look
            weird.");

        if(!idleAnimation) {
            _animation = null;
            Debug.Log("No idle animation found. Turning off
            animations.");
        }
        if(!walkAnimation) {
            _animation = null;
            Debug.Log("No walk animation found. Turning off
            animations.");
        }

        controller = GetComponent<CharacterController>();
}

public virtual void Start ()
{
        Init ();
}
```

```
public virtual void Init ()
{
        // cache the usual suspects
        myBody= rigidbody;
        myGO= gameObject;
        myTransform= transform;

        // add default keyboard input
        default_input= myGO.AddComponent<Keyboard_Input>();

        // cache a reference to the player controller
        myPlayerController= myGO.GetComponent<BasePlayerManager>();

        if(myPlayerController!=null)
            myPlayerController.Init();
}

public void SetUserInput( bool setInput )
{
        canControl= setInput;
}

public virtual void GetInput()
{
        horz= Mathf.Clamp( default_input.GetHorizontal() , -1, 1 );
        vert= Mathf.Clamp( default_input.GetVertical() , -1, 1 );
}

public virtual void LateUpdate()
{
        // we check for input in LateUpdate because Unity recommends
        // this
        if(canControl)
            GetInput();
}

public bool moveDirectionally;

private Vector3 targetDirection;
private float curSmooth;
private float targetSpeed;
private float curSpeed;
private Vector3 forward;
private Vector3 right;

void UpdateSmoothedMovementDirection ()
{
        if(moveDirectionally)
        {
            UpdateDirectionalMovement();
        } else {
            UpdateRotationMovement();
        }
}

void UpdateDirectionalMovement()
{
        // find target direction
        targetDirection= horz * Vector3.right;
```

```
                    targetDirection+= vert * Vector3.forward;

                    // We store speed and direction seperately,
                    // so that when the character stands still we still have a
                    // valid forward direction
                    // moveDirection is always normalized, and we only update it
                    // if there is user input.
                    if (targetDirection != Vector3.zero)
                    {
                        moveDirection = Vector3.RotateTowards(moveDirection,
                        targetDirection, rotateSpeed * Mathf.Deg2Rad * Time.
                        deltaTime, 1000);
                        moveDirection = moveDirection.normalized;
                    }

                    // Smooth the speed based on the current target direction
                    curSmooth= speedSmoothing * Time.deltaTime;

                    // Choose target speed
                    //* We want to support analog input but make sure you can't
                    // walk faster diagonally than just forward or sideways
                    targetSpeed= Mathf.Min(targetDirection.magnitude, 1.0f);

                    _characterState = CharacterState.Idle;

                    // decide on animation state and adjust move speed
                    if (Time.time - runAfterSeconds > walkTimeStart)
                    {
                        targetSpeed *= runSpeed;
                        _characterState = CharacterState.Running;
                    }
                    else
                    {
                        targetSpeed *= walkSpeed;
                        _characterState = CharacterState.Walking;
                    }

                    moveSpeed = Mathf.Lerp(moveSpeed, targetSpeed, curSmooth);

                    // Reset walk time start when we slow down
                    if (moveSpeed < walkSpeed * 0.3f)
                        walkTimeStart = Time.time;

                    // Calculate actual motion
                    Vector3 movement= moveDirection * moveSpeed;
                    movement *= Time.deltaTime;

                    // Move the controller
                    collisionFlags = controller.Move(movement);

                    // Set rotation to the move direction
                    myTransform.rotation = Quaternion.LookRotation(moveDirection);
            }

        void UpdateRotationMovement ()
        {
                    // this character movement is based on the code in the Unity
                    // help file for CharacterController.SimpleMove
                    // http://docs.unity3d.com/Documentation/ScriptReference/
                    // CharacterController.SimpleMove.html
```

```
        myTransform.Rotate(0, horz * rotateSpeed * Time.deltaTime, 0);
    curSpeed = moveSpeed * vert;
        controller.SimpleMove( myTransform.forward * curSpeed );

        // Target direction (the max we want to move, used for
        // calculating target speed)
        targetDirection= vert * myTransform.forward;

        // Smooth the speed based on the current target direction
        float curSmooth= speedSmoothing * Time.deltaTime;

        // Choose target speed
        //* We want to support analog input but make sure you can't
        // walk faster diagonally than just forward or sideways
        targetSpeed= Mathf.Min(targetDirection.magnitude, 1.0f);

        _characterState = CharacterState.Idle;

        // decide on animation state and adjust move speed
        if (Time.time - runAfterSeconds > walkTimeStart)
        {
            targetSpeed *= runSpeed;
            _characterState = CharacterState.Running;
        }
        else
        {
            targetSpeed *= walkSpeed;
            _characterState = CharacterState.Walking;
        }

        moveSpeed = Mathf.Lerp(moveSpeed, targetSpeed, curSmooth);

        // Reset walk time start when we slow down
        if (moveSpeed < walkSpeed * 0.3f)
            walkTimeStart = Time.time;

    }

    void Update ()
    {
        if (!canControl)
        {
            // kill all inputs if not controllable.
            Input.ResetInputAxes();
        }

        UpdateSmoothedMovementDirection();

        // ANIMATION sector
        if(_animation) {
            if(controller.velocity.sqrMagnitude < 0.1f) {
                _animation.CrossFade(idleAnimation.name);
            }
            else
            {
                if(_characterState == CharacterState.Running) {
                    _animation[walkAnimation.name].speed =
                Mathf.Clamp(controller.velocity.magnitude, 0.0f,
                    runMaxAnimationSpeed);
```

```
_animation.CrossFade(walkAnimation.name);
                }
                else if(_characterState == CharacterState.Walking) {
                        _animation[walkAnimation.name].speed =
                        Mathf.Clamp(controller.velocity.magnitude,
                        0.0f, walkMaxAnimationSpeed);

_animation.CrossFade(walkAnimation.name);
                }
            }
        }
    }

    public float GetSpeed ()
    {
            return moveSpeed;
    }

    public Vector3 GetDirection ()
    {
            return moveDirection;
    }

    public bool IsMoving ()
    {
            return Mathf.Abs(vert) + Mathf.Abs(horz) > 0.5f;
    }

    public void Reset ()
    {
            gameObject.tag = "Player";
    }
}
```

5.2.1 Script Breakdown

The script derives from ExtendedCustomMonoBehavior, as described in Chapter 4, and it adds some extra common variables to the class:

```
public class BaseTopDown : ExtendedCustomMonoBehavior
{
```

By using @script RequireComponent, this code tells the Unity engine that it requires the controller specified by RequireComponent. If there is not one already attached to the gameObject this script is attached to, the Unity engine will automatically add an instance of one at runtime, although it is intended that the CharacterController reference be set up in the Unity editor before the script is run:

```
// Require a character controller to be attached to the same game object
// @script RequireComponent(CharacterController)
```

Note that many of the variable declarations will make more sense later in this section, once we get to look at the actual code using them. For that reason, we skip most of them here and just highlight the ones that either stand out or require more information.

The Animation component should be attached to the gameObject that is to be animated. As this may not always be the same object as this script is attached to, the _animation variable used to coordinate animations later in the script is declared as public. Use the Unity editor Inspector window to reference the Animation component:

```
public Animation _animation;
```

The enum keyword is used to declare an enumeration. An enumeration is a set of constants called an enumeration list, which is a method of describing something with words (keeping the code easily readable), yet at the same time, having the inner workings of the engine use numbers to make processing more efficient. At the beginning of the script, we start with the declaration of an enumeration called CharacterState. This will be used to hold the state of the player's animation:

```
enum CharacterState {
        Idle = 0,
        Walking = 1,
        Running = 2,
}
```

Most of the variable declarations are uneventful and do not require full descriptions, although there are a few more variables of note:

CharacterState _characterState	This holds the player's animation state (based on the enumeration list CharacterState shown earlier in this section).
BasePlayerManager myPlayerController	Although the player controller is not used by this script, it holds a reference to it so that other scripts can find it easily.
Keyboard_Input default_input	The default input system is the standard keyboard input script.
CharacterController controller	Unity's built-in character controller is used for the physics simulation of the character controlled by this script.

On to the Awake() function:

```
void Awake ()
{
```

The moveDirection variable is a Vector3 used to tell the character controller which direction to move in. Here, it is given the world forward vector as a default value:

```
moveDirection = transform.TransformDirection(Vector3.forward);
```

The Animation component (a component built into Unity) is used to animate the character. GetComponent() is used to find the instance of the animation component on the gameObject this script is attached to:

```
// if _animation has not been set up in the inspector, we'll try to
// find it on the current gameobject
if(_animation==null)
            _animation = GetComponent<Animation>();
```

```
if(!_animation)
        Debug.Log("The character you would like to control doesn't
        have animations. Moving her might look weird.");
```

Animations for idle, walking, running, and jumping should be referenced by the Inspector window on the character for them to work with this script. If any of them are missing, however, we don't want it to stop working altogether; a message to report what is missing will be written to the debug window instead via Debug.Log:

```
if(!idleAnimation) {
        _animation = null;
        Debug.Log("No idle animation found. Turning off
animations.");
    }
if(!walkAnimation) {
        _animation = null;
        Debug.Log("No walk animation found. Turning off
animations.");
        }
```

Init() caches references to the characters rigidbody, gameObject, and transform before grabbing references to some required scripts. To work within the player structure, Keyboard_Input.cs is used to provide input from the player to move the character around. BasePlayerManager.cs is also referenced in the Init() function, and although this script does not use it directly, it does store a reference to the player manager for other scripts to access:

```
public virtual void Start ()
{
        Init ();
}

public virtual void Init ()
{
        // cache the usual suspects
        myBody= rigidbody;
        myGO= gameObject;
        myTransform= transform;

        // add default keyboard input
        default_input= myGO.AddComponent<Keyboard_Input>();

        // cache a reference to the player controller
        myPlayerController= myGO.GetComponent<BasePlayerManager>();

        if(myPlayerController!=null)
            myPlayerController.Init();
}
```

The SetUserInput() function is used to set canControl, which is used to check whether user input should be disabled or not:

```
public void SetUserInput( bool setInput )
{
        canControl= setInput;
}
```

Having input separated into a single GetInput() function should make it easy to customize inputs if required. Here, the horz, vert, and jumpButton Boolean variables are set by the default_input (a Keyboard_Input.cs instance) functions. These variables are used to control the character controller further in the script:

```
public virtual void GetInput()
{
        horz= Mathf.Clamp( default_input.GetHorizontal() , -1, 1 );
        vert= Mathf.Clamp( default_input.GetVertical() , -1, 1 );
}
```

LateUpdate() is used to call for an update to the input Boolean variables via the GetInput() script. Unity advises LateUpdate as the best place to check for keyboard entry, after the engine has carried out its own input updates:

```
public virtual void LateUpdate()
{
        // we check for input in LateUpdate because Unity recommends
        // this
        if(canControl)
                GetInput();
}
```

This script was adapted from the third-person controller code provided by Unity. Its original behavior was to move the player based on the direction of the camera. For example, when the right key was pressed, the player would move toward the right of the screen based on the camera location and rotation (right being along the camera's x-axis). Player rotation in the original script was determined by the camera rotation, and for the movement to make sense, it was reliant on the camera being behind the player during gameplay. Of course, this control scheme would not work with a top-down camera system or any camera system other than the one it was intended for.

As the script was adapted, the dependence on the camera rotation was removed and replaced with a directional approach. In this system, pressing the right key moves right along the world x-axis and pressing up or down moves up or down along the world z-axis.

For some top-down character-based games, the directional approach is a good one, but the genre is not exactly locked into this scheme so we also provide a rotational movement approach. Whenever moveDirectionally is false, pressing the left or right button will rotate the player left or right around its y-axis. Pressing the up button will walk forward along the player's z-axis, and pressing down will move it backward.

In the UpdateSmoothedMovementDirection() script, the moveDirectionally variable is checked to determine which type of movement function to call to update player movement:

```
void UpdateSmoothedMovementDirection ()
{
        if(moveDirectionally)
        {
                UpdateDirectionalMovement();
        } else {
                UpdateRotationMovement();
        }
}
```

Directional movement uses the world x- and z-axes to decide which way to move; that is, the player moves along the world x- or z-axis based on the button pressed by the player. The UpdateDirectionalMovement() function starts by taking the horizontal and vertical user inputs (from the variables horz and vert) and multiplying them by either the world forward vector or the world right vector, respectively. Note that the targetDirection variable is of Vector3 type and that it starts out being set to the horizontal direction and then has the vertical added to it, encompassing both vertical and horizontal movement into the same vector:

```
void UpdateDirectionalMovement()
{
        // find target direction
        targetDirection= horz * Vector3.right;
        targetDirection+= vert * Vector3.forward;
```

As the code comments will tell you, we store speed and direction separately. By doing so, we can have the character face a particular direction without actually moving, a behavior sometimes useful for this type of game.

The targetDirection variable will be zero when there is no user input, so before calculating any movement amounts, we check that movement is intended first:

```
        // We store speed and direction separately,
        // so that when the character stands still we still have a
        // valid forward direction
        // moveDirection is always normalized, and we only update it
        // if there is user input.
        if (targetDirection != Vector3.zero)
        {
```

The modeDirection vector will be used to move the player around the arena. Its value comes from an interpolation between the current value of moveDirection and the targetDirection calculated earlier from the user inputs. This vector is then multiplied by rotateSpeed, then converted into radians, and again multiplied by Time.deltaTime to make the rotation speed time based. Vector3.RotateTowards is used to make the turn, which ensures that the rotation ends in the exact specified position.

The Unity documentation describes Vector3.RotateTowards as follows:

This function is similar to MoveTowards except that the vector is treated as a direction rather than a position. The current vector will be rotated round toward the target direction by an angle of maxRadiansDelta, although it will land exactly on the target rather than overshoot. If the magnitudes of current and target are different then the magnitude of the result will be linearly interpolated during the rotation. If a negative value is used for maxRadiansDelta, the vector will rotate away from target until it is pointing in exactly the opposite direction, then stop.

The moveDirection vector is then normalized to remove any magnitude from the equation:

```
            moveDirection = Vector3.RotateTowards(moveDirection,
            targetDirection, rotateSpeed * Mathf.Deg2Rad * Time.
            deltaTime, 1000);
            moveDirection = moveDirection.normalized;
        }
```

The next part of the BaseTopDown.cs script deals with speed. The variable curSmooth will be used further in the script to decide how long it takes for the movement speed of the player to go from zero to max speed:

```
// Smooth the speed based on the current target direction
curSmooth= speedSmoothing * Time.deltaTime;
```

The variable targetSpeed is capped to a maximum of 1. To do this, Mathf.Min is fed with the magnitude of the targetDirection and 1. Whichever is least will go into targetSpeed:

```
// Choose target speed
//* We want to support analog input but make sure you can't
// walk faster diagonally than just forwards or sideways
targetSpeed= Mathf.Min(targetDirection.magnitude, 1.0f);
```

The variable _characterState starts out set to CharacterState.Idle:

```
_characterState = CharacterState.Idle;
```

This script allows for two states of movement: running and walking. The transition between running and walking is timed—the character will begin walking and continue walking until vertical input is applied for more than (in seconds) the value of runAfterSeconds. The animation and movement speed will then transition into running and continue to run until the vertical input stops.

Time.time is used to track how long the player has been walking, which means that Time.timeScale will affect it (if the game is paused or time is scaled, this timing will remain relative to the timescale):

```
// decide on animation state and adjust move speed
if (Time.time - runAfterSeconds > walkTimeStart)
{
```

If the state is running, then we multiply the targetSpeed by runSpeed, and then set the animation state to running:

```
    targetSpeed *= runSpeed;
    _characterState = CharacterState.Running;
}
else
{
```

The walkSpeed variable is a multiplier for the targetSpeed when the player is in its walking state:

```
    targetSpeed *= walkSpeed;
    _characterState = CharacterState.Walking;
}
```

The moveSpeed variable was used earlier in the function, but it only gets calculated here because it relies on targetSpeed and curSmooth to have been worked out. It's OK that it gets calculated so late in the function, as although it only gets picked up on the next update, the delay is so small that it is unnoticeable.

moveSpeed is an interpolation (using Mathf.Lerp) between its current value and the variable targetSpeed over an amount of time set by curSmooth.

When moveSpeed drops below the threshold set by walkSpeed (essentially, when the player releases the move input enough to slow movement down), walkTimeStart gets reset so that the walk will start again next time the player moves:

```
moveSpeed = Mathf.Lerp(moveSpeed, targetSpeed, curSmooth);

// Reset walk time start when we slow down
if (moveSpeed < walkSpeed * 0.3f)
        walkTimeStart = Time.time;
```

The final part of the UpdateDirectionalMovement() function tells the character controller to move and sets the rotation of myTransform to match the movement direction. In the original Unity third-person controller script this code was adapted from, this code was in the Update() function. It was moved here for the purpose of keeping all directional movement code within a single function.

The variable movement takes moveDirection and multiplies it by moveSpeed; then, on the next line, the result is multiplied by Time.deltaTime to provide a time-based movement vector with magnitude suitable for passing into the character controller. When the controller is told to Move (with the movement vector passed in as a parameter), it will return a bitmask called CollisionFlags. When a collision occurs with the character controller, the collisionFlags variable may be used to tell where the collision happened; the collisionFlags mask represents None, Sides, Above, or Below. Although the collision data are not used in this version of BaseTopDown.cs, it is implemented for future functionality:

```
// Calculate actual motion
Vector3 movement= moveDirection * moveSpeed;
movement *= Time.deltaTime;

// Move the controller
collisionFlags = controller.Move(movement);
```

In the last line of the function, Quaternion.LookRotation creates a rotation toward moveDirection and sets myTransform.rotation to it—making the player face in the correct direction for the movement:

```
// Set rotation to the move direction
myTransform.rotation = Quaternion.LookRotation(moveDirection);

}
```

The second type of movement in BaseTopDown.cs is rotational movement. UpdateRotationalMovement() uses a combination of transform.Rotate and the character controller's SimpleMove function to provide a control system that rotates the player on its *y*-axis and moves along its *z*-axis (in the case of the humanoid, this is forward and backward walking or running).

5. Building Player Movement Controllers

For horizontal input, the variable horz is multiplied by the variable rotateSpeed and multiplied by Time.deltaTime to be used as the rotation for the player's (myTransform) *y* rotation:

```
void UpdateRotationMovement ()
{
        myTransform.Rotate(0, horz * rotateSpeed * Time.deltaTime, 0);
```

Vertical input (stored in vert) is dealt with next, as vert multiplied by moveSpeed makes up the speed at which to traverse the player's *z*-axis.

Note that moveSpeed is calculated further down in the function, so don't worry about that right away—just keep in mind that moveSpeed is the desired speed of movement:

```
curSpeed = moveSpeed * vert;
```

CharacterController.SimpleMove moves a character controller, taking into account the velocity set by the vector passed into it. In this line, the vector provided to SimpleMove is the player's forward vector multiplied by curSpeed:

```
controller.SimpleMove( myTransform.forward * curSpeed );
```

targetDirection is a Vector3-type variable that determines how much, based on the vert input variable, we would like to move, even though its vector is only used in calculating for its magnitude later on in the function:

```
// Target direction (the max we want to move, used for calculating
// target speed)
targetDirection= vert * myTransform.forward;
```

When the speed changes, rather than changing the animation instantly from slow to fast, the variable curSmooth is used to transition speed smoothly. The variable speedSmoothing is intended to be set in the Unity Inspector window, and it is then multiplied by Time.deltaTime to make the speed transition time based:

```
// Smooth the speed based on the current target direction
float curSmooth= speedSmoothing * Time.deltaTime;
```

The next line of the script caps the targetSpeed at 1. Taking the targetDirection vector from earlier, targetSpeed takes a maximum value of 1 or, if it is less than 1, the value held by targetDirection.magnitude:

```
// Choose target speed
//* We want to support analog input but make sure you can't walk
// faster diagonally than just forwards or sideways
targetSpeed= Mathf.Min(targetDirection.magnitude, 1.0f);
```

The rest of the function transitions between walking and running in the same way that the UpdateDirectionalMovement()function did earlier in this section:

```
_characterState = CharacterState.Idle;

// decide on animation state and adjust move speed
if (Time.time - runAfterSeconds > walkTimeStart)
```

```
        {
                targetSpeed *= runSpeed;
                _characterState = CharacterState.Running;
        }
        else
        {
                targetSpeed *= walkSpeed;
                _characterState = CharacterState.Walking;
        }

        moveSpeed = Mathf.Lerp(moveSpeed, targetSpeed, curSmooth);

        // Reset walk time start when we slow down
        if (moveSpeed < walkSpeed * 0.3f)
                walkTimeStart = Time.time;
}
```

Update() begins with a call to stop input when canControl is set to false. More than anything, this is designed to bring the player to a stop when canControl is set at the end of the game. When the game ends, rather than inputs continuing and the player being left to run around behind the game-over message, inputs are set to zero:

```
void Update ()
{
        if (!canControl)
        {
                // kill all inputs if not controllable.
                Input.ResetInputAxes();
        }
```

UpdateSmoothedMovementDirection(), as described earlier in this chapter, calls one of two movement update scripts, based on the value of the Boolean variable moveDirectionally. After this is called, the final part of the Update() function takes care of coordinating the animation of the player (provided that there is a reference to an animation component in the variable _animation):

```
        UpdateSmoothedMovementDirection();

        // ANIMATION sector
        if(_animation) {
                if(controller.velocity.sqrMagnitude < 0.1f) {
```

The controller's velocity is used to track when it is time to play the idle animation. The _characterState will not come into play if velocity is less than 0.1f, since we can guarantee at this velocity that the idle animation should be playing above anything else. Animation. CrossFade() transitions from the current animation to the new one smoothly or continues to play the current animation if it is the same as the one being passed in.

The actual animation data are stored in their own variables of type AnimationClip: runAnimation, walkAnimation, and idleAnimation. Note that Animation.CrossFade uses the name of the animation rather than the object:

```
        _animation.CrossFade(idleAnimation.name);
                }
                else
                {
```

When the velocity is higher than 0.1, the script relies on _characterState to provide the correct animation for whatever the player is doing. _characterState refers to the enumeration list at the beginning of the script called CharacterState.

The CharacterState animation state held by _characterState is set by the movement scripts (UpdateDirectionalMovement() and UpdateRotationalMovement() functions), but the speeds that the animations play at are decided here using the controller.velocity.magnitude (the speed at which the character controller is moving) clamped to runMaxAnimationSpeed to keep the number reasonable.

First, the _characterState is checked for running, and the run animation is played at the speed of runMaxAnimationSpeed:

```
if(_characterState == CharacterState.Running) {

_animation[walkAnimation.name].speed =
Mathf.Clamp(controller.velocity.magnitude, 0.0f,
runMaxAnimationSpeed);

_animation.CrossFade(walkAnimation.name);
                    }
```

The final state is CharacterState.Walking played at the speed of walkMax AnimationSpeed:

```
else if(_characterState == CharacterState.Walking) {

_animation[walkAnimation.name].speed =
Mathf.Clamp(controller.velocity.magnitude, 0.0f,
walkMaxAnimationSpeed);

_animation.CrossFade(walkAnimation.name);
                            }


                    }
            }
    }
```

At the end of the BaseTopDown.cs script, GetSpeed(), GetDirection(), and IsMoving() are utility functions provided for other scripts to have access to a few of the character's properties:

```
public float GetSpeed ()
{
        return moveSpeed;
}

public Vector3 GetDirection ()
{
        return moveDirection;
}

public bool IsMoving ()
{
        return Mathf.Abs(vert) + Mathf.Abs(horz) > 0.5f;
}
}
```

▋ 5.3 Wheeled Vehicle

The BaseVehicle.cs script relies on Unity's built-in WheelCollider system. WheelCollider components are added to gameObjects positioned in place of the wheels supporting the car body. The WheelCollider components themselves do not have any visual form, and meshes representing wheels are not aligned automatically. WheelColliders are physics simulations; they take care of all of the physics actions such as suspension and wheel friction.

The Unity documentation describes the WheelCollider as

> …a special collider for grounded vehicles. It has built-in collision detection, wheel physics, and a slip-based tire friction model.

The physics and math behind the friction system are beyond the scope of this book, though thankfully, the Unity documentation has an extensive investigation of the subject on the WheelCollider page in the online help (http://docs.unity3d.com/Documentation/ Components/class-WheelCollider.html).

The BaseVehicle.cs script uses four WheelColliders for its drive (in the example games, these are attached to empty gameObjects), and the actual orientation of wheel meshes is dealt with by a separate script called BaseWheelAlignment.cs and will be explained in full later on in the chapter.

BaseVehicle.cs looks like this:

```
using UnityEngine;
using System.Collections;

public class BaseVehicle : ExtendedCustomMonoBehavior
{
        public WheelCollider frontWheelLeft;
        public WheelCollider frontWheelRight;
        public WheelCollider rearWheelLeft;
        public WheelCollider rearWheelRight;

        public float steerMax = 30f;
        public float accelMax = 5000f;
        public float brakeMax = 5000f;

        public float steer = 0f;

        public float motor = 0f;

        public float brake = 0f;

        public float mySpeed;

        public bool isLocked;

        [System.NonSerialized]
        public Vector3 velo;

        [System.NonSerialized]
        public Vector3 flatVelo;

        public BasePlayerManager myPlayerController;
```

```
[System.NonSerialized]
public Keyboard_Input default_input;

public AudioSource engineSoundSource;

public virtual void Start ()
{
        Init ();
}

public virtual void Init ()
{
        // cache the usual suspects
        myBody= rigidbody;
        myGO= gameObject;
        myTransform= transform;

        // add default keyboard input
        default_input= myGO.AddComponent<Keyboard_Input>();

        // cache a reference to the player controller
        myPlayerController= myGO.GetComponent<BasePlayerManager>();

        // call base class init
        myPlayerController.Init();

        // with this simple vehicle code, we set the center of mass
        // low to try to keep the car from toppling over
        myBody.centerOfMass= new Vector3(0,-4f,0);

        // see if we can find an engine sound source, if we need to
        if( engineSoundSource==null )
        {
                engineSoundSource= myGO.GetComponent<AudioSource>();
        }
}

public void SetUserInput( bool setInput )
{
        canControl= setInput;
}

public void SetLock(bool lockState)
{
        isLocked = lockState;
}

public virtual void LateUpdate()
{
        // we check for input in LateUpdate because Unity recommends
        // this
        if(canControl)
                GetInput();

        // update the audio
        UpdateEngineAudio();
}
```

```
public virtual void FixedUpdate()
{
        UpdatePhysics();
}

public virtual void UpdateEngineAudio()
{
        // this is just a 'made up' multiplier value applied to
        // mySpeed.
        engineSoundSource.pitch= 0.5f + ( Mathf.Abs( mySpeed ) *
        0.005f );
}

public virtual void UpdatePhysics()
{
    CheckLock();

        // grab the velocity of the rigidbody and convert it into
        // flat velocity (remove the Y)
        velo= myBody.angularVelocity;

        // convert the velocity to local space so we can see how
        // fast we're moving forward (along the local z axis)
        velo= transform.InverseTransformDirection(myBody.velocity);
        flatVelo.x= velo.x;
        flatVelo.y= 0;
        flatVelo.z= velo.z;

        // work out our current forward speed
        mySpeed= velo.z;

        // if we're moving slow, we reverse motorTorque and remove
        // brakeTorque so that the car will reverse
        if( mySpeed<2 )
        {
                // that is, if we're pressing down the brake key
                // (making brake>0)
                if( brake>0 )
                {
                        rearWheelLeft.motorTorque = -brakeMax *
                        brake;
                rearWheelRight.motorTorque = -brakeMax * brake;

                        rearWheelLeft.brakeTorque = 0;
                rearWheelRight.brakeTorque = 0;

                frontWheelLeft.steerAngle = steerMax * steer;
                frontWheelRight.steerAngle = steerMax * steer;

                        // drop out of this function before applying
                        // the 'regular' non-reversed values to the
                        // wheels
                        return;
                }
        }

        // apply regular movement values to the wheels
        rearWheelLeft.motorTorque = accelMax * motor;
rearWheelRight.motorTorque = accelMax * motor;
```

```
        rearWheelLeft.brakeTorque = brakeMax * brake;
        rearWheelRight.brakeTorque = brakeMax * brake;

        frontWheelLeft.steerAngle = steerMax * steer;
        frontWheelRight.steerAngle = steerMax * steer;
        }
    public void CheckLock()
    {
        if (isLocked)
        {
                // control is locked out and we should be stopped
                steer = 0;
                brake = 0;
                motor = 0;

                // hold our rigidbody in place (but allow the Y to move so
                // the car may drop to the ground if it is not exactly
                // matched to the terrain)
                Vector3 tempVEC = myBody.velocity;
                tempVEC.x = 0;
                tempVEC.z = 0;
                myBody.velocity = tempVEC;
        }
    }

    public virtual void GetInput()
    {
                // calculate steering amount
                steer= Mathf.Clamp( default_input.GetHorizontal() , -1, 1 );

                // how much accelerator?
                Motor= Mathf.Clamp( default_input.GetVertical() , 0, 1 );

                // how much brake?
                Brake= -1 * Mathf.Clamp( default_input.GetVertical() , -1, 0 );
    }

}
```

5.3.1 Script Breakdown

The class derives from ExtendedCustomMonoBehavior (as discussed in Chapter 4), which adds a few commonly used variables.

Each WheelCollider variable is named based on its intended position: front-WheelLeft, frontWheelRight, rearWheelLeft, and rearWheelRight. For the script to function correctly, WheelColliders need to be referenced (dragged and dropped) into the correct variables in the Unity Inspector window on the vehicle script:

```
using UnityEngine;
using System.Collections;

public class BaseVehicle : ExtendedCustomMonoBehavior
{
        public WheelCollider frontWheelLeft;
        public WheelCollider frontWheelRight;
        public WheelCollider rearWheelLeft;
        public WheelCollider rearWheelRight;
```

A player manager (BasePlayerManager.cs) is referenced by this script, but it is unused by the rest of the script and does nothing other than call its initialization function Init(). It is here to fit into the framework and for future development of the script:

```
public BasePlayerManager myPlayerController;
```

The default input system is a keyboard script in which there is no need to serialize because it is only used internally:

```
[System.NonSerialized]
public Keyboard_Input default_input;
```

An AudioSource is required on the vehicle to make an engine noise. To set one up, add an AudioSource to the gameObject (Component → Audio → AudioSource) and reference an engine audio clip. On the AudioSource, check the boxes for Loop and Play On Awake:

```
public AudioSource engineSoundSource;
```

The Start() function is called by the engine automatically. It calls the Init() function, which begins by caching references to commonly used objects:

```
public virtual void Start ()
{
        Init();
}

public virtual void Init ()
{
        // cache the usual suspects
        myBody= rigidbody;
        myGO= gameObject;
        myTransform= transform;
```

GameObject.AddComponent adds the default input controller to the gameObject:

```
        // add default keyboard input
        default_input= myGO.AddComponent<Keyboard_Input>();
```

A BasePlayerManager script should already be attached to the gameObject, as per the standard player setup for the framework, but just to be safe, a null check is made before calling the Init() function:

```
        // cache a reference to the player controller
        myPlayerController= myGO.GetComponent<BasePlayerManager>();

        // call base class init
        if(myPlayerController!=null)
                myPlayerController.Init();
```

The center of mass may be set on a rigidbody to change the way it behaves in the physics simulation. The farther the center of mass is from the center of the rigidbody, the more it will affect the physics behavior. Setting the center of mass down at −4, for example, will help a lot to keep the car stable. This is a method often employed to keep vehicles from toppling over in games, but it comes at a cost. If the car were to roll and flip over, it will roll in an unrealistic way because of the way that the center of mass will affect its movement. Look to the stabilizer bar simulation for a more realistic solution, but for now, this is as far as we go:

```
// with this simple vehicle code, we set the center of mass
// low to try to keep the car from toppling over
myBody.centerOfMass= new Vector3(0,-4f,0);
```

If no engine sound source has been set up via the Inspector window of the Unity editor, the script tries to find it with a call to GameObject.GetComponent(). The sound source will be stored in engineSoundSource and used solely for engine sound effects:

```
    // see if we can find an engine sound source, if we need to
    if( engineSoundSource==null )
    {
            engineSoundSource= myGO.GetComponent<AudioSource>();
    }
}
```

As with all of the movement controllers, SetUserInput sets a flag to decide whether or not inputs should be used to drive the vehicle:

```
public void SetUserInput( bool setInput )
{
        canControl= setInput;
}
```

Unlike other movement controllers from this book so far, this one introduces a lock state. The lock state is for holding the vehicle in place without affecting its y-axis. This differs from just disabling user input as it adds physical constraints to the physics object to hold it still (its purpose being to hold the vehicle during the counting in at the start of a race or other similar scenario):

```
public void SetLock(bool lockState)
{
        isLocked = lockState;
}
```

LateUpdate() starts by checking for input via the GetInput() function, when canControl is set to true. Next, UpdateEngineAudio() is called to update the pitch of the engine sound based on the engine speed:

```
public virtual void LateUpdate()
{
        // we check for input in LateUpdate because Unity recommends
        // this
        if(canControl)
                GetInput();

        // update the audio
        UpdateEngineAudio();
}
```

To keep everything tidy, all of the physics functionality is called from FixedUpdate(), but it actually resides in the UpdatePhysics() function:

```
public virtual void FixedUpdate()
{
        UpdatePhysics();
}
```

Changing the pitch of the engine AudioSource object makes a convincing motor sound. As it may be possible for the variable mySpeed to be negative, Mathf.Abs is used, as well as an arbitrary multiplier to bring the number down to something that changes the pitch in a satisfactory manner. There's no science here! The number was decided by trial and error, just adjusting its value until the motor sounded right:

```
public virtual void UpdateEngineAudio()
{
        // this is just a 'made up' multiplier value applied to
        // mySpeed.
        engineSoundSource.pitch= 0.5f + ( Mathf.Abs( mySpeed ) *
        0.005f );
}
```

The real guts of the script may be found in the UpdatePhysics() function. CheckLock() is called first, which takes care of holding the vehicle in place when the lock is on (the variable is Locked set to true):

```
public virtual void UpdatePhysics()
{
        CheckLock();
```

velo is a variable holding the velocity of the car's rigidbody:

```
        // grab the velocity of the rigidbody and convert it into
        // flat velocity (remove the Y)
        velo= myBody.angularVelocity;
```

The next task is to find out the velocity in the local coordinate space, remove its y-axis, and use its value along the z-axis to put into the variable mySpeed:

```
        // convert the velocity to local space so we can see how fast we're
        // moving forward (along the local z axis)
        velo= transform.InverseTransformDirection(myBody.velocity);
        flatVelo.x= velo.x;
        flatVelo.y= 0;
        flatVelo.z= velo.z;

        // work out our current forward speed
        mySpeed= velo.z;
```

mySpeed is then checked to see whether its value is less than 2. When the speed is slow and the brake key is held down, brakeTorque is no longer applied to the wheels; instead, a reverse amount of the maximum amount of brake torque (brakeMax) is applied to make the vehicle move backwards. Note that brakeMax is both the maximum amount of torque applied into the brakeTorque property of the WheelColliders during braking and the maximum amount of torque applied as motorTorque during reversing:

```
// if we're moving slow, we reverse motorTorque and remove
// brakeTorque so that the car will reverse
if( mySpeed<2 )
{
        // that is, if we're pressing down the brake key (making
        // brake>0)
        if( brake>0 )
        {
                rearWheelLeft.motorTorque = -brakeMax * brake;
        rearWheelRight.motorTorque = -brakeMax * brake;
```

In reverse mode, no brakeTorque will be applied to the WheelColliders so that the vehicle is free to move backward:

```
                rearWheelLeft.brakeTorque = 0;
        rearWheelRight.brakeTorque = 0;
```

When the vehicle is reversing, the steering is applied in reverse to switch over the steering when going backward, as a real car would:

```
        frontWheelLeft.steerAngle = steerMax * steer;
        frontWheelRight.steerAngle = steerMax * steer;
```

If the reverse conditions have been applied to the WheelColliders, this function drops out before the regular (forward) values are applied:

```
        // drop out of this function before applying the 'regular'
        // non-reversed values to the wheels
        return;
    }
  }
```

In this script, driving the wheels of WheelColliders is a case of applying motorTorque and brakeTorque and setting the steerAngle:

```
// apply regular movement values to the wheels
rearWheelLeft.motorTorque = accelMax * motor;
rearWheelRight.motorTorque = accelMax * motor;

rearWheelLeft.brakeTorque = brakeMax * brake;
rearWheelRight.brakeTorque = brakeMax * brake;

frontWheelLeft.steerAngle = steerMax * steer;
frontWheelRight.steerAngle = steerMax * steer;
}
```

The CheckLock() function looks to see whether the Boolean variable isLocked is set to true; when it is, it freezes all inputs to zero and zeroes the x and z velocities of the vehicle's rigidbody. The y velocity is left as is, so that gravity will still apply to the vehicle when it is being held in place. This is important at the start of a race when the vehicle is being held until the 3, 2, 1 counting in finishes. If the velocity along the y-axis were zeroed too, the car would float just above its resting place against the ground until the race started when it would drop down some as gravity is applied:

```
public void CheckLock()
{
        if (isLocked)
        {
                // control is locked out and we should be stopped
                steer = 0;
                brake = 0;
                motor = 0;

                // hold our rigidbody in place (but allow the Y to
                // move so the car may drop to the ground if it is not
                // exactly matched to the terrain)
                Vector3 tempVEC = myBody.velocity;
                tempVEC.x = 0;
                tempVEC.z = 0;
                myBody.velocity = tempVEC;
        }
}
```

steer, motor, and brake are float variables used for moving the vehicle around. GetInput() uses Mathf.Clamp to keep them to reasonable values as they are set by the default input system:

```
public virtual void GetInput()
{
        // calculate steering amount
        steer= Mathf.Clamp( default_input.GetHorizontal() , -1, 1 );

        // how much accelerator?
motor= Mathf.Clamp( default_input.GetVertical() , 0, 1 );

        // how much brake?
        brake= -1 * Mathf.Clamp( default_input.GetVertical() , -1, 0 );
}
}
```

5.3.2 Wheel Alignment

WheelColliders will do a great job of acting like wheels, but if we want to actually see wheels, there is still more work to be done; each wheel mesh needs to be positioned to match that of its WheelCollider counterpart.

The script in full looks like this:

```
// based on work done in this forum post:
// http://forum.unity3d.com/threads/50643-How-to-make-a-physically-real-
// stable-car-with-WheelColliders
// by Edy.

using UnityEngine;
using System.Collections;

public class BaseWheelAlignment : MonoBehavior
```

```
{
        // Define the variables used in the script, the Corresponding
        // collider is the wheel collider at the position of
        // the visible wheel, the slip prefab is the prefab instantiated
        // when the wheels slide, the rotation value is the
        // value used to rotate the wheel around its axle.
        public WheelCollider CorrespondingCollider;
        public GameObject slipPrefab;
        public float slipAmountForTireSmoke= 50f;

        private float RotationValue = 0.0f;
        private Transform myTransform;
        private Quaternion zeroRotation;
        private Transform colliderTransform;
        private float suspensionDistance;

        void Start ()
        {
                // cache some commonly used things...
                myTransform= transform;
                zeroRotation= Quaternion.identity;
                colliderTransform= CorrespondingCollider.transform;
        }

        void Update ()
        {
                // define a hit point for the raycast collision
                RaycastHit hit;
                // Find the collider's center point, you need to do this
                // because the center of the collider might not actually be
                // the real position if the transform's off.
                Vector3 ColliderCenterPoint=
                colliderTransform.TransformPoint( CorrespondingCollider.
                center );

                // now cast a ray out from the wheel collider's center the
                // distance of the suspension, if it hit something, then use
                // the "hit" variable's data to find where the
                // wheel hit, if it didn't, then set the wheel
                // to be fully extended along the suspension.
                if ( Physics.Raycast( ColliderCenterPoint,
                -colliderTransform.up, out hit,
                CorrespondingCollider.suspensionDistance +
                CorrespondingCollider.radius ) ) {
                        myTransform.position= hit.point +
                        (colliderTransform.up *
                        CorrespondingCollider.radius);
                } else {
                        myTransform.position= ColliderCenterPoint -
                        ( colliderTransform.up *
                        CorrespondingCollider.suspensionDistance );
                }

                // now set the wheel rotation to the rotation of the
                // collider combined with a new rotation value. This new value
                // is the rotation around the axle, and the rotation from
                // steering input.
```

```
myTransform.rotation= colliderTransform.rotation *
Quaternion.Euler( RotationValue,
CorrespondingCollider.steerAngle, 0 );

// increase the rotation value by the rotation speed (in
// degrees per second)
RotationValue+= CorrespondingCollider.rpm * ( 360 / 60 ) *
Time.deltaTime;

// define a wheelhit object, this stores all of the data
// from the wheel collider and will allow us to determine
// the slip of the tire.
WheelHit correspondingGroundHit= new WheelHit();
CorrespondingCollider.GetGroundHit( out
correspondingGroundHit );

// if the slip of the tire is greater than 2.0f, and the
// slip prefab exists, create an instance of it on the ground at
// a zero rotation.
if ( Mathf.Abs( correspondingGroundHit.sidewaysSlip ) >
slipAmountForTireSmoke ) {
        if ( slipPrefab ) {
                SpawnController.Instance.Spawn( slipPrefab,
                correspondingGroundHit.point, zeroRotation );
        }
    }

    }
}
```

5.3.3 Script Breakdown

The BaseWheelAlignment.cs script may be used to align the wheel meshes to the wheel colliders, as well as to provide a little extra functionality in spawning tire smoke as the wheel is slipping. The smoke is optional, of course, but it's here in case you need it.

Each wheel should have a BaseWheelAlignment script attached to it (i.e., the wheel mesh not the WheelCollider) and then a reference to the WheelCollider component provided to this script via the Unity editor Inspector window, into the variable named CorrespondingCollider. The wheels should be independent of the WheelColliders for them to move correctly; do not parent the wheel meshes to the colliders.

In the example game *Metal Vehicle Doom*, the vehicle looks like this in the hierarchy window:

Car

    Body

    Colliders (body)

    WheelColliders

        Wheel_FL

        Wheel_FR

Wheel_RL

Wheel_RR

WheelMeshes

Wheel_FL

Wheel_FR

Wheel_RL

Wheel_RR

The script derives from MonoBehavior so that it can tap into the engine's Update() function:

```
using UnityEngine;
using System.Collections;

public class BaseWheelAlignment : MonoBehavior
{
```

Skipping by the variable declarations, we move down to the Start() function. myTransform is a cached reference to the wheel transform, a default rotation value is stored in zeroRotation, and there's also a cached reference to the transform, which has the WheelCollider attached to it, to be stored in the variable colliderTransform:

```
void Start ()
{
        // cache some commonly used things...
        myTransform= transform;
        zeroRotation= Quaternion.identity;
        colliderTransform= CorrespondingCollider.transform;
}
```

This Update() function works by casting a ray down from the center of the WheelCollider with the intention of placing the wheel mesh up from the point of impact. If nothing is picked up by the raycast, the wheel mesh is simply positioned at a point down from the center of the WheelCollider instead:

```
void Update ()
{
        // define a hit point for the raycast collision
        RaycastHit hit;
```

The WheelCollider.center property returns a value from the WheelCollider's local coordinate space, so Transform.TransformPoint is used to convert it into a world space coordinate that we can use to start the ray cast from:

```
        Vector3 ColliderCenterPoint=
        colliderTransform.TransformPoint( CorrespondingCollider.
        center );
```

For a realistic representation of the structure of suspension, the raycast length should be limited to the length of the suspension and to the radius of the wheel. Starting out from the center of the WheelCollider, the ray will travel down the collider transform's negative up vector (i.e., down, as the WheelCollider's transform describes it):

```
if ( Physics.Raycast( ColliderCenterPoint,
-colliderTransform.up, out hit, CorrespondingCollider.
suspensionDistance + CorrespondingCollider.radius ) ) {
```

When Physics.Raycast finds a hit, the position for the wheel is the hit point, plus the wheel collider transform's up vector multiplied by the wheel radius. When the wheel meshes pivot point is at its center, this should position the wheel in the correct place on the ground:

```
myTransform.position= hit.point + (colliderTransform.up *
CorrespondingCollider.radius);
} else {
```

When Physics.Raycast finds nothing, the wheel position is at its default of the suspension length down from the WheelCollider's center point:

```
myTransform.position= ColliderCenterPoint -
( colliderTransform.up * CorrespondingCollider.
suspensionDistance );
}
```

Now that the position is set for the wheel, the rotation needs to be calculated based on the WheelCollider's rotation in the 3D space along with some extra code to produce a rotation angle from the WheelCollider's revolutions per minute (RPM).

The wheel mesh transform's rotation is put together as a result of the WheelCollider's transform rotation multiplied by a new Euler angle formed with Quaternion.Euler. The new angle takes the value in the variable RotationValue as its x-axis, the value of the steerAngle property of the WheelCollider as its y-axis and a zero as its z-axis:

```
myTransform.rotation= colliderTransform.rotation *
Quaternion.Euler( RotationValue, CorrespondingCollider.steerAngle, 0 );
```

RotationValue is a constantly flowing number; it is never reset once the game gets going. Instead, RotationValue is incremented by the WheelCollider's RPM value (CorrespondingCollider.rpm) as it is converted into radians and multiplied by Time.deltaTime to keep the rotation time based.

```
// increase the rotation value by the rotation speed (in degrees
// per second)
RotationValue+= CorrespondingCollider.rpm * ( 360 / 60 ) *
Time.deltaTime;
```

To analyze detailed information from the WheelCollider and its contacts and relationships with the 3D world, Unity provides a structure called WheelHit.

correspondingGroundHit is a new WheelHit formed with the specific purpose of getting to the sidewaysSlip value of the WheelCollider. If its value falls outside a certain threshold, the wheels must be sliding enough to merit some tire smoke to be instantiated:

```
// define a wheelhit object, this stores all of the data from the
// wheel collider and will allow us to determine
// the slip of the tire.
WheelHit correspondingGroundHit= new WheelHit();
```

To fill correspondingGroundHit with the information from this wheel's WheelCollider, the WheelCollider.GetGroundHit() function is used with correspondingGroundHit:

```
CorrespondingCollider.GetGroundHit( out correspondingGroundHit );
// if the slip of the tire is greater than 2.0f, and the slip
// prefab exists, create an instance of it on the ground at
// a zero rotation.
if ( Mathf.Abs( correspondingGroundHit.sidewaysSlip ) >
slipAmountForTireSmoke ) {
        if ( slipPrefab ) {
```

Note that the slipPrefab will be instantiated every step (every update) that the sidewaysSlip value is above the value of slipAmountForTireSmoke. If your tire smoke particle effect is complex, this could be a big slowdown point. For more complex effects, consider staggering the effect based on a timer or simplifying the particle effect itself.

The tire smoke will be instantiated at the point of contact between the ground and the wheel, but its rotation is not matched to the wheel:

```
                SpawnController.Instance.Spawn( slipPrefab,
correspondingGroundHit.point, zeroRotation );
            }
        }

    }
}
```

At this stage, the framework is loaded up for players and movement controllers. In the next chapter, it's time to add some weaponry to the framework.

6 Weapon Systems

The weapon system, or more specifically at this point, the firing system, needs to be capable of dealing with either single or multiple weapons. To be as flexible as possible, we will build a weapon management system that will control individual weapon controllers. Those weapon controllers, in turn, will deal with spawning projectiles, and finally, projectiles will take care of themselves independently. Our weapon management system should function with a single weapon, or we should be able to add many different weapons and switch between them.

Our parent system should work independently of each specific weapon and fire out a generic message to the currently selected one. The selected weapon will deal with the call itself, and the overall weapon management system can continue unaffected.

The weapon controller deals with how weapons are stored or manipulated and passes on messages to the actual weapons themselves. It contains an array containing all weapons and a method to activate and deactivate them as required (switching between them).

Each weapon is a prefab with a script attached that derives from BaseWeaponScript.cs. The weapon should be self-contained except when it receives a call to Fire() in which it should do whatever it is supposed to do. BaseWeaponScript contains the basics for a weapon (ammunition, reload time, and the ability to be disabled or enabled).

■ 6.1 Building the Scripts

For the weapon system, there are just two main scripts:

1. BaseWeaponController.cs

   This is the framework for our weapon control system. It offers everything the system requires, and it is intended to be overridden for customization.

2. BaseWeaponScript.cs

   This script takes care of individual weapon types. If you were to think of the BaseWeaponController as the arms of the player, the BaseWeaponScript would be the design of the weapon it is holding.

6.1.1 BaseWeaponController.cs

Here is the BaseWeaponController.cs script in its completed form:

```
using UnityEngine;
using System.Collections;


public class BaseWeaponController : MonoBehavior
{
        public GameObject[] weapons;


        public int selectedWeaponSlot;
        public int lastSelectedWeaponSlot;


        public Vector3 offsetWeaponSpawnPosition;


        public Transform forceParent;


        private ArrayList weaponSlots;
        private ArrayList weaponScripts;
        private BaseWeaponScript TEMPWeapon;
        private Vector3 TEMPvector3;
        private Quaternion TEMProtation;
        private GameObject TEMPgameObject;


        private Transform myTransform;
        private int ownerNum;


        public bool useForceVectorDirection;
        public Vector3 forceVector;
        private Vector3 theDir;
```

```
public void Start ()
{
        // default to the first weapon slot
        selectedWeaponSlot= 0;
        lastSelectedWeaponSlot= -1;


        // initialize weapon list ArrayList
        weaponSlots= new ArrayList();


        // initialize weapon scripts ArrayList
        weaponScripts= new ArrayList();


        // cache a reference to the transform (looking up a
        // transform each step can be expensive, so this is important!)
        myTransform= transform;


        if(forceParent==null)
        {
                forceParent= myTransform;
        }
        // rather than look up the transform position and rotation
        // of the player each iteration of the loop below,
        // we cache them first into temporary variables
        TEMPvector3= forceParent.position;
        TEMProtation= forceParent.rotation;


        // we instantiate all of the weapons and hide them so that
        // we can activate and use them
        // when needed.
        for( int i=0; i<weapons.Length; i++ )
        {
                // Instantiate the item from the weapons list
                TEMPgameObject= (GameObject) Instantiate( weapons[i],
                TEMPvector3 + offsetWeaponSpawnPosition,
                TEMProtation );


                // make this gameObject that our weapon controller
                // script is attached to, to be the parent of the
                // weapon so that the weapon will move around
                // with the player

                // NOTE: if you need projectiles to be on a
                // different layer from the main gameObject, set the
                // layer of the
                // forceParent object to the layer you want
                // projectiles to be on

                TEMPgameObject.transform.parent= forceParent;
                TEMPgameObject.layer= forceParent.gameObject.layer;
                TEMPgameObject.transform.position= forceParent.
                position;
                TEMPgameObject.transform.rotation= forceParent.
                rotation;
```

```
                    // store a reference to the gameObject in an ArrayList
                    weaponSlots.Add( TEMPgameObject );


                    // grab a reference to the weapon script attached to
                    // the weapon and store the reference in an ArrayList
                    TEMPWeapon= TEMPgameObject.GetComponent<BaseWeapon
                    Script>();
                    weaponScripts.Add( TEMPWeapon );


                    // disable the weapon
                    TEMPgameObject.SetActive( false );
            }


            // now we set the default selected weapon to visible
            SetWeaponSlot(0);
    }


    public void SetOwner(int aNum)
    {
            // used to identify the object firing, if required
            ownerNum= aNum;
    }


    public virtual void SetWeaponSlot (int slotNum)
    {
            // if the selected weapon is already this one, drop out!
            if(slotNum==lastSelectedWeaponSlot)
                    return;


            // disable the current weapon
            DisableCurrentWeapon();


            // set our current weapon to the one passed in
            selectedWeaponSlot= slotNum;


            // make sure sensible values are getting passed in
            if(selectedWeaponSlot<0)
                    selectedWeaponSlot= weaponSlots.Count-1;


            // make sure that the weapon slot isn't higher than the
            // total number of weapons in our list
            if(selectedWeaponSlot>weaponSlots.Count-1)
                    selectedWeaponSlot=weaponSlots.Count-1;


            // we store this selected slot to use to prevent duplicate
            // weapon slot setting
            lastSelectedWeaponSlot= selectedWeaponSlot;
```

```
                // enable the newly selected weapon
                EnableCurrentWeapon();
        }


        public virtual void NextWeaponSlot (bool shouldLoop)
        {
                // disable the current weapon
                DisableCurrentWeapon();


                // next slot
                selectedWeaponSlot++;


                // make sure that the slot isn't higher than the total
                // number of weapons in our list
                if(selectedWeaponSlot==weaponScripts.Count)
                {
                        if(shouldLoop)
                        {
                                selectedWeaponSlot= 0;
                        } else {
                                selectedWeaponSlot= weaponScripts.Count-1;
                        }
                }


                // we store this selected slot to use to prevent duplicate
                // weapon slot setting
                lastSelectedWeaponSlot=selectedWeaponSlot;


                // enable the newly selected weapon
                EnableCurrentWeapon();
        }


        public virtual void PrevWeaponSlot (bool shouldLoop)
        {
                // disable the current weapon
                DisableCurrentWeapon();


                // prev slot
                selectedWeaponSlot--;


                // make sure that the slot is a sensible number
                if( selectedWeaponSlot<0 )
                {
                        if(shouldLoop)
                        {
                                selectedWeaponSlot= weaponScripts.Count-1;
                        } else {
                                selectedWeaponSlot= 0;
                        }
                }
```

```
          // we store this selected slot to use to prevent duplicate
          // weapon slot setting
          lastSelectedWeaponSlot=selectedWeaponSlot;


          // enable the newly selected weapon
          EnableCurrentWeapon();
}


public virtual void DisableCurrentWeapon ()
{
          if(weaponScripts.Count==0)
                  return;


          // grab reference to currently selected weapon script
          TEMPWeapon= ( BaseWeaponScript )weaponScripts[selectedWeapon
          Slot];


          // now tell the script to disable itself
          TEMPWeapon.Disable();


          // grab reference to the weapon's gameObject and disable
          // that, too
          TEMPgameObject= ( GameObject )weaponSlots[selectedWeaponSlot];
          TEMPgameObject.SetActive( false );
}


public virtual void EnableCurrentWeapon ()
{
          if( weaponScripts.Count==0 )
                  return;


          // grab reference to currently selected weapon
          TEMPWeapon= ( BaseWeaponScript )weaponScripts[selectedWeapon
          Slot];


          // now tell the script to enable itself
          TEMPWeapon.Enable();


          TEMPgameObject= ( GameObject )weaponSlots[selectedWeapon
          Slot];
          TEMPgameObject.SetActive( true );
}


public virtual void Fire ()
{
          if(weaponScripts==null)
                  return;
```

```
        if(weaponScripts.Count==0)
                return;


        // find the weapon in the currently selected slot
        TEMPWeapon= ( BaseWeaponScript )weaponScripts[selectedWeapon
        Slot];


        theDir = myTransform.forward;


        if( useForceVectorDirection )
                theDir = forceVector;


        // fire the projectile
        TEMPWeapon.Fire( theDir, ownerNum );
    }
}
```

6.1.1.1 Script Breakdown

The BaseWeaponController class derives from MonoBehavior, utilizing the usual built-in Unity calls (Start(), Update(), FixedUpdate(), etc.):

```
public class BaseWeaponController : MonoBehavior
{
```

Skipping down, past the declarations, to the Start() function, default values are set for the currently selected weapon slot, and the last selected weapon and ArrayList arrays are initialized ready to hold different weapon(s). When the lastSelectedWeaponSlot variable is set to −1, it just lets the weapon system know that it needs to set the weapon (to avoid duplicate calls later on, whenever the weapon slot is set, it checks to make sure that the new weapon it is trying to set is different to the one currently set up—hence the −1 to make the values of selectedWeaponSlot versus lastSelectedWeaponSlot different on initialization):

```
        // default to the first weapon slot
        selectedWeaponSlot= 0;
        lastSelectedWeaponSlot= -1;


        // initialize weapon list ArrayList
        weaponSlots= new ArrayList();


        // initialize weapon scripts ArrayList
        weaponScripts= new ArrayList();
```

Transforms are cached into myTransform, and the variable forceParent is populated with myTransform if it has not been set in the Unity editor Inspector window. The idea here is that there may be occasions where the required parent transform of the weapon may not always be the transform to which this script is attached. The weapon's parent transform may be set by dragging a reference into forceParent from within the Unity editor:

```
myTransform= transform;

if(forceParent==null)
{
        forceParent= myTransform;
}
```

The position and rotation of the parent transform will be used repeatedly in the weapons setup code. To avoid having to look them up over and over again, their values are saved in the variables TEMPvector3 and TEMProtation:

```
TEMPvector3= forceParent.position;
TEMProtation= forceParent.rotation;
```

When the game starts, the prefab references held by the ArrayList array are instantiated and positioned at the parent transform's position.

The for loop uses weapons.Length to get the length of the weapons array and iterate through it:

```
// we instantiate all of the weapons and hide them so that
// we can activate and use them when needed.
for( int i=0; i<weapons.Length; i++ )
{
```

The weapon at position *i* in the array is instantiated at the position of TEMPvector3 with the rotation from TEMProtation:

```
// Instantiate the item from the weapons list
TEMPgameObject= (GameObject) Instantiate( weapons[i],
TEMPvector3 + offsetWeaponSpawnPosition,
TEMProtation );
```

The instantiated weapon is then parented to the transform held in the variable forceParent so that it inherits its position and rotation. In this game, the layer of the parent will also be used to identify where projectiles come from. We'll look at this layer-based identification a little more as the function unfolds, but for now, just make a little note that the layer of the weapon's parent will be copied down to the weapon. Individual weapons scripts will also copy the layer setting onto their projectiles:

```
TEMPgameObject.transform.parent= forceParent;
TEMPgameObject.layer= forceParent.gameObject.layer;
TEMPgameObject.transform.position= TEMPvector3;
TEMPgameObject.transform.rotation= TEMProtation;
```

These new objects are going to be the ones that the script manages, enabling and disabling them as required and calling on them to act as required. Each new weapon is added to a new ArrayList called weaponSlots:

```
// store a reference to the gameObject in an ArrayList
weaponSlots.Add( TEMPgameObject );
```

The BaseWeaponScript instance attached to each weapon in those slots is found (using GameObject.GetComponent()) and stored in another ArrayList named weaponScripts. By putting them in an array, it saves having to look them up every time:

```
// grab a reference to the weapon script attached to
// the weapon and store the reference in an ArrayList
TEMPWeapon= TEMPgameObject.GetComponent<BaseWeapon
Script>();
weaponScripts.Add( TEMPWeapon );
```

The weapons need to start out disabled; otherwise, they will all appear on top of each other and all active. They are disabled here using the GameObject.SetActive() Unity function:

```
        // disable the weapon
        TEMPgameObject.SetActive( false );
}
```

Now that all of the weapons are instantiated, set up, and hidden, the last thing needed for initialization is to set the default weapon slot to the first weapon (index of 0). To set the slot, use the SetWeaponSlot() function:

```
        // now we set the default selected weapon to visible
        SetWeaponSlot(0);
}
```

When a projectile hits an enemy or collides with a player, the object being hit needs to know where the projectile came from in order for it to know how to react to the collision. In the example game *Lazer Blast Survival*, projectile identification is made simply by layer—all player projectiles are set to layer 9, and all enemy projectiles are on layer 17. Set the layer on the gun-mounting-point object (the object that will be the parent to the weapon), and this weapon script will use the same layer when assigning layers to the projectiles.

Another method for checking where projectiles have come from is to assign each player with a unique ID number and to use the SetOwner() function to tell the projectiles who owns each one. This method is employed in the *Interstellar Paranoids* and *Tank Battle* example games. The ID number is passed on to projectiles and stored in the script that each projectile has attached to it, the ProjectileController.cs script:

```
public void SetOwner(int aNum)
{
        // used to identify the object firing, if required
        ownerNum= aNum;
}
```

The function SetWeaponSlot takes an integer to use as an index number to refer to the weapons stored in the ArrayList named weaponSlots. The weaponSlots ArrayList will be in the same order as weapons added to the original weapons array in the Unity editor Inspector window.

The SetWeaponSlot() function starts out by making sure that the weapon we are trying to set (the variable slotNum) is not the weapon that is already active (the variable lastSelectedWeaponSlot). This is done to avoid duplicate calls to activate the same already activated weapon:

```
public virtual void SetWeaponSlot (int slotNum)
{
```

```
// if the selected weapon is already this one, drop out!
if(slotNum==lastSelectedWeaponSlot)
        return;
```

As a new weapon is about to be made active, the current weapon is disabled by a call to the function DisableCurrentWeapon():

```
// disable the current weapon
DisableCurrentWeapon();
```

selectedWeaponSlot is an index used to store the currently active weapon slot. Here it is set to the incoming parameter value of slotNum:

```
// set our current weapon to the one passed in
selectedWeaponSlot= slotNum;
```

The new value of selectedWeaponSlot is then validated to make sure that it is not less than zero or more than the total number of occupied slots taking away one (since the weaponSlots array of weapons starts at zero, we take one off the total to find the last entry). During the validation, if the value of slotNum is found to be outside what is allowed, it will be set to the nearest valid number—that way, the function will not fail in setting the weapon because of a bad value in slotNum but will choose the wrong weapon instead:

```
// make sure sensible values are getting passed in
if(selectedWeaponSlot<0)
        selectedWeaponSlot= weaponSlots.Count-1;

// make sure that the weapon slot isn't higher than the
// total number of weapons in our list
if(selectedWeaponSlot>weaponSlots.Count-1)
        selectedWeaponSlot=weaponSlots.Count-1;
```

Now that selectedWeaponSlot has been set, lastSelectedWeaponSlot needs updating to the latest slot number:

```
// we store this selected slot to use to prevent duplicate
// weapon slot setting
lastSelectedWeaponSlot= selectedWeaponSlot;
```

A call to EnableCurrentWeapon() will take the value of selectedWeaponSlot and activate the currently selected weapon:

```
// enable the newly selected weapon
EnableCurrentWeapon();
}
```

The NextWeaponSlot() takes a Boolean parameter to tell the function whether or not to loop around from the last weapon to the first. If the shouldLoop parameter is false, and the current weapon is already set to the last available weapon, it will return the same weapon instead of looping around to zero and returning the weapon from the first slot:

```
public virtual void NextWeaponSlot (bool shouldLoop)
{
```

First, the current weapon is disabled in anticipation of setting a new one:

```
// disable the current weapon
DisableCurrentWeapon();
```

selectedWeaponSlot index number is incremented and validated to make sure that it now contains a valid index number (this is where the slot number will be looped back to zero if it goes over the total number of available weapons):

```
// next slot
selectedWeaponSlot++;


// make sure that the slot isn't higher than the total
// number of weapons in our list
if(selectedWeaponSlot==weaponScripts.Count)
{
        if(shouldLoop)
        {
                selectedWeaponSlot= 0;
        } else {
                selectedWeaponSlot= weaponScripts.Count-1;
        }
}
```

The lastSelectedWeaponSlot gets updated before the new current weapon is enabled, completing the function:

```
// we store this selected slot to use to prevent duplicate
// weapon slot setting
lastSelectedWeaponSlot=selectedWeaponSlot;

// enable the newly selected weapon
EnableCurrentWeapon();
}
```

PrevWeaponSlot works in almost exactly the same way as NextWeaponSlot(). It has a Boolean parameter to state whether or not to loop around if the current weapon slot drops below zero, and the most obvious difference is that the selectedWeaponSlot variable is decremented rather than incremented:

```
public virtual void PrevWeaponSlot (bool shouldLoop)
{
        // disable the current weapon
        DisableCurrentWeapon();


        // prev slot
        selectedWeaponSlot--;


        // make sure that the slot is a sensible number
        if( selectedWeaponSlot<0 )
        {
                if(shouldLoop)
```

```
            {
                    selectedWeaponSlot= weaponScripts.Count-1;
            } else {
                    selectedWeaponSlot= 0;
            }
    }


    // we store this selected slot to use to prevent duplicate
    // weapon slot setting
    lastSelectedWeaponSlot=selectedWeaponSlot;


    // enable the newly selected weapon
    EnableCurrentWeapon();
}
```

Disabling the current weapon means that it will be both invisible and unable to fire:

```
public virtual void DisableCurrentWeapon ()
{
```

To disable the weapon, the script will need to talk to the BaseWeaponScript.cs attached to it. Since weaponScripts and weaponSlots ArrayLists were created in the same order, the selectedWeaponSlot can be used as the index for either array.

To make sure that there are scripts in the weaponScripts array, its Count property is checked before going any further:

```
if(weaponScripts.Count==0)
        return;
```

A reference to the currently selected weapon slot's weapon script (BaseWeaponScript. cs) is stored in the variable TEMPWeapon as it is retrieved from the weaponScripts ArrayList:

```
// grab reference to currently selected weapon script
TEMPWeapon= ( BaseWeaponScript )weaponScripts[selectedWeapon
Slot];
```

To tell the weapon to disable, it's a call to its Disable() function:

```
// now tell the script to disable itself
TEMPWeapon.Disable();
```

As well as disabling the actual weapon script, it now needs to be hidden from view. First, the variable TEMPgameObject receives a reference to the weapon's gameObject from the weaponSlots ArrayList. The TEMPgameObject variable is then set to inactive by GameObject.SetActive():

```
// grab reference to the weapon's gameObject and disable
// that, too
TEMPgameObject= ( GameObject )weaponSlots[selectedWeaponSlot];
TEMPgameObject.SetActive( false );
}
```

Enabling the currently selected weapon is done by the EnableCurrentWeapon() function, which works almost exactly the same as DisableCurrentWeapon() except that it calls the Enable() function of the BaseWeaponScript instead of Disable():

```
public virtual void EnableCurrentWeapon ()
{
        if ( weaponScripts.Count==0 )
                return;


        // grab reference to currently selected weapon
        TEMPWeapon= ( BaseWeaponScript )weaponScripts[selectedWeapon
        Slot];


        // now tell the script to enable itself
        TEMPWeapon.Enable();


        TEMPgameObject= ( GameObject )weaponSlots[selectedWeapon
        Slot];
        TEMPgameObject.SetActive( true );
}
```

By default, the Fire() function will launch projectiles along the transform's forward axis, but there is support for firing along a fixed vector by setting the useForceVectorDirection to true.

The function takes no parameters, making it easy to call from any other script:

```
public virtual void Fire ()
{
```

The weaponScripts ArrayList is checked to make sure that it has been properly initialized and that it contains entries (a quick count check):

```
        if (weaponScripts==null)
                return;


        if (weaponScripts.Count==0)
                return;
```

TEMPWeapon gets a reference to the currently selected weapon's script from the weaponScripts array:

```
        // find the weapon in the currently selected slot
        TEMPWeapon= ( BaseWeaponScript )weaponScripts[selectedWeapon
        Slot];
```

By default, the firing direction is along the transform's forward vector:

```
        theDir = myTransform.forward;
```

When useForceVectorDirection is set to true, theDir is set to the Vector from the variable forceVector, which should be set in the Unity editor Inspector window on the gameObject:

```
if( useForceVectorDirection )
    theDir = forceVector;
```

The ownerNum variable was mentioned earlier in this section, where it is set by the SetOwner() function. When the call to the currently selected weapon's Fire() function goes out, it takes a Vector3 and the owner ID:

```
        // fire the projectile
        TEMPWeapon.Fire( theDir, ownerNum );
    }
}
```

6.1.2 BaseWeaponScript.cs

Here is the BaseWeaponController.cs script in its completed form:

```
using UnityEngine;
using System.Collections;


public class BaseWeaponScript : MonoBehavior
{
        [System.NonSerialized]
        public bool canFire;


        public int ammo= 100;
        public int maxAmmo= 100;


        public bool isInfiniteAmmo;
        public GameObject projectileGO;
        public Collider parentCollider;


        private Vector3 fireVector;


        [System.NonSerialized]
        public Transform myTransform;


        private int myLayer;


        public Vector3 spawnPosOffset;
        public float forwardOffset= 1.5f;
        public float reloadTime= 0.2f;
        public float projectileSpeed= 10f;
        public bool inheritVelocity;
```

```
[System.NonSerialized]
public Transform theProjectile;


private GameObject theProjectileGO;
private bool isLoaded;
private ProjectileController theProjectileController;


public virtual void Start()
{
        Init();
}


public virtual void Init()
{
        // cache the transform
        myTransform= transform;


        // cache the layer (we'll set all projectiles to avoid this
        // layer in collisions so that things don't shoot themselves!)
        myLayer= gameObject.layer;


        // load the weapon
        Reloaded();
}


public virtual void Enable()
{
        // drop out if firing is disabled
        if( canFire==true )
                return;


        // enable weapon (do things like show the weapons mesh etc.)
        canFire=true;
}


public virtual void Disable()
{
        // drop out if firing is disabled
        if( canFire==false )
                return;


        // hide weapon (do things like hide the weapons mesh etc.)
        canFire=false;
}


public virtual void Reloaded()
{
```

```
          // the 'isLoaded' var tells us if this weapon is loaded and
          // ready to fire
          isLoaded= true;
    }


    public virtual void SetCollider( Collider aCollider )
    {
          parentCollider= aCollider;
    }


    public virtual void Fire( Vector3 aDirection, int ownerID )
    {
          // be sure to check canFire so that the weapon can be
          // enabled or disabled as required!
          if( !canFire )
                return;


          // if the weapon is not loaded, drop out
          if( !isLoaded )
                return;


          // if we're out of ammo and we do not have infinite ammo,
          // drop out...
          if( ammo<=0 && !isInfiniteAmmo )
                return;


          // decrease ammo
          ammo--;


          // generate the actual projectile
          FireProjectile( aDirection, ownerID );


          // we need to reload before we can fire again
          isLoaded= false;


          // schedule a completion of reloading in <reloadTime>
          // seconds:
          CancelInvoke( "Reloaded" );
          Invoke( "Reloaded", reloadTime );
    }


    public virtual void FireProjectile( Vector3 fireDirection, int
    ownerID )
    {
          // make our first projectile
          theProjectile= MakeProjectile( ownerID );


          // direct the projectile toward the direction of fire
```

```
        theProjectile.LookAt( theProjectile.position +
        fireDirection );


        // add some force to move our projectile
        theProjectile.rigidbody.velocity= fireDirection *
        projectileSpeed;
}


public virtual Transform MakeProjectile( int ownerID )
{
        // create a projectile
        theProjectile= SpawnController.Instance.Spawn( projectileGO,
        myTransform.position+spawnPosOffset + ( myTransform.forward
        * forwardOffset ), myTransform.rotation );
        theProjectileGO= theProjectile.gameObject;
        theProjectileGO.layer= myLayer;


        // grab a ref to the projectile's controller so we can pass
        // on some information about it
        theProjectileController= theProjectileGO.GetComponent<Projec
        tileController>();

        // set owner ID so we know who sent it
        theProjectileController.SetOwnerType(ownerID);

        Physics.IgnoreLayerCollision( myTransform.gameObject.layer,
        myLayer );


        // NOTE: Make sure that the parentCollider is a collision
        // mesh which represents the firing object
        // or a collision mesh likely to be hit by a projectile as
        // it is being fired from the vehicle.
        // One limitation with this system is that it only reliably
        // supports a single collision mesh


        if( parentCollider!=null )
        {
                // disable collision between 'us' and our projectile
                // so as not to hit ourselves with it!
                Physics.IgnoreCollision( theProjectile.collider,
                parentCollider );
        }


        // return this projectile in case we want to do something
        // else to it
        return theProjectile;
}


}
```

6.1.2.1 Script Breakdown

The BaseWeaponScript class derives from MonoBehavior:

```
using UnityEngine;
using System.Collections;


public class BaseWeaponScript : MonoBehavior
{
        public virtual void Start()
        {
                Init();
        }
```

Init() begins by grabbing a reference to the transform and to the layer at which this gameObject with this script attached to is set. This will be used to disable collisions between the layer of the weapon and the actual projectile so that the projectile does not just explode as soon as it is instantiated:

```
        public virtual void Init()
        {
                // cache the transform
                myTransform= transform;


                // cache the layer (we'll set all projectiles to avoid this
                // layer in collisions so that things don't shoot
                // themselves!)
                myLayer= gameObject.layer;


                // load the weapon
                Reloaded();
        }
```

The Enable() and Disable() functions set the Boolean variable canFire to true and false, respectively. This will be checked elsewhere in the code before allowing any projectile firing. Note that the visual representation of the weapon is not hidden here; that task is left to the slot control script to deal with rather than to the weapon itself:

```
        public virtual void Enable()
        {
                canFire=true;
        }


        public virtual void Disable()
        {
                canFire=false;
        }
```

When the weapon is fired, the assumption is made that it will not be loaded for a certain period of time (otherwise, you could, in theory, fire out thousands of projectiles each second). To keep track of when the weapon is in a loaded state, this script uses the

Boolean variable isLoaded. A timed call to the Reloaded() function, after firing, will reset the weapon state again:

```
public virtual void Reloaded()
{
        // the 'isLoaded' var tells us if this weapon is loaded and
        // ready to fire
        isLoaded= true;
}
```

SetCollider() is used to set a collider to be ignored by a projectile. For example, when the script is applied to a player, it should ignore the player's collider so as to prevent the newly created projectile from exploding instantly. It should be set, using the Unity editor Inspector window, to a collider that would likely destroy the projectile as it was spawned. If no parentCollider is set, the script will still work, but the projectile will not ignore any collider:

```
public virtual void SetCollider( Collider aCollider )
{
        parentCollider= aCollider;
}
```

The Fire() function takes two parameters, a Vector3 to represent the direction of fire and an integer providing an ID number for its owner (which gets used primarily by collision code to know how to react):

```
public virtual void Fire( Vector3 aDirection, int ownerID )
{
```

The Boolean variable canFire needs to be true (the weapon is allowed to fire) and isLoaded needs to be true also (the weapon is ready to fire) before the function can progress to check the state of ammunition:

```
        // be sure to check canFire so that the weapon can be
        // enabled or disabled as required!
        if( !canFire )
                return;


        // if the weapon is not loaded, drop out
        if( !isLoaded )
                return;
```

If the integer variable ammo is less than zero and the Boolean isInfiniteAmmo has not been set in the Unity editor Inspector window to true, then the function will drop out here, too:

```
        // if we're out of ammo and we do not have infinite ammo,
        // drop out...
        if( ammo<=0 && !isInfiniteAmmo )
                return;
```

Since all of the criteria have been met, the function goes ahead and decrements ammo in anticipation of the projectile about to be generated by the FireProjectile() function. The direction held by aDirection and the owner ID in the variable ownerID also get passed on to the FireProjectile() function as parameters:

```
// decrease ammo
ammo--;


// generate the actual projectile
FireProjectile( aDirection, ownerID );
```

This is where the Boolean variable isLoaded gets reset to false to delay firing for a reasonable amount of time (set by the value held in the variable reloadTime):

```
// we need to reload before we can fire again
isLoaded= false;
```

CancelInvoke is called to make sure that there is never more than one Invoke call to Reloaded() waiting to activate:

```
// schedule a completion of reloading in <reloadTime>
// seconds:
CancelInvoke( "Reloaded" );
Invoke( "Reloaded", reloadTime );
}
```

The FireProjectile() function is where the projectile gets instantiated. It was called by that last function, Fire():

```
public virtual void FireProjectile( Vector3 fireDirection, int
ownerID )
{
```

The function MakeProjectile will do the work in getting a physical projectile into the scene, but it returns a transform that this function can then use to set up with:

```
// make our first projectile
theProjectile= MakeProjectile( ownerID );
```

Now theProjectile contains a transform; the code uses the Transform.LookAt() function to align it along the target trajectory passed in via the parameter variable fireDirection. Since LookAt() requires a world position vector (as opposed to a direction vector), it takes the projectile's current position from theProjectile.position and adds the fireDirection vector to it. This will adjust the new projectile's rotation so that its *z*-axis is facing in the required direction of travel:

```
// direct the projectile toward the direction of fire
theProjectile.LookAt( theProjectile.position + fireDirection );
```

To send the projectile on its way, the projectile's rigidbody has its velocity set to the required firing direction multiplied by projectilSpeed. Setting its velocity directly, rather than applying forces, makes its movement more predictable; how velocity is affected by applied force is strongly influenced by other properties of the rigidbody such as drag, gravity, and mass, whereas velocity will immediately set it in movement at the correct speed in the required direction:

```
// add some force to move our projectile
theProjectile.rigidbody.velocity= fireDirection *
projectileSpeed;
}
```

MakeProjectile() handles the creation of the physical projectile, taking a parameter of the ownerID (to pass on to the projectile) and returning the newly instantiated projectile transform:

```
public virtual Transform MakeProjectile( int ownerID )
{
```

The SpawnController script from Chapter 4 is used to instantiate the projectile through its Spawn() function. For convenience, SpawnController.Instance.Spawn() takes the exact same parameters as Unity's Instantiate function: the prefab reference to spawn, a Vector3 position, and a rotation for the spawned object.

The projectile to spawn is held in the variable projectileGO (typed as a GameObject); the position is found by taking myTransform's position (the position of the weapon) and adding to it the spawnPosOffset vector (a Vector3 intended to be set in the Unity editor Inspector window). The rotation is taken from the weapon's rotation myTransform.rotation, but the projectile will normally be created from the Fire() function and a new rotation applied to it after the projectile is returned:

```
// create a projectile
theProjectile= SpawnController.Instance.Spawn( projectileGO,
myTransform.position+spawnPosOffset + ( myTransform.forward
* forwardOffset ), myTransform.rotation );
```

To set the projectile's layer, access to its gameObject is required since there is no way to set the layer of a transform. theProjectileGO holds a quick temporary reference to theProjectile.gameObject, and the next line sets its layer to the value held by myLayer:

```
theProjectileGO= theProjectile.gameObject;
theProjectileGO.layer= myLayer;
```

The projectile needs to know about the owner ID so that it can be identified during a collision. Before the script can tell the projectile about it, it needs to use GameObject. GetComponent() to find the ProjectileController.cs script instance

```
// grab a ref to the projectile's controller so we can pass
// on some information about it
theProjectileController= theProjectileGO.GetComponent<Projec
tileController>();
```

With the instance reference in theProjectileController, the next line tells the projectile's script about its owner ID:

```
// set owner ID so we know who sent it
theProjectileController.SetOwnerType(ownerID);
```

In an attempt to prevent projectiles from colliding either with the parent object or with other projectiles spawned closely together, Physics.IgnoreLayerCollision() is used.

Physics.IgnoreLayerCollision() takes two layer numbers (both integers) referring to which layers should ignore colliding with each other. The layer numbers come from the Tags and Layers manager accessible via the menu Edit → Project Settings → Tags and Layers or the Unity editor Inspector window by clicking on the layer dropdown and clicking on the Add layer button. This is applied globally, which means that once two layers are on Unity's ignore list, everything placed on those two layers will no longer register collisions.

In this case, the first layer is the weapon's layer from myTransform.gameObject.layer and the second taken from the variable myLayer, which was set in the Init() function of this script:

```
Physics.IgnoreLayerCollision( myTransform.gameObject.layer, myLayer );
```

A better solution to avoiding collisions between the projectile and any parent collider is to set the parentCollider reference in the Unity editor Inspector window. This part of the code checks that parentCollider is not null; then as long as it contains something, Physics. When a collider is accessible to this script via parentCollider (as set in the Unity editor Inspector window), IgnoreCollision is used to tell the engine to ignore collisions between the two specific colliders.

Whereas Physics.IgnoreLayerCollision() worked to disable all collisions between objects on two layers, the Physics.IgnoreCollision() function stops collision events on specified colliders:

```
if( parentCollider!=null )
{
        // disable collision between 'us' and our projectile
        // so as not to hit ourselves with it!
        Physics.IgnoreCollision( theProjectile.collider,
        parentCollider );
}
```

The newly created projectile needs to be returned to the function calling (especially when this is called from the Fire() function shown earlier in this section), and the last bit of code from this script does just that:

```
        // return this projectile in case we want to do something
        // else to it
        return theProjectile;
    }
}
```

Further on in this book, when the example games are examined, these base scripts will come up again and we will see how they can be applied to real game situations. In Chapter 9, we look at adding artificial intelligence (AI) to the game and how the weapon controller can easily be tied into it and controlled by an AI player in a game.

7 Recipe: Waypoints Manager

◼ 7.1 Waypoint System

Both the racing game *Motor Vehicle Doom* and the shoot 'em up *Interstellar Paranoids* will need waypoints for the AI players. In *Motor Vehicle Doom*, we use waypoints for the AI and also for the main player for the following reasons:

1. To check that the main player is heading in the right direction. The car controller code will track the player's position on the track (based on which waypoint has been passed) and check its forward vector to make sure that it is facing the next waypoint along the track. If the player's forward vector is not within a certain tolerance angle, the game will display a wrong way message and eventually respawn the car facing the right way.

2. To enable the respawning system to find a "safe" place along the track to respawn the player as well as to use its rotation to point the respawned car in the right direction along the track.

3. To find out how far the vehicle has traveled around the track, which is used to compare the other players progress amounts to calculate race positions.

Interstellar Paranoids uses waypoints for moving all of the enemies. Enemies are simple path followers that move along a path firing until they reach the end, where they are destroyed.

The Waypoints_Controller.cs script is very similar to the one from my last book, *Game Development for iOS with Unity3D* (also published by CRC Press). The waypoints controller here has been converted over to C# from its original JavaScript form:

```
public class Waypoints_Controller : MonoBehavior
{
        [ExecuteInEditMode]

        // this script simply gives us a visual path to make it easier to edit
        // our waypoints
        private ArrayList transforms; // arraylist for easy access to
                                      //  transforms
        private Vector3 firstPoint; // store our first waypoint so we can
                                    //  loop the path
        private float distance; // used to calculate distance between
                                //  points
        private Transform TEMPtrans; // a temporary holder for a transform
        private int TEMPindex; // a temporary holder for an index number
        private int totalTransforms;

        private Vector3 diff;
        private float curDistance;
        private Transform closest;

        private Vector3 currentPos;
        private Vector3 lastPos;
        private Transform pointT;

        public bool closed=true;
        public bool shouldReverse;

        void Start()
        {
                // make sure that when this script starts that
                // we have grabbed the transforms for each waypoint
                GetTransforms();
        }

        void OnDrawGizmos()
        {
                // we only want to draw the waypoints when we're editing,
                // not when we are playing the game
                if( Application.isPlaying )
                        return;

                GetTransforms();
                // make sure that we have more than one transform in the
                // list, otherwise we can't draw lines between them
                if (totalTransforms < 2)
                                return;

                // draw our path first, we grab the position of the very
                // first waypoint so that our line has a start point
                TEMPtrans = (Transform)transforms[0];
                lastPos = TEMPtrans.position;

                // we point each waypoint at the next, so that we can use
                // this rotation data to find out when the player is going
```

```
            // the wrong way or to position the player after a reset
            // facing the correct direction. So first we need to hold a
            // reference to the transform we are going to point
            pointT = (Transform)transforms[0];

            // also, as this is the first point we store it to use for
            // closing the path later
            firstPoint = lastPos;

            // now we loop through all of the waypoints drawing lines
            // between them
            for (int i = 1; i < transforms.Count; i++)
            {
                    TEMPtrans = (Transform)transforms[i];
                    if(TEMPtrans==null)
                    {
                            GetTransforms();
                            return;
                    }

                    // grab the current waypoint position
                    currentPos = TEMPtrans.position;

                    Gizmos.color=Color.green;
                    Gizmos.DrawSphere(currentPos,2);

                    // draw the line between the last waypoint and this one
                    Gizmos.color=Color.red;
                    Gizmos.DrawLine(lastPos, currentPos);

                    // point our last transform at the latest position
                    pointT.LookAt(currentPos);

                    // update our 'last' waypoint to become this one as we
                    // move on to find the next...
                    lastPos = currentPos;

                    // update the pointing transform
                    pointT=(Transform)transforms[i];
            }
            // close the path
            if(closed)
            {
                    Gizmos.color=Color.red;
                    Gizmos.DrawLine(currentPos, firstPoint);
            }
    }

    public void SetReverseMode(bool rev)
    {
            shouldReverse=rev;
    }

    public void GetTransforms()
    {
            // we store all of the waypoints transforms in an ArrayList,
            // which is initialised here (we always need to do this
            // before we can use ArrayLists)
            transforms=new ArrayList();
```

```
                // now we go through any transforms 'under' this transform,
                // so all of the child objects that act as our waypoints get
                // put into our arraylist
                foreach(Transform t in transform)
                {
                        // add this transform to our arraylist
                        transforms.Add(t);
                }

                totalTransforms=(int)transforms.Count;
        }

        public int FindNearestWaypoint ( Vector3 fromPos, float maxRange)
        {
                // make sure that we have populated the transforms
                // list, if not, populate it
                if(transforms==null)
                        GetTransforms();

                // the distance variable is just used to hold the
                // 'current' distance when we are comparing, so that
                // we can find the closest distance = Mathf.Infinity;

                // Iterate through them and find the closest one
                for(int i = 0; i < transforms.Count; i++)
                {
                        // grab a reference to a transform
                        TEMPtrans = (Transform)transforms[i];

                        // calculate the distance between the current
                        // transform and the passed in transform's
                        // position vector
                        diff = (TEMPtrans.position - fromPos);
                        curDistance = diff.sqrMagnitude;
                        // now compare distances - making sure that
                        // we are not closer than the closest object
                        // (whose distance is held by the variable
                        // (distance)
                        if ( curDistance < distance )
                        {
                                if( Mathf.Abs( TEMPtrans.position.y -
                                fromPos.y ) < maxRange )
                                {
                                        // set our current 'winner'
                                        // (closest transform) to the
                                        // transform we just found
                                        closest = TEMPtrans;

                                        // store the index of this
                                        // waypoint
                                        TEMPindex=i;

                                        // set our 'winning' distance
                                        // to the distance we just
                                        // found
                                        distance = curDistance;
                                }
                        }
                }
```

```
                    // now we make sure that we did actually find
                    // something, then return it
                    if(closest)
                    {
                            // return the waypoint we found in this test
                            return TEMPindex;
                    } else {
                            // no waypoint was found, so return -1 (this
                            // should be accounted for at the other end!)
                            return -1;
                    }
        }


// this function has the addition of a check to avoid finding the
// same transform as one passed in. We use this to make sure that
// when we are looking for the nearest waypoint we don't find the
// same one as we just passed

public int FindNearestWaypoint ( Vector3 fromPos , Transform
exceptThis, float maxRange)
{
                    // make sure that we have populated the transforms
                    // list, if not, populate it
                    if(transforms==null)
                            GetTransforms();

                    // the distance variable is just used to hold the
                    // 'current' distance when we are comparing, so that
                    we can find the closest distance = Mathf.Infinity;

                    // Iterate through them and find the closest one
                    for(int i = 0; i < transforms.Count; i++)
                    {
                            // grab a reference to a transform
                            TEMPtrans = (Transform)transforms[i];

                            // calculate the distance between the current
                            // transform and the passed in transform's
                            // position vector
                            diff = (TEMPtrans.position - fromPos);
                            curDistance = diff.sqrMagnitude;

                            // now compare distances - making sure that
                            // we are not
                            if ( curDistance < distance && TEMPtrans !=
                            exceptThis )
                            {
                                    if( Mathf.Abs( TEMPtrans.position.y -
                                    fromPos.y ) < maxRange )
                                    {
                                            // set our current 'winner'
                                            // (closest transform) to the
                                            // transform we just found
                                            closest = TEMPtrans;

                                            // store the index of this
                                            // waypoint
                                            TEMPindex=i;
```

```
                                    // set our 'winning' distance
                                    // to the distance we just
                                    // found
                                    distance = curDistance;
                           }
                    }
              }

              // now we make sure that we did actually find
              // something, then return it
              if(closest)
              {
                    // return the waypoint we found in this test
                    return TEMPindex;
              } else {
                    // no waypoint was found, so return -1 (this
                    // should be accounted for at the other end!)
                    return -1;
              }
       }

       public Transform GetWaypoint(int index)
       {
              if( shouldReverse )
              {
                    // send back the reverse index'd waypoint
                    index=(transforms.Count-1)-index;

                    if(index<0)
                           index=0;
              }

              // make sure that we have populated the transforms list, if
              // not, populate it
                    if(transforms==null)
                           GetTransforms();

              // first, let's check to see if this index is higher than
              // our waypoint count
              // if so, we return null which needs to be handled on the
              // other side'
              if(index>transforms.Count-1)
                    return null;

              return (Transform)transforms[index];
       }

       public int GetTotal()
       {
              return totalTransforms;
       }

}
```

After variable declarations, the Start() function calls a function called Get Transforms().

```
void Start()
    {
        // make sure that when this script starts that
        // we have grabbed the transforms for each waypoint
        GetTransforms();
    }
```

Jumping ahead in the script, take a look at GetTransforms() function now so that it is clear what happens when this class first starts:

```
public void GetTransforms()
    {
        // we store all of the waypoints transforms in an ArrayList,
        // which is initialised here (we always need to do this
        // before we can use ArrayLists)
        transforms=new ArrayList();
```

To make the waypoints control script easy to use, we need to make sure that our waypoints are set up in a particular way in the scene where we want to use them. This format is an empty gameObject with the WaypointsController.cs component attached to it, with all waypoints as its children. The waypoints controller script expects to find all of the waypoints it is going to use, as child objects under it. All of the transforms found in the GetTransforms() function are added to an ArrayList variable named transforms like this:

```
        foreach(Transform t in transform)
        {
            // add this transform to our arraylist
            transforms.Add(t);
        }

        totalTransforms=(int)transforms.Count;
    }
```

At the end of GetTransforms, we store the total number of transforms in an integer for easy access later on (so that we don't have to count the ArrayList each time we need to know how many transforms it contains).

If you have never dealt with gizmos before, they are quite simply little icons or helper objects and switches to make editing easier. Unity relies quite heavily on gizmos for the editor and how you interact with it, as well as to provide a nice interface for you to build your own custom types.

All gizmo drawing needs to be done in one of two functions (called automatically by the engine):

| OnDrawGizmos | Called every frame. All gizmos are pickable. |
| OnDrawGizmosSelected | Called only when the object with the script attached is selected. |

The OnDrawGizmos() function is a runtime class (called automatically by the game engine) where we can draw our own gizmos and do some editor-based manipulation. In this case, the OnDrawGizmos function of the Waypoints_Controller.cs script will render the waypoint positions and draw lines between each one so that we have a simple visual representation of the path when we come to build or edit it in the Unity editor:

```
void OnDrawGizmos()
{
        // we only want to draw the waypoints when we're editing,
        // not when we are playing the game
        if( Application.isPlaying )
                return;
```

Application.Playing can be checked to find out whether or not Unity is in edit mode or playing your game. There is no point in wasting time or CPU cycles drawing waypoints when the game is running, so we did a quick check to drop out whenever we are not in edit mode.

The next steps are to keep the transforms up to date (just in case they are moved or new ones added in the editor). Also, when you first build a path, obviously it will start with a single waypoint. With only one point, there is no end point for rendering a line in the editor, so this function checks that there are enough waypoints to actually draw a line and drops out when totalTransforms is less than 2.

```
GetTransforms();

// make sure that we have more than one transform in the
// list, otherwise we can't draw lines between them
if (totalTransforms < 2)
        return;

// draw our path first, we grab the position of the very
// first waypoint so that our line has a start point
TEMPtrans = (Transform)transforms[0];
lastPos = TEMPtrans.position;

// we point each waypoint at the next, so that we can use
// this rotation data to find out when the player is going
// the wrong way or to position the player after a reset
// facing the correct direction. So first we need to hold a
// reference to the transform we are going to point
pointT = (Transform)transforms[0];
// also, as this is the first point we store it to use for
// closing the path later
firstPoint = lastPos;

// now we loop through all of the waypoints drawing lines
// between them
for (int i = 1; i < totalTransforms; i++)
{
        TEMPtrans = (Transform)transforms[i];
        if(TEMPtrans==null)
        {
                GetTransforms();
                return;
        }

        // grab the current waypoint position
        currentPos = TEMPtrans.position;
```

Having all of the gizmos, lines, and editor helper graphics, the same colors would make life harder. For that reason, Unity provides the Gizmos.color function to set their colors. It takes just one call to Gizmos.color (passing in a Color object) and everything after that point will be rendered using it.

```
Gizmos.color=Color.green;
```

Gizmos.DrawSphere does exactly that. It draws a nice sphere at a set position and radius like this:

```
Gizmos.DrawSphere(currentPos,2);

// draw the line between the last waypoint and this
// one
Gizmos.color=Color.red;
Gizmos.DrawLine(lastPos, currentPos);
```

Gizmos.DrawLine is another utility provided by Unity to draw a simple line between two 3D vectors. The gizmo drawing system has a few more options available to make editing easier.

According to the Unity documentation, the Gizmo interface provides the following functions:

DrawCube	Draw a solid box with center and size.
DrawFrustum	Draw a camera frustum using the currently set Gizmos.matrix for its location and rotation.
DrawGUITexture	Draw a texture in the scene.
DrawIcon	Draw an icon at a position in the scene view.
DrawLine	Draw a line starting at from toward to.
DrawRay	Draw a ray starting at from to from + direction.
DrawSphere	Draw a solid sphere with center and radius.
DrawWireCube	Draw a wireframe box with center and size.
DrawWireSphere	Draw a wireframe sphere with center and radius.

As stated earlier in this chapter, the waypoints are used at one stage as respawn points for vehicles that may be stuck or off track. Their rotations are also used to ensure that the repositioned vehicle is facing in the correct direction; for that reason, we need the waypoints to face "forward." To make sure that the rotations of our waypoints are correct, we go through and point each one forward toward the next one:

```
pointT.LookAt(currentPos);
```

You can easily rotate a transform so that its forward points toward another transform by using the transform.LookAt() function. It takes one or two parameters, the first being the transform you want to point toward and the second an optional up vector.

Note that having this functionality happening all the time during OnDrawGizmos() can make drag-and-drop editing difficult, as objects pivot around automatically when you drag waypoints. Comment out the line above if you find you are having trouble with automatically rotating points.

As the function continues, we continue to iterate through the waypoints and then close the path, if the Boolean variable closed is set to true (you can set that in the Inspector window of the editor when the gameObject that has this script attached is selected):

```
                              // update our 'last' waypoint to become this one as
                              // we move on to find the next...
                              lastPos = currentPos;

                              // update the pointing transform
                              pointT=(Transform)transforms[i];
            }

      // close the path
      if(closed)
      {
                  Gizmos.color=Color.red;
                  Gizmos.DrawLine(currentPos, firstPoint);
      }
}
```

After the GetTransforms() function discussed earlier, the rest of the class is made up of publically accessible utility functions for other scripts to access:

SetReverseMode	Sets the value of a Boolean variable called shouldReverse, which determines whether or not the path should be reversed.
FindNearestWaypoint	Finds the nearest waypoint to a given position, within a given distance, and returns its index number as an integer.
	There are two implementations of the FindNearestWaypoint function, one of which adds the extra parameter of exceptThis. The function will find the closest waypoint as normal, but when exceptThis is used it will ignore the specified transform.
GetWaypoint	Returns the transform of the waypoint at the index number passed in (as an integer).
GetTotal	Returns an integer value representing the total number of waypoints this class has control over.

```
public void SetReverseMode(bool rev)
{
        shouldReverse=rev;
}

public int FindNearestWaypoint (Vector3 fromPos, float maxRange)
{
                  // make sure that we have populated the transforms
                  // list, if not, populate it
                  if(transforms==null)
                        GetTransforms();
```

```
// the distance variable is just used to hold the
// 'current' distance when we are comparing, so that
// we can find the closest
distance = Mathf.Infinity;
```

To find the nearest waypoint to the 3D vector fromPos, the variable distance starts out at a very large number—Mathf.Infinity. We use this to compare distances during the iteration loop below:

```
// Iterate through them and find the closest one
for(int i = 0; i < transforms.Count; i++)
{
        // grab a reference to a transform
        TEMPtrans = (Transform)transforms[i];

        // calculate the distance between the current
        // transform and the passed in transform's
        // position vector
        diff = (TEMPtrans.position - fromPos);
        curDistance = diff.sqrMagnitude;

        // now compare distances - making sure that
        // we are not
        if ( curDistance < distance )
        {
```

As Mathf.Infinity is, well, infinity, this condition will always be satisfied at least once. There should always be something closer than infinity, meaning that as long as there are transforms to compare, we should always get at least some kind of return result no matter how far away they are in the 3D world.

```
if( Mathf.Abs( TEMPtrans.position.y -
fromPos.y ) < maxRange )
{
```

In some case, returning far away transforms may not always be the desired result, so maxRange is provided to at least have some kind of cap on distance if needed.

```
                // set our current 'winner'
                // (closest transform) to the
                // transform we just found
                closest = TEMPtrans;

                // store the index of this
                // waypoint
                TEMPindex=i;

                // set our 'winning' distance
                // to the distance we just
                // found
                distance = curDistance;
        }
    }
}
```

With the addition of the maxRange check, we can no longer be 100% sure of a return result, so a quick check makes sure that closest has something other than a zero in it before returning the result:

```
// now we make sure that we did actually find
// something, then return it
if(closest)
{
        // return the waypoint we found in this test
        return TEMPindex;
} else {
        // no waypoint was found, so return -1 (this
        // should be accounted for at the other end!)
        return -1;
}
}

// this function has the addition of a check to avoid finding the
// same transform as the one passed in. We use this to make sure
// that when we are looking for the nearest waypoint we don't find
// the same one as we just passed
```

It is possible to have two different implementations of the same function, each with its own set of required parameters. Here, a second version of the FindNearestWaypoint() function follows almost the same course as the first with the exception of a new transform passed in via the exceptThis parameter discussed earlier in this section.

```
public int FindNearestWaypoint (Vector3 fromPos , Transform
exceptThis, float maxRange)
{
        // make sure that we have populated the transforms
        // list, if not, populate it
        if(transforms==null)
                GetTransforms();

        // the distance variable is just used to hold the
        // 'current' distance when we are comparing, so that
        // we can find the closest
        distance = Mathf.Infinity;

        // Iterate through them and find the closest one
        for(int i = 0; i < transforms.Count; i++)
        {
                // grab a reference to a transform
                TEMPtrans = (Transform)transforms[i];

                // calculate the distance between the current
                // transform and the passed in transform's
                // position vector
                diff = (TEMPtrans.position - fromPos);
                curDistance = diff.sqrMagnitude;

                // now compare distances - making sure that
                // we are not
                if ( curDistance < distance && TEMPtrans !=
                exceptThis )
```

```
                                {
                                        if( Mathf.Abs( TEMPtrans.position.y -
                                        fromPos.y ) < maxRange )
                                        {
                                                // set our current 'winner'
                                                // (closest transform) to the
                                                // transform we just found
                                                closest = TEMPtrans;

                                                // store the index of this
                                                // waypoint
                                                TEMPindex=i;

                                                // set our 'winning' distance
                                                // to the distance we just
                                                // found
                                                distance = curDistance;
                                        }
                                }
                        }

                        // now we make sure that we did actually find
                        // something, then return it
                        if(closest)
                        {
                                // return the waypoint we found in this test
                                return TEMPindex;
                        } else {
                                // no waypoint was found, so return -1 (this
                                // should be accounted for at the other end!)
                                return -1;
                        }
        }
```

GetWaypoint() returns the transform of the waypoint at the index passed in via the integer index.

```
        public Transform GetWaypoint(int index)
        {
                if( shouldReverse )
                {
```

This is the only place in the class where shouldReverse is used. GetWaypoint will reverse the index numbers of the waypoints when shouldReverse is true (i.e., using GetWaypoint to get a waypoint with the index number of zero would return the last waypoint in the path, instead of the first).

To reverse the index passed in to this function, the variable index is modified by subtracting it from the number of transforms in totalTransforms.

```
                        // send back the reverse index'd waypoint
                        index=(totalTransforms)-index;

                        if(index<0)
                                index=0;
                }
```

Obviously, before trying to access the waypoint transforms to send out as a return value, it is important to make sure that they have been set up; so there's a quick check to make sure that transforms is not null. If transforms is null, we know that there will be no transforms to work with so GetTransforms() is called to get everything set up:

```
// make sure that we have populated the transforms list, if
// not, populate it
    if(transforms==null)
        GetTransforms();
```

If the index being requested is too high, rather than return a wrong waypoint it will return a null value. The code on the requesting side can then check for a null return value and act accordingly:

```
// first, let's check to see if this index is higher than
// our waypoint count
// if so, we return null which needs to be handled on the
// other side'
if(index>totalTransforms-1)
        return null;
```

Now that everything has been set up correctly (the transforms list contains waypoints and the index number is within range), all that is left to do is return the transform from the array:

```
    return (Transform)transforms[index];
}
```

The final piece in the waypoints controller script is GetTotal(), which is used by other scripts to find out how many waypoints there are:

```
public int GetTotal()
{
        return totalTransforms;
}
}
```

8 Recipe: Sound Manager

Audio can make or break a video game. Good audio can provide a deeper level of immersion by reinforcing the themes of the game world and filling out environments into living, noise-making places. On the other hand, bad audio can irritate players and turn a good gameplay experience into something repetitive and empty.

Most commercial games have several different layers of audio playing at the same time, transitioning or changing contextually. To achieve commercial levels of audio, Unity's audio system will need a lot of help. Out of the box, it isn't exactly an easy process to do some simple tasks, such as fading audio in and out or controlling volume levels. To accomplish even basic functionality, extra audio management code is required.

The audio code in this book provides the following functionality to our framework:

1. To provide a single audio source for multiple audio clips

2. To be able to manage audio clips from a single source

3. To be able to play, pause, or stop an audio clip

4. To be able to play, pause, or stop music streaming from disc

5. To provide volume control functions to set volume and fade music in and out

6. To provide accessibility, by being a static singleton instance, so that all calls to audio are of the same format

There are two scripts in this book related to the playback and management of audio. One is the sound controller, intended for sound effects, BaseSoundController.cs. The second is intended for music control, the script MusicController.cs.

▌ 8.1 The Sound Controller

In the example framework for this book, it is assumed that each scene has a sound controller, an empty gameObject with the BaseSoundController.cs script attached to it. The component has an array populated in the Unity editor Inspector window by the sounds required for the game (their AudioClips). When a sound is required by another script, it calls upon the sound manager to play it, passing in the index of the AudioClip as it stands in the array:

```
BaseSoundController.Instance.PlaySoundByIndex( the index number from the
array of sounds );
```

Centralizing the audio playback avoids dealing with properties in multiple places, such as having to set the volume level on every AudioSource when a user changes it in the options menu. When audio is centralized like this, one volume setting and one volume script can easily change all of the game audio.

Below is the full sound controller script:

```
using UnityEngine;
using System.Collections;

public class SoundObject
{
        public AudioSource source;
        public GameObject sourceGO;
        public Transform sourceTR;

        public AudioClip clip;
        public string name;

        public SoundObject(AudioClip aClip, string aName, float aVolume)
        {
                // in this (the constructor) we create a new audio source
                // and store the details of the sound itself
                sourceGO= new GameObject("AudioSource_"+aName);
                sourceTR= sourceGO.transform;
                source= sourceGO.AddComponent<AudioSource>();
                source.name= "AudioSource_"+aName;
                source.playOnAwake= false;
                source.clip= aClip;
                source.volume= aVolume;
                clip= aClip;
                name= aName;
        }

        public void PlaySound(Vector3 atPosition)
        {
                sourceTR.position= atPosition;
                source.PlayOneShot(clip);
        }
```

```
        }

public class BaseSoundController : MonoBehavior
{
        public static BaseSoundController Instance;

        public AudioClip[] GameSounds;

        private int totalSounds;
        private ArrayList soundObjectList;
        private SoundObject tempSoundObj;

        public float volume= 1;
        public string gamePrefsName= "DefaultGame"; // DO NOT FORGET TO SET
                                                     // THIS IN THE EDITOR!!

        public void Awake()
        {
                Instance= this;
        }

        void Start ()
        {
                // we will grab the volume from PlayerPrefs when this script
                // first starts
                volume= PlayerPrefs.GetFloat(gamePrefsName+"_SFXVol");
                Debug.Log ("BaseSoundController gets volume from prefs
                "+gamePrefsName+"_SFXVol at "+volume);
                soundObjectList=new ArrayList();

                // make sound objects for all of the sounds in GameSounds
                // array
                foreach(AudioClip theSound in GameSounds)
                {
                        tempSoundObj= new SoundObject(theSound,
                        theSound.name, volume);
                        soundObjectList.Add(tempSoundObj);
                        totalSounds++;
                }
        }

        public void PlaySoundByIndex(int anIndexNumber, Vector3 aPosition)
        {
                // make sure we're not trying to play a sound indexed higher
                // than exists in the array
                if(anIndexNumber>soundObjectList.Count)
                {
                        Debug.LogWarning("BaseSoundController>Trying to do
                        PlaySoundByIndex with invalid index number. Playing
                        last sound in array, instead.");
                        anIndexNumber= soundObjectList.Count-1;
                }

                tempSoundObj= (SoundObject)soundObjectList[anIndexNumber];
                tempSoundObj.PlaySound(aPosition);
        }
}
```

8.1.1 Script Breakdown

This script should be attached to an empty gameObject somewhere in the scene. For the volume control to work correctly, the gamePrefsName should be set to a name suitable for describing the game. That way, it will use PlayerPrefs to grab volume levels.

AudioClips should be dragged into the GameSounds array via the Inspector window in the Unity editor. Each AudioClip in the array will have its own AudioSource and GameObject instantiated when the BaseSoundController.cs script first runs. Think of each sound as having its own audio channel to avoid overlaps or too many different sounds playing on a single AudioSource. Internally, a class called SoundObject is used to store information about the audio sources and their gameObjects. When the main sound controller script needs to access each one, the references in SoundObject are used to avoid having to repeatedly look for them.

The SoundObject class is declared at the top of the script:

```
using UnityEngine;
using System.Collections;

public class SoundObject
{
        public AudioSource source;
        public GameObject sourceGO;
        public Transform sourceTR;

        public AudioClip clip;
        public string name;

        public SoundObject(AudioClip aClip, string aName, float aVolume)
        {
                // in this (the constructor) we create a new audio source
                // and store the details of the sound itself
                sourceGO= new GameObject("AudioSource_"+aName);
                sourceTR= sourceGO.transform;
                source= sourceGO.AddComponent<AudioSource>();
                source.name= "AudioSource_"+aName;
                source.playOnAwake= false;
                source.clip= aClip;
                source.volume= aVolume;
                clip= aClip;
                name= aName;
        }
```

The SoundObject single function is to PlaySound(). A position is passed in as a parameter, and AudioSource.PlayOneShot() is used to start the AudioClip playback.

PlayOneShot() is a simple method for getting the AudioSource to play the desired clip without having to set its AudioClip property permanently. To get it to play in the correct location in the 3D world, the position of the AudioSource is set just before the call to play it happens:

```
        public void PlaySound(Vector3 atPosition)
        {
                sourceTR.position= atPosition;
                source.PlayOneShot(clip);
        }
}
```

BaseSoundController derives from MonoBehavior so that it can use the Awake() and Start() functions called by the Unity engine:

```
public class BaseSoundController : MonoBehavior
{
        public static BaseSoundController Instance;

        public AudioClip[] GameSounds;

        private int totalSounds;
        private ArrayList soundObjectList;
        private SoundObject tempSoundObj;

        public float volume= 1;
        public string gamePrefsName= "DefaultGame"; // DO NOT FORGET TO SET
                                                     // THIS IN THE EDITOR!!
```

The variable named Instance is static typed, accessible from anywhere, which makes playing a sound possible from any other script in the game. When the script's Awake() function is called, Instance is set to the instance of the script. The assumption is that each scene requiring sound effects will contain one instance of this script in a scene, attached to an empty gameObject or similar. Since this script does not check for multiple instances, care must be taken to ensure that there is only one instance in a scene:

```
        public void Awake()
        {
                Instance= this;
        }

        void Start ()
        {
```

PlayerPrefs saves a file to the user's hard drive, which can be accessed at any time for saving trivial data. The Unity documentation has the following information on where PlayerPrefs files are stored:

Editor/Standalone

On Mac OS X PlayerPrefs are stored in ~LibraryPreferences folder, in a file named unity. [company name].[product name].plist, where company and product names are the names set up in Project Settings. The same .plist file is used for both Projects run in the Editor and standalone players.

On Windows, PlayerPrefs are stored in the registry under HKCU\Software\[company name]\[product name] key, where company and product names are the names set up in Project Settings.

On Linux, PlayerPrefs can be found in ~/.confignunity3d[CompanyName]/[ProductName]. confignunity3d again using the company and product names specified in the Project Settings.

WebPlayer

On Web players, PlayerPrefs are stored in binary files in the following locations:
Mac OS X: ~LibraryPreferencesUnityWebPlayerPrefs
Windows: %APPDATA%\Unity\WebPlayerPrefs

There is one preference file per Web player URL and the file size is limited to 1 MB. If this limit is exceeded, SetInt, SetFloat, and SetString will not store the value and throw a PlayerPrefsException.

The filename for the preference files this script uses is made up of a combination of the contents of the string named gamePrefsName and a suffix of _SFXVol. The gamePrefs-Name string should be set in the Unity editor so that each game has a unique preferences file.

PlayerPrefs may be formatted in three different ways: floats, integers, or strings, in this case, a float between 0 and 1 to represent sound volume:

```
// we will grab the volume from PlayerPrefs when this script
// first starts
volume= PlayerPrefs.GetFloat(gamePrefsName+"_SFXVol");
```

To store SoundObject instances, an ArrayList is used. The ArrayList needs to be initialized before any attempts to access it:

```
soundObjectList=new ArrayList();
```

Next, the script iterates through the array of AudioClips set in the Unity editor and builds the SoundObject instances to hold information about each sound. The soundObjectList ArrayList is populated by the new SoundObject instances.

A foreach loop iterates through each AudioClip in the GameSounds array:

```
foreach(AudioClip theSound in GameSounds)
{
```

The constructor function of the SoundObject takes three parameters: the AudioClip, the name of the sound, and its intended volume (based on the volume value read earlier from the PlayerPrefs and stored in the variable named volume):

```
tempSoundObj= new SoundObject(theSound,
theSound.name, volume);
soundObjectList.Add(tempSoundObj);
```

The integer variable totalSounds counts how many sounds go into the ArrayList to save having to recount the array each time we need it:

```
totalSounds++;
    }
}
```

To play a sound, the function PlaySoundByIndex takes two parameters: an index number (integer) and a position. The index number refers to an AudioClip's position in the original AudioClip array:

```
public void PlaySoundByIndex(int anIndexNumber, Vector3 aPosition)
{
```

For safety, the index number is checked to make sure that it is valid so that it won't raise a null reference exception because of a mistake with the call. The index number will be set to the last AudioClip in the array if it is higher than it should be and a warning logged in the console to raise attention to it:

```
if(anIndexNumber>soundObjectList.Count)
{
        Debug.LogWarning("BaseSoundController>Trying to do
        PlaySoundByIndex with invalid index number. Playing
        last sound in array, instead.");
        anIndexNumber= soundObjectList.Count-1;
}
```

A temporary AudioClip is made to hold the required sound as it is played with AudioSource.PlaySound():

```
        tempSoundObj= (SoundObject)soundObjectList[anIndexNumber];
        tempSoundObj.PlaySound(aPosition);
    }
}
```

There is still some way to go before this sound controller provides a complete solution to game audio, but it should serve as a good, solid start.

■ 8.2 The Music Player

The MusicController.cs script is intended for playing music. It will set the volume according to a PlayerPrefs value and handle volume fading and audio clip looping.

Below is the full script:

```
using UnityEngine;
using System.Collections;

public class MusicController : MonoBehavior
{
        private float volume;
        public string gamePrefsName= "DefaultGame"; // DO NOT FORGET TO SET
                                                     // THIS IN THE EDITOR!!

        public AudioClip music;

        public bool loopMusic;

        private AudioSource source;
        private GameObject sourceGO;

        private int fadeState;
        private int targetFadeState;

        private float volumeON;
        private float targetVolume;

        public float fadeTime=15f;
        public bool shouldFadeInAtStart= true;
```

```
void Start ()
{
        // we will grab the volume from PlayerPrefs when this script
        // first starts
        volumeON= PlayerPrefs.GetFloat(gamePrefsName+"_MusicVol");

        // create a game object and add an AudioSource to it, to
        // play music on
        sourceGO= new GameObject("Music_AudioSource");
        source= sourceGO.AddComponent<AudioSource>();
        source.name= "MusicAudioSource";
        source.playOnAwake= true;
        source.clip= music;
        source.volume= volume;

        // the script will automatically fade in if this is set
        if(shouldFadeInAtStart)
        {
                fadeState=0;
                volume=0;
        } else {
                fadeState=1;
                volume=volumeON;
        }

        // set up default values
        targetFadeState=1;
        targetVolume=volumeON;
        source.volume=volume;
}

void Update ()
{
        // if the audiosource is not playing and it's supposed to
        // loop, play it again (Sam?)
        if( !source.isPlaying && loopMusic )
                source.Play();

        // deal with volume fade in/out
        if(fadeState!=targetFadeState)
        {
                if(targetFadeState==1)
                {
                        if(volume==volumeON)
                                fadeState=1;
                } else {
                        if(volume==0)
                                fadeState=0;
                }

                volume=Mathf.Lerp(volume, targetVolume,
                Time.deltaTime * fadeTime);
                source.volume=volume;
        }
}

public void FadeIn ( float fadeAmount )
{
```

```
                volume=0;
                fadeState=0;
                targetFadeState=1;
                targetVolume=volumeON;
                fadeTime=fadeAmount;
        }

        public void FadeOut ( float fadeAmount )
        {
                volume=volumeON;
                fadeState=1;
                targetFadeState=0;
                targetVolume=0;
                fadeTime=fadeAmount;
        }
}
```

8.2.1 Script Breakdown

The MusicController.cs script should be added to an empty gameObject in a scene. It derives from MonoBehavior to use the Start() and Update() functions called by the engine:

```
public class MusicController : MonoBehavior
{
```

The MusicController script can automatically fade music in when it loads, making for a nicer transition into the scene. shouldFadeInAtStart should be set in the Unity editor Inspector window on the component:

```
        public bool shouldFadeInAtStart= true;

        void Start ()
        {
```

As with the sound controller, it is important to set the gamePrefsName string to load and save preferences correctly:

```
                // we will grab the volume from PlayerPrefs when this script
                // first starts
                volumeON= PlayerPrefs.GetFloat(gamePrefsName+"_MusicVol");
```

In the next part of the script, a new gameObject is created and an AudioSource added to it. The AudioSource is set to play on awake so that the music starts automatically at the start of the scene. The music variable should be set in the Unity editor Inspector window, so that the music AudioClip can be carried over to the new source:

```
                // create a game object and add an AudioSource to it, to
                // play music on
                sourceGO= new GameObject("Music_AudioSource");
                source= sourceGO.AddComponent<AudioSource>();
                source.name= "MusicAudioSource";
```

```
source.playOnAwake= true;
source.clip= music;
source.volume= volume;
```

The final part of the Start() function deals with setting up the default fade settings. When shouldFadeInAtStart is set to true, the volume will start at 0, and the fadeState will be 0. The fader variables will be explained in full along with the fader code further down within the Update() loop:

```
// the script will automatically fade in if this is set
if(shouldFadeInAtStart)
{
        fadeState=0;
        volume=0;
} else {
        fadeState=1;
        volume=volumeON;
}
// set up default values
targetFadeState=1;
targetVolume=volumeON;
```

The AudioSource created to play music needs to have its volume set at the beginning for it to start out at the volume set by the preference file:

```
        source.volume=volume;
}
```

The Update() function begins by checking to see whether the AudioSource in the variable source is playing by polling its AudioSource.isPlaying property. If this is false and the music is set to loop (by the loopMusic variable), the next line makes a call to Play() on the AudioSource, restarting the music:

```
void Update ()
{
        // if the audiosource is not playing and it's supposed to
        // loop, play it again (Sam?)
        if( !source.isPlaying && loopMusic )
                source.Play();
```

The fader works by having a fadeState variable and a targetFadeState. When targetFade State is different to fadeState, it gets to work on fading the volume in whichever direction it needs to go until it reaches the target volume. When the volume is at the target volume, fadeState and targetFadeState will be the same. The target volume is decided by the state of targetFadeState. When targetFadeState is 0, the target volume will be 0. When targetFade State is 1, the target volume will be the value of the variable volumeON, which was given its value back in the Start() function when the volume was grabbed from PlayerPrefs:

```
        // deal with volume fade in/out
        if(fadeState!=targetFadeState)
        {
                if(targetFadeState==1)
```

```
        {
                if(volume==volumeON)
                        fadeState=1;
        } else {
                if(volume==0)
                        fadeState=0;
        }
```

A quick interpolation between the current volume and the targetVolume, with the time it takes to fade decided by Time.deltaTime multiplied by fadeTime:

```
        volume=Mathf.Lerp(volume, targetVolume,
        Time.deltaTime * fadeTime);
        source.volume=volume;
    }
}
```

The last two functions in the MusicController class set up the fader variables for either fading in or fading out through code. The single parameter fadeAmount is a value for which to decide how long it should fade in or out:

```
public void FadeIn ( float fadeAmount )
{
        volume=0;
        fadeState=0;
        targetFadeState=1;
        targetVolume=volumeON;
        fadeTime=fadeAmount;
}

public void FadeOut ( float fadeAmount )
{
        volume=volumeON;
        fadeState=1;
        targetFadeState=0;
        targetVolume=0;
        fadeTime=fadeAmount;
}
}
```

■ 8.3 Adding Sound to the Weapons

There are two places that may, at first glance, make good sound trigger points for weapons. One is when the fire button is pressed in the player script, and the other is when the projectile itself is created.

Making a sound when the fire button is pressed may seem like a good idea, but to do that, we have to make sure that the projectile actually makes it into the world. After the fire button is pressed, it may be that there is no ammunition left in the weapon or that the weapon is in its reloading period. Making the sound without firing the projectile would be rather silly.

Making a sound when the projectile is spawned may in fact be a better option, as it will only make a sound when a projectile is successfully made. Also, the sound can be

---

tailored to suit the projectile. For example, perhaps a small laser blast has a less powerful sound effect than a larger blast, or perhaps a green laser sounds different from a red laser.

In the example project for this book, the code to play a firing sound from the projectile will already be in place. The code resides within the ProjectileController.cs script.

Note that placing the call to play the projectile sound in the Awake() or Start() function may cause problems because of the time it takes to initialize versus the time it takes for the script creating the projectile to get around to position it correctly in the 3D world. To ensure that the projectile will have been positioned correctly when the audio is played, this code goes into the Update() loop with a simple Boolean flag to stop the sound getting played more than once.

The variable declarations related to the firing effect, to go with the other declarations at the beginning of the script, are as follows:

```
private bool didPlaySound;
private int whichSoundToPlayOnStart= 0;
```

The code to play the sound is placed at the top of the Update() function. It checks first to make sure that the sound has not already been played and then makes a call out to the BaseSoundController static variable Instance. The PlaySoundByIndex parameters are the contents of the integer whichSoundToPlayOnStart variable and the projectile transform's position. After the sound call, didPlaySound is set to true to prevent duplicate calls to play:

```
if(!didPlaySound)
{
BaseSoundController.Instance.PlaySoundByIndex(whichSoundToPlayOnStart,
myTransform.position);
                didPlaySound=true;
}
```

9 AI Manager

When computer scientist John McCarthy coined the term artificial intelligence (AI) in the mid-1950s, I doubt anything like the path-finding killer robot cars we will be building in this book would have been on his mind.

The AI Controller in this book is a basic state machine, focused on function rather than on any kind of emotional simulation. For it to work for the example games later on in the book, our AI controller will be able to perform several different actions. It will need to be able to control a vehicle (as in a body, a spaceship, or other moving entity) by turning and moving forward and backward and using vision to try to avoid obstacles. When we need the controller to follow a specific path, it should be capable of turning toward and moving in the direction of waypoints.

Achieving this will require the controller to act differently in several different states. The BaseAIController.cs states are as follows:

1. moving_looking_for_target

   Moves forward, continuously checking the distance between this object and the target. If the distance is below a set chase distance (maxChaseDistance), then the AI uses raycasting to check the line of sight between object and target. If the target is visible, the AIState changes to chasing_target.

   Two "feeler" raycasts will be made out from the front of this object, looking for obstacles. If an obstacle is found on the right, the AIState changes to turn left. If an obstacle is found on the left, the AIState changes to turn right. If obstacles are found to be on both sides, the AIState will change to backing_up_looking_for_target. The AI will back up until it no longer detects any obstacles.

2. chasing_target

The AI will turn to face the target and move forward toward it. If the target falls out of range, the AIState returns to moving_looking_for_target.

3. backing_up_looking_for_target

In this state, the AI moves backward until no obstacles are found by its forward raycasting. When no obstacles are found, the AIState switches randomly to either stopped_turning_left or stopped_turning_right. This is randomized to help reduce situations where backing up and turning in a particular direction are unsuccessful in getting the AI away from an obstacle. Repeated backing up and turning should eventually free the AI. As it does this, the code still checks to see whether its target is within range (and if it is, the AIState will change to chasing_target).

4. stopped_turning_left

The AI will turn to its left until no obstacles are found by the forward raycasts. Although this state means that the AI is not moving, the code checks to see whether its target is within range (and if it is, the AIState will change to chasing_target instead).

5. stopped_turning_right

The AI will turn to its right until no obstacles are found. If its target is within range, the AIState will change to chasing_target.

6. paused_looking_for_target

The AI does not move in this state but continues to check to see whether the target is within range to chase.

7. translate_along_waypoint_path

Waypoints (managed by an instance of the Waypoints_Controller.cs script component, discussed in Chapter 7) are used as targets to aim for. Transform.Translate is used to move the AI around, and the BaseAIController.TurnTowardTarget() is used to control rotation. The AI will move forward toward a waypoint and move on to the next waypoint when it gets close to it.

8. steer_to_waypoint

This state is similar to the translate_along_waypoint_path except that it does not use TurnTowardTarget() for steering. Instead, input values are calculated (in the same format as user input values would be) so that a player controller script can use them and deal with turning itself.

9. steer_to_target

This state is similar to steer_to_waypoint except that it does not have any waypoint checking incorporated into it. Instead, it will provide input values for steering the AI toward its target. There is no obstacle checking in this state either, only steering.

10. paused_no_target

In this state, the AI does quite literally nothing. It does not move or look for a target.

As the BaseAIController.cs script encompasses so much functionality, it's is one of the biggest, if not the biggest, in the book; there are over 50 lines just in the variable declarations! It may seem rather intimidating at first, but remember that not all of this script will be running at any one time. Within the main Update() function, we only actually run whichever segment of code is activated within the case statement, and most of the additional functions either are there as helper functions for other scripts or are used to set up the AI with such things as waypoints or enemy target transforms.

▌ 9.1 The AI State Control Script

Before getting to the main BaseAIController.cs script, take a look at AIStates.cs below. It contains all of the AIStates from the previous section stored in an enumerator list similar to the one used by the character controller from Chapter 5. This list will be used by the AI to determine its current required behavior. The list is in its own file (the AIStates.cs file) and in a namespace called AIStates so that we can easily make it accessible from any script used by the game:

```
using UnityEngine;

namespace AIStates
{
        public enum AIState
        {
                moving_looking_for_target,
                chasing_target,
                backing_up_looking_for_target,
                stopped_turning_left,
                stopped_turning_right,
                paused_looking_for_target,
                translate_along_waypoint_path,
                paused_no_target,
                steer_to_waypoint,
                steer_to_target,
        }
}
```

■ 9.2 The Base AI Control Script

The BaseAIController.cs script includes the standard namespaces along with the addition of AIStates, so that the AI controller can easily have access to the behavior enumerator list.

The full AI controller script looks like this:

```
using UnityEngine;
using System.Collections;
using AIStates;

[AddComponentMenu("Base/AI Controller")]

public class BaseAIController : ExtendedCustomMonoBehavior {

        // AI states are defined in the AIStates namespace

        private Transform proxyTarget;
        private Vector3 relativeTarget;
        private float targetAngle;
        private RaycastHit hit;
        private Transform tempTransform;
        private Vector3 tempDirVec;

        public float horz;
        public float vert;

        private int obstacleHitType;

        // editor changeable / visible
        public bool isStationary;

        public AIState currentAIState;

        public float patrolSpeed= 5f;
        public float patrolTurnSpeed= 10f;
        public float wallAvoidDistance= 40f;

        public Transform followTarget;

        public float modelRotateSpeed= 15f;
        public int followTargetMaxTurnAngle= 120;

        public float minChaseDistance= 2f;
        public float maxChaseDistance= 10f;
        public float visionHeightOffset= 1f;

        [System.NonSerialized]
        public Vector3 moveDirection;

        // waypoint following related variables
        public Waypoints_Controller myWayControl;

        public int currentWaypointNum;

        [System.NonSerialized]
        public Transform currentWaypointTransform;
```

```
        private int totalWaypoints;

        private Vector3 nodePosition;
        private Vector3 myPosition;
        private Vector3 diff;
        private float currentWayDist;

        [System.NonSerialized]
        public bool reachedLastWaypoint;
        private Vector3 moveVec;
        private Vector3 targetMoveVec;
        private float distanceToChaseTarget;

        public float waypointDistance= 5f;
        public float moveSpeed= 30f;
        public float pathSmoothing= 2f;
        public bool shouldReversePathFollowing;
        public bool loopPath;
        public bool destroyAtEndOfWaypoints;

        public bool faceWaypoints;
        public bool startAtFirstWaypoint;
        [System.NonSerialized]
        public bool isRespawning;

        private int obstacleFinderResult;
        public Transform rotateTransform;

        [System.NonSerialized]
        public Vector3 RelativeWaypointPosition;

        public bool AIControlled;

        public void Start ()
        {
                Init ();
        }

        public virtual void Init ()
        {
                // cache ref to gameObject
                myGO= gameObject;

                // cache ref to transform
                myTransform= transform;

                // rotateTransform may be set if the object we rotate is
                // different to the main transform
                if( rotateTransform==null )
                    rotateTransform= myTransform;

                // cache a ref to our rigidbody
                myBody= myTransform.rigidbody;

                // init done!
                didInit= true;
        }
```

```csharp
public void SetAIControl( bool state )
{
        AIControlled= state;
}

// set up AI parameters --------------------

public void SetPatrolSpeed( float aNum )
{
        patrolSpeed= aNum;
}

public void SetPatrolTurnSpeed( float aNum )
{
        patrolTurnSpeed= aNum;
}

public void SetWallAvoidDistance( float aNum )
{
        wallAvoidDistance= aNum;
}

public void SetWaypointDistance( float aNum )
{
        waypointDistance= aNum;
}

public void SetMoveSpeed( float aNum )
{
        moveSpeed=aNum;
}

public void SetMinChaseDistance( float aNum )
{
        minChaseDistance= aNum;
}

public void SetMaxChaseDistance( float aNum )
{
        maxChaseDistance= aNum;
}

public void SetPathSmoothing( float aNum )
{
        pathSmoothing= aNum;
}

// ------------------------------------------

public virtual void SetAIState( AIState newState )
{
        // update AI state
        currentAIState= newState;
}

public virtual void SetChaseTarget( Transform theTransform )
{
        // set a target for this AI to chase, if required
```

```
            followTarget= theTransform;
      }

      public virtual void Update ()
      {
            // make sure we have initialized before doing anything
            if( !didInit )
                  Init ();

            // check to see if we're supposed to be controlling the player
            if( !AIControlled )
                  return;

            // do AI updates
            UpdateAI();
      }

      public virtual void UpdateAI()
      {
            // reset our inputs
            horz=0;
            vert=0;

            int obstacleFinderResult= IsObstacleAhead();

            switch( currentAIState )
            {
            // ----------------------------
            case AIState.moving_looking_for_target:
                  // look for chase target
                  if( followTarget!=null )
                        LookAroundFor( followTarget );

                  // the AvoidWalls function looks to see if there's
                  // anything in front. If there is, it will
                  // automatically change the value of moveDirection
                  // before we do the actual move
                  if( obstacleFinderResult==1 ){ // GO LEFT
                        SetAIState( AIState.stopped_turning_left );
                  }
                  if( obstacleFinderResult==2 ){ // GO RIGHT
                        SetAIState( AIState.stopped_turning_right );
                  }
                  if( obstacleFinderResult==3 ){ // BACK UP
                        SetAIState( AIState.backing_up_looking_for_
                        target );
                  }

                  // all clear! head forward
                  MoveForward();
                  break;
            case AIState.chasing_target:
                  // chasing in case mode, we point toward the target
                  // and go right at it!

                  // quick check to make sure that we have a target
                  // (if not, we drop back to patrol mode)
                  if( followTarget==null )
```

```
                    SetAIState( AIState.moving_looking_for_
                    target );

            // the TurnTowardTarget function does just that, so
            // to chase we just throw it the current target
            TurnTowardTarget( followTarget );

            // find the distance between us and the chase target
            // to see if it is within range
            distanceToChaseTarget= Vector3.Distance( myTransform.
            position, followTarget.position );

            // check the range
            if( distanceToChaseTarget>minChaseDistance )
            {
                    // keep charging forward
                    MoveForward();
            }

            // here we do a quick check to test the distance
            // between AI and target. If it's higher than
            // our maxChaseDistance variable, we drop out of
            // chase mode and go back to patrolling.
            if( distanceToChaseTarget>maxChaseDistance ||
            CanSee( followTarget )==false )
            {
                    // set our state to 1 - moving_looking_for_
                    // target
                    SetAIState( AIState.moving_looking_for_
                    target );
            }

        break;
// ----------------------------

case AIState.backing_up_looking_for_target:

        // look for chase target
        if( followTarget!=null )
                LookAroundFor( followTarget );

        // backing up
        MoveBack ();

        if( obstacleFinderResult==0 )
        {
                // now we've backed up, let's randomize
                // whether to go left or right
                if( Random.Range (0,100)>50 )
                {
                        SetAIState( AIState.stopped_turning_
                        left );
                } else {
                        SetAIState( AIState.stopped_turning_
                        right );
                }
        }
        break;
```

```
case AIState.stopped_turning_left:
        // look for chase target
        if( followTarget!=null )
                LookAroundFor( followTarget );

        // stopped, turning left
        TurnLeft();

        if( obstacleFinderResult==0 )
        {
                SetAIState( AIState.moving_looking_for_
                target );
        }
        break;
case AIState.stopped_turning_right:
        // look for chase target
        if( followTarget!=null )
                LookAroundFor( followTarget );

        // stopped, turning right
        TurnRight ();

        // check results from looking, to see if path ahead
        // is clear
        if( obstacleFinderResult==0 )
        {
                SetAIState( AIState.moving_looking_for_
                target );
        }
        break;
case AIState.paused_looking_for_target:
        // standing still, with looking for chase target
        // look for chase target
        if( followTarget!=null )
                LookAroundFor( followTarget );
        break;

case AIState.translate_along_waypoint_path:
        // following waypoints (moving toward them, not
        // pointing at them) at the speed of moveSpeed

        // make sure we have been initialized before trying
        // to access waypoints
        if( !didInit && !reachedLastWaypoint )
                return;

        UpdateWaypoints();

        // move the ship
        if( !isStationary )
        {
                targetMoveVec = Vector3.Normalize
                ( currentWaypointTransform.position -
                myTransform.position );
                moveVec= Vector3.Lerp( moveVec, targetMoveVec,
                Time.deltaTime * pathSmoothing );
                myTransform.Translate( moveVec * moveSpeed *
                Time.deltaTime );
```

```
                    MoveForward();

                    if( faceWaypoints )
                    {
                            TurnTowardTarget
                            ( currentWaypointTransform );
                    }
            }
            break;

    case AIState.steer_to_waypoint:

            // make sure we have been initialized before trying
            // to access waypoints
            if( !didInit && !reachedLastWaypoint )
                    return;

            UpdateWaypoints();

            if( currentWaypointTransform==null )
            {
                    // it may be possible that this function gets
                    // called before waypoints have been set up,
                    // so we catch any nulls here
                    return;
            }

            // now we just find the relative position of the
            // waypoint from the car transform, that way we can
            // determine how far to the left and right the
            // waypoint is.
            RelativeWaypointPosition= transform.InverseTransform
            Point( currentWaypointTransform.position );

            // by dividing the horz position by the magnitude,
            // we get a decimal percentage of the turn angle
            // that we can use to drive the wheels
            horz= ( RelativeWaypointPosition.x /
            RelativeWaypointPosition.magnitude );

            // now we do the same for torque, but make sure that
            // it doesn't apply any engine torque when going
            // around a sharp turn...
            if ( Mathf.Abs( horz ) < 0.5f ) {
                    vert= RelativeWaypointPosition.z / Relative
                    WaypointPosition.magnitude - Mathf.Abs( horz );
            }else{
                    NoMove();
            }
    break;

    case AIState.steer_to_target:

            // make sure we have been initialized before trying
            // to access waypoints
            if( !didInit )
                    return;

            if( followTarget==null )
```

```
                {
                        // it may be possible that this function gets
                        // called before a target has been set up, so
                        // we catch any nulls here
                        return;
                }

                // now we just find the relative position of the
                // waypoint from the car transform, that way we can
                // determine how far to the left and right the
                // waypoint is.
                RelativeWaypointPosition= transform.
                InverseTransformPoint( followTarget.position );

                // by dividing the horz position by the magnitude,
                // we get a decimal percentage of the turn angle
                // that we can use to drive the wheels
                horz= ( RelativeWaypointPosition.x /
                RelativeWaypointPosition.magnitude );

                // if we're outside of the minimum chase distance,
                // drive!
                if( Vector3.Distance( followTarget.position,
                myTransform.position )>minChaseDistance )
                {
                        MoveForward();
                } else {
                        NoMove();
                }

                if( followTarget!=null )
                        LookAroundFor( followTarget );

                // the AvoidWalls function looks to see if there's
                // anything in front. If there is, it will
                // automatically change the value of moveDirection
                // before we do the actual move
                if( obstacleFinderResult==1 ){ // GO LEFT
                        TurnLeft ();
                }

                if( obstacleFinderResult==2 ){ // GO RIGHT
                        TurnRight ();
                }

                if( obstacleFinderResult==3 ){ // BACK UP
                        MoveBack ();
                }
        }

break;

case AIState.paused_no_target:
        // paused_no_target
        break;

default:
        // idle (do nothing)
        break;
```

```
        }
}

public virtual void TurnLeft ()
{
        horz= -1;
}

public virtual void TurnRight ()
{
        horz= 1;
}

public virtual void MoveForward ()
{
        vert= 1;
}

public virtual void MoveBack ()
{
        vert= -1;
}

public virtual void NoMove ()
{
        vert= 0;
}

public virtual void LookAroundFor(Transform aTransform)
{
        // here we do a quick check to test the distance between AI
        // and target. If it's higher than our maxChaseDistance
        // variable, we drop out of chase mode and go back to
        // patrolling.
        if( Vector3.Distance( myTransform.position, aTransform.
        position ) < maxChaseDistance )
        {
                // check to see if the target is visible before
                // going into chase mode
                if( CanSee( followTarget )==true )
                {
                        // set our state to chase the target
                        SetAIState( AIState.chasing_target );
                }
        }
}

private int obstacleFinding;

public virtual int IsObstacleAhead()
{
        obstacleHitType=0;

        // quick check to make sure that myTransform has been set
        if( myTransform==null )
        {
                return 0;
        }
```

```
        // draw this raycast so we can see what it is doing
        Debug.DrawRay(myTransform.position, ((myTransform.forward +
        (myTransform.right * 0.5f)) * wallAvoidDistance));
        Debug.DrawRay(myTransform.position, ((myTransform.forward +
        (myTransform.right * -0.5f)) * wallAvoidDistance));

        // cast a ray out forward from our AI and put the 'result'
        // into the variable named hit
        if(Physics.Raycast( myTransform.position, myTransform.
        forward + ( myTransform.right * 0.5f ), out hit,
        wallAvoidDistance ))
        {
                // obstacle
                // it's a left hit, so it's a type 1 right now (though
                // it could change when we check on the other side)
                obstacleHitType=1;
        }

        if(Physics.Raycast( myTransform.position,myTransform.forward +
        ( myTransform.right * -0.5f ), out hit, wallAvoidDistance ))
        {
                // obstacle
                if( obstacleHitType==0 )
                {
                        // if we haven't hit anything yet, this is a
                        // type 2
                        obstacleHitType=2;
                } else {
                        // if we have hits on both left and right
                        // raycasts, it's a type 3
                        obstacleHitType=3;
                }
        }

        return obstacleHitType;
}

public void TurnTowardTarget( Transform aTarget )
{
        if(aTarget==null)
                return;

        // Calculate the target position relative to the
        // target of this transform's coordinate system.
        // e.g. a positive x value means the target is to
        // to the right of the car, a positive z means
        // the target is in front of the car
        relativeTarget = rotateTransform.InverseTransformPoint
        ( aTarget.position ); // note we use rotateTransform as a
                              // rotation object rather than
                              // myTransform!

        // Calculate the target angle
        targetAngle = Mathf.Atan2 ( relativeTarget.x,
        relativeTarget.z );

        // Atan returns the angle in radians, convert to degrees
        targetAngle *= Mathf.Rad2Deg;
```

```csharp
                    // The wheels should have a maximum rotation angle
                    targetAngle = Mathf.Clamp ( targetAngle, -followTarget
                    MaxTurnAngle-targetAngle, followTargetMaxTurnAngle );

                    // turn towards the target at the rate of modelRotateSpeed
                    rotateTransform.Rotate( 0, targetAngle * modelRotateSpeed *
                    Time.deltaTime, 0 );
          }

          public bool CanSee( Transform aTarget )
          {
                    // first, let's get a vector to use for raycasting by
                    // subtracting the target position from our AI position
                    tempDirVec=Vector3.Normalize( aTarget.position - myTransform.
                    position );

                    // let's have a debug line to check the distance between the
                    // two manually, in case you run into trouble!
                    Debug.DrawLine( myTransform.position, aTarget.position );

                    // cast a ray from our AI, out toward the target passed in
                    // (use the tempDirVec magnitude as the distance to cast)
                    if( Physics.Raycast( myTransform.position +
                    ( visionHeightOffset * myTransform.up ), tempDirVec, out
                    hit, maxChaseDistance ))
                    {
                              // check to see if we hit the target
                              if( hit.transform.gameObject.layer == aTarget.
                              gameObject.layer )
                              {
                                        return true;
                              }
                    }

                    // nothing found, so return false
                    return false;
          }

          public void SetWayController( Waypoints_Controller aControl )
          {
                    myWayControl=aControl;
                    aControl=null;

                    // grab total waypoints
                    totalWaypoints = myWayControl.GetTotal();

                    // make sure that if you use SetReversePath to set
                    // shouldReversePathFollowing that you call SetReversePath
                    // for the first time BEFORE SetWayController, otherwise it
                    // won't set the first waypoint correctly

                    if( shouldReversePathFollowing )
                    {
                              currentWaypointNum= totalWaypoints-1;
                    } else {
                              currentWaypointNum= 0;
                    }

                    Init();
```

```
        // get the first waypoint from the waypoint controller
        currentWaypointTransform= myWayControl.
        GetWaypoint( currentWaypointNum );

        if( startAtFirstWaypoint )
        {
                // position at the currentWaypointTransform position
                myTransform.position= currentWaypointTransform.
                position;
        }
}

public void SetReversePath( bool shouldRev )
{
        shouldReversePathFollowing= shouldRev;
}

        public void SetSpeed( float aSpeed )
{
        moveSpeed= aSpeed;
}

public void SetPathSmoothingRate( float aRate )
{
        pathSmoothing= aRate;
}

public void SetRotateSpeed( float aRate )
{
        modelRotateSpeed= aRate;
}


void OnDrawGizmos ()
{
        Gizmos.DrawWireSphere ( transform.position, waypointDistance );
}

void UpdateWaypoints()
{
        // If we don't have a waypoint controller, we safely drop out
        if( myWayControl==null )
                return;

        if( reachedLastWaypoint && destroyAtEndOfWaypoints )
        {
                // destroy myself(!)
                Destroy( gameObject );
                return;
        } else if( reachedLastWaypoint )
        {
                currentWaypointNum= 0;
                reachedLastWaypoint= false;
        }

        // because of the order that scripts run and are
        // initialised, it is possible for this function to be called
        // before we have actually finished running the waypoints
```

```
// initialization, which means we need to drop out to avoid
// doing anything silly or before it breaks the game.
if( totalWaypoints==0 )
{
        // grab total waypoints
        totalWaypoints= myWayControl.GetTotal();
        return;
}

if( currentWaypointTransform==null )
{
        // grab our transform reference from the waypoint
        // controller
        currentWaypointTransform= myWayControl.GetWaypoint
        ( currentWaypointNum );
}

// now we check to see if we are close enough to the current
// waypoint to advance on to the next one
myPosition= myTransform.position;
myPosition.y= 0;

// get waypoint position and 'flatten' it
nodePosition= currentWaypointTransform.position;
nodePosition.y= 0;

// check distance from this to the waypoint

currentWayDist= Vector3.Distance( nodePosition,myPosition );

if ( currentWayDist < waypointDistance ) {
        // we are close to the current node, so let's move
        // on to the next one!

        if( shouldReversePathFollowing )
        {
                currentWaypointNum--;
                // now check to see if we have been all the
                // way around
                if( currentWaypointNum<0 ){
                        // just in case it gets referenced
                        // before we are destroyed, let's
                        // keep it to a safe index number
                        currentWaypointNum= 0;
                        // completed the route!
                        reachedLastWaypoint= true;
                        // if we are set to loop, reset the
                        // currentWaypointNum to 0
                        if(loopPath)
                        {
                                currentWaypointNum=
                                totalWaypoints;

                                // the route keeps going in a
                                // loop, so we don't want
                                // reachedLastWaypoint to ever
                                // become true
                                reachedLastWaypoint= false;
                        }
```

```
                                        // drop out of this function before
                                        // we grab another waypoint into
                                        // currentWaypointTransform, as
                                        // we don't need one and the index
                                        // may be invalid
                                        return;
                            }
                } else {
                            currentWaypointNum++;
                            // now check to see if we have been all the
                            // way around
                            if( currentWaypointNum>=totalWaypoints ){
                                        // completed the route!
                                        reachedLastWaypoint= true;
                                        // if we are set to loop, reset the
                                        // currentWaypointNum to 0
                                        if(loopPath)
                                        {
                                                    currentWaypointNum= 0;

                                                    // the route keeps going in a
                                                    // loop, so we don't want
                                                    // reachedLastWaypoint to ever
                                                    // become true
                                                    reachedLastWaypoint= false;
                                        }
                                        // drop out of this function before
                                        // we grab another waypoint into
                                        // currentWaypointTransform, as
                                        // we don't need one and the index
                                        // may be invalid
                                        return;
                            }
                }

                // grab our transform reference from the waypoint
                // controller
                currentWaypointTransform= myWayControl.GetWaypoint
                ( currentWaypointNum );

        }
}

public float GetHorizontal()
{
        return horz;
}

public float GetVertical()
{
        return vert;
}
}
```

9.2.1 Script Breakdown

The AI script begins with the usual namespaces (default ones added by Unity to all C# scripts) as well as AIStates seen earlier in this chapter. By including AIStates as a namespace, it may be accessed as though it were part of the same script:

```
using UnityEngine;
using System.Collections;
using AIStates;
```

There are a lot of variables to declare, so don't worry about those right away. We will see how they are used later in the breakdown.

The Init() function takes care of making cached references to the gameObject, the transform, and its rigidbody (note that the script assumes that there will always be a rigidbody attached to the AI gameObject):

```
public virtual void Init ()
        {
                // cache ref to gameObject
                myGO= gameObject;

                // cache ref to transform
                myTransform= transform;

                // cache a ref to our rigidbody
                myBody= myTransform.rigidbody;
```

rotateTransform is an optional parameter that may be set in the Unity editor Inspector window to provide a transform for rotation that is different from the one to which the script is attached. This is used in cases where we do not wish to rotate the main transform:

```
                // rotateTransform may be set if the object we rotate is
                // different to the main transform
                if( rotateTransform==null )
                        rotateTransform= myTransform;
```

As with all of the other scripts in this book, didInit is a Boolean variable used to determine whether or not the Init() function has successfully completed.

```
                // init done!
                didInit= true;
        }
```

A Boolean variable named AIControlled is used to decide whether or not this script should take control. The SetAIControl() function just provides an easy way for other scripts to enable or disable AI control:

```
        public void SetAIControl( bool state )
        {
                AIControlled= state;
        }
```

The script continues with some functions to set several of the main parameters used in the AI behavior. Those are the following:

patrolSpeed (float)	Determines how quickly the bot should move when it is patrolling.
patrolTurnSpeed (float)	Determines how quickly the bot should turn when patrolling.
wallAvoidDistance (float)	Determines, in 3D units, how far the bot should look ahead in its attempts to avoid running into walls when it is patrolling.

wayPointDistance (float)	Determines, in 3D units, how close the bot will be allowed to get to a waypoint before it advances to the next waypoint.
moveSpeed (float)	Indicates the speed at which the bot will move when it is moving along a path of waypoints.
minChaseDistance (float)	Determines, in 3D units, how close the bot should get to its target, when chasing a target, before it stops moving toward it. This is to prevent the bot from getting too close and pushing the player around.
maxChaseDistance (float)	Determines, in 3D units, how far away from its target the bot is allowed to get before it gives up chasing and goes back into patrolling mode.
pathSmoothing (float)	When the bot is following along a waypoint path, the rotation between each waypoint is damped (rather than the bot jumping to a point directly at each point). This variable is used to decide how much to interpolate this.

The functions to set them are as follows:

```
// set up AI parameters --------------------

public void SetPatrolSpeed( float aNum )
{
        patrolSpeed= aNum;
}

public void SetPatrolTurnSpeed( float aNum )
{
        patrolTurnSpeed= aNum;
}

public void SetWallAvoidDistance( float aNum )
{
        wallAvoidDistance= aNum;
}

public void SetWaypointDistance( float aNum )
{
        waypointDistance= aNum;
}

public void SetMoveSpeed( float aNum )
{
        moveSpeed=aNum;
}

public void SetMinChaseDistance( float aNum )
{
        minChaseDistance= aNum;
}
public void SetMaxChaseDistance( float aNum )
{
        maxChaseDistance= aNum;
}

public void SetPathSmoothing( float aNum )
{
        pathSmoothing= aNum;
}
```

There will be times when we may need to force the state of the bot from another script, such as telling it which state to start in when the game begins. Use the function SetAIState for that, passing in an AIState.

```
public virtual void SetAIState( AIState newState )
{
        // update AI state
        currentAIState= newState;
}
```

If chasing is required, the SetChaseTarget() function should be used to pass in a reference to the transform that needs chasing. It gets stored into a variable named followTarget.

```
public virtual void SetChaseTarget( Transform theTransform )
{
        // set a target for this AI to chase, if required
        followTarget= theTransform;
}
```

The Update() function is called by Unity at each frame update, but we need to be sure that the script has properly initialized before doing anything significant with it because it may be possible for Update to be called before Init() has finished its run.

```
public virtual void Update ()
{
        // make sure we have initialized before doing anything
        if( !didInit )
                Init ();
```

If AIControlled is not set to true, the function drops out before it has a chance to call for an update to the AI—with the Boolean variable AIControlled, it makes it possible to turn on or off the AI control at will. This functionality is useful in situations where we might want AI code to take control of a player but not at the start of the game; for example, AI might take over at the end of a racing game when a race is complete, and we want the player's car to continue driving without any player input.

```
        // check to see if we're supposed to be controlling the player
        if( !AIControlled )
                return;

        // do AI updates
        UpdateAI();
}
```

UpdateAI() is right at the core of the script—it is called by the Update() function shown earlier and deals with coordinating the bot to do what it should:

```
public virtual void UpdateAI()
{
```

In some cases, the AI script does not manipulate its object directly but rather acts as an input provider. The reason it works this way is so that AI can use the same movement controllers as the player without having to recode movement each time. For example, in the example game *Metal Vehicle Doom* in Chapter 11, the AI cars use the same car physics as the player. When a car is set to use AI, input is used from the AI script rather than from an input controller.

The AI script uses horz and vert (both floats) to store horizontal and vertical input, which are the standard variable names used in other scripts in this book:

```
// reset our inputs
horz=0;
vert=0;
```

Later in this section, we will look at the IsObstacleAhead() function. It uses raycasting to check for any obstacles in front of the bot and returns a number back:

0	No obstacles were found.
1	An obstacle was detected front, left side only.
2	An obstacle was detected front, right side only.
3	Obstacle or obstacles detected on both sides.

On the next line of code, the IsObstacleAhead() result is placed into the temporary variable obstacleFinderResult (an integer) for use later in the UpdateAI() function:

```
int obstacleFinderResult= IsObstacleAhead();
```

Next in the script, a switch statement determines exactly what the AI should be doing based on the state held in the variable currentAIState (which is of type AIState):

```
switch( currentAIState )
{
// ----------------------------
```

The first case is AIState.moving_looking_for_target, which tells the bot to move forward through the level until it finds the target specified in the variable followTarget:

```
case AIState.moving_looking_for_target:
        // look for chase target
        if( followTarget!=null )
```

LookAroundFor() is a function we will look at in detail later in this section. For now, let's us just say that it looks for the target transform in followTarget. The function has no return value and will change the AIState directly, if the target transform should be chased:

```
LookAroundFor( followTarget );
```

At the start of the UpdateAI() function, the call to IsObstacleAhead() was made and its return value placed into obstacleFinderResult. The next lines react to that result, changing the AIState to turn left or right depending on whether obstacles have been detected:

```
// the AvoidWalls function looks to see if there's
// anything in front. If there is, it will
```

```
// automatically change the value of moveDirection
// before we do the actual move
if( obstacleFinderResult==1 ){ // GO LEFT
        SetAIState( AIState.stopped_turning_left );
}
if( obstacleFinderResult==2 ){ // GO RIGHT
        SetAIState( AIState.stopped_turning_right );
}
```

When obstacles are detected on both the left and right sides of the bot, the return result from IsObstacleAhead() is 3. Instead of trying to turn to avoid whatever is blocking the way forward, the bot goes into a reverse state—AIState.backing_up_looking_for_target:

```
if( obstacleFinderResult==3 ){ // BACK UP
        SetAIState( AIState.backing_up_looking_for_
        target );
}
```

Now that the bot has finished deciding whether or not to turn or back up to avoid obstacles, all that is left for it to do is move forward. The MoveForward() function is called as we break for the next case:

```
// all clear! head forward
MoveForward();
break;
```

The next state is AIState.chasing_target:

```
case AIState.chasing_target:
        // chasing in case mode, we point toward the target
        // and go right at it!
```

As this mode's main objective is to chase the transform in followTarget, we need to first make sure that there is an actual transform in there to follow. If followTarget is null, the script changes the state back to AIState.moving_looking_for_target:

```
// quick check to make sure that we have a target
// (if not, we drop back to patrol mode)
if( followTarget==null )
        SetAIState( AIState.moving_looking_for_
        target );
```

TurnTowardTarget() will rotate the transform toward the target transform passed into the function as a parameter, at the speed set by the float variable modelRotateSpeed. Note that the transform to be rotated will be the transform held by the variable rotate-Transform, as described in the Init() function earlier in this section, not specifically the transform to which the script is attached:

```
// the TurnTowardTarget function does just that, so
// to chase we just throw it the current target
TurnTowardTarget( followTarget );
```

Unity's Vector3.Distance function is used to check that the position of the transform in followTarget is not too close or too far away:

```
// find the distance between us and the chase target
// to see if it is within range
distanceToChaseTarget= Vector3.Distance
( myTransform.position, followTarget.position );
```

If the target is further than minChaseDistance 3D units away, the bot will continue to move forward. The MoveForward() function takes care of keeping things moving:

```
// check the range
if( distanceToChaseTarget>minChaseDistance )
{
        // keep charging forward
        MoveForward();
}
```

When the target transform is too far away, the AIState needs to switch back to the search/patrol state of AIState.moving_looking_for_target:

```
// here we do a quick check to test the distance
// between AI and target. If it's higher than
// our maxChaseDistance variable, we drop out of
// chase mode and go back to patrolling.
if( distanceToChaseTarget>maxChaseDistance ||
CanSee( followTarget )==false )
{
        // set our state to 1 - moving_looking_for_
        // target
        SetAIState( AIState.moving_looking_for_target );
}

break;
// ----------------------------
```

The next case is AIState.backing_up_looking_for_target, which calls upon the MoveBack() function to take care of moving the bot backward:

```
case AIState.backing_up_looking_for_target:

        // look for chase target
        if( followTarget!=null )
                LookAroundFor( followTarget );

        // backing up
        MoveBack ();
```

Once IsObstacleAhead() returns a zero (no obstacles) into obstacleFinderResult, we try to avoid hitting the same obstacles again by going into turning mode. Which direction to turn is randomized in the hope that if one way proves unsuccessful in getting the bot out of the trap situation, perhaps turning the other way will free it. To randomize, we use Random.Range(min,max) to represent a 50/50 percentage split over which direction it will turn:

```
if( obstacleFinderResult==0 )
{
        // now we've backed up, let's randomize
        // whether to go left or right
        if( Random.Range (0,100)>50 )
```

```
                    {
                            SetAIState( AIState.stopped_turning_
                            left );
                    } else {
                            SetAIState( AIState.stopped_turning_
                            right );
                    }
            }
            break;
```

Functions for turning left and right, TurnLeft() and TurnRight(), respectively, are used by the cases for AIState.stopped_turning_left and AIState.stopped_turning_right. The two cases also check obstacleFinderResult to see whether the path ahead is clear. If the path is clear (when obstacleFinderResult contains zero), the state is changed to AIState. moving_looking_for_target:

```
case AIState.stopped_turning_left:
        // look for chase target
        if( followTarget!=null )
                LookAroundFor( followTarget );

        // stopped, turning left
        TurnLeft();

        if( obstacleFinderResult==0 )
        {
            SetAIState( AIState.moving_looking_for_target );
        }
        break;

case AIState.stopped_turning_right:
        // look for chase target
        if( followTarget!=null )
                LookAroundFor( followTarget );

        // stopped, turning right
        TurnRight ();

        // check results from looking, to see if path ahead
        // is clear
        if( obstacleFinderResult==0 )
        {
            SetAIState( AIState.moving_looking_for_target );
        }
        break;
```

The AIState.paused_looking_for_target state does a check to make sure that follow Target is not null and then makes a call out to the LookAroundFor() function to see whether the target is within range to chase. This code contains no movement code, and when the bot is in this state, it should just stand still and wait for the player to get close, as though it were standing guard:

```
case AIState.paused_looking_for_target:
        // standing still, while looking for chase target
        // look for chase target
```

```
if( followTarget!=null )
        LookAroundFor( followTarget );
break;
```

So far, the AI code has dealt with patrolling and standing guard, but the script also supports waypoint-following and -steering behaviors.

The first method of waypoint following is AIState.translate_along_waypoint_path, which moves the bot along a path without rotation:

```
case AIState.translate_along_waypoint_path:
        // following waypoints (moving toward them, not
        // pointing at them) at the speed of moveSpeed
```

Before trying to follow any sort of path, it is a good idea to check that the initialization function was completed (didInit will be true) and that the last waypoint has not been reached. If didInit is false or the last waypoint has been reached, the path-following should stop and the function returns:

```
// make sure we have been initialized before trying
// to access waypoints
if( !didInit && !reachedLastWaypoint )
        return;
```

The UpdateWaypoints() function is called to check the distance from the bot to the waypoint and update which waypoint to follow, as needed:

```
UpdateWaypoints();
```

isStationary is a Boolean variable used to provide a method of keeping the AI bot stationary, if required. When it is set to true, the bot will not be moved. Note that this state does not have any rotation code or provide input values for its movement; it uses Unity's Transform.Translate to directly translate the transform toward each waypoint, instead. It will use the transform held in the variable myTransform:

```
// move the ship
if( !isStationary )
{
```

A Vector3 called targetMoveVec provides a vector for the bot to move along, toward the waypoint. This movement vector is calculated by subtracting the position of the bot from the current waypoint transform's position. The vector is then normalized with Unity's Vector3.Normalize function to strip away the magnitude. Note that the waypoint's transform is held in the variable currentWaypointTransform, put there by that earlier call to the UpdateWaypoints() function:

```
targetMoveVec = Vector3.Normalize
( currentWaypointTransform.position -
myTransform.position );
```

The actual amount we move is an interpolated vector somewhere between the current value of moveVec (the current amount being moved) and the vector we just calculated in targetMoveVec. pathSmoothing is a float variable used to determine how long the interpolation takes (the Time.deltaTime multiplied by pathSmoothing) and therefore how much the rotation along the waypoint path should be smoothed out:

```
moveVec= Vector3.Lerp( moveVec,
targetMoveVec, Time.deltaTime *
pathSmoothing );
```

When the actual translation of the transform happens, the moveVec vector is multiplied by moveSpeed and, in turn, multiplied by Time.deltaTime to keep everything time based:

```
myTransform.Translate( moveVec * moveSpeed *
Time.deltaTime );
MoveForward();
```

Rotating myTransform toward the target waypoint is optional. The faceWaypoints Boolean variable is intended to be set in the Unity editor Inspector window. When face-Waypoints is true, the rotation is carried out by a call to TurnTowardTarget, passing in the current waypoint transform:

```
if( faceWaypoints )
{
        TurnTowardTarget
        ( currentWaypointTransform );
}
}
break;
```

Next in the UpdateAI() function are the steering behaviors, all ready for use by the example games from this book, *Metal Vehicle Doom* and *Tank Battle*.

AIState.steer_to_waypoint starts by checking that the initialization occurred (didInit should be true) and that the last waypoint has not been reached. If all is well, a call to UpdateWaypoints() will make sure that the current waypoint held by the variable current WaypointTransform is the correct one:

```
case AIState.steer_to_waypoint:

        // make sure we have been initialized before trying
        // to access waypoints
        if( !didInit && !reachedLastWaypoint )
                return;

        UpdateWaypoints();
```

It may be possible that currentWaypointTransform does not contain a waypoint. If that is the case, the function drops out:

```
if( currentWaypointTransform==null )
{
        // it may be possible that this function gets
        // called before waypoints have been set up,
        // so we catch any nulls here
        return;
}
```

The next step is to find out the relative position of the waypoint from the (myTransform) transform. Transform.InverseTransformPoint converts a position from world space into local space. In this case, we take the position of the waypoint and convert it into the local space of myTransform.

The result of the Transform.InverseTransformPoint space conversion is stored in a Vector3 type variable called RelativeWaypointPosition. This vector now represents the direction that the AI would need to travel to reach the next waypoint.

By dividing the *x* value of RelativeWaypointPosition by its magnitude, we end up with a number that, in layman's terms, says how much we would need to turn left or right to be facing the waypoint, a number that is perfect for use as horizontal input to a steering or turning system. The code below places the calculated steer value into the variable horz (the variable name used for horizontal input throughout this book):

```
RelativeWaypointPosition= myTransform.
InverseTransformPoint( currentWaypointTransform.
position );
// by dividing the horz position by the magnitude,
// we get a decimal percentage of the turn angle
// that we can use to drive the wheels
horz= ( RelativeWaypointPosition.x /
RelativeWaypointPosition.magnitude );
```

Now that horz contains the amount required to turn toward the next waypoint, this value may be used to slow down the bot if it is moving too fast.

The absolute (never negative) value of horz is checked against 0.5 to decide whether or not acceleration should be used. If the turn is more than 0.5, acceleration is set to 0. The acceleration put into the variable vert is calculated by taking the RelativeWaypointPosition *z* value divided by its magnitude, with the horizontal turn amount subtracted from it. The idea is that, even though the distance to the waypoint along the AI bot's *z*-axis is taken into account, the more the turn is, the less the acceleration value will be. In many cases, this should help the AI to get around corners without crashing:

```
// now we do the same for torque, but make sure that
// it doesn't apply any engine torque when going
// around a sharp turn...
if ( Mathf.Abs( horz ) < 0.5f ) {
        vert= RelativeWaypointPosition.z /
        RelativeWaypointPosition.magnitude -
        Mathf.Abs( horz );
}else{
        NoMove();
}
break;
```

AIState.steer_to_target works in the exact same way as the waypoint-steering code above, except that it uses followTarget to aim for instead of the waypoint in the current-WaypointTransform variable:

```
case AIState.steer_to_target:

        // make sure we have been initialized before trying
        // to access waypoints
```

```
if( !didInit )
        return;

if( followTarget==null )
{
        // it may be possible that this function gets
        // called before a target has been set up, so
        // we catch any nulls here
        return;
}

// now we just find the relative position of the
// waypoint from the car transform,
// that way we can determine how far to the left and
// right the waypoint is.
RelativeWaypointPosition= transform.
InverseTransformPoint( followTarget.position );

// by dividing the horz position by the magnitude,
// we get a decimal percentage of the turn angle
// that we can use to drive the wheels
horz= ( RelativeWaypointPosition.x /
RelativeWaypointPosition.magnitude );

// if we're outside of the minimum chase distance,
// drive!
if( Vector3.Distance( followTarget.position,
myTransform.position )>minChaseDistance )
{
        MoveForward();
} else {
        NoMove();
}
```

As this state is following a target around and not traveling along a fixed waypoint path, it includes some logic to react to obstacles (just in case the target decides to hide behind a wall or something like that):

```
if( followTarget!=null )
        LookAroundFor( followTarget );
```

It uses the same code as the obstacle detection in AIState.moving_looking_for_target, explained earlier in this section:

```
// the AvoidWalls function looks to see if there's
// anything in front. If there is, it will
// automatically change the value of moveDirection
// before we do the actual move
if( obstacleFinderResult==1 ){ // GO LEFT
        TurnLeft ();
}

if( obstacleFinderResult==2 ){ // GO RIGHT
        TurnRight ();
}
```

When both left and right sides ahead are blocked by an obstacle, the bot will simply back up. This behavior may not be ideal in all situations, but for the *Tank Battle* example game in this book, I saw it as the equivalent of making the AI wait for its target to come back out from behind the wall. This code tends to make the bot hang around until it eventually turns to face its target:

```
if( obstacleFinderResult==3 ){ // BACK UP
        MoveBack ();
}

break;
```

The AIState.paused_no_target state does literally nothing. It doesn't aim or move— none of that!

```
case AIState.paused_no_target:
        // paused_no_target
        break;
```

Just in case something falls through the cracks, this function provides a default behavior similar to your average politician—that of doing nothing:

```
default:
        // idle (do nothing)
        break;
    }
}
```

That's is the UpdateAI() function all wrapped up. Next, there is a collection of functions to set inputs for turning left and right or moving forward and backward. The reason that these have their own functions rather than just setting them in the UpdateAI() code is so that it would be easy to deal with other types of control systems by overriding them in a derived class. In this script, it is literally a case of setting the values of the horz and vert variables as required:

```
public virtual void TurnLeft ()
{
        horz= -1;
}

public virtual void TurnRight ()
{
        horz= 1;
}

public virtual void MoveForward ()
{
        vert= 1;
}

public virtual void MoveBack ()
{
        vert= -1;
}
```

```
public virtual void NoMove ()
{
        vert= 0;
}
```

The LookAroundFor() function starts out by using a distance check (using Unity's Vector3.Distance function) to find out whether or not the bot's transform (in myTransform) position is within maxChaseDistance 3D units:

```
public virtual void LookAroundFor(Transform aTransform)
{
        // here we do a quick check to test the distance between AI
        // and target. If it's higher than our maxChaseDistance
        // variable, we drop out of chase mode and go back to
        // patrolling.
        if( Vector3.Distance( myTransform.position, aTransform.
        position ) < maxChaseDistance )
        {
```

When the target transform is close enough (within maxChaseDistance), the next step is to find out whether or not it is visible to this bot. The CanSee() function takes care of this, returning true or false depending on whether the bot "can see" the target transform or not:

```
                // check to see if the target is visible before
                // going into chase mode
                if( CanSee( followTarget )==true )
                {
```

At this stage, we know that there is a target within range and that it is visible to this bot (there are no obstacles between the bot and the target) so we can switch over to AIState. chasing_target to start the chase:

```
                        // set our state to chase the target
                        SetAIState( AIState.chasing_target );
                }
        }
}
```

One of the core components of the AI controller is the IsObstacleAhead() function. In this part, Physics.Raycast is used to raycast out ahead (and slightly to the left or right) to check for obstacles. It returns an integer, expressing its findings with the following values:

0	No obstacles were found.
1	An obstacle was detected front, left side only.
2	An obstacle was detected front, right side only.
3	Obstacle or obstacles detected on both sides.

The beginning of the function checks to make sure that we have an actual transform in myTransform to start with:

```
private int obstacleFinding;
```

```
public virtual int IsObstacleAhead()
{
        obstacleHitType=0;

        // quick check to make sure that myTransform has been set
        if( myTransform==null )
        {
                return 0;
        }
```

Along the way, doubts may set in as to whether or not things are working as they should with the AI—to make it easier to visualize what is happening, the function includes some Debug.DrawRay calls that will make lines appear in the editor where the rays are being cast. This will only happen in the editor when Gizmos are set to true (use the Gizmos icon above the window to set this):

```
        // draw this raycast so we can see what it is doing
        Debug.DrawRay(myTransform.position, ((myTransform.forward +
        (myTransform.right * 0.5f)) * wallAvoidDistance));
        Debug.DrawRay(myTransform.position, ((myTransform.forward +
        (myTransform.right * -0.5f)) * wallAvoidDistance));
```

The actual raycasting happens next, using the AI bot's forward vector—myTransform. forward—with an offset to the side—myTransform.right multiplied by half so that the angle goes diagonally out from the bot—with the ray starting at myTransform.position.

The Physics.Raycast function as used here is given as follows:

```
bool Physics.Raycast( Vector3 origin, Vector3 direction, RayCastHit
hitInfo, distance)
```

The variable wallAvoidDistance is used as the distance parameter for raycasting, which may be set in the Unity editor Inspector window. When the AI moves faster, it will usually help the patrolling if this value is higher as the bot can look ahead further for obstacles.

If a call to Physics.Raycast finds something, it will return true, meaning we can easily use it in an if statement:

```
        // cast a ray out forward from our AI and put the 'result'
        // into the variable named hit
        if(Physics.Raycast( myTransform.position, myTransform.
        forward + ( myTransform.right * 0.5f ), out hit,
        wallAvoidDistance ))
        {
```

When the Raycast function finds an obstacle, the variable obstacleHitType is set to 1. This represents an obstacle on the left side. At the end of this section, the value of obstacleHitType will form the return value for the function:

```
                // obstacle
                // it's a left hit, so it's a type 1 right now
                // (though it could change when we check on the
                // other side)
                obstacleHitType=1;
        }
```

Now a ray is cast on the other side of the bot:

```
if(Physics.Raycast( myTransform.position,myTransform.forward +
( myTransform.right * -0.5f ), out hit, wallAvoidDistance ))
        {
```

When the ray is cast here, the code checks obstacleHitType to see whether it has been set by the previous raycast. If it has not yet been set, its value will be at 0; this tells us that this ray is the first one to get a hit and that the function has only found an obstacle on this side—obstacleHitType gets set to 2:

```
// obstacle
if( obstacleHitType==0 )
{
        // if we haven't hit anything yet, this is a
        // type 2
        obstacleHitType=2;
} else {
```

If we have found something on this side via the raycast and obstacleHitType is not at 0, we know that both raycasts have found obstacles (since the first raycast set obstacle-HitType to 1 if it found something earlier). To represent obstacles found on both sides, obstacleHitType gets set to 3:

```
        // if we have hits on both left and right
        // raycasts, it's a type 3
        obstacleHitType=3;
}
}
```

The return result of this function is the value of obstacleHitType. Earlier in this chapter, the main UpdateAI() function used this return result to decide which way to turn or whether to go into reverse mode.

```
return obstacleHitType;
}
```

The next part of BaseAIController.cs is TurnTowardTarget(). This function does exactly what it seems—it will turn the bot (more specifically, the transform set in the variable rotateTransform) toward the transform passed to it as a parameter:

```
public void TurnTowardTarget( Transform aTarget )
{
        if(aTarget==null)
                return;
```

Earlier in this chapter, in the UpdateAI() function, we looked at how AIState.translate_along_waypoint calculated the relative position of its target—it's the same here, with the relative position of the target calculated with Unity's Transform.InverseTransformPoint() function:

```
relativeTarget = rotateTransform.InverseTransformPoint
( aTarget.position ); // note we use rotateTransform as a rotation
                      // object rather than myTransform!
```

The newly calculated relativeTarget vector is then used with Mathf.Atan2 to find an angle of rotation:

```
// Calculate the target angle
targetAngle = Mathf.Atan2 ( relativeTarget.x,
relativeTarget.z );

// Atan returns the angle in radians, convert to degrees
targetAngle *= Mathf.Rad2Deg;
```

To enforce limits on the amount of rotation to apply in one step, the function uses Mathf.Clamp to keep the angle less than the value of the float variable followTargetMaxAngle:

```
// The wheels should have a maximum rotation angle
targetAngle = Mathf.Clamp ( targetAngle,
-followTargetMaxTurnAngle-targetAngle,
followTargetMaxTurnAngle );
```

The next step is to use Transform.Rotate to turn the bot. targetAngle is multiplied by modelRotateSpeed and again multiplied by Time.deltaTime to make the rotation time based. This value is used by the Rotate function to turn the rotateTransform transform (which takes three float parameters for *x*, *y*, and *z* rotation amounts):

```
// turn towards the target at the rate of modelRotateSpeed
rotateTransform.Rotate( 0, targetAngle * modelRotateSpeed *
Time.deltaTime, 0 );
}
```

CanSee() does a simple line-of-sight check to see whether anything is between the bot and its target. This is useful for cutting off chases when the target goes behind a wall or somewhere unreachable by the AI bot.

It creates a normalized vector from the two positions and then uses this to cast a ray from the bot out at the length from the maxChaseDistance variable:

```
public bool CanSee( Transform aTarget )
{
    // first, let's get a vector to use for raycasting by
    // subtracting the target position from our AI position
    tempDirVec=Vector3.Normalize( aTarget.position -
    myTransform.position );

    // let's have a debug line to check the distance between the
    // two manually, in case you run into trouble!
    Debug.DrawLine( myTransform.position, aTarget.position );

    // cast a ray from our AI, out toward the target passed in
    // (use the tempDirVec magnitude as the distance to cast)
    if( Physics.Raycast( myTransform.position +
    ( visionHeightOffset * myTransform.up ), tempDirVec, out
    hit, maxChaseDistance ))
    {
```

When a hit occurs in the raycast, all this code does is check to see whether the hit object is the target. If it is the target, we now know that there is nothing blocking the way so it can return true; otherwise, it falls through to return false at the end of the function:

```
                    // check to see if we hit the target
                    if( hit.transform.gameObject == aTarget.gameObject )
                    {
                            return true;
                    }
            }

            // nothing found, so return false
            return false;
    }
```

The AI controller incorporates waypoints control into the mix using the Waypoints_Controller.cs script to manage them. Since the AI bot does not know which waypoints to use, another script (such as the game controller) will call SetWayController and pass in a Waypoints_Controller object:

```
    public void SetWayController( Waypoints_Controller aControl )
    {
            myWayControl=aControl;
            aControl=null;
```

totalWaypoints contains a cached value of the total number of waypoints from the waypoints controller to save having to look it up every time it is needed by this script:

```
            // grab total waypoints
            totalWaypoints = myWayControl.GetTotal();
```

If shouldReversePathFollowing is true, the starting waypoint will be the last one found in the list of waypoints made by the Waypoints_Controller script:

```
            if( shouldReversePathFollowing )
            {
                    currentWaypointNum= totalWaypoints-1;
            } else {
                    currentWaypointNum= 0;
            }
```

Among other things, the Init() function in this class caches a reference to the AI bot's transform in the variable myTransform. The SetWayController() function calls Init() to make sure that the reference is set up and ready for it to use, as it repositions myTransform at the first waypoint (when the Boolean variable startAtFirstWaypoint is set to true):

```
            Init();

            // get the first waypoint from the waypoint controller
            currentWaypointTransform= myWayControl.GetWaypoint( current
            WaypointNum );

            if( startAtFirstWaypoint )
            {
                    // position at the currentWaypointTransform position
                    myTransform.position= currentWaypointTransform.
                    position;
            }
    }
```

The next four functions in the class are interface functions for other scripts to change values, if needed:

```
public void SetReversePath( bool shouldRev )
{
        shouldReversePathFollowing= shouldRev;
}

public void SetSpeed( float aSpeed )
{
        moveSpeed= aSpeed;
}

public void SetPathSmoothingRate( float aRate )
{
        pathSmoothing= aRate;
}

public void SetRotateSpeed( float aRate )
{
        modelRotateSpeed= aRate;
}
```

UpdateWaypoints() takes care of keeping the current target waypoint up to date and carries out self-destruction, if required, when the AI reaches the end of the path.

It begins with a check to make sure that myWayControl (a reference to an instance of Waypoints_Controller.cs) is not null, which should mean that the SetWayController() function has been called by another script and set up successfully:

```
void UpdateWaypoints()
{
        // If we don't have a waypoint controller, we safely drop out
        if( myWayControl==null )
                return;
```

The AI controller script has the option to automatically destroy itself when the last waypoint is reached. When destroyAtEndOfWaypoints is set to true, the gameObject is destroyed, and this code drops out of the UpdateWaypoints() script immediately.

When destroyAtEndOfWaypoints is false, the assumption is that waypoint following should go back to the beginning; currentWaypointNum is set to zero, reachedLastWaypoint is reset, and the AI is free to start over again:

```
        if( reachedLastWaypoint && destroyAtEndOfWaypoints )
        {
                // destroy myself(!)
                Destroy( gameObject );
                return;
        } else if( reachedLastWaypoint )
        {
                currentWaypointNum= 0;
                reachedLastWaypoint= false;
        }
```

To keep this function safe (just in case it is somehow called before the waypoints have been correctly set up by the Waypoints_Controller.cs script), there is a check to make sure that more than one waypoint was found. If totalWaypoints is zero, another attempt is made to get the total from the myWayControl object before it drops out of the UpdateWaypoints() function:

```
if( totalWaypoints==0 )
{
        // grab total waypoints
        totalWaypoints= myWayControl.GetTotal();
        return;
}
```

If no currentWaypointTransform object has been set up at this point, myWay-Control is called upon to provide one with the index number held in the variable currentWaypointNum:

```
if( currentWaypointTransform==null )
{
        // grab our transform reference from the waypoint
        // controller
        currentWaypointTransform=
        myWayControl.GetWaypoint( currentWaypointNum );
}
```

Calculating the distance between two transforms will take into account x, y, and z coordinates. For the examples in this book, waypoint following needs only to work on a two-dimensional plane and the y-axis may be done away with completely. Doing so can solve problems with ground-based games where the height combined with the x- and y-axis differences end up not advancing the current waypoint at the right times. If you were making a game based in the air, you would most likely need to comment this part out and use x, y, and z.

Both myPosition, a cached Vector3 of the bot's position, and nodePosition, the cached waypoint position, are stripped of the y-axis in the code below:

```
// now we check to see if we are close enough to the current
// waypoint to advance on to the next one

myPosition= myTransform.position;
myPosition.y= 0;

// get waypoint position and 'flatten' it
nodePosition= currentWaypointTransform.position;
nodePosition.y= 0;
```

The distance between the AI bot and the next waypoint is calculated using the two cached position variables below. When the resulting currentWayDist value is less than the value of waypointDistance, it means that the bot is close enough to the current waypoint to advance to the next one:

```
currentWayDist= Vector3.Distance( nodePosition,myPosition );

if ( currentWayDist < waypointDistance ) {
        // we are close to the current node, so let's move
        // on to the next one!
```

Before advancing to the next waypoint, shouldReversePathFollowing is checked to see which direction along the path it needs to go. When its value is true, the value of currentWaypointNum is decremented:

```
if( shouldReversePathFollowing )
{
        currentWaypointNum--;
```

If the path is reversed, when currentWaypointNum drops below zero, it needs to get reset to the waypoint at the other end of the path (only when loopPath is set). To make this happen, currentWaypointNum will be set to the value of the variable totalWaypoints.

Something else that happens in this chunk of code, when we know that the end of the path has been reached, is that the value of reachedLastWaypoint is set to true. This will be checked on the next UpdateWaypoints() call to carry out any actions that need to be done at the end of the path (such as destroying the gameObject when destroyAtEndOfWaypoints is set to true):

```
// now check to see if we have been all the way around
if( currentWaypointNum<0 ){
        // just in case it gets referenced before we
        // are destroyed, let's keep it to a safe
        // index number
        currentWaypointNum= 0;
        // completed the route!
        reachedLastWaypoint= true;
        // if we are set to loop, reset the
        // currentWaypointNum to 0
        if(loopPath)
        {
                currentWaypointNum= totalWaypoints;

                // the route keeps going in a loop,
                // so we don't want reachedLastWaypoint
                // to ever become true
                reachedLastWaypoint= false;
        }
        // drop out of this function before we grab
        // another waypoint into currentWaypoint
        // Transform, as we don't need one and the
        // index may be invalid
        return;
} else {
```

The shouldReversePathFollowing Boolean must have been set to false for the following code to be executed, meaning that the currentWaypointNum has gone past the final waypoint in the list held by the waypoints controller and that currentWaypointNum needs to be reset to zero if the variable loopPath is set to true:

```
currentWaypointNum++;
// now check to see if we have been all the way around
if( currentWaypointNum>=totalWaypoints ){
```

```
                    // completed the route!
                    reachedLastWaypoint= true;
                    // if we are set to loop, reset the current
                    // WaypointNum to 0
                    if(loopPath)
                    {
                            currentWaypointNum= 0;

                            // the route keeps going in a loop, so we
                            // don't want reachedLastWaypoint to ever
                            // become true
                            reachedLastWaypoint= false;
                    }
                    // drop out of this function before we grab another
                    // waypoint into currentWaypointTransform, as we
                    // don't need one and the index may be invalid
                    return;
            }
        }
```

With all of the manipulations to currentWaypointNum now complete, we can use it as an index number to ask the waypoint controller myWayControl to provide the transform for the next waypoint. currentWaypointTransform is set to the result of a call to the Waypoint_Controller.cs function GetWaypoint():

```
                // grab our transform reference from the waypoint
                // controller
                currentWaypointTransform= myWayControl.GetWaypoint
                ( currentWaypointNum );


        }
    }
```

Finally, in this epic BaseAIController.cs script, two small functions provide access to the horizontal and vertical input variables:

```
    public float GetHorizontal()
    {
            return horz;
    }

    public float GetVertical()
    {
            return vert;
    }
}
```

■ 9.3 Adding Weapon Control to the AI Controller

The BaseArmedEnemy.cs script is intended to be added to a player to take control of the weapons system and deal with firing. It does not specifically reference or require the AI controller, and it works independently, relying only on the Standard_SlotWeaponController. cs script to operate the weapon and a separate class named AIAttackStates.

The AIAttackStates.cs script stores an enumerated list of the possible states for the armed enemy to take:

```csharp
using UnityEngine;

namespace AIAttackStates
{
        public enum AIAttackState
        {
                random_fire,
                look_and_destroy,
                no_attack,
        }
}
```

Below is the BaseArmedEnemy.cs script:

```csharp
using AIAttackStates;

using UnityEngine;
using System.Collections;

public class BaseArmedEnemy : ExtendedCustomMonoBehavior
{
        [System.NonSerialized]
        public bool doFire;

        public bool onlyFireWhenOnscreen;

        public int pointsValue=50;
        public int thisEnemyStrength= 1;
        public bool thisGameObjectShouldFire;

        // we use a renderer to test whether or not the ship is on screen
        public Renderer rendererToTestAgainst;


        public Standard_SlotWeaponController weaponControl;
        public GameObject mesh_parentGO;

        private bool canFire;

        public float fireDelayTime =1f;

        public BasePlayerManager myPlayerManager;
        public BaseUserManager myDataManager;

        public bool isBoss= false;

        public int tempINT;

        // default action is to attack nothing
        public AIAttackState currentState= AIAttackState.random_fire;

        public string tagOfTargetsToShootAt;

        public void Start ()
        {
                // now call our script-specific init function
                InitThis ();
        }
```

```
public void InitThis()
{
        // cache our transform
        myTransform= transform;

        // cache our gameObject
        myGO= gameObject;

        if(weaponControl==null)
        {
                // try to find weapon controller on this gameObject
                weaponControl= myGO.GetComponent
                <Standard_SlotWeaponController>();
        }

        if(rendererToTestAgainst==null)
        {
                // we need a renderer to find out whether or not we
                // are on screen, so let's try and find one in our
                // children if we don't already have one set in the
                // editor
                rendererToTestAgainst= myGO.GetComponentInChildren
                <Renderer>();
        }

        // if a player manager is not set in the editor, let's try
        // to find one
        if(myPlayerManager==null)
        {
                myPlayerManager= myGO.AddComponent
                <BasePlayerManager>();
        }

        myDataManager= myPlayerManager.DataManager;
        myDataManager.SetName("Enemy");
        myDataManager.SetHealth(thisEnemyStrength);

        canFire=true;
        didInit=true;
}

private RaycastHit rayHit;

public virtual void Update ()
{
        // if we are not allowed to control the weapon, we drop out
        // here
        if(!canControl)
                return;

        if(thisGameObjectShouldFire)
        {
                // we use doFire to determine whether or not to fire
                // right now
                doFire=false;

                // canFire is used to control a delay between firing
                if( canFire )
```

```
        {
                if( currentState==AIAttackState.random_fire )
                {
                        // if the random number is over x,
                        // fire
                        if( Random.Range(0,100)>98 )
                        {
                                doFire=true;
                        }
                } else if( currentState==AIAttackState.
                look_and_destroy )
                {
                        if(Physics.Raycast( myTransform.
                        position, myTransform.forward, out
                        rayHit ))
                        {
                                // is it an opponent to be
                                // shot at?
                        if( rayHit.transform.CompareTag
                        ( tagOfTargetsToShootAt ) )
                        {
                                // we have a match on the tag, so
                                // let's shoot at it
                                doFire=true;
                        }
                }
        }

} else {
        // if we're not set to random fire or look and
        // destroy, just fire whenever we can
        doFire=true;
}
}

if( doFire )
{
        // we only want to fire if we are on screen, visible on the
        // main camera
        if(onlyFireWhenOnscreen && !rendererToTestAgainst.
        IsVisibleFrom( Camera.mainCamera ))
        {
                doFire=false;
                return;
        }

                        // tell weapon control to fire, if we have a
                        // weapon controller
                        if(weaponControl!=null)
                        {
                                // tell weapon to fire
                                weaponControl.Fire();
                        }
                        // set a flag to disable firing temporarily
                        // (providing a delay between firing)
                        canFire= false;
                        // invoke a function call in <fireDelayTime>
                        // to reset canFire back to true, allowing
                        // another firing session
```

```
                                        Invoke ( "ResetFire", fireDelayTime );
                        }
                }
        }

        public void ResetFire ()
        {
                canFire=true;
        }
}
```

9.3.1 Script Breakdown

BaseArmedEnemy.cs uses the namespace AIAttackStates from the AIAttackStates.cs script seen earlier in this section. The advantage of using the namespace is that this script can access the AIAttackStates enumerated list as though it were declared in this class. To tell Unity that we want to refer to this namespace, we use the using keyword:

```
using AIAttackStates;
```

The main BaseArmedEnemy.cs script is derived from ExtendedCustomMono Behavior, which extends the base functionality of MonoBehavior to include some helper variables:

```
public class BaseArmedEnemy : ExtendedCustomMonoBehavior
{
```

The Start() function calls Init():

```
        public void Start ()
        {
                // now call our script-specific init function
                Init();
        }
```

As with most of the Init() functions in this book, it starts by caching references to the gameObject and transform to which this script component is applied:

```
        public void Init()
        {
                // cache our transform
                myTransform= transform;

                // cache our gameObject
                myGO= gameObject;
```

This class's prime objective is to manage the weapons system for the AI players, so a reference to the weapon controller script is essential. If one has not been set in the Unity editor Inspector window on this script's gameObject, the code below will find out and try to find it with a call to gameObject.GetComponent():

```
                if(weaponControl==null)
                {
                        // try to find weapon controller on this gameObject
```

```
                        weaponControl= myGO.GetComponent<Standard_SlotWeapon
                        Controller>();
        }
```

The option is provided with this class to only fire the weapon when a specified renderer is on screen. The intention is that the main enemy mesh renderer is used for this, so that weapon firing only happens when the enemy is on screen. If the variable (of type Renderer) renderToTestAgainst has not been set in the Unity editor Inspector window, the code here uses GameObject.GetComponentInChildren() to try and find a renderer to use instead:

```
        if(rendererToTestAgainst==null)
        {
                // we need a renderer to find out whether or not we
                // are on screen, so let's try and find one in our
                // children if we don't already have one set in the
                // editor
                rendererToTestAgainst= myGO.GetComponentInChildren
                <Renderer>();
        }
```

The player manager for this enemy will be used to deal with this enemy's health amount. The enemy is not technically a player, but as it does share some scripts and behaviors, the lines become blurry and some logic is interchangeable between the two types.

Since it is going to be firing projectiles, it may be likely that it will be receiving hits from them, too. The BaseArmedEnemy.cs script itself does not manipulate health, but in Chapter 14, you will see how a script derived from this one will add full support for health and hits.

myPlayerManager holds a reference to the BasePlayerManager script, which will also be populated in this code if it has not been set in the Unity editor Inspector window (making its value null):

```
        // if a player manager is not set in the editor, let's try
        // to find one
        if(myPlayerManager==null)
        {
                myPlayerManager= myGO.AddComponent
                <BasePlayerManager>();
        }
```

Once the reference to the player manager script has been made, some default properties are set up for this enemy, including an integer amount used for health from the variable thisEnemyStrength:

```
        myDataManager= myPlayerManager.DataManager;
        myDataManager.SetName("Enemy");
        myDataManager.SetHealth(thisEnemyStrength);
```

With the Init() function complete, canFire allows this enemy to fire from now on and didInit is set to true so that other functions or scripts can tell that this Init() function has been completed:

```
        canFire=true;
        didInit=true;
    }
```

Since most of the core logic takes place in the Update() function, which is automatically called by the Unity engine at each frame, it is declared here as a virtual function that will almost certainly be overridden by any class deriving from the BaseArmedEnemy class:

```
public virtual void Update ()
{
```

If canControl is false, no weapon control is allowed so this function drops out early:

```
// if we are not allowed to control the weapon, we drop out
// here
if(!canControl)
        return;
```

It may seem redundant having a canControl variable that will drop out of this function along with a variable to decide whether or not to actually execute the firing code, but the reason is consistency; all of the player control scripts use canControl, and it is used here too. Although this script in its current form only deals with weapon control, there is nothing to stop it growing into something more complex later on. To make sure that the script remains extensible for potential future use, the logic to fire is dependent on thisGameObjectShouldFire being set to true:

```
if(thisGameObjectShouldFire)
{
```

Depending on the AIAttackState this enemy is currently set to use, it may be required to be able to have a line of sight to a potential target before firing. doFire is a Boolean variable used to tell whether or not the conditions to fire (such as line of sight) have been satisfied and firing is allowed. Before fire condition checking starts, the assumption is made that firing will not be allowed, and doFire is set to false:

```
// we use doFire to determine whether or not to fire
// right now
doFire=false;
```

There will always be a pause in-between firing. The Boolean variable canFire is used to determine whether or not the script should be allowed to fire at this time.

```
if( canFire )
{
```

AIAttackState.random_fire means just that—there is no checking other than to generate a random number and see whether it turns out to be over a set number (98, in this case). When the randomly generated number is high enough, doFire is set to true so that firing happens:

```
if( currentState==AIAttackState.random_fire )
    {
            // if the random number is over x, fire
            if( Random.Range(0,100)>98 )
            {
                    doFire=true;
            }
    } else
```

AIAttackState.look_and_destroy will use raycasting to look out forward from this enemy's transform to see whether a potential target is in front. tagOfTargetsToShootAt is set to hold a tag applied to enemies (via the Unity editor Inspector window Tag drop-down), and Transform.CompareTag() is used to make sure that an object hit by a raycast has the correct tag in place:

```
if( currentState==AIAttackState.look_and_destroy )
            {
                    if(Physics.Raycast( myTransform.position,
                    myTransform.forward, out rayHit ))
                    {
                            // is it an opponent to be shot at?
                            if( rayHit.transform.CompareTag
                            ( tagOfTargetsToShootAt ) )
                                    {
```

When an object is found in front of this transform with the correct tag applied, doFire is set to true, and firing can happen later in the function:

```
                                    doFire=true;
                            }
                    }

            } else {
```

The else condition is provided as a catch-all. If in doubt, fire it out! If AIAttackState makes no sense, the function will just keep firing:

```
                    // if we're not set to random fire or look and
                    // destroy, just fire whenever we can
                    doFire=true;
            }
        }
```

The state of doFire is a condition for executing the next chunk of code:

```
                    if( doFire )
                    {
```

The Boolean variable onlyFireWhenOnScreen suggests whether or not this enemy should be allowed to fire when not being drawn by the camera. The renderer component referenced by rendererToTestAgainst is checked using the Renderer.IsVisibleFrom() function provided by Unity. IsVisibleFrom() takes a camera as a parameter and will return true if the renderer is visible from that camera (and, of course, false when it is not).

The code sets doFire to false when onlyFireWhenOnScreen is true and the renderer is not visible on screen. If firing is cancelled in this way, it also drops out with a return statement since there is no value left in executing the script further on this pass:

```
                    if(onlyFireWhenOnscreen && !rendererToTestAgainst.
                    IsVisibleFrom( Camera.mainCamera ))
                    {
                            doFire=false;
                            return;
                    }
```

If weaponControl is not null (suggesting that a weapon control script exists, and we have a usable reference to it), the script now goes ahead and makes the call to weapon Control.Fire():

```
// tell weapon control to fire, if we have a weapon
// controller
if(weaponControl!=null)
{
        // tell weapon to fire
        weaponControl.Fire();
}
```

After the call to fire the weapon has been made, canFire is set to false to delay firing until the function ResetFire() is called to set it back to true again. An Invoke call sets up the call to ResetFire at a time set by fireDelayTime:

```
        // set a flag to disable firing temporarily (providing a
        // delay between firing)
        canFire= false;
        // invoke a function call in <fireDelayTime> to reset
        // canFire back to true, allowing another firing session
        Invoke ( "ResetFire", fireDelayTime );
    }
  }
}
```

canFire is reset by ResetFire(), meaning that after the delay set by fireDelayTime, this enemy can fire its weapon again:

```
public void ResetFire ()
{
        canFire=true;
}
}
```

10 Menus and User Interface

In this chapter, first up is a full breakdown of the main menu used for all of the example games. The main menu structure should provide a perfect starting place for any main menu system.

The second part of this chapter will look at in-game UI and how the example games derive from a class that helps to store useful data.

▌ 10.1 The Main Menu

First impressions last. When you walk by a store, its appearance may influence your decision whether to go in and browse or to keep walking. If the outside of the store looks run-down or badly kept, it may also affect how you feel about the goods inside. A quick visit to an Apple Store can demonstrate the extreme of this idea, where everything is arranged to exacting, some may say extreme, levels of detail. It was no coincidence that many of Apple's initial retail team came from the clothing store Gap, a company well known for its cool image and stylish branding.* Owing to the nature of electronics (hardly stylish to go cable shopping, for example), the appearance of electronics stores had taken a back seat to function before Apple came along and changed things. Apple brought emotion, humanity, function, and style to electronics. Steve Jobs said in a video tour of the first Apple store that "[p]eople don't just want to buy personal computers anymore, they want to know what

---

* http://online.wsj.com/article/SB10001424052702304563104576364071955678908.html.

they can do with them." With this approach in mind, Apple stores attempted to convey the lifestyle just as much as the product, using clever layout and styling to reinforce the key themes of the experience, such as using natural materials to bring a more earthy, organic feel to their casual and clutter-free open plan designs.

Just like the exterior and layout of a high-end store, your menus and interface can dramatically affect how people feel about the game "inside." Thematically unsuitable graphics, a broken menu, or a difficult menu flow can frustrate players even before the game starts, leading to a heightened sense of frustration during initial gameplay. An unpolished interface may lower expectations or change the perception of quality of work that has gone into the game. We want to avoid these situations and set the user up to feel as good as possible. To encourage a positive start, we should try to make sure that menu systems are tidy and functional, and that they attempt to reinforce the main themes of the game world in every aspect.

Building quality user interface and menu screens can be a time-consuming process. If you look at most modern videogames, the menus are filled with little touches that only developers would ever notice, like particle effects, slide-on transitions, and animations. Most games have dedicated teams for building the menus and interface systems. Artists (sometimes both 2D and 3D) work hand in hand with developers to build exciting new experiences. All this comes at a cost, and it may take months of work just for the single main menu screen of a commercial title.

Some studios reuse their menu and interface code from game to game, changing the layout and graphics but keeping the underlying code and/or menu structure. Reuse of menu code makes a lot of sense in an industry where we need to pack in as much gameplay as possible and where customers demand a lot more bang for their buck.

The menu system we will be building in this chapter will not be winning any awards or enticing players in to play. But it will serve perhaps as a structural beginning and as a functional method for configuring the example games and getting them started. The great thing about this menu is that it's completely open to interpretation. It could be built out to work for just about any kind of game with the addition of some graphics and sounds. As you develop your games and develop your style, having an operational menu will help during testing.

The main menu system is used by all of the example games in this book. It is easy to port between games and have submenus for audio and graphics options. The full screen flow for the entire main menu and its submenus is shown in Figure 10.1.

The flow requirements are almost identical for each game, although there are a few things that need to be variable. These are

1. Game name.

2. Which scene to load when we press the start game button.

3. The filename of the prefs we save out to store options (volume and graphics levels).

4. In the case of *Interstellar Paranoids*, the menu needs to have a Start Co-Op Game button, too.

Options menu uses PlayerPrefs to save and load any information we need to store or retrieve related to audio and graphics settings. The menu code should check to see that

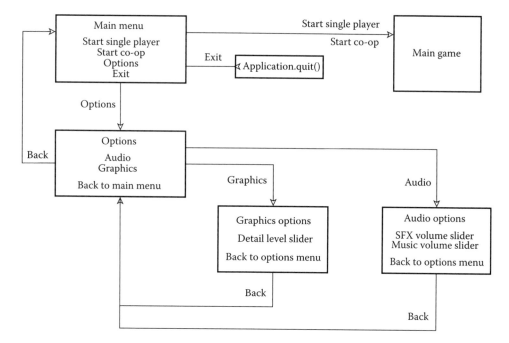

Figure 10.1 The menu flow.

these saved values exist and, in cases where the data have not yet been saved, create new PlayerPrefs saved data as required.

We can use the same exit button and exit confirmation (a simple "Are you sure you want to quit?" yes/no menu), and the options will be exactly the same. It may be beneficial to add the option to display an image instead of just text for the name of the game and it would be easy to implement, so we should take care of that, too.

The menus will be built with Unity GUI, for the sake of simplicity, although the basic reusable menu principles could easily be applied to a GUI using a custom or third-party solution such as NGUI. Menus should also have the option to play some music in the background as well as play a sound effect whenever buttons are clicked, and the background music should continue to play between menus without restarting or breaking.

The menu is a single class to keep it simple and to allow for easy expansion or porting between projects. It is capable of displaying all different screens that make up the main menu by using a variable to state which menu should be displayed, which is checked by a case statement, and the correct screen composed within the OnGUI function.

To help make customization and stylization easier, the menu system uses a Unity GUI skin named MenuGUIskin, which defines the font to use and any custom layout requirements.

The options menu uses QualitySettings.names to find out how many different graphics preferences are available and present them as a slider bar for easy modification by players. Getting all of the available settings from QualitySettings.names (rather than hard coding them) allows for a greater level of flexibility when porting between games, as there may not always be the same number of graphics detail levels available (they are configurable in the Unity editor by going to the menus Edit → Project Settings → Quality and editing each quality setting as a list in the Inspector window).

The main menu class is in a script called MainMenuController.cs. It is derived from MonoBehavior and looks like this:

```
using UnityEngine;
using System.Collections;

public class MainMenuController : MonoBehavior
{
        public int whichMenu= 0;

        public GUISkin menuSkin;

        public string gameDisplayName= "- DEFAULT GAME NAME -";
        public string gamePrefsName= "DefaultGame";

        public string singleGameStartScene;
        public string coopGameStartScene;

        public float default_width= 720;
        public float default_height= 480;

        public float audioSFXSliderValue;
        public float audioMusicSliderValue;

        public float graphicsSliderValue;
        private int detailLevels= 6;

        void Start()
        {
                // set up default options, if they have been saved out to
                // prefs already
                if(PlayerPrefs.HasKey(gamePrefsName+"_SFXVol"))
                {
                        audioSFXSliderValue= PlayerPrefs.
                        GetFloat(gamePrefsName+"_SFXVol");
                } else {
                        audioSFXSliderValue= 1;
                }
                if(PlayerPrefs.HasKey(gamePrefsName+"_MusicVol"))
                {
                        audioMusicSliderValue= PlayerPrefs.
                        GetFloat(gamePrefsName+"_MusicVol");
                } else {
                        audioMusicSliderValue= 1;
                }
                if(PlayerPrefs.HasKey(gamePrefsName+"_GraphicsDetail"))
                {
                        graphicsSliderValue= PlayerPrefs.
                        GetFloat(gamePrefsName+"_GraphicsDetail");
                } else {
                        string[] names = QualitySettings.names;
                        detailLevels= names.Length;
                        graphicsSliderValue= detailLevels;
                }
```

10. Menus and User Interface

```
            // set the quality setting
            QualitySettings.SetQualityLevel( (int)graphicsSliderValue,
            true);
    }

    void OnGUI()
    {
            float resX = Screen.width / default_width;
            float resY = Screen.height / default_height;
            GUI.matrix = Matrix4x4.TRS (new Vector3(0, 0, 0),
            Quaternion.identity, new Vector3 (resX, resY, 1));

            // set the GUI skin to use our custom menu skin
            GUI.skin= menuSkin;

            switch(whichMenu)
            {
            case 0:
                    GUI.BeginGroup (new Rect (default _width / 2 - 150,
                    default _height / 2 - 250, 500, 500));

                    // All rectangles are now adjusted to the group.
                    // (0,0) is the topleft corner of the group.

                    GUI.Label(new Rect( 0, 50, 300, 50 ),
                    gameDisplayName, "textarea");

                    if(GUI.Button(new Rect( 0, 200, 300, 40 ),"START
                    SINGLE", "button"))
                    {
                            PlayerPrefs.SetInt( "totalPlayers", 1 );
                            LoadLevel( singleGameStartScene );
                    }

                    if(coopGameStartScene!="")
                    {
                            if(GUI.Button(new Rect(0, 250, 300,
                            40 ),"START CO-OP"))
                            {
                                    PlayerPrefs.SetInt("totalPlayers",2);
                                    Load Level( coopGameStartScene );
                            }

                            if(GUI.Button(new Rect(0,300,300,40),"OPTIONS"))
                            {
                                    ShowOptionsMenu();
                            }
                    } else {
                            if(GUI.Button(new Rect(0,250,300,40),"OPTIONS"))
                            {
                                    ShowOptionsMenu();
                            }
                    }


                    if(GUI.Button(new Rect(0, 400, 300, 40 ),"EXIT"))
                    {
```

```
                        ConfirmExitGame();
                }

                // End the group we started above. This is very
                // important to remember!
                GUI.EndGroup ();

        break;

        case 1:
                // Options menu
                GUI.BeginGroup (new Rect (native_width / 2 - 150,
                native_height / 2 - 250, 500, 500));

                // Are you sure you want to exit?
                GUI.Label(new Rect( 0, 50, 300, 50 ), "OPTIONS",
                "textarea");

                if(GUI.Button(new Rect(0, 250, 300, 40 ),"AUDIO
                OPTIONS"))
                {
                        ShowAudioOptionsMenu();
                }

                if(GUI.Button(new Rect(0, 300, 300, 40 ),"GRAPHICS
                OPTIONS"))
                {
                        ShowGraphicsOptionsMenu();
                }

                if(GUI.Button(new Rect(0, 400, 300, 40 ),"BACK TO
                MAIN MENU"))
                {
                        GoMainMenu();
                }

                GUI.EndGroup ();

        break;

        case 2:
                GUI.BeginGroup (new Rect (default_width / 2 - 150,
                default_height / 2 - 250, 500, 500));

                // Are you sure you want to exit?
                GUI.Label(new Rect( 0, 50, 300, 50 ), "Are you sure
                you want to exit?", "textarea");

                if(GUI.Button(new Rect(0, 250, 300, 40 ),"YES, QUIT
                PLEASE!"))
                {
                        ExitGame();
                }

                if(GUI.Button(new Rect(0, 300, 300, 40 ),"NO, DON'T
                QUIT"))
                {
                        GoMainMenu();
```

```
                }

                GUI.EndGroup ();

        break;

        case 3:
                // AUDIO OPTIONS
                GUI.BeginGroup (new Rect (default_width / 2 - 150,
                default_height / 2 - 250, 500, 500));

                GUI.Label(new Rect ( 0, 50, 300, 50 ), "AUDIO
                OPTIONS", "textarea");

                GUI.Label(new Rect(0, 170, 300, 20), "SFX volume:");
                audioSFXSliderValue = GUI.HorizontalSlider (new
                Rect( 0, 200, 300, 50 ), audioSFXSliderValue, 0.0f,
                1f);

                GUI.Label(new Rect(0, 270, 300, 20), "Music
                volume:");
                audioMusicSliderValue = GUI.HorizontalSlider (new
                Rect( 0, 300, 300, 50 ), audioMusicSliderValue,
                0.0f, 1f);

                if(GUI.Button(new Rect(0, 400, 300, 40 ),"BACK TO
                OPTIONS MENU"))
                {
                        SaveOptionsPrefs();
                        ShowOptionsMenu();
                }

                GUI.EndGroup ();
        break;

        case 4:
                // GRAPHICS OPTIONS
                GUI.BeginGroup (new Rect (default_width / 2 - 150,
                default_height / 2 - 250, 500, 500));

                GUI.Label(new Rect ( 0, 50, 300, 50 ), "GRAPHICS
                OPTIONS", "textarea");

                GUI.Label(new Rect(0, 170, 300, 20), "Graphics
                quality:");
                graphicsSliderValue = Mathf.RoundToInt(GUI.
                HorizontalSlider (new Rect( 0, 200, 300, 50 ),
                graphicsSliderValue, 0, detailLevels));


                if(GUI.Button(new Rect(0, 400, 300, 40 ),"BACK TO
                OPTIONS MENU"))
                {
                        SaveOptionsPrefs();
                        ShowOptionsMenu();
                }

                GUI.EndGroup ();
```

```
                break;

        } // <- end switch
}

void LoadLevel( string whichLevel )
{
        Application.LoadLevel( whichLevel );
}

void GoMainMenu()
{
        whichMenu=0;
}

void ShowOptionsMenu()
{
        whichMenu=1;
}

void ShowAudioOptionsMenu()
{
        whichMenu=3;
}

void ShowGraphicsOptionsMenu()
{
        whichMenu=4;
}

void SaveOptionsPrefs()
{
        PlayerPrefs.SetFloat(gamePrefsName+"_SFXVol",
        audioSFXSliderValue);
        PlayerPrefs.SetFloat(gamePrefsName+"_MusicVol",
        audioMusicSliderValue);
        PlayerPrefs.SetFloat(gamePrefsName+"_GraphicsDetail",
        graphicsSliderValue);

        // set the quality setting
        QualitySettings.SetQualityLevel( (int)graphicsSliderValue,
        true);
}

void ConfirmExitGame()
{
        whichMenu=2;
}

void ExitGame()
{
        // tell level loader to shut down the game for us
        Application.Quit();
}
}
```

10.1.1 Script Breakdown

After all of the variable declarations, the first part of this script does the initial setup within a Start() function. Remember that, in Unity, the Start function is automatically called by the engine after a script is initialized and before the first update. Here, the script checks to see whether or not PlayerPrefs data have already been saved to disk. If it finds PlayerPrefs keys that exist, it loads them in and applies the saved values to our local variables. To store slider values from the options menu, there are three variables used. These are:

1. audioSFXSliderValue, a float, with a value between 0 and 1, for the sound effects volume level.

2. audioMusicSliderValue, a float, with a value between 0 and 1, for the music volume level.

3. graphicsSliderValue, an integer to store the level of graphics detail. The number acts as an index used to set Unity's QualitySettings quality level with the SetQualityLevel function.

```
void Start()
    {
            // set up default options, if they have been saved out to
            // prefs already
            if(PlayerPrefs.HasKey(gamePrefsName+"_SFXVol"))
            {
                    audioSFXSliderValue= PlayerPrefs.
                    GetFloat(gamePrefsName+"_SFXVol");
            } else {
                    audioSFXSliderValue= 1;
            }
            if(PlayerPrefs.HasKey(gamePrefsName+"_MusicVol"))
            {
                    audioMusicSliderValue= PlayerPrefs.
                    GetFloat(gamePrefsName+"_MusicVol");
            } else {
                    audioMusicSliderValue= 1;
            }
            if(PlayerPrefs.HasKey(gamePrefsName+"_GraphicsDetail"))
            {
                    graphicsSliderValue= PlayerPrefs.
                    GetFloat(gamePrefsName+"_GraphicsDetail");
            } else {
                    string[] names = QualitySettings.names;
                    detailLevels= names.Length;
                    graphicsSliderValue= detailLevels;
            }

            // set the quality setting
            QualitySettings.SetQualityLevel( (int)graphicsSliderValue,
            true);
    }
```

When you start a Unity project and the screen resolution box appears, there is a drop-down menu for the quality settings, usually something along the lines of Fastest, Fast, Simple, Good, Beautiful, and Fantastic (the default names and quality types). You can modify these in the Unity Inspector window by going through the menus Edit → Project Settings → Quality, deleting or adding new settings levels as you see fit. What this means is that there is no guarantee of there being the same number of quality settings from game to game—for example, you may choose to only have Good, Bad, and Ugly. To find out how many settings there are, QualitySettings.names is used to return an array containing all of the available quality names, and its .Length property tells us how many items are in the array. This number of available quality settings is held in the variable named detailLevels. In the Start() function, the code to do this looks like this:

```
string[] names = QualitySettings.names;
detailLevels= names.Length;
```

By default, the function also uses the highest quality level as a default setting for quality when no PlayerPrefs key is found.

```
graphicsSliderValue= detailLevels;
```

The actual graphics quality level (QualitySettings.SetQualityLevel) is set in the last line of the function:

```
QualitySettings.SetQualityLevel( (int)graphicsSliderValue, true);
```

Next up, we move straight on to the OnGUI function:

```
void OnGUI()
    {
            float resX = Screen.width / default_width;
            float resY = Screen.height / default _height;
            GUI.matrix = Matrix4x4.TRS (new Vector3(0, 0, 0),
            Quaternion.identity, new Vector3 (resX, resY, 1));
```

The Matrix 4 × 4 function is complicated, and I am not about to try to explain it here (trust me, I am no mathematician!), but the simplest explanation I have is as follows.

The default width and height are the resolution at which you designed the UI for (so, if you intend the default screen resolution to be 1024 × 768, you would make the default_ width and default_height variables equal to 1024 and 768, respectively).

The multipliers to use with the GUI.matrix function are established by taking the width and height of the screen and dividing it by your default width and height values. The line that does all the hard work is where Unity sets the GUI.matrix. It takes your values and stretches the UI to fill the screen. This, of course, means that there will be some stretching at different aspect ratios, but the UI will at least scale to suit every resolution. It is probably the easiest way to deal with multiple screen resolutions without having to design multiple user interfaces.

Once the GUI.matrix is set, everything we draw in the OnGUI function will be scaled accordingly so we can go on and start drawing the menus.

To set a GUI skin, we need to tell Unity about it in the OnGUI function. You can use as many different skins as you like, and changing/setting the skin is as easy as

```
// set the GUI skin to use our custom menu skin
GUI.skin= menuSkin;
```

In our UI function, menuSkin is a public variable so that we can set the GUI skin value in the Inspector window of the editor.

The next step is to check the variable whichMenu to see "which menu" we need to render. There are four different screens we may display here, the first one being the main menu (case 0):

```
switch(whichMenu)
            {
            case 0:
```

To help us to position the menu and for the most flexibility, we will render it within a group. Using a group is similar to drawing the UI inside a window, which may be moved around with its contents keeping the same layout. The coordinate system for the GUI contents within the group starts at 0,0 in the top left of the group and remains to be unaffected by screen positioning (which continues to be determined by the group rather than by its content).

```
GUI.BeginGroup (new Rect (default _width / 2 - 150, default _height /
2 - 250, 500, 500));
```

Putting content into a group is simple. Use GUI.BeginGroup() within an OnGUI function to start the content and GUI.EndGroup() once the content is complete.

```
GUI.Label(new Rect( 0, 50, 300, 50 ), gameDisplayName, "textarea");
```

One way to get text onto the screen is to use GUI.Label. In the line above, we define a rectangle where we are going to render (keep in mind that this is happening within a group, so the coordinate system starts at 0,0 top left of the group). As this is the name of the game, we are using a string to hold the game name called gameDisplayName. Using a public string in this way means that we can change the game name in the Unity editor's Inspector window without having to edit the script.

The final part of the GUI.Label line is a GUIStyle. This is just a string that refers to a style defined in a GUISkin. In this case, it's the style called "textarea," and it just makes sure that when this text is rendered that it uses the correct font, size, and text alignment.

The next part of the script renders and acts on a button. The code to draw and check for a button press is all in just a single line:

```
if(GUI.Button(new Rect( 0, 200, 300, 40 ),"START SINGLE", "button"))
```

GUI.Button uses the defined rectangle to draw a button with the specified text "START SINGLE" in it. Again, you can see here that, to encourage predictability, we specify the GUIStyle of "button." Notice that this line acts like a Boolean in this conditional statement, and if the button is pressed, everything within the curly brackets occurs:

```
PlayerPrefs.SetInt( "totalPlayers", 1 );
LoadLevel( singleGameStartScene );
```

The PlayerPrefs call saves out the total number of players for the game, which is there only as a formality (it doesn't actually do anything or get called) in all but the example game *Interstellar Paranoids*. As the game has a cooperative game mode, we use the total-Players pref to decide which mode to start in. None of the other example games uses this key, although you could utilize it if you add multiplayer modes later on.

The next line calls on a function called LoadLevel and passes in the name of the scene to load. The variable singleGameStartScene is used, again a public string for easy editing in the Unity editor Inspector window, to determine which scene to load for a single player game. In this menu system, we also have a variable named coopGameStartScene that, when used, will branch off and display a different layout (with the addition of a "Start Co-op game" button) and will be used to launch a co-op game. It may well be that, in future games, you launch both types of games via the same scene and opt to use the total-Players pref key or another system like that, but the additional string is provided as a "just in case" as well as a simple way to determine whether or not to show that co-op start button with a slightly different menu layout:

```
if(coopGameStartScene!="")
{
        if(GUI.Button(new Rect(0, 250, 300,
40 ),"START CO-OP"))
        {
                PlayerPrefs.SetInt("totalPlayers",2);
                LoadLevel( coopGameStartScene );
        }

        if(GUI.Button(new Rect(0,300,300,40),"OPTIONS"))
        {
                ShowOptionsMenu();
        }
} else {
        if(GUI.Button(new Rect(0,250,300,40),"OPTIONS"))
        {
                ShowOptionsMenu();
        }
}
```

In the code above, we also added an options button to the menu group. If the options button is pressed, a function named ShowOptionsMenu() is called. This function has a single purpose, which is to set whichMenu to 1 (to display the options menu). This may make you wonder why it even exists as a function when we could just as easily set whichMenu in the button codes; the reason is simply to keep things neat and easy to extend later on. Perhaps in future menu code, you may want to play a sound, start a screen transition, or play an animation. Putting all those codes into the button detect can get messy and confusing, making the script harder to debug, hence why the ShowOptionsMenu function exists.

Now that we have dealt with starting the game and changing to the options menu, all that is left to do is show an exit button, end the group, and finish the case statement:

```
if(GUI.Button(new Rect(0, 400, 300, 40),"EXIT"))
        {
```

```
                                ConfirmExitGame();
                        }

                        // End the group we started above. This is very
                        // important to remember!
                        GUI.EndGroup ();

                break;
```

To make sure that our players don't accidentally exit the game, this script provides a separate menu screen to show a simple exit confirmation with "yes" and "no" buttons. The ConfirmExitGame() function sets whichMenu to 2, used by the switch statement to show the confirm screen.

GUI.EndGroup() ends the UI group—important to remember to include this call; otherwise, any additional UI rendered after this line will be within this group's coordinate system and part of this group.

When the variable whichMenu is set to 1, our OnGUI function contains a code to render a simple options menu. The base menu system allows players to change audio and graphics. The menu also uses a back button to go back to the main menu:

```
        case 1:
                // Options menu
                GUI.BeginGroup (new Rect (native_width / 2 - 150,
                native_height / 2 - 250, 500, 500));

                // Are you sure you want to exit?
                GUI.Label(new Rect(0, 50, 300, 50), "OPTIONS",
                "textarea");

                if(GUI.Button(new Rect(0,250,300,40),"AUDIOOPTIONS"))
                {
                        ShowAudioOptionsMenu();
                }

                if(GUI.Button(new Rect(0, 300, 300, 40),"GRAPHICS
                OPTIONS"))
                {
                        ShowGraphicsOptionsMenu();
                }

                if(GUI.Button(new Rect(0, 400, 300, 40),"BACK TO
                MAIN MENU"))
                {
                        GoMainMenu();
                }

                GUI.EndGroup ();
```

ShowAudioOptionsMenu(), ShowGraphicsOptionsMenu() and GoMainMenu() are functions that simply set the variable whichMenu for the different menu screens.

The next menu case is a simple confirm-exit screen, a text label with two buttons that call either the ExitGame() function or the GoMainMenu() function:

```
case 2:
        GUI.BeginGroup (new Rect (default_width / 2 - 150,
        default_height / 2 - 250, 500, 500));

        // Are you sure you want to exit?
        GUI.Label(new Rect(0, 50, 300, 50), "Are you sure
        you want to exit?", "textarea");

        if(GUI.Button(new Rect(0, 250, 300, 40),"YES, QUIT
        PLEASE!"))
        {
                ExitGame();
        }

        if(GUI.Button(new Rect(0, 300, 300, 40),"NO, DON'T
        QUIT"))
        {
                GoMainMenu();
        }

        GUI.EndGroup ();

break;
```

The audio options menu is a little different from the ones we've seen so far in this chapter, as it calls for two horizontal sliders to set the sound effect and music volume levels:

```
case 3:
        // AUDIO OPTIONS
        GUI.BeginGroup (new Rect (default_width / 2 - 150,
        default_height / 2 - 250, 500, 500));

        GUI.Label(new Rect(0, 50, 300, 50), "AUDIO OPTIONS",
        "textarea");

        GUI.Label(new Rect(0, 170, 300, 20), "SFX volume:");
```

After setting up the group and rendering two labels, we move on to the code to render the horizontal slider, which looks like this:

```
audioSFXSliderValue = GUI.HorizontalSlider (new Rect( 0, 200, 300, 50 ),
audioSFXSliderValue, 0.0f, 1f);
```

Here, we set the audioSFXSliderValue variable (a float) to the return value that the GUI.HorizontalSlider gives back. A slider may take up to five parameters as follows:

1. A rectangle defining the size of the area the slider will take up.

2. The current value at which to render the slider handle. The audioSFXSliderValue variable is used here, and it's OK for the GUI.HorizontalSlider to send feedback to itself, as we set audioSFXSliderValue to the return value of the slider and at the same time set the value of the handle to the same variable.

3. The value at the left end of the slider. Your slider can start anywhere, but in this case, we need it to start at 0.

4. The value at the right end of the slider. The maximum volume we would need to set our audio to would be 1. That's why we set the right end of the slider to 1(f).

5. If you wanted to set a GUIStyle, a fifth optional parameter (a string containing the name of the GUIStyle) may be used here, too.

A little further down in the script, we draw another label and the second horizontal slider, using the variable audioMusicSliderValue to store its value. Notice that the slider starts at 0 and ends with a maximum value of 1, the highest amount we would ever need to which to set the volume property of an AudioSource object:

```
GUI.Label(new Rect(0, 270, 300, 20), "Music volume:");
audioMusicSliderValue = GUI.HorizontalSlider (new
Rect( 0, 300, 300, 50 ), audioMusicSliderValue,
0.0f, 1f);
```

Now all that's left to do is provide a method to get back to the options menu and to end the group. When the button is pressed, we call on two functions: SaveOptionsPrefs() and ShowOptionsMenu().

```
if(GUI.Button(new Rect(0, 400, 300, 40),"BACK TO
OPTIONS MENU"))
{
        SaveOptionsPrefs();
        ShowOptionsMenu();
}

GUI.EndGroup ();
break;
```

Getting back to the OnGUI menu switch statement, the next menu case is the graphics options menu:

```
case 4:
```

First, a group is set up for the UI to be rendered in:

```
// GRAPHICS OPTIONS
GUI.BeginGroup (new Rect (default_width / 2 - 150,
default_height / 2 - 250, 500, 500));
```

The labels for the screen are drawn next, with GUI.Label:

```
GUI.Label(new Rect(0, 50, 300, 50), "GRAPHICS
OPTIONS", "textarea");

GUI.Label(new Rect(0, 170, 300, 20), "Graphics
quality:");
```

For the graphics detail, the GUI.HorizontalSlider function is used with the variable graphicsSliderValue:

```
graphicsSliderValue = Mathf.RoundToInt(GUI.
HorizontalSlider (new Rect(0, 200, 300, 50),
graphicsSliderValue, 0, detailLevels));
```

The back button (which leads out of this menu and back to the options menu) also makes a call to SaveOptionsPrefs() to store any data updated by the user as this screen was active:

```
if(GUI.Button(new Rect(0, 400, 300, 40),"BACK TO
OPTIONS MENU"))
{
        SaveOptionsPrefs();
        ShowOptionsMenu();
}
```

Finally, the GUI group is ended as the case breaks out:

```
        GUI.EndGroup ();
    break;
```

A LoadLevel() function uses Application.LoadLevel to load in a new scene:

```
void LoadLevel( string whichLevel )
{
        Application.LoadLevel( whichLevel );
}
```

The functions GoMainMenu(), ShowOptionsMenu(), ShowAudioOptionsMenu(), and ShowGraphicsOptionsMenu() set the value of the variable whichMenu so that the case statement from the main OnGUI function will render the required menu:

```
void GoMainMenu()
{
        whichMenu=0;
}

void ShowOptionsMenu()
{
        whichMenu=1;
}

void ShowAudioOptionsMenu()
{
        whichMenu=3;
}

void ShowGraphicsOptionsMenu()
{
        whichMenu=4;
}
```

PlayerPrefs is used for saving out data we will need later on. In SaveOptionsPrefs(), the values for sound volume, music volume, and graphics detail level are saved to disk. You may have noticed some of these PlayerPrefs names from earlier chapters of this book, where they were used to set volume levels and graphics settings:

```
void SaveOptionsPrefs()
{
        PlayerPrefs.SetFloat(gamePrefsName+"_SFXVol",
        audioSFXSliderValue);
        PlayerPrefs.SetFloat(gamePrefsName+"_MusicVol",
        audioMusicSliderValue);
        PlayerPrefs.SetFloat(gamePrefsName+"_GraphicsDetail",
        graphicsSliderValue);

        // set the quality setting
        QualitySettings.SetQualityLevel((int)graphicsSliderValue,true);
}
```

PlayerPrefs is used to save our settings to disk. The example games in this book use an optional string variable called gamePrefsName to attach a prefix to the PlayerPrefs key names so that our preferences will be saved individually for each game. This is completely optional—Unity saves preferences on a per-game basis, so your preferences will never be shared across projects. In this case, as all of the game examples in this book are saved into a single Unity project, the prefix ensures that each game will save its settings individually despite them all being lumped into the same project preferences file.

QualitySettings.SetQualityLevel is used to set Unity's quality level. SetQualityLevel takes an integer index number with its second parameter being a Boolean value to set whether or not expensive changes should be applied. These are settings that may cause the game to stall. It may not always be a good idea to cause stalling (e.g., where SetQualityLevel is used for real-time dynamic quality switching based on frame rate), but in this case, it will have no noticeable impact for the player, so we can go ahead and apply all settings here.

▋ 10.2 In-Game User Interface

The user interface used for the games in this book is extremely basic but entirely functional. Each script derives from a class called BaseUIDataManager, which declares several common variables and provides some basic functions to deal with them. Those are

player_score	The player's score
player_lives	The amount of health or lives that the player has
player_highscore	The highest score achieved in the game so far
gamePrefsName	A string to prefix all PlayerPrefs references (see the earlier section in this chapter for a more in-depth discussion on how PlayerPrefs is used)

The BaseUIDataManager.cs script looks like this:

```
using UnityEngine;
using System.Collections;

public class BaseUIDataManager : MonoBehavior
{
        // the actual UI drawing is done by a script deriving from this one

        public int player_score;
        public int player_lives;
```

```
public int player_highscore;

public string gamePrefsName= "DefaultGame"; // DO NOT FORGET TO SET
                                            // THIS IN THE EDITOR!!

public void UpdateScoreP1( int aScore )
{
        player_score=aScore;
        if( player_score>player_highscore )
                player_highscore = player_score;
}

public void UpdateLivesP1( int alifeNum )
{
        player_lives = alifeNum;
}

public void UpdateScore( int aScore )
{
        player_score = aScore;
}

public void UpdateLives( int alifeNum )
{
        player_lives = alifeNum;
}

public void LoadHighScore()
{
        // grab high score from prefs
        if( PlayerPrefs.HasKey( gamePrefsName+"_highScore" ) )
        {
                player_highscore = PlayerPrefs.GetInt
                ( gamePrefsName+"_highScore" );
        }
}

public void SaveHighScore()
{
        // as we know that the game is over, let's save out the high
        // score too
        PlayerPrefs.SetInt ( gamePrefsName+"_highScore", player_
        highscore );
}
}
```

For an example of an in-game user interface script using this system, look at the next chapter or any of the other example games for a full breakdown.

11 Dish: *Lazer Blast Survival*

In the late 1970s came a turn-based game called *Robots* from Berkeley Software Distribution (BSD). In *Robots*, the player must escape from a swarm of enemies that move in closer toward the player at each turn. In the original version of the game, the player moves around the arena in an attempt to avoid contact between enemies and player, which would end the game.

Robots is often referred to as the beginning of the arena shooter—a term used to describe a top-down shoot 'em up game with the action locked into a limited area similar to an arena. There were derivatives of the *Robots* concept, but the overall idea of escaping from hoards of enemies in an enclosed area remained the same and the game was perfect for the low-spec computers of the time. Before long, it was inevitable that it would evolve into something faster—and in real time. In 1980, Stern Electronics introduced the world to *Berserk*.

Berserk started out as an arcade game but quickly moved to home consoles such as the Atari 2600, 5200, and Vectrex systems. It was, in essence, the evolution of *Robots* into a real-time arcade shooter. In this version, the player makes his way through a randomly generated maze, zapping enemies. Each screen contained a number of enemies, which could be either destroyed or left behind as the player made his way to the edge of the screen to move on to the next part of the maze. There was no scrolling; movement between each section was by a screen swap. One of *Berserk*'s most outstanding and well-remembered features was a speech synthesis system in the arcade machines that allowed the robots to talk. Arcades everywhere rumbled to random robot phrases and kids like me put on their best robot voices to say "Get the humanoid", "The intruder must not escape", and "Flight like a robot!".

The video game *Robotron 2048* arrived in 1982 and was made by a company called Williams Electronics. *Robotron* featured the same basic structure as *Berserk* and *Robots*, with screens full of robots moving toward the player. Designed by Eugene Jarvis and Larry DeMar, the game introduced dual-stick controls to the genre, which have become a common component in today's arena shooters.

Today, the arena shooter genre is alive and well. Over the last few years, there has been quite the renaissance in the arena shooter, mostly in zombie survival shooters. Games such as *Geometry Wars* on Xbox360 and a *Robotron* remake have spun off into a new genre known as the psychedelic arena shooter. I was lucky enough to get to work with Robert Fearon, a true leader in the genre, on bringing his masterpiece *Death Ray Manta* to iOS and Android devices (as shown in Figure 11.1).

Lazer Blast Survival (see Figure 11.2) is a basic template for a top-down shooter, which borrows heavily from its predecessors; the action has a single player moving around an arena fighting off hoards of killer robots.

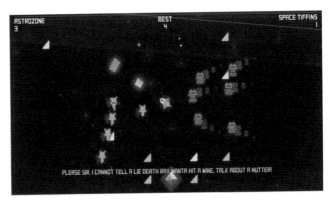

Figure 11.1 *Death Ray Manta* by Rob Fearon, iOS version, published by PsychicParrot Games.

Figure 11.2 *Lazer Blast Survival.*

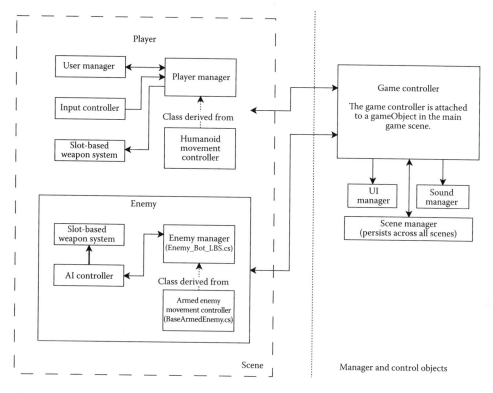

Figure 11.3 The game structure for *Lazer Blast Survival*.

This game may be found in the example games project, its game scenes in the Scenes/ Lazer Blast Survival folder named level_1, level_2 and menu_IP.

Its prefabs are located in the Prefabs/Games/Lazer Blast Survival folder.

A genre-familiar directional control system drives the action—that is, when you press the left or right key, the player moves toward the left or right of the play area and when you press the up or down key the player moves toward the top or bottom of the play area. There is a teleportation particle effect to pre-warn the player as to where the next attack wave will be appearing, which makes the spawning system fair—without the pre-warning effects it would be too easy for the player to be standing right where a new enemy spawns and for it to be killed instantly.

Additions to the core framework are minimal, and you can see the structure of the game in Figure 11.3.

■ 11.1 Main Menu Scene

Lazer Blast Survival works across just two scenes. The main menu scene loads a game scene containing an arena 3D environment and everything to make the game work how it should.

▮ 11.2 Main Game Scene

Rather than loading different scenes for each attach wave, the game works by instantiating prefabs full of enemies into the same scene over and over until the player has no lives remaining.

The main menu consists of a single gameObject, and the main menu script is shown in Chapter 10.

The main game scene Hierarchy structure looks like this:

- ARENA
  - (Models that make up the environment)
- Arena_Colliders
  - (Colliders for the level)
- Directional light
- GameController
- Main Camera
- MusicController
- Player_Startpoint
- SoundController
- SpawnController
- UI
  - Game Over Graphic
  - Get Ready Graphic

Note that the game controller dynamically creates players and enemies when the game starts. References to several prefabs and gameObjects are set in the Unity Inspector window:

- Game controller prefabs
  - Explosion prefab (a particle effect for explosions)
  - Player Prefab List array containing a reference to the Top_Down_Player prefab
  - StartPoints array containing a reference to the Player_Startpoint gameObject in the scene

- The Radar Control Script contains a reference to the Main Camera (which, in turn, has an instance of the RadarGUI.cs component attached to it)

- The BaseSoundController.cs script attached to the Sound Controller gameObject has an array called Game Sounds, containing references to:

  - shoot1

  - explode2

  - player_explode

  - powerup

  - spawner 1

- The Spawn Controller gameObject has an instance of WaveSpawner.cs attached to it, with the following references in its Spawn Object Prefabs array:

  - Spawn_Structure1

  - Spawn_Structure2

  - Spawn_Structure3

- The UI gameObject has a script named UI_LBS.cs attached to it. It refers to

  - GAMEOVER_GRAPHIC gameObject

  - GETREADY_GRAPHIC gameObject

██ 11.3 Prefabs

The prefabs that make up the game are

ENEMIES

  EnemyBot

ENEMY WAVES

  Spawn_Structure 1

  Spawn_Structure 2

  Spawn_Structure 3

PLAYERS

  Top_down_player

Top_down_player_ALT

PROJECTILES

Blast

Blast2

WEAPONS

Blaster

Blaster_1

EXPLOSION PREFAB (not specific to this game; the explosion prefab is in the PARTICLE_EFFECTS folder)

The rest of this chapter will look at the scripts and the programming behind the script components within the prefabs and gameObjects looked at so far.

◼ 11.4 Ingredients

Lazer Blast Survival uses the following ingredients:

1. Game Controller. The game controller script for this game derives from BaseGameController.cs

2. The Main Player. The player rig is based on a Unity character controller and the scripts used to control the main player are as follows:

    a. A main player script derived from BaseTopDown.cs (found in Chapter 5, Section 5.2.)

    b. The player data manager BasePlayerManager.cs (found in Chapter 3, Section 3.3.)

    c. The weapon controller Standard_Slot_Weapon_Controller.cs

3. The enemy bots. The enemies are made of the following scripts:

    a. Enemy bot controller derived from BaseArmedEnemy.cs

    b. BaseAIController.cs for patrolling and target chasing logic.

    c. SimpleBotMover.cs to make the bot move around.

    d. A rigidbody component.

    e. The weapon controller Standard_Slot_Weapon_Controller.cs

    f. A box collider component.

4. Wave spawning. Attack waves are made from prefabs containing groups of enemies. A wave spawner script named Wave_Spawner.cs instantiates the prefabs in a random order and keeps track of how many enemies there are in the level so that it knows when to spawn the next wave. Another small script called WaveProperties. cs is attached to the enemy wave prefabs to tell the spawner how many enemies it contains.

5. Projectiles. The projectiles are made up of the following:

   a. Automatic Destroy Object script AutomaticDestroyObject.cs

   b. ProjectileController.cs

   c. Rigidbody component.

   d. A sphere collider component.

6. User Interface. The user interface for in-game will derive from the BaseUI DataManager script from Chapter 10, Section 10.2, which adds data management. The main menu uses the main menu system outlined in Chapter 10.

7. Top Down Camera. One of the camera scripts from Chapter 4.

8. Sound Controller. The sound controller script from Chapter 8.

9. Music Controller. The music controller script from Chapter 8.

There are other pieces to the puzzle, such as an empty gameObject to act as a starting position for the player named SpawnPosition (its transform position will be used as the location to spawn the player at). As the scripts are broken down later in this chapter, the other components should become apparent.

Note that those components already described in detail elsewhere in this book will not be covered in this section (the full list of ingredients, from early in this section, states which scripts are from elsewhere).

■ 11.5 Game Controller

The Game Controller is a central communications hub for the game. It derives from BaseGameController, overriding some of the base functions as well as adding some of its own.

The full GameController_LBS.cs script looks like this:

```
using UnityEngine;
using System.Collections;

public class GameController_LBS : BaseGameController
{
        public string mainMenuSceneName = "menu_LBS";
        public GameObject[] playerPrefabList;
```

```
    public Wave_Spawner WaveSpawnController;

    public Transform playerParent;
public Transform [] startPoints;

    [System.NonSerialized]
public GameObject playerGO1;

    private Vector3[] playerStarts;
    private Quaternion[] playerRotations;

private ArrayList playerList;
    private ArrayList playerTransforms;

    private Player_LBS thePlayerScript;
    private Player_LBS focusPlayerScript;

    [System.NonSerialized]
    public BaseUserManager mainPlayerDataManager1;

    private int numberOfPlayers;

    public UI_LBS UIControl;

    [System.NonSerialized]
    public static GameController_LBS Instance;

    public float gameSpeed=1;

    public RadarGUI theRadarControlScript;

    public GameController_LBS()
    {
            Instance=this;
    }

    public void Start()
    {
            Init();
            Time.timeScale=gameSpeed;
    }

    public void Init()
    {
            Invoke ("StartPlayer",1);

            SpawnController.Instance.Restart();

            numberOfPlayers= playerPrefabList.Length;

            // initialize some temporary arrays we can use to set up the
            // players
        Vector3 [] playerStarts = new Vector3 [numberOfPlayers];
        Quaternion [] playerRotations = new Quaternion [numberOfPlayers];

            // we are going to use the array full of start positions that must
            // be set in the editor, which means we always need to
```

```
    // make sure that there are enough start positions for the number
    // of players

    for ( int i = 0; i < numberOfPlayers; i++ )
    {
        // grab position and rotation values from start position
        // transforms set in the inspector
        playerStarts [i] = (Vector3) startPoints [i].position;
        playerRotations [i] = ( Quaternion ) startPoints [i].rotation;
    }

SpawnController.Instance.SetUpPlayers( playerPrefabList,
playerStarts, playerRotations, playerParent, numberOfPlayers );

        playerTransforms=new ArrayList();

        // now let's grab references to each player's controller
        // script
        playerTransforms =
        SpawnController.Instance.GetAllSpawnedTransforms();

        playerList=new ArrayList();

        for ( int i = 0; i < numberOfPlayers; i++ )
    {
                Transform tempT= (Transform)playerTransforms[i];
                Player_LBS tempController=
                tempT.GetComponent<Player_LBS>();
                playerList.Add(tempController);
                tempController.Init ();
        }

// grab a ref to the player's gameobject for later
playerGO1 = SpawnController.Instance.GetPlayerGO( 0 );

// grab a reference to the focussed player's controller script, so
// that we can do things like access its speed variable
thePlayerScript = ( Player_LBS )
playerGO1.GetComponent<Player_LBS>();

// assign this player the id of 0
thePlayerScript.SetID( 0 );

// set player control
thePlayerScript.SetUserInput( true );

// as this is the user, we want to focus on this for UI etc.
focusPlayerScript = thePlayerScript;

        // see if we have a camera target object to look at
        Transform aTarget=
        playerGO1.transform.FindChild("CamTarget");

        if(aTarget!=null)
        {
                // if we have a camera target to aim for, instead of
                // the main player, we use that instead
```

```
                    Camera.main.SendMessage("SetTarget", aTarget );
            } else {
            // tell the camera script to target the player
                    Camera.main.SendMessage("SetTarget",
                    playerGO1.transform );
            }

            // finally, tell the radar about the new player
            theRadarControlScript.SetCenterObject( playerGO1.transform );
    }

    void StartPlayer()
    {
            // grab a reference to the main player's data manager so we
            // can update its values later on (scoring, lives etc.)
            mainPlayerDataManager1=
            playerGO1.GetComponent<BasePlayerManager>().DataManager;

            // all ready to play, let's go!
            thePlayerScript.GameStart();
    }

    public override void EnemyDestroyed ( Vector3 aPosition,
    int pointsValue, int hitByID )
    {
            // tell our sound controller to play an explosion sound
            BaseSoundController.Instance.PlaySoundByIndex( 1, aPosition );

            // tell main data manager to add score
            mainPlayerDataManager1.AddScore( pointsValue );

            // update the score on the UI
            UpdateScoreP1( mainPlayerDataManager1.GetScore() );

            // play an explosion effect at the enemy position
            Explode ( aPosition );

            // tell spawn controller that we're one enemy closer to the
            // next wave
            WaveSpawnController.Fragged();
    }

    public void PlayerHit(Transform whichPlayer)
    {
            // tell our sound controller to play an explosion sound
            BaseSoundController.Instance.PlaySoundByIndex( 2,
            whichPlayer.position );

            // call the explosion function!
            Explode( whichPlayer.position );
    }

    public void AddEnemyToRadar( Transform aTransform )
    {
            theRadarControlScript.AddEnemyBlipToList( aTransform );
    }
```

```
public void RemoveEnemyFromRadar( Transform aTransform )
{
        theRadarControlScript.RemoveEnemyBlip( aTransform );
}

public Player_LBS GetMainPlayerScript ()
{
        return focusPlayerScript;
}

public Transform GetMainPlayerTransform ()
{
        return playerGO1.transform;
}

public GameObject GetMainPlayerGO ()
{
        return playerGO1;
}

public void PlayerDied(int whichID)
{
        // this is a single player game, so just end the game now
        // both players are dead, so end the game
        UIControl.ShowGameOver();
        Invoke ("Exit",5);
}

void Exit()
{
        Application.LoadLevel( mainMenuSceneName );
}

// UI update calls
//
public void UpdateScoreP1( int aScore )
{
        UIControl.UpdateScoreP1( aScore );
}

public void UpdateLivesP1( int aScore )
{
        UIControl.UpdateLivesP1( aScore );
}
}
```

11.5.1 Script Breakdown

GameController_LBS.cs derives from BaseGameController, which, in turn, derives from MonoBehavior so that it can tap into some of Unity's built-in calls to functions like Update(), Awake() and Start(), etc.:

```
using UnityEngine;
using System.Collections;
```

```
public class GameController_LBS : BaseGameController
{
```

When the game has finished, the string type variable mainMenuSceneName is used to load the main menu. The main menu scene of this game is named "menu_LBS":

```
public string mainMenuSceneName = "menu_LBS";
```

Skipping past the variable declarations (as their functions should become obvious as the script is analyzed later in this section), there is a constructor for GameController_LBS. When this script is attached to a GameObject, the constructor will be called when the game first starts (as constructors are called when an instance of a script is made).

The constructor sets the static variable named Instance to the instance of the script that this function is being called on. From here on, when another script needs to talk to the game controller it can do so through GameController_LBS.Instance():

```
public GameController_LBS()
{
        Instance=this;
}
```

Time.timeScale need not always be set to 1. gameSpeed is a public variable which may be used to set the game timing to one that makes for a specific type of game play experience. When Start() is called by the Unity engine, the time scale is set just after Init() is called:

```
public void Start()
{
        Init();
        Time.timeScale=gameSpeed;
}
```

The player will not be allowed to move straight away, and the Init() function schedules a call, with the Invoke method, to start player movement 1 second later.

This Init() function will be called when the game restarts. When the game restarts, SpawnController may still hold references to the old objects it has spawned. By calling Restart() on its instance, everything gets cleared out ready for a new round:

```
public void Init()
{
        Invoke ("StartPlayer",1);
        SpawnController.Instance.Restart();
```

Rather than hard-coding a player prefab or specific player objects, to keep things flexible the game controller uses an array named playerPrefabList. Player prefab references are added via the Inspector window in the Unity editor, and the game controller uses the array to spawn them when the game starts. numberOfPlayers holds a count of the players in the playerPrefabList array:

```
numberOfPlayers= playerPrefabList.Length;
```

As with players, gameObjects used to define player start positions are also stored in an array called startPoints (again, its references are set in the Inspector window of the Unity editor). Note that there needs to be at least the same amount of start positions as players for this function to work (as each player will need one).

The function iterates through the start position objects to get at positions and rotations from them and store each one into the arrays playerStarts and playerRotations:

```
                // initialize some temporary arrays we can use to set up the
                // players
        Vector3 [] playerStarts = new Vector3 [numberOfPlayers];
        Quaternion [] playerRotations = new Quaternion [numberOfPlayers];

                // we are going to use the array full of start positions that must
                // be set in the editor, which means we always need to make sure
                // that there are enough start positions for the number of players

        for ( int i = 0; i < numberOfPlayers; i++ )
        {
            // grab position and rotation values from start position
            // transforms set in the inspector
            playerStarts [i] = (Vector3) startPoints [i].position;
            playerRotations [i] = ( Quaternion ) startPoints [i].rotation;
        }
```

Now that the function has arrays for players, start positions and start rotations, it can call upon the SpawnController instance's SetUpPlayers() function to bring them into the game scene:

```
        SpawnController.Instance.SetUpPlayers( playerPrefabList,
playerStarts, playerRotations, playerParent, numberOfPlayers );
```

At some point, it is inevitable that this script will need to communicate with the players. The player transforms get stored in an ArrayList called playerTransforms and references to their control scripts (instances of Player_LBS.cs) held in an array named playerList.

The SpawnController instance returns an ArrayList() back from GetAllSpawned Transforms() that we use to iterate through to get to each Player_LBS instance with GetComponent():

```
        playerTransforms=new ArrayList();

        // now let's grab references to each player's controller script
        playerTransforms =
        SpawnController.Instance.GetAllSpawnedTransforms();

        playerList=new ArrayList();

        for ( int i = 0; i < numberOfPlayers; i++ )
        {
                Transform tempT= (Transform)playerTransforms[i];
                Player_LBS tempController=
                tempT.GetComponent<Player_LBS>();
                playerList.Add(tempController);
                tempController.Init ();
        }
```

The first player object added to the list of players in the Unity editor Inspector window needs to be the main player, in gaming terms we might call this "player one". When players are generated, the SpawnController stores their objects in an array so they can be accessed later on, from other scripts. Access to the array is provided by the function GetPlayerGO(index number). Here, we call upon the SpawnController to return the main player object to be stored in playerGO1:

```
// grab a ref to the player's gameobject for later
playerGO1 = SpawnController.Instance.GetPlayerGO( 0 );
```

GetComponent() is used to grab a reference to the main player's control script, which is stored in the variable named thePlayerScript:

```
// grab a reference to the focussed player's controller script, so
// that we can do things like access its speed variable
// thePlayerScript = ( Player_LBS ) playerGO1.GetComponent<Player_
LBS>();
```

The next line assigns an ID number to the player, used later to identify the origin of projectiles:

```
// assign this player the id of 0
thePlayerScript.SetID( 0 );
```

To allow control of the main player by the user, SetUserInput is called. We also keep a reference to this player script in the variable named focusPlayerScript, since it is the player that the game controller will be focused on when providing data to the UI and the player that the camera needs to focus on, too:

```
// set player control
thePlayerScript.SetUserInput( true );

// as this is the user, we want to focus on this for UI etc.
focusPlayerScript = thePlayerScript;
```

The script looks for a reference to a gameObject named CamTarget attached to the main player. If it exists, it will be used as a target for the camera. If not, the player is set to be the camera target instead:

```
// see if we have a camera target object to look at
Transform aTarget= playerGO1.transform.FindChild("CamTarget");

if(aTarget!=null)
{
        // if we have a camera target to aim for, instead of
        // the main player, we use that instead
        Camera.main.SendMessage("SetTarget", aTarget );
} else {
// tell the camera script to target the player
        Camera.main.SendMessage("SetTarget",
        playerGO1.transform );
}
```

The radar system needs to know which object to center on. A quick call to its SetCenterObject() function is made, with the parameter being the player's transform:

```
                // finally, tell the radar about the new player
                theRadarControlScript.SetCenterObject( playerGO1.transform );
        }
```

Invoked by the Start() function, the StartPlayer() function will tell the player when it should begin the game. This function also grabs a reference to the player's data manager and keeps it in a variable named mainPlayerDataManager1. This will be used by the game controller later on for things like displaying the player's score in the UI:

```
        void StartPlayer()
        {
                // grab a reference to the main player's data manager so we
                // can update its values later on (scoring, lives etc.)
                mainPlayerDataManager1=
                playerGO1.GetComponent<BasePlayerManager>().DataManager;
```

Each player script incorporates a function called GameStart(), used to finalize whatever it needs to start the game:

```
                // all ready to play, let's go!
                thePlayerScript.GameStart();
        }
```

The EnemyDestroyed() function is overridden from its original form in the BaseGameController.cs script. It will be called whenever an enemy gets destroyed and will be used to make an explosion effect, to update scoring, and to tell the wave spawner that the player is one less enemy closer to completing the wave. Its parameters are the position of the enemy when it was impacted, the enemy points value, and the ID of the projectile it was hit by:

```
        public override void EnemyDestroyed ( Vector3 aPosition,
        int pointsValue, int hitByID )
        {
```

The enemy explosion sound is the second item set in array via the Unity editor, making its index number 1:

```
                // tell our sound controller to play an explosion sound
                BaseSoundController.Instance.PlaySoundByIndex( 1, aPosition );
```

Add the score to the main player's data manager:

```
                // tell main data manager to add score
                mainPlayerDataManager1.AddScore( pointsValue );
```

A call to update the UI is made via the function later in this script called UpdateScoreP1(). To get at the player's score, the data manager provides the GetScore() function:

```
                // update the score on the UI
                UpdateScoreP1( mainPlayerDataManager1.GetScore() );

                // play an explosion effect at the enemy position
                Explode ( aPosition );
```

The wave spawn controller (in the variable WaveSpawnController) keeps track of how many enemies there are, so that it knows when to spawn new ones. Each time an enemy is destroyed, the game controller needs to call its Fragged() function once:

```
        // tell spawn controller that we're one enemy closer to the
        // next wave
        WaveSpawnController.Fragged();
}
```

The PlayerHit() function makes an explosion sound via the BaseSoundController instance, then spawns an explosion wherever the player is. The player control script will call this function when it collides with an enemy projectile:

```
public void PlayerHit(Transform whichPlayer)
{
        // tell our sound controller to play an explosion sound
        BaseSoundController.Instance.PlaySoundByIndex( 2,
        whichPlayer.position );

        // call the explosion function!
        Explode( whichPlayer.position );
}
```

Each time a new enemy is added to the world, it needs to tell the radar to track it. The game controller acts as a go-between in its AddEnemyToRadar() function, which takes the transform of the new object to be added and passes it on to the radar via its AddEnemyBlipToList() function:

```
public void AddEnemyToRadar( Transform aTransform )
{
        theRadarControlScript.AddEnemyBlipToList( aTransform );
}
```

When an enemy is destroyed, the radar has no way to tell whether or not to keep trying to track it. The game controller uses this RemoveEnemyFromRadar function to tell the radar to stop tracking the transform passed in as a parameter:

```
public void RemoveEnemyFromRadar( Transform aTransform )
{
        theRadarControlScript.RemoveEnemyBlip( aTransform );
}
```

There may be occasions when the main player script, its gameObject, or its transform needs to be accessed through other scripts, so game controller provides the GetMainPlayerScript(), GetMainPlayerTransform(), and GetMainPlayerGO() functions:

```
public Player_LBS GetMainPlayerScript ()
{
        return focusPlayerScript;
}

public Transform GetMainPlayerTransform ()
{
        return playerGO1.transform;
```

```
        }

        public GameObject GetMainPlayerGO ()
        {
                return playerGO1;
        }
```

When the main player is destroyed, the PlayerDied() function is called. It tells the UI controller to display a message (a game-over message) and schedules the exiting of the game 5 seconds from the time that the call is made.

The ID of the player is passed into this function, though it remains unused in its current form. This is purely to maintain a standardized system, where under other circumstances (such as local multiplayer games) the ID might be checked to see which player died and react accordingly. In this case, as we know that there is only one player (it is a single-player game example, after all!), it is assumed that the game is over without having to check IDs:

```
        public void PlayerDied(int whichID)
        {
                // this is a single player game, so just end the game now
                // both players are dead, so end the game
                UIControl.ShowGameOver();
                Invoke ("Exit",5);
        }
```

When the Exit() function is called (as scheduled by the PlayerDied() function earlier), Application.LoadLevel will switch scenes away from the game and in to the main menu. The mainMenuSceneName string should be set by the Inspector window in the Unity editor to the name of the main menu scene, although its default declaration early in this script will, by default, be set to the name of the main menu in the example game:

```
        void Exit()
        {
                Application.LoadLevel( mainMenuSceneName );
        }
```

The UIControl.cs script will be analyzed in full later in this chapter. Game controller needs to tell it about lives and score changes, which it does so through the functions UpdateScoreP1() and UpdateLivesP1():

```
        // UI update calls
        //
        public void UpdateScoreP1( int aScore )
        {
                UIControl.UpdateScoreP1( aScore );
        }

        public void UpdateLivesP1( int aScore )
        {
                UIControl.UpdateLivesP1( aScore );
        }
}
```

■ 11.6 Player Controller

Lazer Blast Survival uses an animated human player model from the Unity3d *Angry Bots* tutorial, included with Unity. It uses a class that derives from the top-down controller script shown in Chapter 5, adding custom game-specific scripting to it and a separate class to take care of animating the character model.

The player class Player_LBS derives from the controller script BaseTopDown.cs, a modified version of the third-person controller script included with Unity that uses Unity's built-in character controller for physics. BaseTopDown.cs is detailed in full in Chapter 5 (Building Player Movement Controllers).

Player_LBS.cs looks like this:

```
using UnityEngine;
using System.Collections;

public class Player_LBS : BaseTopDown
{
        private bool isInvulnerable;
        private bool isRespawning;

        public BasePlayerManager myPlayerManager;
        public BaseUserManager myDataManager;


        public bool godMode =false;
        public GameObject theMeshGO;

        public Standard_SlotWeaponController weaponControl;
        public bool canFire;

        public bool isFinished;

        public override void Init ()
        {
                base.Init();

                // do god mode, if needed)
                if(!godMode)
                {
                        MakeVulnerable();
                } else {
                        MakeInvulnerable();
                }

                // start out with no control from the player
                canControl=false;

                // get a ref to the weapon controller
                weaponControl=
                myGO.GetComponent<Standard_SlotWeaponController>();

                // if a player manager is not set in the editor, let's try
                // to find one
                if(myPlayerManager==null)
                        myPlayerManager=
                        myGO.GetComponent<BasePlayerManager>();
```

```
            // set up the data for our player
            myDataManager= myPlayerManager.DataManager;
            myDataManager.SetName("Player");
            myDataManager.SetHealth(3);

            isFinished= false;

            // tell game control to update the lives UI
    GameController_LBS.Instance.UpdateLivesP1(myDataManager.GetHealth());
    }

    public override void GetInput()
    {
            if(isFinished || isRespawning)
            {
                    horz=0;
                    vert=0;
                    return;
            }

            // drop out if we're not supposed to be controlling this player
            if(!canControl)
                    return;

            // grab inputs from the default input provider
            horz= Mathf.Clamp( default_input.GetHorizontal() , -1, 1 );
            vert= Mathf.Clamp( default_input.GetVertical() , -1, 1 );

            // fire if we need to
            if( default_input.GetFire() && canFire )
            {
                    // tell weapon controller to deal with firing
                    weaponControl.Fire();
            }
    }

    public void GameStart()
    {
            // this function is called by the game controller to tell us
            // when we can start moving
            canControl=true;
    }

    void LostLife()
    {
            isRespawning=true;

            // blow us up!
            GameController_LBS.Instance.PlayerHit( myTransform );

            // reduce lives by one
            myDataManager.ReduceHealth(1);
    GameController_LBS.Instance.UpdateLivesP1( myDataManager.GetHealth() );

            if(myDataManager.GetHealth()<1) // <- game over
            {
```

```
                    // stop movement, as long as rigidbody is not
                    // kinematic (otherwise it will have no velocity and we
                    // will generate an error message trying to set it)
                    if( !myPlayerController.rigidbody.isKinematic )
                    myPlayerController.rigidbody.velocity=Vector3.zero;

                    // hide ship body
                    theMeshGO.SetActive(false);

                    // disable and hide weapon
                    weaponControl.DisableCurrentWeapon();

                    // do anything we need to do at game finished
                    PlayerFinished();
            } else {
                    // hide ship body
                    theMeshGO.SetActive(false);

                    // disable and hide weapon
                    weaponControl.DisableCurrentWeapon();

                    // respawn
                    Invoke("Respawn",2f);
            }
    }

    void Respawn()
    {
            // reset the 'we are respawning' variable
            isRespawning= false;

            // we need to be invulnerable for a little while
            MakeInvulnerable();

            Invoke ("MakeVulnerable",3);
            // show ship body again
            theMeshGO.SetActive(true);

            // revert to the first weapon
            weaponControl.SetWeaponSlot(0);

            // show the current weapon (since it was hidden when the
            // ship explosion was shown)
            weaponControl.EnableCurrentWeapon();
    }

    void OnCollisionEnter(Collision collider)
    {
            // MAKE SURE that weapons don't have colliders
            // if you are using primitives, only use a single collider
            // on the same gameobject which has this script on

            // when something collides with our ship, we check its layer
            // to see if it is on 11 which is our projectiles
            // (Note: remember when you add projectiles set the layer
            correctly!)
            if(collider.gameObject.layer==11 && !isRespawning &&
            !isInvulnerable)
```

```
                {
                        LostLife();
                }
        }

        void MakeInvulnerable()
        {
                isInvulnerable=true;
        }

        void MakeVulnerable()
        {
                isInvulnerable=false;
        }

        public void PlayerFinished()
        {
                // tell the player controller that we have finished
                GameController_LBS.Instance.PlayerDied( id );

                isFinished=true;
        }
}
```

11.6.1 Script Breakdown

The player derives from BaseTopDown.cs, which was described back in Chapter 5. The game-specific Player_LBS script adds weapon control, respawning, invulnerability, and a data manager:

```
public class Player_LBS : BaseTopDown
{
```

Skipping down past the variable declarations, we can see that the Init() function comes first. Notice that there is no Start() function attached to this script; expected behavior might be to call the Init() function from Start(), but in this case the player's Init() function will be called from the game controller so there is no need for a Start() function in this class:

```
        public override void Init ()
        {
```

Calling base.Init() means that the Init() function in the base class (the one that this script is derived from) will be called. It's a good way to keep all of the setup code from the original function without having to duplicate or override it:

```
                base.Init();
```

The game's god mode gives unlimited invulnerability to the player. It is provided purely to make the game easier to test, as there is currently no way to activate this in-game and it is assumed that the godMode checkbox should be set in the Inspector window of the Unity editor on the component:

```
// do god mode, if needed)
if(!godMode)
{
        MakeVulnerable();
} else {
        MakeInvulnerable();
}
```

canControl will be used to determine whether or not the user can move this player around via whichever input is attached:

```
// start out with no control from the player
canControl=false;
```

The standard slot weapon controller (as described in Chapter 6) is used by this player. For this weapon controller to work correctly, its forceParent variable needs to be set to an empty gameObject named GunMountPoint and the layer of that gameObject set to layer number 9, the layer named "enemy projectile." This will ensure that weapons are parented to the right part of the player character and that the projectiles they fire may be identified correctly.

Expand out the player's gameObject in the Hierarchy window of the Unity editor and you will see quite a lot of objects in it. As you get deeper into the hierarchy of gameObjects, you will start to expand the bones of the skeleton used to animate the player. Deep down under the object Bip 001 Right Hand is an empty gameObject named GunMountPoint. The GunMountPoint is where weapons will be attached and it will move around with the right hand, moving the weapon around as though the player character was holding it.

GunMountPoint gameObject is stored in the forceParent variable of the Standard_SlotWeaponController component attached to the player (see Figure 11.4) and the gameObject that will act as parent to all weapons in the game. By changing its layer, all projectiles belong to that layer, too. This is how the game identifies which projectiles are the player's and which are fired by the enemy.

The variable weaponControl will provide the reference we need to communicate with it, as required:

```
// get a ref to the weapon controller
weaponControl= myGO.GetComponent<Standard_SlotWeaponController>();
```

As discussed in Chapter 3, the player manager script deals with all of the data associated with a player. Next in the script, if it does not already have a reference set up, myPlayer Manager is set up with a reference to an instance of BasePlayerManager for health/damage and scoring. We then set its name with SetName() and its health with SetHealth(). The health value is used a little differently than you may think in that it is treated more as a lives system than as health points. It is set to 3, and each time the player hits a projectile it will be respawned and a single health unit taken away; when there is no health left the game will end:

```
// if a player manager is not set in the editor, let's try
// to find one
if(myPlayerManager==null)
myPlayerManager= myGO.GetComponent<BasePlayerManager>();
```

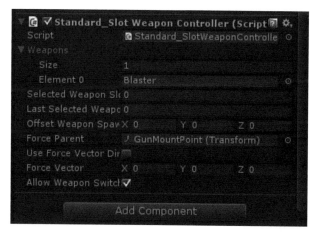

Figure 11.4 The Standard_SlotWeaponController attached to the player prefab.

```
// set up the data for our player
myDataManager= myPlayerManager.DataManager;
myDataManager.SetName("Player");
myDataManager.SetHealth(3);
```

isFinished is used to tell this player whether or not to act like it is playing the game. When the game ends, isFinished is set to true and the user will no longer have control:

```
isFinished= false;
```

The last part of this function tells the game controller to update the lives display to the health set within the data manager. This needs to happen for the lives display to be populated with the right amount when the game first starts:

```
// tell game control to update the lives UI
GameController_LBS.Instance.UpdateLivesP1(myDataManager.GetHealth());
}
```

The GetInput() function overrides the one from the base class (BaseTopDown.cs) to provide support for respawning and firing.

When the game has finished and isFinished is true, or when the player is respawning, all of the inputs are set to zero so that the user cannot move the player around:

```
public override void GetInput()
{
        if(isFinished || isRespawning)
        {
                horz=0;
                vert=0;
                return;
        }
```

Before going through to check for input, the function will drop out if canControl is false. canControl means that the user is not supposed to control this player:

```
// drop out if we're not supposed to be controlling this
// player
if(!canControl)
        return;
```

The actual input values come in from the default input controller held in the default_input variable. The variable default_input is declared as type Keyboard_Input.

The values returned from a call to default_input.GetHorizontal() and default_input. GetVertical() are clamped with Mathf.Clamp as a precaution, even though the keyboard controller this example game uses should never return anything other than a number between –1 and 1:

```
// grab inputs from the default input provider
horz= Mathf.Clamp( default_input.GetHorizontal() , -1, 1 );
vert= Mathf.Clamp( default_input.GetVertical() , -1, 1 );
```

default_input checks for the fire button, too. Next, the code checks to see whether the fire button is pressed and whether or not firing is actually possible. The Boolean variable canFire is standardized across the example games as a method to be set in the Unity editor Inspector window to state whether or not this player should be allowed to fire or not.

If the fire button is pressed and canFire is set to true, the function Fire() is called on the weaponControl object. This should tell the weapon system to fire the currently selected weapon:

```
// fire if we need to
if( default_input.GetFire() && canFire )
{
        // tell weapon controller to deal with firing
        weaponControl.Fire();
}
}
```

The game controller has an Invoke statement in its Start() function, which calls StartPlayer() and, in turn, calls this GameStart() function:

```
public void GameStart()
{
```

canControl is set to true, meaning that the player now has control:

```
        // this function is called by the game controller to tell us
        // when we can start moving
        canControl=true;
}
```

Respawning the player starts when LostLife() is called by this script's collision function. We will look at OnCollisionEnter further in this section.

When LostLife() is called, the first thing that happens is the Boolean variable isRespawning is set to true. You may recall this from the input function earlier when input was locked out if the player is respawning.

Earlier in this chapter when we looked at the game controller, PlayerHit() was one of the functions used to display an explosion effect. Here, we access the static game controller variable GameController_LBS.Instance and call PlayerHit(), passing in this player's transform:

```
void LostLife()
{
        isRespawning=true;

        // blow us up!
        GameController_LBS.Instance.PlayerHit( myTransform );
```

The data manager gets a call next, to reduce the lives count by 1:

```
        // reduce lives by one
        myDataManager.ReduceHealth(1);
```

As the health has changed, we now need to update the UI and tell the user about it:

```
    GameController_LBS.Instance.UpdateLivesP1( myDataManager.GetHealth() );
```

In this code, the data manager function GetHealth() returns an integer health value. When health is less than 1, it's time to stop the player from moving (setting its velocity to zero) and end the game. The player mesh is hidden too (via SetActive):

```
    if(myDataManager.GetHealth()<1) // <- game over
    {
            // stop movement, as long as rigidbody is not
            // kinematic (otherwise it will have no velocity and we
            // will generate an error message trying to set it)
            if( !myPlayerController.rigidbody.isKinematic )
            myPlayerController.rigidbody.velocity=Vector3.zero;

            // hide ship body
            theMeshGO.SetActive(false);
```

The weapon system is shut down so that firing doesn't happen anymore, followed by a call to the PlayerFinished() function to take care of finalizing the game for this player:

```
            // disable and hide weapon
            weaponControl.DisableCurrentWeapon();

            // do anything we need to do at game finished
            PlayerFinished();
```

If the player's health amount is more than 0, the player's model is hidden, the weapon system is disabled and a respawn is scheduled 2 seconds from here (via an Invoke statement to call the Respawn() function):

```
    } else {
            // hide ship body
            theMeshGO.SetActive(false);

            // disable and hide weapon
            weaponControl.DisableCurrentWeapon();
```

```
                                // respawn
                                Invoke("Respawn",2f);
                    }
        }
```

Respawn() will reposition the player at its starting position and reset all of the variables required to put the player back to the state it was at the beginning of the level:

```
        void Respawn()
        {
                    // reset the 'we are respawning' variable
                    isRespawning= false;
```

When a player respawns, it may often be placed in a position where there is already an enemy or some laser fire. It could be unfair to respawn the player and have it destroyed immediately, so when respawning happens the opportunity for a spawn problem is alleviated by making the player invulnerable for a short period of time. A call to MakeInvulnerable() starts this, with an Invoke call to activate the MakeVulnerable function to counter its effect 3 seconds later:

```
                    // we need to be invulnerable for a little while
                    MakeInvulnerable();

                    Invoke ("MakeVulnerable",3);
```

The player mesh was hidden when the player was destroyed, so as it respawns the SetActive() function is used to show it again:

```
                    // show ship body again
                    theMeshGO.SetActive(true);
```

As well as the player model being hidden on its destruction, the weapon controller was disabled. To re-enable it, the weapon slot is set to the first one (zero) to reset it, and a call to weaponControl.EnableCurrentWeapon() is made to get it going again:

```
                    // revert to the first weapon
                    weaponControl.SetWeaponSlot(0);

                    // show the current weapon (since it was hidden when the
                    // ship explosion was shown)
                    weaponControl.EnableCurrentWeapon();
        }
```

The OnCollisionEnter function will detect when an object first collides with the player. The layer of the object colliding with it is checked to see whether it is a projectile (on layer 11) and we make sure that the player is not respawning.

The simple invulnerability system comes into play in this function; the state of isInvulnerable decides whether or not it should react to the collision.

If all conditions are met, the LostLife() function is called:

```
        void OnCollisionEnter(Collision collider)
        {
                    // MAKE SURE that weapons don't have colliders
```

```
                    // if you are using primitives, only use a single collider
                    // on the same gameobject which has this script on

                    // when something collides with our ship, we check its layer
                    // to see if it is on 11 which is our projectiles
                    // (Note: remember when you add projectiles set the layer
                    // correctly!)
                    if(collider.gameObject.layer==11 && !isRespawning &&
                    !isInvulnerable)
                    {
                            LostLife();
                    }
            }
```

MakeInvulnerable() and MakeVulnerable() simply set the Boolean isInvulnerable variable to true or false, respectively:

```
            void MakeInvulnerable()
            {
                    isInvulnerable=true;
            }

            void MakeVulnerable()
            {
                    isInvulnerable=false;
            }
```

The final part of the script informs the game controller when this player is completely finished with. This player will be inactive until its isFinished Boolean variable is reset to false:

```
            public void PlayerFinished()
            {
                    // tell the player controller that we have finished
                    GameController_LBS.Instance.PlayerDied( id );

                    isFinished=true;
            }
    }
```

■ 11.7 Enemies

EnemyBot_LBS.cs is a surprisingly straightforward script, thanks to the BaseAIController.cs and the BaseArmedEnemy.cs scripts it uses at its core:

```
public class EnemyBot_LBS : BaseArmedEnemy
{
        public void Start ()
        {
                base.Start ();

                // let's find our AI controller
                BaseAIController aControl= (BaseAIController)
                gameObject.GetComponent<BaseAIController>();
```

```
                        // and tell it to chase our player around the screen (we get
                        // the player transform from game controller)
        aControl.SetChaseTarget( GameController_LBS.Instance.GetMainPlayerTransform() );

                        // now get on and chase it!
                        aControl.SetAIState( AIStates.AIState.chasing_target );

                        // we also need to add this enemy to the radar, so we will
                        // tell game controller about it and some code in game
                        // controller will do this for us
                        GameController_LBS.Instance.AddEnemyToRadar( myTransform );
                }

                // game controller specifics (overridden for our laser blast
                survival game controller)
                // -------------------------------------------------------------
                public override void TellGCEnemyDestroyed()
                {
                        // tell the game controller we have been destroyed
                        GameController_LBS.Instance.EnemyDestroyed( myTransform.
                        position, pointsValue, tempINT );

                        // remove this enemy from the radar
                        GameController_LBS.Instance.RemoveEnemyFromRadar(
                        myTransform );
                }

                public override void TellGCBossDestroyed()
                {
                        // tell the game controller we have been destroyed (and that
                        // we are a boss!)
                        GameController_LBS.Instance.BossDestroyed();

                        // remove this enemy from the radar
                        GameController_LBS.Instance.RemoveEnemyFromRadar(
                        myTransform );
                }
        }
}
```

11.7.1 Script Breakdown

The EnemyBot_LBS class derives from BaseArmedEnemy, as described in Chapter 4 of
this book:

```
public class EnemyBot_LBS : BaseArmedEnemy
{
        public void Start ()
        {
                base.Start ();

                // let's find our AI controller
                BaseAIController aControl= (BaseAIController) gameObject.Get
                Component<BaseAIController>();

                // and tell it to chase our player around the screen (we get
                // the player transform from game controller)
        aControl.SetChaseTarget( GameController_LBS.Instance.GetMainPlayerTransform() );

                // now get on and chase it!
```

```
        aControl.SetAIState( AIStates.AIState.chasing_target );

        // we also need to add this enemy to the radar, so we will
        // tell game controller about it and
        // some code in game controller will do this for us
        GameController_LBS.Instance.AddEnemyToRadar( myTransform );
    }
```

As all of the games have different custom game controller scripts, it is not possible for all of the player scripts to try to call their game controllers in the same way. Instead, some functions need to be designed to talk to a specific game controller. The enemy needs to tell the game controller when it is destroyed by calling its EnemyDestroyed() or BossDestroyed() function when the enemy is set to a boss. When an enemy is destroyed, it also needs to tell the game controller to remove its transform from the list of transforms that are being tracked by the radar:

```
    // game controller specifics (overridden for our laser blast
    // survival game controller)
    // ------------------------------------------------------------

    public override void TellGCEnemyDestroyed()
    {
        // tell the game controller we have been destroyed
        GameController_LBS.Instance.EnemyDestroyed( myTransform.
        position, pointsValue, tempINT );

        // remove this enemy from the radar
        GameController_LBS.Instance.RemoveEnemyFromRadar
        ( myTransform );
    }

    public override void TellGCBossDestroyed()
    {
        // tell the game controller we have been destroyed (and that
        // we are a boss!)
        GameController_LBS.Instance.BossDestroyed();

        // remove this enemy from the radar
        GameController_LBS.Instance.RemoveEnemyFromRadar
        ( myTransform );
    }
}
```

▌ 11.8 Wave Spawning and Control

Here is the Wave_Spawner.cs script in full:

```
using UnityEngine;
using System.Collections;

public class Wave_Spawner : MonoBehavior
{
    public bool randomSpawning;

    public float timeBeforeFirstSpawn=1f;

    public GameObject[] spawnObjectPrefabs;
```

```csharp
        private int totalSpawnObjects;
        private int currentObjectNum;

        public int currentWave;

        void Start ()
        {
                // count how many objects we have lined up in the spawn
                // object list
                foreach( GameObject go in spawnObjectPrefabs )
                {
                        totalSpawnObjects++;
                }

                Debug.Log("Wave_Spawner.cs found "+totalSpawnObjects+" spawn
                objects to choose from.");

                // schedule first attack wave
                Invoke("LaunchWave",timeBeforeFirstSpawn);
        }

        public void LaunchWave()
        {
                CancelInvoke("LaunchWave");

                if( randomSpawning )
                {
                        currentObjectNum= Random.Range ( 0,
                        totalSpawnObjects-1 );
                } else {
                        currentObjectNum++;

                        // loop back to 0 when we reach the end of the
                        // current 'run' of things to spawn
                        if( currentObjectNum > totalSpawnObjects-1 )
                        {
                                currentObjectNum=0;
                        // you could also implement something to tell
                        // game control that all waves have finished if
                        // you were making a game that only lasted until
                        // that happens
                        }
                }

                // create an object
                GameObject tempObj=
        SpawnController.Instance.SpawnGO( spawnObjectPrefabs[currentObjectNum],
                Vector3.zero, Quaternion.identity );

        WaveProperties tempProps= tempObj.GetComponent<WaveProperties>();
                currentWave= tempProps.enemiesInWave;
        }

        public void Fragged()
        {
                // one enemy down
                currentWave--;
```

```
            if( currentWave<=0 )
            {
                    // this wave is done, let's start the next one!
                    LaunchWave ();
            }
    }
}
```

11.8.1 Script Breakdown

The way attack waves are made in *Lazer Blast Survival* is by having a preset layout of enemies made previously in the Unity editor, parented to a single gameObject and saved out as a single prefab. When it comes time to add a new wave of enemies to the scene, the prefab is instantiated and the wave spawner script keeps track of how many enemies there are until it is time to spawn new ones.

This is an arena-based shooter and the action is intended to go on and on until the player runs out of lives. In this example game, there are just a few enemy wave prefabs (meaning that there are only just a few different types of attack waves), but there could just as easily be tens or hundreds of different layouts as required. The array spawnObjectPrefabs contains references to all of the attack wave prefabs.

Wave_Spawner.cs derives from MonoBehavior to take advantage of some of Unity's built-in function calls:

```
using UnityEngine;
using System.Collections;

public class Wave_Spawner : MonoBehavior
{
```

When the Start() function is called, the first thing that happens is that all of the attack wave prefabs are counted and the result stored in the integer variable totalSpawnObjects:

```
    void Start ()
    {
            // count how many objects we have lined up in the spawn
            // object list
            foreach( GameObject go in spawnObjectPrefabs )
            {
                    totalSpawnObjects++;
            }

            Debug.Log("Wave_Spawner.cs found "+totalSpawnObjects+" spawn
            objects to choose from.");
```

Once counting has finished, the first attack wave is scheduled using timeBeforeFirst-Spawn to tell the Invoke statement how long to wait:

```
            // schedule first attack wave
            Invoke("LaunchWave",timeBeforeFirstSpawn);
    }
```

OK, so there's no actual launching of anything here, just prefab instantiating. It may not be as exciting as its name sounds, but the LaunchWave() function is at the core of the game:

```
public void LaunchWave()
{
```

We make a quick call to CancelInvoke just in case there have been any duplicate calls to LaunchWave(). If more than one attack wave was spawned into the same level, our spawner would have trouble tracking how many enemies are left before the next wave and the system wouldn't work. If there are any previous Invoke calls to LaunchWave() queued up, they will be cancelled out by CancelInvoke:

```
CancelInvoke("LaunchWave");
```

The spawner may work in two different ways. One is to pick random items from the spawnPrefabObjects array and spawn them; the other is to progressively go through the array starting at zero and loop back to zero once the list is exhausted.

If the Boolean variable randomSpawning is true, the variable currentObjectNum is set to a random number between 0 and the total number of objects in the spawnPrefabObjects array (using Random.Range). If randomSpawning is set to false, the currentObjectNum is incremented and a check is made to ensure that it loops back to zero when it is incremented higher than the total number of objects in the array:

```
if( randomSpawning )
{
        currentObjectNum= Random.Range ( 0,
        totalSpawnObjects-1 );
} else {
        currentObjectNum++;

        // loop back to 0 when we reach the end of the
        // current 'run' of things to spawn
        if( currentObjectNum > totalSpawnObjects-1 )
        {
        // currentObjectNum=0;
        // you could also implement something to tell
        // game control that all waves have finished if
        // you were making a game that only lasted until
        // that happens
        }
}
```

The next step is to instantiate the attack wave prefab. For this, an instance of the spawn controller (outlined in full back in Chapter 4, Section 4.3.1) is used and its SpawnGO (spawn game object) function. The parameters for SpawnGO are the prefab object to be spawned, a position and a Quaternion rotation:

```
// create an object
GameObject tempObj=
SpawnController.Instance.SpawnGO( spawnObjectPrefabs[currentObjectNum],
Vector3.zero, Quaternion.identity );
```

Once the attack wave is in the scene, we use GameObject.GetComponent to find the WaveProperties script that needs to be attached to the parent gameObject of the attack wave prefab. This script has a single variable that we need to get at: enemiesInWave. As long as enemiesInWave is set correctly on the prefab, the wave spawner can use the variable currentWave to store how many enemies the player needs to destroy to progress to the next wave:

```
WaveProperties tempProps=
tempObj.GetComponent<WaveProperties>();
currentWave= tempProps.enemiesInWave;
}
```

Whenever an enemy is destroyed, the game-specific game controller makes a call to the following Fragged() function (see earlier in this chapter GameController_LBS.cs):

```
public void Fragged()
{
```

We decrease the value of currentWave, which holds how many enemies are in the current wave:

```
// one enemy down
currentWave--;
```

Then the value of currentWave is checked to see whether it is less than or equal to 0. If this is true, it must be time to spawn the next attack wave so a call goes out to the LaunchWave() function:

```
if( currentWave<=0 )
{
        // this wave is done, let's start the next one!
        LaunchWave ();
}
    }
}
```

11.9 Wave Properties

The Wave_Spawner.cs script outlined in the last section showed that we need to know how many enemies there are in each attack wave. To take care of this, a simple WaveProperties script is attached to the attack wave prefab. It contains just a single integer named enemiesInWave that we set in the Unity editor Inspector window. The game controller script will access this value whenever a new wave is spawned, and it will use the value of enemiesInWave to keep track of enemies in each wave.

WaveProperties.cs looks like this:

```
public class WaveProperties : MonoBehavior
{
        public int enemiesInWave;
}
```

11.10 Weapons and Projectiles

The main weapon (a prefab named Blaster) has a gun mesh with a single script attached to it—BaseWeaponScript.cs—and it contains a reference to a projectile named Blast that will be instantiated whenever it fires.

The projectile is made from a cube, colored red to look more like laser fire. Attached to the projectile are several scripts:

- Automatic Destroy Object

    Destroys the gameObject after a set amount of time (to stop any projectiles that never hit anything from travelling off into infinite space!).

- Projectile Controller

    As discussed in full in Chapter 6.

- Rigidbody

    The rigidbody has only 0.1 mass and no drag at all. The rigidbody is set to interpolate its movement (in an attempt to help improve collisions). One other point of note is that its collision method is set to Continuous. When projectiles are moving as quickly as they do in this game, it is very probable that they will sometimes go through other meshes with no registered collision. The Continuous collision setting will mean increased accuracy but at a small processing cost. In a game like this, the difference in performance is negligible but you should use continuous collisions sparingly and as little as possible.

- Sphere Collider

    The collider is a standard sphere collider.

11.11 User Interface

The main script looks like this:

```
using UnityEngine;
using System.Collections;

[AddComponentMenu("Sample Game Glue Code/Laser Blast Survival/In-Game UI")]

public class UI_LBS : BaseUIDataManager
{
        public GameObject gameOverMessage;
        public GameObject getReadyMessage;

        void Awake()
        {
                Init();
        }
```

```
void Init()
{
        LoadHighScore();

        HideMessages ();

        Invoke("ShowGetReady",1);
        Invoke("HideMessages",2);

}

public void HideMessages()
{
        gameOverMessage.SetActive(false);
        getReadyMessage.SetActive(false);
}

public void ShowGetReady()
{
        getReadyMessage.SetActive(true);
}

public void ShowGameOver()
{
        SaveHighScore();

        // show the game over message
        gameOverMessage.SetActive(true);
}

void OnGUI()
{
        GUI.Label(new Rect (10,10,100,50),"PLAYER 1");
        GUI.Label(new Rect (10,40,100,50),"SCORE "+player_score);
        GUI.Label(new Rect (10,70,200,50),"HIGH SCORE "+player_
        highscore);

        GUI.Label(new Rect (10,100,100,50),"LIVES "+player_lives);
}
}
```

11.11.1 Script Breakdown

The script derives from BaseUIDataManager, the standard UI script shown in Chapter 10. The BaseUIDataManager declares several common variables and provides some basic functions to deal with them:

```
using UnityEngine;
using System.Collections;

public class UI_LBS : BaseUIDataManager
{
```

In the example games, the game-over message and get-ready messages are GUITexture objects. In the Unity editor Inspector window, the gameOverMessage and getReadyMessage variables are set to their objects in the scene:

```
public GameObject gameOverMessage;
public GameObject getReadyMessage;

void Awake()
{
        Init();
}
```

Before showing the main UI, the player_highscore variable needs to be populated with the high score saved in a PlayerPrefs file. The function LoadHighScore() is called to set that up:

```
void Init()
{
        LoadHighScore();
```

Both messages (gameOverMessage and getReadyMessage) are hidden at the start of the game by calling the HideMessages() function:

```
        HideMessages ();
```

The message to get ready (the reference to which is in the getReadyMessage) will be on screen in 1 second after this function call, as set up by the Invoke command:

```
        Invoke("ShowGetReady",1);
```

The get-ready message stays on the screen for another second before the following Invoke call is activated and the message hidden from view:

```
        Invoke("HideMessages",2);

}
```

In HideMessages(), both messages are hidden using the GameObject.SetActive() function:

```
public void HideMessages()
{
        gameOverMessage.SetActive(false);
        getReadyMessage.SetActive(false);
}
```

The function dedicated to showing the get-ready message is called from the Init() function via Invoke:

```
public void ShowGetReady()
{
        getReadyMessage.SetActive(true);
}
```

When the game has ended, ShowGameOver() gets called. The high score is saved out into the PlayerPrefs file and the message set to active (shown) via GameObject.SetActive():

```
public void ShowGameOver()
{
```

```
            SaveHighScore();

            // show the game over message
            gameOverMessage.SetActive(true);
    }
```

The UI code uses OnGUI() to render, which is a function called automatically by the Unity engine. The problem with OnGUI() is that it may be called several times every frame, which causes a huge performance hit on mobile devices. If you are intending on converting the game over to run on a mobile system, you may want to look at other GUI solutions instead.

GUI.Label is a simple method for drawing text onto the screen. For this example game, it is used for all of the UI:

```
    void OnGUI()
    {
            GUI.Label(new Rect (10,10,100,50),"PLAYER 1");
            GUI.Label(new Rect (10,40,100,50),"SCORE "+player_score);
            GUI.Label(new Rect (10,70,200,50),"HIGH SCORE "+player_
            highscore);

            GUI.Label(new Rect (10,100,100,50),"LIVES "+player_lives);
    }
}
```

12 Dish: *Metal Vehicle Doom*

As anyone who knows me will tell you, racing is my favorite genre of video games. I like genuine, no-frills racing where the focus is about getting your car from the start to the finish as quickly as possible—you can keep all the fancy stuff, I'm only here for the racing! The types I enjoy the most are the low- to no-budget quirky little racers, games that aren't afraid to just be racing games and not feel like they have to innovate for the sake of it or innovate to grab extra buyers. I like visceral, honest racing, games like Bugbear Entertainment's *FlatOut 1, 2* and *Ultimate Carnage*; Black Box's *Need for Speed Carbon*; or Team6 Game Studios' *European Street Racer*. Throughout my career, I have been involved in the creation of numerous racing games, from promotional free browser-based titles to console games and retail games. As an independent developer in 2012, I single-handedly made my own ambitious racing game called *Headlong Racing* (see Figure 12.1).

In my last book, *Game Development for iOS with Unity3d*, I built a simple mobile-ready kart racing game using box colliders on a rigid body that slid around a zero-friction environment. In this book, the racing is more ambitious. *Metal Vehicle Doom* (Figure 12.2) features everything a fully featured no-nonsense racer might need—AI opponents, a respawning system, wrong-way detection, and modern video game car physics using Unity's wheel colliders for suspension and car control.

The overall structure of *Metal Vehicle Doom* adds the Global Race Controller to the scheme, with Race Controller objects added to the player (see Figure 12.3).

This game may be found in the example games project and its game scenes in the Scenes/Metal Vehicle Doom folder named game_MVD and menu_MVD.

Figure 12.1 *Headlong Racing* by PsychicParrot Games.

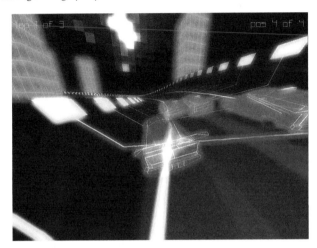

Figure 12.2 *Metal Vehicle Doom.*

Its prefabs are located in the Prefabs/Games/Metal Vehicle Doom folder.

12.1 Main Menu Scene

The game works over two scenes, a main menu and the main track scene. The scene named menu_MVD contains a single camera called Main Camera. The MainMenuController.cs script component is attached to the camera object and deals with rendering the menu to the screen and dealing with interaction.

12.2 Main Game Scene

The menu loads a scene containing the track and environmental specifics such as a light and any collision meshes. When the game starts, the game controller adds the racers to the scene (instantiating their prefabs) as the game begins.

The main menu consists of a single gameObject and the main menu script is shown in Chapter 10.

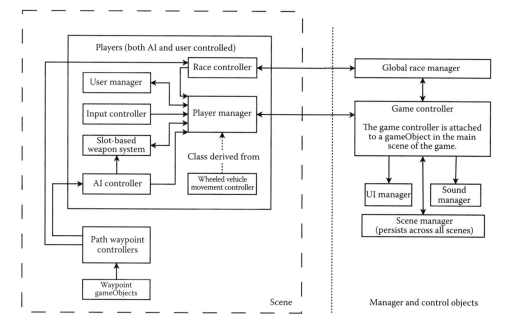

Figure 12.3 Game structure.

The main game scene Hierarchy structure looks like this:

- GameController

- LEVEL

  - (Models that make up the environment)

- Main Camera

- Player_StartPoints

- START_FINISH_LINE

  - Cube (for display only)

  - Cube (for display only)

  - Cube (for display only)

  - TRIGGER_STARTLINE

- UI

  - Final_Position

  - GAMEOVER_GRAPHIC

- GETREADY_GRAPHIC

- in_1

- in_2

- in_3

- Text_Lap

- Text_Position

- WrongWay

- Waypoints

  - All of the transforms used as waypoints for path finding, progress checking, etc.

As with the other example games in this book, players and enemies are dynamically created by the game controller when the game starts. References to several prefabs and gameObjects are set in the Unity editor Inspector window. These are

- Game controller Unity editor Inspector window references:

  - Explosion Prefab—A particle effect for explosions.

  - Player Parent—An empty gameObject that will act as a parent object for players. This is just to keep things neat—when the game is running, if for any reason you need to look at a particular player you can easily access it by expanding the player parent object.

  - Start Points—These are gameObjects in the scene that the game controller can use to get position and rotation information from, for use with positioning the cars at the start of the game.

  - Camera Script—This refers to the camera, which has an instance of the script Camera_Third_Person.cs attached to it. The game controller requires this reference to be set up to communicate with the camera.

  - Lap Text—A gameObject with the GUIText component attached, which renders the user's current lap to the screen.

  - Pos Text—A gameObject with the GUITexture component attached, which renders the user's current position in the race.

  - Count 3—A gameObject used to display the number 3 during the 3-2-1 countdown at the start of the race.

  - Count 2—A gameObject used to display the number 2 at the start of the race.

- Count 1—A gameObject used to display the number 1 at the start of the race.

- Final Position Text—A gameObject with the GUIText component attached, used to show the position of the user at the end of the race.

- Player Prefab List—All of the player prefabs to be instantiated to make the game happen.

- Waypoint Controller—The waypoint control system from Chapter 7.

- Wrong Way Sign—A gameObject, with a GUIText component attached, to be displayed whenever the game detects that the user is going in the wrong direction around the track.

12.2.1 Prefabs

The prefabs for this game are

FX

ExplosionParticleEffect

PLAYERS

Car

Car_AI_Rig

Car_AI_Rig_ARMED

Car_ARMED

PROJECTILES

Ground_Follower

WEAPONS

FastProjectileBlaster

▐█ 12.3 Ingredients

Metal Vehicle Doom uses these ingredients:

1. Game Controller—The game controller script for this game derives from BaseGameController.cs.

2. Race Manager—Each player has a race controller script attached to it, which holds information relevant to its race stats (position/waypoint, etc.). The race manager talks to all of the player's race controllers and tracks global information on the state of the race, such as player race positions and whether or not the race is still in progress.

---

3. Vehicles:

   a. Main player

   b. AI opponents

   All vehicles use the weapon controller Standard_Slot_Weapon_Controller.cs

4. User Interface—The user interface for in-game will derive from the Base UIDataManager script from Chapter 4, which adds data management. The main menu uses the main menu system outlined in Chapter 10.

5. Sound Controller—The sound controller script from Chapter 8.

6. Music Controller

12.3.1 Game Controller

The game controller script GameController_MVD.cs looks like this:

```
using UnityEngine;
using System.Collections;

public class GameController_MVD : BaseGameController
{
    public string mainMenuSceneName = "menu_MVD";
    public int totalLaps = 3;
    public int numberOfRacers = 4;

    public Transform playerParent;
    public Transform [] startPoints;
    public Camera_Third_Person cameraScript;

    [System.NonSerialized]
    public GameObject playerGO1;

    private CarController_MVD thePlayerScript;
    private CarController_MVD focusPlayerScript;

    private ArrayList playerList;
        private ArrayList playerTransforms;

    private float aSpeed;

    public GUIText lapText;
    public GUIText posText;
    // position checking
    private int myPos;
    private int theLap;

        private bool isAhead;
```

```
private CarController_MVD car2;
private int focusPlayerRacePosition;

public GameObject count3;
public GameObject count2;
public GameObject count1;

public GUIText finalPositionText;

public GameObject [] playerPrefabList;

[System.NonSerialized]
public static GameController_MVD Instance;

    public Waypoints_Controller WaypointControllerForAI;

// scale time here
public float gameSpeed = 1;
    private bool didInit;

    public GameObject wrongWaySign;
    private bool oldIsWrongWay;

public GameController_MVD ()
{
    Instance = this;
}

void Start ()
{
    Init();
}

void Init ()
{
    // in case we need to change the timescale, it gets set here
    Time.timeScale = gameSpeed;

        // tell race manager to prepare for the race
        GlobalRaceManager.Instance.InitNewRace( totalLaps );

    // initialize some temporary arrays we can use to set up the
    // players
    Vector3 [] playerStarts = new Vector3 [numberOfRacers];
    Quaternion [] playerRotations = new Quaternion [numberOfRacers];

    // we are going to use the array full of start positions that must
    // be set in the editor, which means we always need to make sure
    // that there are enough start positions for the number of players

    for ( int i = 0; i < numberOfRacers; i++ )
    {
        // grab position and rotation values from start position
        // transforms set in the inspector
        playerStarts [i] = (Vector3) startPoints [i].position;
        playerRotations [i] = ( Quaternion ) startPoints [i].rotation;
    }
```

```
SpawnController.Instance.SetUpPlayers( playerPrefabList,
playerStarts, playerRotations, playerParent, numberOfRacers );

        playerTransforms=new ArrayList();

        // now let's grab references to each player's controller
        //script
        playerTransforms = SpawnController.Instance.
        GetAllSpawnedPlayers();

        playerList=new ArrayList();

        for ( int i = 0; i < numberOfRacers; i++ )
{
                Transform tempT= (Transform)playerTransforms[i];
                CarController_MVD tempController= tempT.
                GetComponent<CarController_MVD>();

                playerList.Add(tempController);

                BaseAIController
                tempAI=tempController.GetComponent<BaseAIControl
                ler>();

                // tell each player where to find the waypoints
                tempAI.SetWayController(WaypointControllerForAI);

                tempController.Init ();

                // tell the car controller script about the waypoint
                // controller so it can pass it on to the
                // racecontroller (!)
            tempController.SetWayController(WaypointControllerForAI);
        }

// grab a ref to the player's gameobject for later use
playerGO1 = SpawnController.Instance.GetPlayerGO( 0 );

        // add an audio listener to the first car so that the audio
        // is based from the car rather than from the main camera
        playerGO1.AddComponent<AudioListener>();

        // look at the main camera and see if it has an audio
        // listener attached
        AudioListener tempListener=
        Camera.main.GetComponent<AudioListener>();

        // if we found a listener, let's destroy it
        if( tempListener!=null )
                Destroy(tempListener);

// grab a reference to the focussed player's car controller script,
// so that we can do things like access its speed variable
thePlayerScript = ( CarController_MVD )
playerGO1.GetComponent<CarController_MVD>();

// assign this player the id of 0
thePlayerScript.SetID( 0 );
```

```
                // set player control
                thePlayerScript.SetUserInput( true );

                // as this is the user, we want to focus on this for UI etc.
                focusPlayerScript = thePlayerScript;

                // tell the camera script to target this new player
                cameraScript.SetTarget( playerGO1.transform );

                // do initial lap counter display
                UpdateLapCounter( 1 );

                // lock all the players on the spot until we're ready to go
                SetPlayerLocks( true );

                // start the game in 3 seconds from now
                Invoke( "StartRace"      , 4 );

                // update positions throughout the race, but we don't need
                // to do this every frame, so just do it every half a second
                // instead
                InvokeRepeating( "UpdatePositions", 0.5f, 0.5f );

                // hide our count in numbers
                HideCount();

                // schedule count in messages
                Invoke( "ShowCount3", 1 );
                Invoke( "ShowCount2", 2 );
                Invoke( "ShowCount1", 3 );
                Invoke( "HideCount", 4 );

                // hide final position text
                finalPositionText.gameObject.SetActive( false );
                doneFinalMessage = false;

                // start by hiding our wrong way message
                wrongWaySign.SetActive( false );

                        didInit=true;
        }

        void StartRace ()
        {
                // the SetPlayerLocks function tells all players to unlock
                SetPlayerLocks( false );

                        // tell the global race manager that we are now racing
                        GlobalRaceManager.Instance.StartRace();
        }
        void SetPlayerLocks ( bool aState )
        {
                // tell all of the players to set their locks
                for ( int i = 0; i < numberOfRacers; i++ )
                {
                        thePlayerScript = ( CarController_MVD ) playerList [i];
                        thePlayerScript.SetLock( aState );
```

```
            }
        }

    void UpdatePositions()
    {
            // here we need to talk to the race controller to get what
            // we need to display on screen
            focusPlayerRacePosition=
            GlobalRaceManager.Instance.GetPosition(1);
            theLap= GlobalRaceManager.Instance.GetLapsDone(1) +1;

            // update the display
            UpdateRacePositionText();
            UpdateLapCounter(theLap);
    }

void UpdateLapCounter ( int theLap )
{
    // if we've finished all the laps we need to finish, let's cap the
    // number so that we can have the AI cars continue going around the
    // track without any negative implications
    if ( theLap > totalLaps )
        theLap = totalLaps;

    // now we set the text of our GUIText object lap count display
    lapText.text = "Lap " + theLap.ToString() + " of " +
    totalLaps.ToString();
}

void UpdateRacePositionText ()
{
    posText.text = "Pos " + focusPlayerRacePosition.ToString() + " of
    "+ numberOfRacers.ToString();
}

private bool doneFinalMessage;

public void RaceComplete ( int finalPosition )
{
    if ( !doneFinalMessage )
    {
            if ( finalPosition == 1 )
                finalPositionText.text = "FINISHED 1st";

            if ( finalPosition == 2 )
                finalPositionText.text = "FINISHED 2nd";

            if ( finalPosition == 3 )
                finalPositionText.text = "FINISHED 3rd";

            if ( finalPosition >= 4 )
                finalPositionText.text = "FINISHED";

            doneFinalMessage = true;

            finalPositionText.gameObject.SetActive(true);
```

12. Dish: *Metal Vehicle Doom*

```
                        // drop out of the race scene completely in 10
                        // seconds...
                        Invoke( "FinishRace", 10 );
        }
    }

    void FinishRace ()
    {
        Application.LoadLevel( "menu_MVD" );
    }

    void ShowCount1 ()
    {
        count1.SetActive( true );
        count2.SetActive( false );
        count3.SetActive( false );
    }
    void ShowCount2 ()
    {
        count1.SetActive( false );
        count2.SetActive( true );
        count3.SetActive( false );
    }
    void ShowCount3 ()
    {
        count1.SetActive( false );
        count2.SetActive( false );
        count3.SetActive( true );
    }
    void HideCount ()
    {
        count1.SetActive( false );
        count2.SetActive( false );
        count3.SetActive( false );
    }

    public void UpdateWrongWay ( bool isWrongWay )
    {
                if( isWrongWay==oldIsWrongWay)
                    return;

                if ( isWrongWay )
        {
            wrongWaySign.SetActive( true );
        }
        else
        {
            wrongWaySign.SetActive( false );
        }

                oldIsWrongWay=isWrongWay;
    }
        public void PlayerHit (Transform whichPlayer)
        {
                // tell our sound controller to play an explosion sound
                BaseSoundController.Instance.PlaySoundByIndex( 1,
                whichPlayer.position );
```

```
                // call the explosion function!
                Explode( whichPlayer.position );
        }

        public void PlayerBigHit(Transform whichPlayer)
        {
                // tell our sound controller to play an explosion sound
                BaseSoundController.Instance.PlaySoundByIndex( 2,
                whichPlayer.position );

                // call the explosion function!
                Explode( whichPlayer.position );
        }

        public void Explode ( Vector3 aPosition )
        {
                // instantiate an explosion at the position passed into this
                // function
                Instantiate( explosionPrefab,aPosition, Quaternion.identity );
        }
}
```

12.3.1.1 Script Breakdown

The script derives from BaseGameController.cs:

```
using UnityEngine;
using System.Collections;

public class GameController_MVD : BaseGameController
{
```

The variable Instance is set to this instance of the script when it is first created and the script's constructor gets called:

```
public GameController_MVD ()
{
    Instance = this;
}
```

A call to Init() is made:

```
void Start ()
{
    Init();
}
```

The Init() function starts by setting Time.timeScale, in this example game gameSpeed is set to make the game run a little faster:

```
void Init ()
{
    // in case we need to change the timescale, it gets set here
    Time.timeScale = gameSpeed;
```

This game uses a race manager script. As discussed at the beginning of this chapter, the race manager tracks race state for both the individual players and the race overall. The game controller needs to tell the race manager, held in the variable GlobalRaceManager, that the race is beginning, and a new race should be initialized:

```
// tell race manager to prepare for the race
GlobalRaceManager.Instance.InitNewRace( totalLaps );
```

The spawn system requires two arrays to be passed into it for spawning the players, for the start positions and the start rotations. In this code, the arrays are initialized and populated with positions and rotations from the startPoints array:

```
// initialize some temporary arrays we can use to set up the
// players
Vector3 [] playerStarts = new Vector3 [numberOfRacers];
Quaternion [] playerRotations = new Quaternion [numberOfRacers];

// we are going to use the array full of start positions that must
// be set in the editor, which means we always need to make sure
// that there are enough start positions for the number of players

for ( int i = 0; i < numberOfRacers; i++ )
{
    // grab position and rotation values from start position
    // transforms set in the inspector
    playerStarts [i] = (Vector3) startPoints [i].position;
    playerRotations [i] = ( Quaternion ) startPoints [i].rotation;
}
```

Now that the script has positions and rotations for the players, an instance of SpawnController may be called upon to add the players to the scene:

```
SpawnController.Instance.SetUpPlayers( playerPrefabList,
playerStarts, playerRotations, playerParent, numberOfRacers );
```

playerTransforms is filled with all of the transforms for the players. We get to them by calling SpawnController.Instance.GetAllSpawnedPlayers(), which returns all of the player transforms created by the spawn controller:

```
playerTransforms=new ArrayList();

// now let's grab references to each player's controller
// script
playerTransforms =
SpawnController.Instance.GetAllSpawnedPlayers();
```

When the game controller needs to communicate with the players, it uses references to them from an array called playerList. The next part of the code iterates through the playerTransforms array (using the value held in numberOfRacers as a total count) and uses GameObject. GetComponent() to find each instance of the CarController_MVD.cs script attached to each player. As the code steps through each player, it also uses GetComponent() to find its AI controller script to tell it which waypoint control script to use and calls its Init() function:

```
playerList=new ArrayList();
```

```
                    for ( int i = 0; i < numberOfRacers; i++ )
    {
                Transform tempT= (Transform)playerTransforms[i];
                CarController_MVD tempController=
                tempT.GetComponent<CarController_MVD>();

                playerList.Add(tempController);

                BaseAIController tempAI=tempController.GetComponent<
                BaseAIController>();

                // tell each player where to find the waypoints
                tempAI.SetWayController(WaypointControllerForAI);

                tempController.Init ();

                // tell the car controller script about the waypoint
                // controller so it can pass it on to the
                // racecontroller (!)
```

The variable WaypointControllerForAI should be set to reference the waypoint controller in the main scene (via the Unity editor Inspector window):

```
                tempController.SetWayController(WaypointControllerForAI);
    }
```

playerGO1 will store a reference to the main player's gameObject, which is returned by the spawn controller when we ask for it by index:

```
        // grab a ref to the player's gameobject for later use
        playerGO1 = SpawnController.Instance.GetPlayerGO( 0 );
```

Once a reference to the main player is established, the game controller adds an AudioListener component to it. By default, Unity adds an audio listener to the main camera of the scene. This is great for a start, but in this case, it makes more sense to have the listener attached to the player; the user is supposed to be in the car, not in the camera:

```
        // add an audio listener to the first car so that the audio
        // is based from the car rather than from the main camera
        playerGO1.AddComponent<AudioListener>();
```

Next, the game controller looks to try to find the default AudioListener component attached to the camera. If it finds one, the next part of the code uses the Destroy() function to remove it. Removing the listener from the camera is important, as Unity only allows for a single listener per scene, and if there is more than one listener, a warning will be written to the console:

```
        // look at the main camera and see if it has an audio
        // listener attached
        AudioListener tempListener=
        Camera.main.GetComponent<AudioListener>();

        // if we found a listener, let's destroy it
        if( tempListener!=null )
                Destroy(tempListener);
```

To access the user's car controller script quickly, the game controller stores a reference to it in the variable focusPlayerScript, so named because it is the player on which the game controller will focus:

```
focusPlayerScript = ( CarController_MVD )
playerGO1.GetComponent<CarController_MVD>();
```

The user's player script is given an ID number of 0, and user input is allowed with a call to SetUserInput():

```
// assign this player the id of 0
focusPlayerScript.SetID( 0 );

// set player control
focusPlayerScript.SetUserInput( true );
```

For the camera to follow the player during the game, the camera control script needs to know about its target. This script uses the SetTarget() function to do that, passing in the transform from playerGO1:

```
// tell the camera script to target this new player
cameraScript.SetTarget( playerGO1.transform );
```

UpdateLapCounter is used to set the current lap to be displayed by the UI code. Its default value of 1 gets set here so that the display is correct when the game starts:

```
// do initial lap counter display
UpdateLapCounter( 1 );
```

Players need to be held in place until the 3-2-1 countdown at the start of the race has finished. The function SetPlayerLocks will loop through all of the players in the game and tell them whether or not they should be locked in place:

```
// lock all the players on the spot until we're ready to go
SetPlayerLocks( true );
```

The 3-2-1 countdown is about to begin. It will take 4 s to go through it so the game controller schedules a call to StartRace in 4 s time using the Invoke function:

```
// start the game in 3 seconds from now
Invoke( "StartRace", 4 );
```

There is no need for the user interface to update every frame or every step. It would be an unnecessary load on the CPU to update positions like that, so instead, the game controller schedules a repeating call to the UpdatePositions() every half second. The InvokeRepeating function takes three parameters: the name of the function to call, the time from the call to the first function call, and the time between each function call after that and ongoing until either this script instance is destroyed or CancelInvoke is called to stop the continuing calls:

```
// update positions throughout the race, but we don't need
// to do this every frame, so just do it every half a second
// instead
InvokeRepeating( "UpdatePositions", 0.5f, 0.5f );
```

All three of the 3-2-1 countdown numbers should be hidden at the start of the game (otherwise, we'll just have a big blob of all three numbers on the screen at the same time!). A call to the game controller's HideCount() function takes care of that:

```
// hide our count in numbers
HideCount();
```

The code to make the 3-2-1 countdown happen is made simple by Unity's Invoke function. The functions that the game controller uses to display each number will hide each previously displayed number, so all that needs to be done is some staggered calling to each one followed by a final call to HideCount() to hide the final number at the end of the countdown sequence:

```
// schedule count in messages
Invoke( "ShowCount3", 1 );
Invoke( "ShowCount2", 2 );
Invoke( "ShowCount1", 3 );
Invoke( "HideCount", 4 );
```

When the race is over, the finalPositionText gameObject will be shown. It contains a GUIText component to display text telling the user what his/her final race position was. Of course, at the start of the race, this should be hidden. GameObject.SetActive() hides it here:

```
// hide final position text
finalPositionText.gameObject.SetActive( false );
```

After the final position message has been shown, a Boolean variable called done-FinalMessage will be set to avoid multiple calls for it to be shown. Here in the Init() function, doneFinalMessage gets reset to false:

```
doneFinalMessage = false;
```

The final in-game message that needs to be hidden is the wrong-way message. Its gameObject is referenced in the wrongWaySign variable and GameObject.SetActive() is used to hide it:

```
// start by hiding our wrong way message
wrongWaySign.SetActive( false );
```

The Init() function is done, so didInit gets set to true so that other scripts (and other parts of this script) know that the game should be ready to go:

```
    didInit=true;
}
```

When the race actually starts (after the 3-2-1 countdown), all of the cars need to be unlocked. SetPlayerLocks() is called here in the StartRace() function, setting all players' lock states to false.

The GlobalRaceManager race manager script instance gets a call to StartRace(), too, so that its management of the race states can get started:

```
void StartRace ()
{
        // the SetPlayerLocks function tells all players to unlock
    SetPlayerLocks( false );

        // tell the global race manager that we are now racing
        GlobalRaceManager.Instance.StartRace();
}
```

Called a few times by the script already in this section, the SetPlayerLocks() function tells players whether or not they should be locked in place. As discussed in Chapter 5, when the vehicle controller is outlined, locking the vehicles will constrain them along their x- and z-axes but not on the y-axis. This is so that the vehicle will still be affected by gravity; it can use its own suspension code, and the car will look natural at the beginning of the game. If the vehicle's y-axis were locked too, the car would sit exactly at its start position in the game world (which may be slightly above ground or perhaps too low) and not in its natural resting spot against the ground.

In SetPlayerLocks(), all of the play scripts held in the playerList array are called on with the SetLock() function to pass on the required lock state:

```
void SetPlayerLocks ( bool aState )
{
    // tell all of the players to set their locks
    for ( int i = 0; i < numberOfRacers; i++ )
    {
                thePlayerScript = ( CarController_MVD ) playerList
                [i];
        thePlayerScript.SetLock( aState );
    }
}
```

UpdatePositions() asks the global race manager for the position of the first player (since we know that the main player was added to the game before any of the others as it was the top of the list). The focusPlayerRacePosition variable takes the return value of the call:

```
void UpdatePositions()
{
        // here we need to talk to the race controller to get what
        // we need to display on screen
        focusPlayerRacePosition=
        GlobalRaceManager.Instance.GetPosition(1);
```

theLap is an integer. Here it is set to the return value from a call to the race manager asking for how many laps player number 1 has completed. We also add an extra lap to this return value, since we are looking to find out which lap the player is currently at, not how many laps the player has completed:

```
        theLap= GlobalRaceManager.Instance.GetLapsDone(1) +1;
```

Now that this function has the player's race position and current lap number, these numbers are fed to the UI system to be displayed on screen:

```
        // update the display
        UpdateRacePositionText();
        UpdateLapCounter(theLap);
}
```

The game controller for this game also deals with updating the text on the user interface lap counter directly. The current lap number is passed into UpdateLapCounter() as a parameter, and then it gets checked to make sure that the lap number is within the total laps for the race. If it is too high, it will be capped at the value of totalLaps before the user interface text is set:

```
void UpdateLapCounter ( int theLap )
{
    // if we've finished all the laps we need to finish, let's cap the
    // number so that we can have the AI cars continue going around the
    // track without any negative implications
    if ( theLap > totalLaps )
        theLap = totalLaps;

    // now we set the text of our GUIText object lap count display
    lapText.text = "Lap " + theLap.ToString() + " of " +
    totalLaps.ToString();
}
```

The UpdateRacePositionText() function updates the text on the position display (the object posText is of type GUIText, referenced via the Unity editor Inspector window). The string is composed of the value of focusPlayerRacePosition and the numberOfRacers. Note that the function uses .ToString() to make the conversion between the value and the string. This appears to be optional in Unity, but it is used here as security just in case this changes in the future:

```
void UpdateRacePositionText ()
{
    posText.text = "Pos " + focusPlayerRacePosition.ToString() + " of "
    + numberOfRacers.ToString();
}
```

When the race is over, RaceComplete() gets called with an integer parameter containing the main player's final position. This is used to compose a message to relay the final position back to the user via the GUI object finalPositionText.

The function begins by checking doneFinalMessage to make sure that the message is not already being displayed (that should not happen, but I prefer to check it to keep everything safe against any unforeseen calls):

```
public void RaceComplete ( int finalPosition )
    {
        if ( !doneFinalMessage )
        {
```

There is no need to report back to the user past third position in this game, so specific messages end there. Any position higher than third will display a message simply saying "Finished" instead:

```
if ( finalPosition == 1 )
        finalPositionText.text = "FINISHED 1st";

if ( finalPosition == 2 )
        finalPositionText.text = "FINISHED 2nd";

if ( finalPosition == 3 )
        finalPositionText.text = "FINISHED 3rd";

if ( finalPosition >= 4 )
        finalPositionText.text = "FINISHED";
```

Here's the doneFinalMessage Boolean variable again, being set to true now that the message has been set up:

```
doneFinalMessage = true;
```

The finalPositionText object's gameObject was set inactive (hidden) at the start of this class by the Init() function. Since we need to display it again now, the call goes out to GameObject.SetActive() again, this time setting it to true so the message is visible:

```
finalPositionText.gameObject.SetActive(true);
```

The race is done. We know this, as the RaceComplete() function only gets called once at the end of the race. After it is called, the code below schedules a call to FinishRace() in 10 s time via Unity's Invoke function:

```
        // drop out of the race scene completely in 10
        // seconds...
        Invoke( "FinishRace", 10 );
    }
}
```

When it is called, FinishRace() will load the main menu, effectively ending the game altogether:

```
void FinishRace ()
{
    Application.LoadLevel( mainMenuSceneName );
}
```

The ShowCount1(), ShowCount2(), and ShowCount3() functions switch the active states of the user interface objects used to display the numbers during the 3-2-1 countdown at the start of the race:

```
void ShowCount1 ()
{
    count1.SetActive( true );
    count2.SetActive( false );
```

```
        count3.SetActive( false );
    }
    void ShowCount2 ()
    {
        count1.SetActive( false );
        count2.SetActive( true );
        count3.SetActive( false );
    }
    void ShowCount3 ()
    {
        count1.SetActive( false );
        count2.SetActive( false );
        count3.SetActive( true );
    }
```

HideCount() hides all three of the UI objects from the 3-2-1 countdown:

```
    void HideCount ()
    {
        count1.SetActive( false );
        count2.SetActive( false );
        count3.SetActive( false );
    }
```

To hide or show a message to the user that the main player is driving the wrong way on the track, the UpdateWrongWay() function uses GameObject.SetActive(). For that reason, the user interface objects active states only need to be updated whenever there is a change, as opposed to constant resetting. To track the changes, oldIsWrongWay holds the value of isWrongWay but only gets set if it is not the same. We can decide early on to drop out of the function, whenever isWrongWay is equal to oldIsWrongWay:

```
    public void UpdateWrongWay ( bool isWrongWay )
    {
            if( isWrongWay==oldIsWrongWay)
                return;
```

If the script execution reaches this point, the value of wrong way must have changed so the script may go ahead and set the active state of the UI gameObject referenced by wrongWaySign:

```
            if ( isWrongWay )
        {
            wrongWaySign.SetActive( true );
        }
        else
        {
            wrongWaySign.SetActive( false );
        }

            oldIsWrongWay=isWrongWay;
    }
```

The PlayerHit() and PlayerBigHit() functions are not required for a racing game, but they are here for a good reason. What they do is play an explosion sound effect and call the Explode() function to instantiate a small particle effect. When the weapons system in this book is used, these PlayerHit() and PlayerBigHit() functions will provide feedback for projectile hits:

```
public void PlayerHit(Transform whichPlayer)
{
        // tell our sound controller to play an explosion sound
        BaseSoundController.Instance.PlaySoundByIndex( 1,
        whichPlayer.position );

        // call the explosion function!
        Explode( whichPlayer.position );
}

public void PlayerBigHit(Transform whichPlayer)
{
        // tell our sound controller to play an explosion sound
        BaseSoundController.Instance.PlaySoundByIndex( 2,
        whichPlayer.position );

        // call the explosion function!
        Explode( whichPlayer.position );
}
```

For a standard racing game, just as with PlayerHit() and PlayerBigHit(), the Explode() function is not actually a requirement but instead is provided to make sure that the game controller can support the weapons system:

```
public void Explode ( Vector3 aPosition )
{
        // instantiate an explosion at the position passed into this
        // function
        Instantiate( explosionPrefab,aPosition, Quaternion.identity );
}
}
```

12.3.2 Race Controller

The race controller works with the global race manager. The RaceController.cs script is attached to each player that needs its race position and state managed by the race manager, which will be looked at in the next section:

```
using UnityEngine;
using System.Collections;

public class RaceController : MonoBehavior
{
    private bool isFinished;
        private bool isLapDone;
        private float currentWaypointDist;
        private int currentWaypointNum;

        private float waypointDistance= 110f;

        private Vector3 myPosition;
        private Vector3 diff;
```

```
            private int totalWaypoints;

            private Waypoints_Controller waypointManager;
            private Transform currentWaypointTransform;
            private Transform myTransform;
            private Vector3 nodePosition;
            private float targetAngle;
            private int lapsComplete;
            public bool goingWrongWay;
            public bool oldWrongWay;
            public bool raceRunning;
            public float timeWrongWayStarted;

            private bool doneInit;

            // we default myID to -1 so that we will know if the script hasn't
            // finished initializing when another script tries to GetID
            private int myID =-1;

            public RaceController ()
            {
                    myID= GlobalRaceManager.Instance.GetUniqueID( this );

                    Debug.Log ("ID assigned is "+myID);
            }

            public void Init()
            {
                    myTransform= transform;
                    doneInit= true;
            }

            public int GetID ()
            {
                    return myID;
            }

            public bool IsLapDone ()
            {
                    return isLapDone;
            }

            public void RaceFinished ()
            {
                    isFinished=true;
                    raceRunning=true;

                    // find out which position we finished in
                    int finalRacePosition=
                    GlobalRaceManager.Instance.GetPosition( myID );

                    // not the cleanest solution, but it means we don't have to
                    // hardwire in the game controller script type
                    // or the player control script at least. Here, we take our
                    // object and do a SendMessage call to it, to say the lap
                    // finished
```

```
                    // NOTE: if you change the name of the function
                    // PlayerFinishedRace, make sure it isn't the same as any
                    // functions in any other script attached to the
                    // player, or you could cause problems
                    gameObject.SendMessageUpwards("PlayerFinishedRace",
    finalRacePosition, SendMessageOptions.DontRequireReceiver);
        }

        public void RaceStart ()
        {
                isFinished=false;
                raceRunning=false;
        }

        public bool IsFinished ()
    {
        return isFinished;
    }

    public int GetCurrentLap ()
    {
        return GlobalRaceManager.Instance.GetLapsDone(myID) +1;
    }

        public void ResetLapCounter()
        {
                GlobalRaceManager.Instance.ResetLapCount(myID);
        }

    public int GetCurrentWaypointNum ()
    {
        return currentWaypointNum;
    }

    public float GetCurrentWaypointDist ()
    {
        return currentWaypointDist;
    }

        public bool GetIsFinished ()
        {
                return isFinished;
        }

        public bool GetIsLapDone ()
        {
                return isLapDone;
        }

        public void UpdateRaceState( bool aState )
        {
                raceRunning= aState;
        }

        public void SetWayController ( Waypoints_Controller aControl )
        {
                waypointManager= aControl;
```

```
}

public Transform GetWaypointTransform ()
{
        // if we have no waypoint transform already 'in the system'
        // then we need to grab one
        if(currentWaypointTransform==null)
        {
                currentWaypointNum=0;
                currentWaypointTransform=
                waypointManager.GetWaypoint(currentWaypointNum);
        }

        return currentWaypointTransform;
}

public Transform GetRespawnWaypointTransform ()
{
        // if we are past the first waypoint, let's go back a
        // waypoint and return that one rather than the
        // current one. That way, the car will appear roughly where
        // it despawned rather than ahead of it.
        if(currentWaypointNum>0)
                currentWaypointNum--;

        currentWaypointTransform=
        waypointManager.GetWaypoint(currentWaypointNum);

        return currentWaypointTransform;
}

public void UpdateWaypoints()
{
        if(!doneInit)
                Init();

        // quick check to make sure that we have a reference to the
        // waypoint manager
        if( waypointManager==null )
                return;

        // because of the order that scripts run and are
        // initialized, it is possible for this function
        // to be called before we have actually finished running the
        // waypoints initialization, which means we need to drop out
        // to avoid doing anything silly or before it breaks the
        // game.
        if(totalWaypoints==0)
        {
                // grab total waypoints
                totalWaypoints = waypointManager.GetTotal();
                return;
        }

        // here, we deal with making sure that we always have a
        // waypoint set up and if not take the steps to find out
        // what our current waypoint should be
        if(currentWaypointTransform==null)
```

```
            {
                    currentWaypointNum=0;
                    currentWaypointTransform=waypointManager.GetWaypoint
                    (currentWaypointNum);
            }

            // now we need to check to see if we are close enough to the
            // current waypoint to advance on to the next one

            myPosition = myTransform.position;
            myPosition.y=0;

            // get waypoint position and 'flatten' it
            nodePosition = currentWaypointTransform.position;
            nodePosition.y=0;

            // check distance from this car to the waypoint

            currentWaypointDist = Vector3.Distance(nodePosition,
            myPosition);

            if (currentWaypointDist < waypointDistance) {
                    // we are close to the current node, so let's move
                    // on to the next one!
                    currentWaypointNum++;

                    // now check to see if we have been all the way
                    // around the track and need to start again

                    if(currentWaypointNum>=totalWaypoints){
                            // completed a lap! set the lapDone flag to
                            // true, which will be checked when we go over
                            // the first waypoint (so that you can't
                            // almost complete a race then go back around
                            // the other way to confuse it)
                            isLapDone=true;

                            // reset our current waypoint to the first
                            // one again
                            currentWaypointNum=0;
                    }

                    // grab our transform reference from the waypoint
                    // controller
currentWaypointTransform=waypointManager.GetWaypoint(currentWaypointNum);

            }

        // position our debug box at the current waypoint so we can
        // see it (uncomment if you're debugging!)
    // debugBox.transform.position=currentWaypointTransform.position;
    }


    public void CheckWrongWay()
    {
            if(currentWaypointTransform==null)
                return;
```

```
                Vector3 relativeTarget = myTransform.InverseTransformPoint
                (currentWaypointTransform.position);
                // Calculate the target angle for the wheels,
                // so they point towards the target
                targetAngle = Mathf.Atan2 (relativeTarget.x,
                relativeTarget.z);
                // Atan returns the angle in radians, convert to degrees
                targetAngle *= Mathf.Rad2Deg;

                if(targetAngle<-90 || targetAngle>90){
                        goingWrongWay=true;
                } else {
                        goingWrongWay=false;
                        timeWrongWayStarted=-1;
                }

                if(oldWrongWay!=goingWrongWay)
                {
                        // store the current time
                        timeWrongWayStarted= Time.time;
                }

                oldWrongWay=goingWrongWay;
        }

        public void OnTriggerEnter( Collider other )
        {
                // if the trigger we just hit is the start line trigger, we
                // can increase our lap counter when lapDone is true
                // check the name of the trigger and make sure lapDone is
                // true
                if(     other.name=="TRIGGER_STARTLINE" && isLapDone==true)
                {
                        // increase lap counter
                        lapsComplete++;

                        // reset our lapDone flag ready for when we finish
                        // the next lap
                        isLapDone=false;

                        // tell race controller we just finished a lap and
                        // which lap we are now on
                        GlobalRaceManager.Instance.CompletedLap(myID);

                        // not the cleanest solution, but it means we don't
                        // have to hardwire in the game controller script
                        // type or the player control script at least. Here,
                        // we take our object and do a SendMessage call to
                        // it, to say the lap finished
                        gameObject.SendMessageUpwards("LapFinished",SendMess
                        ageOptions.DontRequireReceiver);

                }
        }
}
```

12.3.2.1 Script Breakdown

The RaceController.cs script is going to be tracking everything we need for a race game (other than players). It derives from MonoBehavior so that it can tap into the automated system calls to Update(), Start(), etc.:

```
using UnityEngine;
using System.Collections;

public class RaceController : MonoBehavior
{
```

Every racer will be given a unique ID by the global race manager (covered later in this chapter). When the script is on its first run, the myID variable is set to –1 so that any other scripts trying to access it will instantly know that it is not ready to be accessed. Once the script's Init() function has completed, the ID should no longer be –1, and it should be set correctly:

```
// we default myID to -1 so that we will know if the script hasn't
// finished initializing when another script tries to GetID
private int myID =-1;
```

RaceController() is automatically called by the engine when the script is first instanced. To get the player set up with an ID number as soon as possible before the race actually begins, myID is set up in the constructor (whereas it might normally be set a little later on in the Init() function).

To get a unique ID, the global race manager contains a function called GetUniqueID(). The logic behind this function ensures that each player will be awarded a unique ID at the start of each game. Its ID may then be used to identify it elsewhere. Note that GlobalRaceManager.Instance is a static variable. The race manager uses some nifty code to ensure that there is only ever one instance of the script in action at any time, which will be looked at in detail later on in this section, so don't worry about that just now.

myID is an integer, set by a call to GlobalRaceManager.Instance.GetUniqueID(). The parameter it takes is this instance of the script, so that the race manager will be able to link the ID to the script from here on:

```
public RaceController ()

{
        myID= GlobalRaceManager.Instance.GetUniqueID( this );

        Debug.Log ("ID assigned is "+myID);
}
```

Init() grabs a cached reference to myTransform and sets its doneInit Boolean to true:

```
public void Init()
{
        myTransform= transform;
        doneInit= true;
}
```

There may be occasions where other scripts need to get this player's unique ID number, which is why the GetID() function returns the value of myID:

```
public int GetID ()
{
        return myID;
}
```

When the player passes by all of the waypoints around the track, the variable isLapDone is set to true. This Boolean is used when the player hits the trigger on the start/finish line to see whether or not the lap should be increased. Increasing laps in this way (rather than just incrementing the current lap counter at the start/finish line) ensures that the player has driven all the way around the track and crosses the finish line:

```
public bool IsLapDone ()
{
        return isLapDone;
}
```

RaceFinished() is the function responsible for finding out the player's final race position and for telling the player when it is time to stop racing.

First, our internal variables are set up for use in other scripts, that is, isFinished, race Running, and finalRacePosition:

```
public void RaceFinished ()
{
        isFinished=true;
        raceRunning=true;
```

finalRacePosition gets its value by hitting up the GlobalRaceManager for its race position via GetPosition (passing in this player's ID from myID):

```
// find out which position we finished in
int finalRacePosition=
GlobalRaceManager.Instance.GetPosition( myID );
```

To tell the player that the race has finished, this script uses Unity's function gameObject.SendMessageUpwards(). What this does is send a message from this script to this gameObject and every ancestor of it. If there is a component script attached to the same gameObject this script is attached to, containing a function naming the message being sent, in this case, PlayerFinishedRace(), then it will be called.

This part of the code could have stored a reference to the player's control script directly, but that would mean hard coding the player script, which reduces the overall flexibility of this script. For example, the player control script for this game is named PlayerController_MVD. The player control script for the example game *Tank Battle* is named PlayerController_TB. If we wanted to make a reference to the player's script for this game, it would need to be held in a variable of type PlayerController_MVD, and for the *Tank Battle* game, it would need to be in a variable of a different type: PlayerController_TB. To make this script work for both games would mean that we needed to create either two separate references to the two different player scripts or two different versions of the script. Instead, SendMessageUpwards() will send out the message to everything without caring about what type of script it is talking to. Just in case there is no script attached to the same gameObject with the function PlayerFinishedRace(), the parameter SendMessageOptions.DontRequireReciever is used, which means that no errors or warnings will occur if there is no script to receive the message:

```
gameObject.SendMessageUpwards("PlayerFinishedRace",
finalRacePosition, SendMessageOptions.DontRequireReceiver);
}
```

At RaceStart(), our internal state variables isFinished and raceRunning are set to false. Note that raceRunning starts out false because it will be set by another function, a little further on from the initialization of this script:

```
public void RaceStart ()
{
        isFinished=false;
        raceRunning=false;
}
```

Other scripts may need to know whether this player has finished racing. The IsFinished() function will return a Boolean to that effect:

```
public bool IsFinished ()
{
    return isFinished;
}
```

When other scripts need to find out what the player's current lap is, the GetCurrentLap() function gets the latest information to be calculated by the GlobalRaceManager object instance. It passes in this player's ID as a parameter (so that the global race manager knows who is asking for their lap count) and adds 1 because the return value from GlobalRaceManager.Instance.GetLapsDone() will be how many laps are completed, not what the current lap is:

```
public int GetCurrentLap ()
{
    return GlobalRaceManager.Instance.GetLapsDone(myID) +1;
}
```

The game could be reset by another script, calling for the lap counter for this player to be reset, too. The GlobalRaceManager object provides the ResetLapCount() function for this, with its parameter being the player's unique ID from myID:

```
public void ResetLapCounter()
{
        GlobalRaceManager.Instance.ResetLapCount(myID);
}
```

This race controller script tracks where the player is on the track by monitoring its progress along a path of waypoints. In the example game here, those waypoints are the same ones used to drive the AI players around. By keeping tabs on the waypoints, this script may be accessed to find out where the car is and compare it to where other cars are and calculate race positions. GetCurrentWaypointNum() will return the player's current-WaypointNum integer typed variable:

```
public int GetCurrentWaypointNum ()
{
    return currentWaypointNum;
}
```

currentWaypointDist is a floating point variable containing the current distance from the player to its current waypoint in 3D units. The GetCurrentWaypointDist() simply returns its value as a float:

```
public float GetCurrentWaypointDist ()
{
    return currentWaypointDist;
}
```

GetIsFinished() and GetIsLapDone() both return Boolean values and will be used by the global race manager:

```
public bool GetIsFinished ()
{
        return isFinished;
}

public bool GetIsLapDone ()
{
        return isLapDone;
}
```

When the game starts or stops, the global race manager will call the UpdateRaceState function to tell this script whether or not the race is running:

```
public void UpdateRaceState ( bool aState )
{
        raceRunning= aState;
}
```

The waypointManager (of type Waypoints_Controller) is set up in this function, which is called by the game controller to pass in the waypoints to use for race position/ progress tracking.

```
public void SetWayController ( Waypoints_Controller aControl )
{
        waypointManager= aControl;
}
```

The current waypoint transform may be retrieved by a call to GetWaypoint-Transform(). If there is no transform already in the currentWaypointTransform variable, this function will detect that and retrieve the transform from the waypointManager object:

```
public Transform GetWaypointTransform ()
{
        // if we have no waypoint transform already 'in the system'
        // then we need to grab one
        if(currentWaypointTransform==null)
        {
                currentWaypointNum=0;
```

```
                    currentWaypointTransform=
                    waypointManager.GetWaypoint(currentWaypointNum);
        }

            return currentWaypointTransform;
    }
```

It is inevitable that a player will need to respawn at some point. This might be due to a player getting stuck, a player falling out of the game area, or perhaps a user choosing to respawn when the car is facing the wrong way along the track. Whatever the reason, there should be a little penalty involved in respawning to stop players from using it as an escape button when trouble hits.

GetRespawnWaypointTransform() is used to return a reference to a transform that the respawning code uses for positioning and rotation data. It does not return the current waypoint but instead the last waypoint passed. When this happens, it is also important to change the value of currentWaypointNum too, so that the current waypoint is not too far away from the respawn point.

When the function is called, it first checks that currentWaypointNum is more than 0 so that it can be decremented without breaking the code:

```
        public Transform GetRespawnWaypointTransform ()
        {
                // if we are past the first waypoint, let's go back a
                // waypoint and return that one rather than the
                // current one. That way, the car will appear roughly where
                // it despawned rather than ahead of it.
```

As long as it is above 0, currentWaypointNum gets decremented by 1 here:

```
        if(currentWaypointNum>0)
                currentWaypointNum--;
```

The new current waypoint is returned by the waypointManager via its GetWaypoint() function and then held in the currentWaypointTransform variable ready to be returned at the end of this function:

```
                    currentWaypointTransform=
                    waypointManager.GetWaypoint(currentWaypointNum);

            return currentWaypointTransform;
        }
```

The next function is UpdateWaypoints(), which deals with keeping track of which waypoint the player should be aiming for and updates the waypoint counter as needed. UpdateWaypoints() is called by the player control script as part of its own update sequence:

```
        public void UpdateWaypoints()
        {
```

Before any waypoint checking can happen, the class must have run its initialization Init() function and doneInit set to true:

```
        if(!doneInit)
                Init();
```

The variable waypointManager must contain a reference to a waypoint controller to continue:

```
// quick check to make sure that we have a reference to the
// waypoint manager
if( waypointManager==null )
        return;
```

It may be possible for this function to be called before the waypoint controller has finished setting up, so to avoid any problems we check to see if there are any waypoints set up and, if not, make a quick call out to waypointManager.GetTotal() to get the total waypoints and drop out of the function:

```
// because of the order that scripts run and are
// initialized, it is possible for this function
// to be called before we have actually finished running the
// waypoints initialization, which means we need to drop out
// to avoid doing anything silly or before it breaks the game.
if(totalWaypoints==0)
{
        // grab total waypoints
        totalWaypoints = waypointManager.GetTotal();
        return;
}
```

If there is no transform referenced in the currentWaypointTransform, this code assumes that this is the first run and sets currentWaypointNum to 0 before making a call out to the waypointManager.GetWaypoint() function to return a usable transform:

```
// here, we deal with making sure that we always have a
// waypoint set up and if not take the steps to find out
// what our current waypoint should be
if(currentWaypointTransform==null)
{
        currentWaypointNum=0;
        currentWaypointTransform=waypointManager.GetWaypoint
        (currentWaypointNum);
}
```

The waypoint checking works by looking at the distance between the player and the waypoint and moving on to the next waypoint when that distance gets too low. For this type of waypoint following, where steering is employed to turn left or right depending on the direction of the waypoint, the *y*-axis may be discounted. It will serve only to make the distance checking more complicated (since it would be on three axes instead of two) so the first part of this code takes the positions of the player and waypoint and copies them into variables. The copies have the *y* positions set to 0, removing the *y*-axis from any further calculation:

```
// now we need to check to see if we are close enough to the
// current waypoint to advance on to the next one

myPosition = myTransform.position;
myPosition.y=0;
```

```
// get waypoint position and 'flatten' it
nodePosition = currentWaypointTransform.position;
nodePosition.y=0;
```

The Unity function Vector3.Distance takes two Vector3 positions and returns the distance between them:

```
// check distance from this car to the waypoint

currentWaypointDist = Vector3.Distance(nodePosition,
myPosition);
```

When the distance in currentWaypointDist drops below waypointDistance, it increments currentWaypointNum, advancing to the next waypoint:

```
if (currentWaypointDist < waypointDistance) {
        // we are close to the current node, so let's move
        // on to the next one!
        currentWaypointNum++;
```

When currentWaypointNum is greater than or equal to the number in totalWaypoints, we know that the player has been all the way around the track. This is not the place to increase the lap counter, however, as the player needs to cross the start/finish line before the lap may be increased. Instead, when the currentWaypointNum goes beyond the total number of waypoints, the variable isLapDone is set to true, and the value of currentWaypointNum is set back to 0 ready to aim for the next waypoint (which is now the first waypoint):

```
// now check to see if we have been all the way
// around the track and need to start again

if(currentWaypointNum>=totalWaypoints){
        // completed a lap! set the lapDone flag to
        // true, which will be checked when we go over
        // the first waypoint (so that you can't
        // almost complete a race then go back around
        // the other way to confuse it)
        isLapDone=true;
        // reset our current waypoint to the first
        // one again
        currentWaypointNum=0;
}
```

The next part of the code will deal with the updating of the currentWaypointTransform variable to reflect any changes to currentWaypointNum. Here the code calls upon waypointManager.GetWaypoint() and stores the return value in the currentWaypointTransform variable:

```
// grab our transform reference from the waypoint
// controller
currentWaypointTransform=waypointManager.GetWaypoint(currentWaypointNum);

}
```

If you need to debug waypoint-following code, uncommenting the code below will give a visual representation of where the vehicle should be aiming. When uncommented, it will position a gameObject named debugBox at the position of the current waypoint:

```
// position our debug box at the current waypoint so we can
// see it (uncomment if you're debugging!)
// debugBox.transform.position=currentWaypointTransform.
position;
}
```

To make sure that the player is always heading in the right direction around the track, the CheckWrongWay() function uses the waypoints system to look ahead to the next way-point and check the angle of the vehicle versus the ideal angle to reach the waypoint. When the angle goes over a certain threshold (here, it is set to 90°), then the wrong-way message is displayed.

First up, the function checks that currentWaypointTransform has something in it. If this reference was at null, it would break the code. Rather than that, the check will return out of the function instead:

```
public void CheckWrongWay()
{
    if(currentWaypointTransform==null)
        return;
```

The script will use the waypoint from currentWaypointTransform to check that the vehicle is traveling in the right direction. The first step in doing that is to calculate a vector, relative to the vehicle, with Transform.InverseTransformPoint(). Essentially, what happens here is that the world vector provided by currentWaypointTransform.position is converted to the local space belonging to myTransform (the vehicle), providing relativeTarget with its vector:

```
Vector3 relativeTarget =
myTransform.InverseTransformPoint (currentWaypointTransform.
position);
```

Though a technical description of Mathf.Atan2 would be complicated, its use here can be summarized relatively easily; in this code, Atan2 is used to convert the x and z values of the vector relativeTarget into an angle:

```
targetAngle = Mathf.Atan2 (relativeTarget.x,
relativeTarget.z);
```

The result of Mathf.Atan2 will be in radians, so a quick call to Mathf.Rad2Deg is required to convert it over to degrees:

```
targetAngle *= Mathf.Rad2Deg;
```

Since relativeTarget was a vector relative to the vehicle, we can assume that the value of targetAngle of 0° will be forwarded along the vehicle's forward axis and that 90° or −90° will be out to its right or left. In effect, targetAngle now holds the result of how many degrees the vehicle (along its forward vector) is out from facing the waypoint. The next block of code looks to see whether targetAngle is −90° or 90° out and will set the going-WrongWay Boolean variable accordingly:

```
if(targetAngle<-90 || targetAngle>90){
        goingWrongWay=true;
} else {
        goingWrongWay=false;
```

If a vehicle is going the wrong way for a set amount of time, it will be automatically respawned by the game code. timeWrongWayStarted is used to hold the time at which the vehicle heading in the wrong way is first detected.

When the code no longer detects the vehicle going in the wrong direction, time-WrongWayStarted is set to −1 so as to avoid a respawn:

```
        timeWrongWayStarted=-1;
}
```

timeWrongWayStarted is, in effect, a timestamp. When the detection of a wrong way first happens, oldWrongWay will not be equal to goingWrongWay so it is safe to start the timestamp at this point. timeWrongWayStarted is set to Time.time and it will be compared to the current value of Time.time (in the CarController_MVD.cs script) to see how long has passed since the wrong way began:

```
if(oldWrongWay!=goingWrongWay)
{
        // store the current time
        timeWrongWayStarted= Time.time;
}
```

It's the end of the CheckWrongWay() function, and oldWrongWay may now be set to the current value of goingWrongWay:

```
oldWrongWay=goingWrongWay;
}
```

As discussed earlier in this section, the current lap will not be increased as soon as the player reaches the end of its waypoints. The player also needs to cross the start/finish line before the lap counter will be updated, and a simple trigger collider is used on an invisible box crossing the track. When the player hits the trigger, the OnTriggerEnter function is automatically called by the Unity engine:

```
public void OnTriggerEnter( Collider other )
{
```

Using a string to find out whether or not the trigger is hit is a bit of an inefficient way of doing things, but in this case, as there are hardly any triggers in the game, it should have little or no noticeable impact on performance. If you were building a game with many triggers, I would recommend switching this out and using either layer checking (with constants) or another method that does not involve string checking every time a trigger gets hit.

When OnTriggerEnter is called, the call contains information about the Collider that the transform has hit. The variable other is of type Collider, which means it has all the properties of a Collider and may be accessed as one. The function starts out by looking at the name of the Collider to see whether it was the start/finish line trigger. If isLapDone is true and the start/finish line trigger was hit, the code continues by incrementing the lap counter in the variable lapsComplete:

```
if(     other.name=="TRIGGER_STARTLINE" && isLapDone==true)
{
        // increase lap counter
        lapsComplete++;
```

As the lap is incremented, the end of this lap has been reached so we need to use the isLapDone variable to track the next lap. It is reset to false here:

```
        // reset our lapDone flag ready for when we finish
        // the next lap
        isLapDone=false;
```

The GlobalRaceManager instance needs to know when a lap completes so it can keep tabs on each player's current lap situation. The following line makes a call out to the GlobalRaceManager's CompletedLap() function and passes in this vehicle's unique ID to identify itself:

```
        // tell race controller we just finished a lap and
        // which lap we are now on
        GlobalRaceManager.Instance.CompletedLap(myID);
```

Finally, the function lets the player script know that a lap has been completed by sending a message upward through the component hierarchy. GameObject.SendMessageUpwards is used to call a function named LapFinished with the optional parameter to ignore whether or not the message ever actually gets received, to be safe:

```
        // not the cleanest solution, but it means we don't
        // have to hardwire in the game controller script
        // type or the player control script at least. Here,
        // we take our object and do a SendMessage call to
        // it, to say the lap finished
        gameObject.SendMessageUpwards("LapFinished",
        SendMessageOptions.DontRequireReceiver);

    }
  }
}
```

12.3.3 Global Race Manager

The race controller script manages data for each player and registers itself with the global race manager as it instantiates. The global race manager then takes care of managing the bigger picture, dealing with comparing players to calculate race positions and keeping tabs on laps and global race state.

Below is the GlobalRaceManager.cs script in full:

```
using UnityEngine;
```

```csharp
using System.Collections;

public class GlobalRaceManager : ScriptableObject
{
        public int totalLaps;
        private int currentID;

        private Hashtable raceControllers;
        private Hashtable racePositions;
        private Hashtable raceLaps;
        private Hashtable raceFinished;

        private int numberOfRacers;

        private int myPos;
        private bool isAhead;
        private RaceController tempRC;
        private RaceController focusPlayerScript;
        private bool raceRunning;

        private static GlobalRaceManager instance;

        public static GlobalRaceManager Instance
        {
                get
                {
                        if (instance == null)
                        {
                                instance =  ScriptableObject.CreateInstance
                                <GlobalRaceManager>();
                        }
                        return instance;
                }
        }

        public void OnApplicationQuit ()
        {
                instance = null;
        }

        public void InitNewRace( int howManyLaps )
        {
                // initialize our hashtables ready for putting objects into
                racePositions= new Hashtable();
                raceLaps= new Hashtable();
                raceFinished= new Hashtable();
                raceControllers= new Hashtable();

                totalLaps= howManyLaps;
        }

        public int GetUniqueID(RaceController theRaceController)
        {
                // whenever an id is requested, we increment the ID counter.
                // This value never gets reset, so it should always return a
                // unique id (NOTE: these are unique to each race)
                currentID++;
```

```
        // now set up some default data for this new player

        // this player will be on its first lap
        raceLaps.Add(currentID, 1);

        // this player will be in last position
        racePositions.Add(currentID, racePositions.Count + 1);

        // store a reference to the race controller, to talk to later
        raceControllers.Add ( currentID, theRaceController );

        // default finished state
        raceFinished[currentID]=false;

        // increment our racer counter so that we don't have to do
        // any counting or lookup whenever we need it
        numberOfRacers++;

        // pass this id back out for the race controller to use
        return currentID;
}

public int GetRacePosition(int anID)
{
        // just returns the entry for this ID in the racePositions
        // hashtable
        return (int)racePositions[anID];
}

public int GetLapsDone(int anID)
{
        // just returns the entry for this ID in the raceLaps
        // hashtable
        return (int)raceLaps[anID];
}

public void CompletedLap(int anID)
{
        // if should already have an entry in race laps, let's just
        // increment it
        raceLaps[anID] = (int)raceLaps[anID] + 1;

        // here, we check to see if this player has finished the
        // race or not (by checking its entry in
        // raceLaps against our totalLaps var) and if it has
        // finished, we set its entry in raceFinished hashtable
        // to true. Note that we always have to declare the object's
        // type when we get it from the hashtable, since
        // hashtables store objects of any type and the system
        // doesn't know what they are unless we tell it!
        if((int)raceLaps[anID]==totalLaps)
        {
                raceFinished[anID]= true;
                // tell the race controller for this ID that it is
                // finished racing
                tempRC = (RaceController) raceControllers [anID];
                tempRC.RaceFinished();
        }
```

```
        }

    public void ResetLapCount(int anID)
    {
            // if there's ever a need to restart the race and reset laps
            // for this player, we reset its entry
            // in the raceLaps hashtable here
            raceLaps[anID]=0;
    }

    public int GetPosition ( int ofWhichID )
{
            // first, let's make sure that we are ready to go (the
            // hashtables may not have been set up yet, so it's
            // best to be safe and check this first)
            if(raceControllers==null)
            {
                    Debug.Log ("GetPosition raceControllers is NULL!");
                    return -1;
            }

            if(raceControllers.ContainsKey(ofWhichID)==false)
            {
                    Debug.Log ("GetPosition says no race controller
                    found for id "+ofWhichID);
                    return -1;
            }

            // first, we need to find the player that we're trying to
            // calculate the position of
            focusPlayerScript= (RaceController)
            raceControllers[ofWhichID];

            // start with the assumption that the player is in last
            // place and work up
    myPos = numberOfRacers;

    // now we step through each racer and check their positions to
    // determine whether or not our focussed player is in front of them
    // or not
    for ( int b = 1; b <= numberOfRacers; b++ )
    {
        // assume that we are behind this player
        isAhead = false;

        // grab a temporary reference to the 'other' player we want to
        // check against
        tempRC = (RaceController) raceControllers [b];
                    // if car 2 happens to be null (deleted for example)
                    // here's a little safety to skip this iteration in
                    // the loop
                    if(tempRC==null)
                            continue;

        if ( focusPlayerScript.GetID() != tempRC.GetID() )
        { // <-- make sure we're not trying to compare same objects!

            // is the focussed player a lap ahead?
```

```csharp
                if ( focusPlayerScript.GetCurrentLap() >
                tempRC.GetCurrentLap() )
                    isAhead = true;

                // is the focussed player on the same lap, but at a higher
                // waypoint number?
                if ( focusPlayerScript.GetCurrentLap() ==
                tempRC.GetCurrentLap() &&
                focusPlayerScript.GetCurrentWaypointNum() > tempRC.
                GetCurrentWaypointNum() && !tempRC.IsLapDone() )
                    isAhead = true;

                // is the focussed player on the same lap, same waypoint,
                // but closer to it?
                if ( focusPlayerScript.GetCurrentLap() ==
                tempRC.GetCurrentLap() &&
                focusPlayerScript.GetCurrentWaypointNum() ==
                tempRC.GetCurrentWaypointNum() && focusPlayerScript.
                GetCurrentWaypointDist() < tempRC.GetCurrentWaypointDist()
                && !tempRC.IsLapDone() )
                    isAhead = true;

                // has the player completed a lap and is getting ready to
                // move onto the next one?
                if ( focusPlayerScript.GetCurrentLap() ==
                tempRC.GetCurrentLap() &&
                focusPlayerScript.GetCurrentWaypointNum() ==
        tempRC.GetCurrentWaypointNum() && ( focusPlayerScript.IsLapDone() ==
                true && tempRC.IsLapDone() == false ) )
                    isAhead = true;

                if ( focusPlayerScript.GetCurrentLap() ==
                tempRC.GetCurrentLap() && ( focusPlayerScript.IsLapDone() ==
                true && !tempRC.IsLapDone() ) )
                    isAhead = true;

                if ( isAhead )
                {
                    myPos--;
                }
            }

        }

            return myPos;
    }

    public void StartRace()
    {
            raceRunning=true;

            UpdateRacersRaceState();
    }

    public void StopRace()
    {
            raceRunning=false;
            UpdateRacersRaceState();
```

```
        }

        void UpdateRacersRaceState()
        {
                for ( int b = 1; b <= numberOfRacers; b++ )
                {
                        tempRC = (RaceController) raceControllers [b];
                        tempRC.UpdateRaceState(raceRunning);
                }
        }
}
```

12.3.3.1 Script Breakdown

The race manager has no need for system functions such as Update(), Start(), or LateUpdate(), etc., and everything it does will be activated by calls from other scripts. For that reason, it derives not from Monobehavior but from ScriptableObject instead:

```
using UnityEngine;
using System.Collections;

public class GlobalRaceManager : ScriptableObject
{
```

This script should always be accessed via its static variable Instance. Its constructor ensures that only one instance of the script exists at any time by checking to see whether its static variable named instance is null or not:

```
        public static GlobalRaceManager Instance
        {
                get
                {
                        if (instance == null)
                        {
                                instance = ScriptableObject.CreateInstance
                                <GlobalRaceManager>();
                        }
```

Once we are sure that instance contains a reference to an instance of Global = RaceManager, it can go ahead and return it:

```
                        return instance;
                }
        }
```

When a race is started, the game controller calls InitNewRace() to get Global = RaceManager ready for tracking. The parameter for this function is an integer for how many laps the race should go on for:

```
        public void InitNewRace( int howManyLaps )
        {
```

Several variables of type Hashtable are used for access to the various objects that the script will need to access. Note that we always have to declare the object type when retrieving data from the Hashtables, as Hashtables store objects of any type, and the system does not know what type they are supposed to be unless we tell it.

Hashtables have a key and a value, which makes them ideal for storing player-related info or objects. Each player's unique ID can be used to look up entries quickly in the Hashtable. They must be initialized before use:

```
// initialize our hashtables ready for putting objects into
racePositions= new Hashtable();
raceLaps= new Hashtable();
raceFinished= new Hashtable();
raceControllers= new Hashtable();

totalLaps= howManyLaps;
}
```

GetUniqueID() does more than provide a unique ID for each player of the game. When the RaceController script (RaceController.cs—discussed earlier in this chapter) calls in, it passes in a reference to itself (its instance) as a parameter. This function then stores a reference to it in the raceControllers Hashtable, with the key being its ID. We also use the unique ID to set up entries for raceLaps, racePositions, and raceFinished, which will be used by this class to track player state:

```
public int GetUniqueID(RaceController theRaceController)
{
```

Making each ID number unique is a case of incrementing an ID counter called currentID whenever an ID is called for:

```
currentID++;

// now set up some default data for this new player
```

The raceLaps Hashtable stores the current lap each racer is attempting to complete, starting at 1:

```
// this player will be on its first lap
raceLaps.Add(currentID, 1);
```

racePositions is a Hashtable for storing the current race position of each player. It is in no order, so although it is similar to a score table, there will need to be some ordering to find out who is winning the race. The default position for all of the players is in last place (note that positions start at 1 in this function, not at 0 as per arrays—for that reason, the last place is racePositions.Count+1):

```
// this player will be in last position
racePositions.Add(currentID, racePositions.Count + 1);
```

raceControllers holds all of the references to the RaceController script components attached to each player:

```
// store a reference to the race controller, to talk to
// later
raceControllers.Add ( currentID, theRaceController );
```

As the race is just beginning, not ending, the raceFinished state of this player is defaulted to false:

```
// default finished state
raceFinished[currentID]=false;
```

We may as well keep a count of how many players there are here, since all new players will have to be fed through this function. It will save having to count any array later to find out how many players there are, as the integer numberOfRacers will hold the count:

```
// increment our racer counter so that we don't have to do
// any counting or lookup whenever we need it
numberOfRacers++;
```

The currentID is returned to the RaceController calling this function, and the race controller will use it for its unique ID number throughout the game:

```
// pass this id back out for the race controller to use
return currentID;
}
```

GetRacePosition() takes an ID as a parameter and returns the race position of that player, as stored in the racePositions Hashtable. Accessing data from the Hashtable is a straightforward exercise of providing the key within square brackets:

```
public int GetRacePosition(int anID)
{
    // just returns the entry for this ID in the racePositions
    // hashtable
    return (int)racePositions[anID];
}
```

Just like GetRacePosition(), the GetLapsDone() function takes an ID as a parameter and returns the current lap count of that player, as stored in the raceLaps Hashtable:

```
public int GetLapsDone(int anID)
{
    // just returns the entry for this ID in the raceLaps
    // hashtable
    return (int)raceLaps[anID];
}
```

CompletedLap() is called by a RaceController when the player passes all of the waypoints and crosses the start/finish line. The parameter it takes is an integer, the player's unique ID:

```
public void CompletedLap(int anID)
{
```

The entry for anID in the raceLaps Hashtable is incremented by adding 1 to its current value:

```
// if should already have an entry in race laps, let's just
// increment it
raceLaps[anID] = (int)raceLaps[anID] + 1;
```

Here we check to see whether this player has finished the race (by checking its entry in raceLaps against the variable totalLaps), and if it has finished, this player's entry in the raceFinished Hashtable is updated to true:

```
if((int)raceLaps[anID]==totalLaps)
{
        raceFinished[anID] = true;
```

The function now retrieves this player's race controller from the raceControllers Hashtable, so that it can call on its RaceFinished() function to let it know that this player's race is over:

```
        // tell the race controller for this ID that it is
        // finished racing
        tempRC = (RaceController) raceControllers [anID];
        tempRC.RaceFinished();
    }
}
```

If there is ever a need to restart the race for a specific player, ResetLapCount() takes a player ID number and resets its entry in the raceLaps Hashtable to 0:

```
public void ResetLapCount(int anID)
{
        // if there's ever a need to restart the race and reset laps
        // for this player, we reset its entry
        // in the raceLaps hashtable here
        raceLaps[anID]=0;
}
```

The way this function calculates race positions is an on-demand system whereby it is only updated when a position is requested. When GetPosition() is called, the code checks that raceControllers is not null, making sure that everything has been set up correctly:

```
public int GetPosition ( int ofWhichID )
{
        // first, let's make sure that we are ready to go (the
        // hashtables may not have been set up yet, so it's
        // best to be safe and check this first)
        if(raceControllers==null)
        {
                Debug.Log ("GetPosition raceControllers is NULL!");
                return -1;
        }
```

We need to know for sure that the raceControllers Hashtable contains an entry for the ID being passed in as a parameter to this function call, or else the function will fail further along in the code:

```
        if(raceControllers.ContainsKey(ofWhichID)==false)
        {
                Debug.Log ("GetPosition says no race controller
                found for id "+ofWhichID);
                return -1;
        }
```

The first step is to grab the RaceController script instance for the player ID held by ofWhichID, from the Hashtable raceControllers. The resulting RaceController instance will be held by focusPlayerScript. The waypoint and position of the vehicle belonging to focusPlayerScript will be compared to the other racers to calculate race position:

```
            // first, we need to find the player that we're trying to
            // calculate the position of
            focusPlayerScript= (RaceController)
raceControllers[ofWhichID];
```

myPos is an integer that starts out set to the value of the variable numberOfRacers and will be decremented based on how close the race controller script reports the player is along the track:

```
            // start with the assumption that the player is in last
            // place and work up
        myPos = numberOfRacers;
```

A loop (b) goes from 1 to the value of numberOfRacers. The value of b will be used to retrieve RaceController references from the raceController Hashtable. At the start of the position calculations, we assume that the main player (focusPlayerScript) is not ahead of any other car, so the Boolean isAhead is set to false:

```
    // now we step through each racer and check their positions to
    // determine whether or not our focussed player is in front of them
    // or not
    for ( int b = 1; b <= numberOfRacers; b++ )
    {
        // assume that we are behind this player
        isAhead = false;
```

focusPlayerScript is the main player we are interested in (based on the ID passed in as a parameter), and it is the vehicle that will be compared to all the other vehicles in this main section of the function to find out whether the player is ahead of the other players or not. Here tempRC is populated with a reference to a RaceController script from another player that will be compared to the main player using the loop's variable b as its ID:

```
            // grab a temporary reference to the 'other' player we want to
            // check against
            tempRC = (RaceController) raceControllers [b];
```

To keep the function safe, tempRC is null checked just in case one of the players has somehow been removed from the game. If it is null, the continue command will move on to the next iteration of the loop without continuing to execute the rest of the code in subsequent lines:

```
            // if car 2 happens to be null (deleted for example)
            // here's a little safety to skip this iteration in
            // the loop
            if(tempRC==null)
                    continue;
```

The race controller instance held by tempRC is taken from the Hashtable based on the value of b from the loop, which means eventually tempRC will hit upon the same RaceController instance as the one held by focusPlayerScript. Before any position or waypoint checking can happen, the script compares the IDs of focusPlayerScript and tempRC to make sure that they are not the same:

```
if ( focusPlayerScript.GetID() != tempRC.GetID() )
{ // <-- make sure we're not trying to compare same objects!
```

There are several conditions we test against to find out whether the player within focusPlayerScript is ahead of the one that the loop is currently looking at.

The first condition is whether the current lap of the focused player is higher than the lap of the race controller in tempRC—if it is, we know that focusPlayerScript is ahead of tempRC:

```
// is the focussed player a lap ahead?
if ( focusPlayerScript.GetCurrentLap() >
tempRC.GetCurrentLap() )
    isAhead = true;
```

The next condition checks to see whether the current lap of the focused player is the same as the lap of the race controller in tempRC. If they are both on the same lap, we look to the waypoints to see whether the focusPlayerScript waypoint index number is greater than that of tempRC. If it is, we know that focusPlayerScript is ahead of tempRC because its waypoint is further along the track, in which case, isAhead is set to true:

```
// is the focussed player on the same lap, but at a higher
// waypoint number?
if ( focusPlayerScript.GetCurrentLap() ==
tempRC.GetCurrentLap() &&
focusPlayerScript.GetCurrentWaypointNum() > tempRC.
GetCurrentWaypointNum() && !tempRC.IsLapDone() )
    isAhead = true;
```

The third condition checks that focusPlayerScript and tempRC are on the same lap as well as on the same waypoint. From there, it checks to see whether the distance between focusPlayerScript and its target waypoint is less than tempRC's distance to its waypoint. If focusPlayerScript is closer to its waypoint (which is the same waypoint as tempRC) and tempRC has not finished its lap, then we know that focusPlayerScript must be ahead, and the script can go ahead, and set isAhead to true. Note that IsLapDone() is checked on the tempRC object because its distance may be off when the waypoint has switched over to the next lap:

```
// is the focussed player on the same lap, same waypoint,
// but closer to it?
if ( focusPlayerScript.GetCurrentLap() ==
tempRC.GetCurrentLap() &&
focusPlayerScript.GetCurrentWaypointNum() == tempRC.GetCurrentWaypointNum()
    && focusPlayerScript.GetCurrentWaypointDist() <
tempRC.GetCurrentWaypointDist() && !tempRC.IsLapDone() )
    isAhead = true;
```

The fourth condition checks that both players are on the same lap and on the same waypoint, but this time looks to see whether the focus player has registered a lap done before tempRC. If focusPlayerScript.IsLapDone() is true and tempRC.IsLapDone() is false, the script sets isAhead to true:

```
                // has the player completed a lap and is getting ready to
                // move onto the next one?
                if ( focusPlayerScript.GetCurrentLap() ==
                tempRC.GetCurrentLap() &&
focusPlayerScript.GetCurrentWaypointNum() == tempRC.GetCurrentWaypointNum()
                && ( focusPlayerScript.IsLapDone() == true &&
                tempRC.IsLapDone() == false ) )
                    isAhead = true;
```

A fifth and final condition does a similar check to the last one, only this time omitting any waypoint checking. Here the code focuses on whether the two players are on the same lap and, when they are on the same lap, whether the focusPlayerScript has finished its lap or not. When focusPlayerScript.IsLapDone() is true and tempRT.IsLapDone() is false, we know that the focused player is ahead and can go ahead and set isAhead to true:

```
                if ( focusPlayerScript.GetCurrentLap() ==
                tempRC.GetCurrentLap() && ( focusPlayerScript.IsLapDone() ==
                true && !tempRC.IsLapDone() ) )
                    isAhead = true;
```

At this point, isAhead tells us whether or not the player represented by focusPlayerScript is ahead of the current player represented by tempRC. If isAhead is true, the script can reduce the value of myPos to move the player's race position up to one:

```
                if ( isAhead )
                {
                    myPos--;
                }
            }
        }
```

By the time this loop has iterated all the way through the players, myPos shows exactly which race position the focused player is in. The function ends, returning myPos out:

```
                return myPos;
        }
```

Both functions StartRace() and StopRace() change the value of raceRunning (to true or false, respectively) and call the UpdateRacerState() function to tell the players about the change:

```
        public void StartRace()
        {
                raceRunning=true;

                UpdateRacersRaceState();
        }

        public void StopRace()
        {
                raceRunning=false;
                UpdateRacersRaceState();
        }
```

The UpdateRacersRaceState() function is used to tell all of the drivers when there is a change in the state of the race running. When it is called, each race control script, from the Hashtable raceControllers, receives a function call to UpdateRaceState(), passing in a parameter of raceRunning, the Boolean variable holding a state of whether or not the race is still running:

```
void UpdateRacersRaceState()
{
        for ( int b = 1; b <= numberOfRacers; b++ )
        {
                tempRC = (RaceController) raceControllers [b];
                tempRC.UpdateRaceState(raceRunning);
        }
}
```

12.3.4 Vehicle/Custom Player Control

The main player script, CarController_MVD.cs, hooks into the AI controller system from Chapter 9, to provide both a user- and an AI-controlled vehicle system all in one. As if that weren't enough, it also hooks into the weapon control system from Chapter 6. The script in full looks like this:

```
using UnityEngine;
using System.Collections;

public class CarController_MVD : BaseVehicle
{
        public Standard_SlotWeaponController weaponControl;

        public bool canFire;
        public bool isRespawning;
        public bool isAIControlled;
        public bool isInvulnerable;
        public BaseAIController AIController;

        public int startHealthAmount= 50;

        public BasePlayerManager myPlayerManager;
        public BaseUserManager myDataManager;

        public float turnTorqueHelper= 90;
        public float TurnTorqueHelperMaxSpeed= 30;

        public float catchUpAccelMax= 8000;
        public float originalAccelMax= 5000;
        public float resetTime= 4;

        public LayerMask respawnLayerMask;

        private BaseArmedEnemy gunControl;
        private RaceController raceControl;
        private int racerID;
```

```csharp
        private int myRacePosition;
        private bool isRaceRunning;
        private float resetTimer;
        private bool canRespawn;
        private bool canPlayFireSound;
        public float timeBetweenFireSounds= 0.25f;

        public override void Start ()
        {
                // we are overriding the Start function of BaseVehicle
                // because we do not want to initialize from here! Game
                // controller will call Init when it is ready

                myBody= rigidbody;
                myGO= gameObject;
                myTransform= transform;
        }
        public override void Init ()
        {
                Debug.Log ("CarController_MVD Init called.");

                // cache the usual suspects
                myBody= rigidbody;
                myGO= gameObject;
                myTransform= transform;

                // allow respawning from the start
                canRespawn=true;

                // save our accelMax value for later use, in case we need to
                // change it to do AI catch up
                originalAccelMax= accelMax;

                // add default keyboard input if we don't already have one
                if( default_input==null )
                        default_input= myGO.AddComponent<Keyboard_Input>();

                // cache a reference to the player controller
                myPlayerController= myGO.GetComponent<BasePlayerManager>();

                // call base class init
                myPlayerController.Init();

                // with this simple vehicle code, we set the center of mass
                // low to try to keep the car from toppling over
                myBody.centerOfMass= new Vector3(0,-3.5f,0);

                // see if we can find an engine sound source, if we need to
                if( engineSoundSource==null )
                {
                        engineSoundSource= myGO.GetComponent<AudioSource>();
                }

                AddRaceController();

        // reset our lap counter
```

```
raceControl.ResetLapCounter();

        // get a ref to the weapon controller
        weaponControl=
        myGO.GetComponent<Standard_SlotWeaponController>();

        // if a player manager is not set in the editor, let's try
        // to find one
        if(myPlayerManager==null)
            myPlayerManager= myGO.GetComponent<BasePlayerManager>();

        // cache ref to data manager
        myDataManager= myPlayerManager.DataManager;

        // set default data
        myDataManager.SetName("Player");
        myDataManager.SetHealth(startHealthAmount);

        if(isAIControlled)
        {
                // set our name to an AI player
                myDataManager.SetName("AIPlayer");

                // set up AI
                InitAI();
        }
}

void InitAI()
{
        // cache a reference to the AI controller
        AIController= myGO.GetComponent<BaseAIController>();

        // check to see if we found an AI controller component, if
        // not we add one here
        if(AIController==null)
                AIController= myGO.AddComponent<BaseAIController>();

        // initialize the AI controller
        AIController.Init();

        // tell the AI controller to go into waypoint steering mode
        AIController.SetAIState( AIStates.AIState.steer_to_waypoint );

        // disable our default input method
        default_input.enabled=false;

        // add an AI weapon controller
        gunControl= myGO.GetComponent<BaseArmedEnemy>();

        // if we don't already have a gun controller, let's add one
        // to stop things breaking but
        // warn about it so that it may be fixed
        if( gunControl==null )
        {
                gunControl= myGO.AddComponent<BaseArmedEnemy>();
```

```
                    Debug.LogWarning("WARNING! Trying to initialize car
                    without a BaseArmedEnemy component attached. Player
                    cannot fire!");
            }

            // tell gun controller to do 'look and destroy'
            gunControl.currentState=
            AIAttackStates.AIAttackState.look_and_destroy;
    }

    public void AddRaceController()
    {
            if(myGO==null)
                    myGO=gameObject;

            // add a race controller script to our object
            raceControl= myGO.AddComponent<RaceController>();

            // grab our racer ID from the race control script, so we
            // don't have to look it up whenever we communicate with the
            // global race controller
            racerID=raceControl.GetID();

            // set up a repeating invoke to update our race position,
            // rather than calling it every single tick or update
            InvokeRepeating("UpdateRacePosition",0, 0.5f);
    }

    public void UpdateRacePosition()
    {
            // grab our race position from the global race manager
    myRacePosition=GlobalRaceManager.Instance.GetPosition( racerID );
    }

    public override void UpdatePhysics ()
    {
            if(canControl)
            base.UpdatePhysics();

            // if we are moving slow, apply some extra force to turn the
            // car quickly so we can do donuts (!) - note that since
            // there is no 'ground detect' it will apply it in the air,
            // too (bad!)
            if( mySpeed < TurnTorqueHelperMaxSpeed )
            {
                    myBody.AddTorque( new Vector3( 0, steer *
                    myBody.mass * turnTorqueHelper * motor, 0 ) );
            }
    }

    private float timedif;

    public override void LateUpdate()
    {
            // get the state of the race from the race controller
            isRaceRunning= raceControl.raceRunning;

            if(isRaceRunning)
```

```
        {
                // check to see if we've crashed and are upside
                // down/wrong(!)
                Check_If_Car_Is_Flipped();

                // make sure that gunControl has been told it can
                // fire
                if(isAIControlled)
                        gunControl.canControl=true;

                // we check for input in LateUpdate because Unity
                // recommends this
                if(isAIControlled)
                {
                        GetAIInput();
                } else {
                        GetInput();
                }
        } else {
                if(isAIControlled)
                {
                        // since the race is not running, we'll tell
                        // the AI gunControl not to fire yet
                        gunControl.canControl=false;

                }
        }

        // tell the race controller to update
        raceControl.UpdateWaypoints();

        // see if our car is supposed to be held in place
        CheckLock();

        // tell race control to see if we're going the wrong way
        raceControl.CheckWrongWay();

        // check to see if we're going the wrong way and act on it
        if(raceControl.goingWrongWay)
        {
                if (!isAIControlled)
                GameController_MVD.Instance. UpdateWrongWay(true);

                // if going the wrong way, compare time since wrong
                // way started to see if we need to respawn
                if(raceControl.timeWrongWayStarted!=-1)
                        timedif= Time.time -
                        raceControl.timeWrongWayStarted;

                if(timedif>resetTime)
                {
                        // it's been x resetTime seconds in the wrong
                        // way, let's respawn this thing!
                        Respawn();

                }
        } else if (!isAIControlled){
                GameController_MVD.Instance.UpdateWrongWay(false);
        }
```

```
                accelMax= originalAccelMax;

        // do catch up if this car is falling behind in the race
        if(isRaceRunning && isAIControlled)
        {
                if(myRacePosition>3)
                {
                        // speed up
                        accelMax= catchUpAccelMax;
                } else {
                        accelMax= originalAccelMax;
                }

                // first place, let's slow you down!
                if(myRacePosition<2)
                {
                        accelMax= originalAccelMax*0.25f;
                }
        }

        // update the audio
        UpdateEngineAudio();
}

public override void GetInput()
{
        // calculate steering amount
        steer= Mathf.Clamp( default_input.GetHorizontal() , -1, 1 );

        // how much accelerator?
 motor= Mathf.Clamp( default_input.GetVertical() , 0, 1 );

        // how much brake?
     brake= -1 * Mathf.Clamp( default_input.GetVertical() , -1, 0 );

        if( default_input.GetRespawn() && !isRespawning &&
        canRespawn)
        {
                isRespawning=true;
                Respawn();
                canRespawn=false;
                Invoke ("resetRespawn",2);
        }

        // first, we make sure that a weapon controller exists
        // (otherwise no need to fire!)
        if( weaponControl != null )
        {

                // fire if we need to
                if( default_input.GetFire() && canFire )
                {
                        // tell weapon controller to deal with firing
                        weaponControl.Fire();
                }
        }
}
```

```
        void resetRespawn()
        {
                canRespawn=true;
        }

    public void GetAIInput ()
    {
            // calculate steering amount
            steer= Mathf.Clamp( AIController.GetHorizontal(), -1, 1 );

            // how much accelerator?
        motor= Mathf.Clamp( AIController.GetVertical() , 0, 1 );
        }

public void FinishedRace ()
{
    // stop allowing control for the vehicle
    canControl = false;
    brake = 1;
    motor = 0;

    // set a flag so it's easy to tell when we are done
    raceControl.RaceFinished();
}

public void SetAIInput (bool aiFlag)
{
    isAIControlled = aiFlag;
}

public bool IsFinished ()
{
    return raceControl.GetIsFinished();
}

public int GetCurrentLap ()
{
    return raceControl.GetCurrentLap();
}

public int GetCurrentWaypointNum ()
{
    return raceControl.GetCurrentWaypointNum();
}

public float GetCurrentWaypointDist ()
{
    return raceControl.GetCurrentWaypointDist();
}

public bool IsLapDone ()
{
    return raceControl.GetIsLapDone();
}

    public void SetWayController( Waypoints_Controller aControl )
    {
            raceControl.SetWayController(aControl);
    }
```

```
void OnCollisionEnter(Collision collider)
{
        // MAKE SURE that weapons don't have colliders
        // if you are using primitives, only use a single collider
        // on the same gameobject which has this script on

        // when something collides with our ship, we check its layer
        // to see if it is on 11 which is our projectiles
        // (Note: remember when you add projectiles set the layer
        // correctly!)
        if(isAIControlled)
        {
                if(collider.gameObject.layer==9 && !isRespawning &&
                !isInvulnerable)
                {
                        Hit();
                }
        } else {
                if(collider.gameObject.layer==17 && !isRespawning &&
                !isInvulnerable)
                {
                        Hit();
                }
        }
}

public void OnTriggerEnter( Collider other )
{

        int objLayerMask = (1 << other.gameObject.layer);

        if ((respawnLayerMask.value & objLayerMask) > 0)
        {
                Respawn();
        }
}

void Hit()
{
        // reduce lives by one
        myDataManager.ReduceHealth(1);

        if(myDataManager.GetHealth()<1) // <- destroyed
        {
                isRespawning=true;

                // blow up!
                myBody.AddExplosionForce(myBody.mass * 2000f,
                myBody.position, 100);
                myBody.angularVelocity=new Vector3( Random.Range
                (-100,100), Random.Range (-100,100), Random.Range
                (-100,100) );

                // tell game controller to do a nice big explosion
                GameController_MVD.Instance.PlayerBigHit(myTransform );
```

```
                                  // respawn
                                  Invoke("Respawn",4f);

                                  // reset health to full
                                  myDataManager.SetHealth(startHealthAmount);

                        } else {

                                  // tell game controller to do small scale hit
                                  GameController_MVD.Instance.PlayerHit( myTransform );
                        }
              }

              void Respawn()
              {
                        // reset the 'we are respawning' variable
                        isRespawning= false;

                        // reset our velocities so that we don't reposition a
                        // spinning vehicle
                        myBody.velocity=Vector3.zero;
                        myBody.angularVelocity=Vector3.zero;

                        // get the waypoint to respawn at from the race controller
                        tempTR= raceControl.GetRespawnWaypointTransform();
                        tempVEC= tempTR.position;

                        // cast a ray down from the waypoint to try to find the
                        // ground
                        RaycastHit hit;
                        if(Physics.Raycast(tempVEC + (Vector3.up * 300), -Vector3.up,
                        out hit)){
                                  tempVEC.y=hit.point.y+15;
                        }

                        // reposition the player at tempVEC (the waypoint position
                        // with a corrected y value via raycast)
                        // and also we set the player rotation to the waypoint's
                        // rotation so that we are facing in the right
                        // direction after respawning
                        myTransform.rotation= tempTR.rotation;
                        myTransform.position= tempVEC;

                        // we need to be invulnerable for a little while
                        MakeInvulnerable();

                        Invoke ("MakeVulnerable",3);

                        // revert to the first weapon
                        if( weaponControl!=null )
                                  weaponControl.SetWeaponSlot(0);
              }

              void MakeInvulnerable()
              {
                        isInvulnerable=true;
              }
```

```
        void MakeVulnerable()
        {
                isInvulnerable=false;
        }

        public void PlayerFinished()
        {
                // disable this vehicle
                isAIControlled= false;
                canControl= false;
                canFire= false;
                AIController.canControl= false;
                motor= 0;
                steer= 0;
        }

        void Check_If_Car_Is_Flipped()
        {
                if((myTransform.localEulerAngles.z > 80 &&
                myTransform.localEulerAngles.z < 280) || (myTransform.
                localEulerAngles.x >  80 && myTransform.localEulerAngles.x
                < 280)){
                        resetTimer += Time.deltaTime;
                } else {
                        resetTimer = 0;
                }

                if(resetTimer > resetTime)
                        Respawn();
        }

        void PlayerFinishedRace( int whichPositionDidFinish )
        {
                if( !isAIControlled )
                {
                        // tell game controller that the game is finished
                        GameController_MVD.Instance.RaceComplete
                        (whichPositionDidFinish );

                        // take over the car with AI control
                        isAIControlled=true;
                        InitAI();
                }
        }
}
```

12.3.4.1 Script Breakdown

Its script derives from the BaseVehicle class, a vehicle movement controller outlined in Chapter 5. It builds on the functionality of the base vehicle to provide the extra code needed for it to fit into the game framework and work as a game player rather than just a simple vehicle control script:

```
using UnityEngine;
using System.Collections;
```

```
public class CarController_MVD : BaseVehicle
{
```

After the variable declarations, the Start() function here overrides the Start() from the BaseVehicle class. Even though this overridden version features no actual functionality, it is important to do so since the original function (the function we are overriding) called Init() immediately, and we do not want to do that here. The Init() function will be called by the game controller for this game instead:

```
public override void Start ()
{
        // we are overriding the Start function of BaseVehicle
        // because we do not want to initialize from here! Game
        // controller will call Init when it is ready

}
```

For the CarController_MVD class, there are two Init() functions, one for the general initialization and another called InitAI() for dealing with the initialization of the AI system.

Init() begins by caching common variables:

```
public override void Init ()
{
        Debug.Log ("CarController_MVD Init called.");

        // cache the usual suspects
        myBody= rigidbody;
        myGO= gameObject;
        myTransform= transform;
```

The variable canRespawn is used to restrict respawning when a respawn is already in progress. At the start of the game, we allow respawning:

```
        // allow respawning from the start
        canRespawn=true;
```

The maximum acceleration value used for AI players will be altered to make for a more interesting race, such as speeding up an AI car so that it can catch up when it falls too far behind. For this reason, the original acceleration value needs to be stored for when we want to put the maximum acceleration value back to its original amount:

```
        // save our accelMax value for later use, in case we need to
        // change it to do AI catch up
        originalAccelMax= accelMax;
```

A default input controller is added to all players, the Keyboard_Input class:

```
        // add default keyboard input if we don't already have one
        if( default_input==null )
                default_input= myGO.AddComponent<Keyboard_Input>();
```

The BasePlayerManager should be attached to the player's gameObject. It will be needed later, so we store a reference to it in myPlayerController, then call its Init() function for the player manager to initialize:

```
// cache a reference to the player controller
myPlayerController= myGO.GetComponent<BasePlayerManager>();

// call base class init
myPlayerController.Init();
```

The car physics are very simple in this game. In a commercial racing game, there may be all manner of physics helper scripts running just to keep it upright around corners and behaving like a real car should. Advanced car physics are beyond the scope of this book, so instead we set the physics rigidbody's center of mass in such a way as to encourage the car to stay upright. If you were to comment out this line and play *Metal Vehicle Doom*, the first thing you would notice might be how easy it is to make the car roll over onto its roof when going around a corner. Changing the center of mass can have strange effects on the physics, although with a little trial and error, you may be able to reach a good enough level of stability without too much strangeness in terms of physical reaction:

```
// with this simple vehicle code, we set the center of mass
// low to try to keep the car from toppling over
myBody.centerOfMass= new Vector3(0,-3.5f,0);
```

An AudioSource is attached to the player to make a sound for the engine. The AudioClip referenced by the source should be a looping sound that will sound good when its pitch is moved up or down depending on the speed of the vehicle:

```
// see if we can find an engine sound source, if we need to
if( engineSoundSource==null )
{
        engineSoundSource= myGO.GetComponent<AudioSource>();
}
```

The RaceController (as discussed earlier in this chapter) is added next by another function called AddRaceController():

```
AddRaceController();
```

As a matter of protocol, the lap counter within the race controller is reset:

```
// reset our lap counter
raceControl.ResetLapCounter();
```

This script is set up to work with the weapon system, and we keep a reference to the weapon controller component (Standard_SlotWeaponController) in the variable weapon-Control. This code uses GameObject.GetComponent to find it:

```
// get a ref to the weapon controller
weaponControl=
myGO.GetComponent<Standard_SlotWeaponController>();
```

Next in the code, if no player manager component has been set in the Unity editor Inspector window, the code uses GameObject.GetComponent() to try to find the BasePlayerManager component. Once a player manager script is found, myDataManager is set to the data manager object belonging to the player manager.

Data manager is used to store player information (see Chapter 3 for a full breakdown on this):

```
// if a player manager is not set in the editor, let's try
// to find one
if(myPlayerManager==null)
    myPlayerManager= myGO.GetComponent<BasePlayerManager>();

// cache ref to data manager
myDataManager= myPlayerManager.DataManager;
```

This code sets up the player name and default health amount from the variable startHealthAmount. The player name is not used in this game, but we set it here as a matter of consistency across the examples:

```
// set default data
myDataManager.SetName("Player");
myDataManager.SetHealth(startHealthAmount);
```

When the isAIControlled Boolean is set to true, the player's name is set to AIPlayer and the script needs to run an InitAI() function to get the AI controller all ready to go:

```
if(isAIControlled)
{
        // set our name to an AI player
        myDataManager.SetName("AIPlayer");

        // set up AI
        InitAI();
}
}
```

AI players need a little more initialization setup than users. The InitAI() function starts out by using GameObject.GetComponent() to find the BaseAIController component:

```
void InitAI()
{
        // cache a reference to the AI controller
        AIController= myGO.GetComponent<BaseAIController>();
```

For the AI control to work, it is essential that a BaseAIController component is added to the player. Rather than error out, the script goes ahead and uses GameObject. AddComponent() to add a BaseAIController if one is not already there:

```
// check to see if we found an AI controller component, if
// not we add one here
if(AIController==null)
        AIController= myGO.AddComponent<BaseAIController>();
```

Call Init() on the controller (for more on what actually happens during Init() of the AIController, take a look at the AI system in Chapter 9):

```
// initalize the AI controller
AIController.Init();
```

Like its real-life counterpart, our cars use a steering system to move them left or right. Rather than force the car toward a particular direction, the AIController will supply inputs that our CarController_MVD script can use as though they were user inputs. As you may recall from Chapter 9, the AI system has a specific state for providing steering inputs based on waypoints. Here the AIController object is called to set its state to AIStates.AIState.steer_to_waypoint:

```
// tell the AI controller to go into waypoint steering
// mode
AIController.SetAIState( AIStates.AIState.steer_to_waypoint );
```

As this is an AI controller vehicle, the default input method needs to be disabled (otherwise, the AI may have to fight along with the player input!):

```
// disable our default input method
default_input.enabled=false;
```

The BaseArmedEnemy script from Chapter 9, Section 9.3 is used as a weapon controller. If one is not already attached to the player, one will be added:

```
// add an AI weapon controller
gunControl= myGO.GetComponent<BaseArmedEnemy>();

// if we don't already have a gun controller, let's add one
// to stop things breaking but warn about it so that it may
// be fixed
if( gunControl==null )
{
        gunControl= myGO.AddComponent<BaseArmedEnemy>();
        Debug.LogWarning("WARNING! Trying to initialize car
        without a BaseArmedEnemy component attached. Player
        cannot fire!");
}
```

The gun controller needs to shoot whenever it sees an enemy in front of it. For this, the script here sets its currentState to AIAttackStates.AIAttackState.look_and_destroy:

```
// tell gun controller to do 'look and destroy'
gunControl.currentState=
AIAttackStates.AIAttackState.look_and_destroy;
}
```

Any game could use the race controller script. It does not need to be vehicles racing either; it could be humanoids, robots, or just about anything else that moves. The race controller is attached to all players that need to be tracked in a race, and then the global race manager talks to them and tracks the race situation. No extra work required!

That said, we need to make sure that our players actually have race controllers attached to them. AddRaceController() starts by using GameObject.AddComponent() to add an instance of RaceController to this player:

```
public void AddRaceController()
{
        if(myGO==null)
                myGO=gameObject;
```

```
// add a race controller script to our object
raceControl= myGO.AddComponent<RaceController>();
```

It is also a good idea to grab the ID from the race controller to use elsewhere, keeping any ID numbers the same. racerID is an integer that gets set to the ID returned from raceControl.GetID():

```
// grab our racer ID from the race control script, so we
// don't have to look it up whenever we communicate with the
// global race controller
racerID=raceControl.GetID();
```

Every half second, this player script will call upon UpdateRacePosition() to update its position from the global race manager. An InvokeRepeating call is used to set this up on a recurring basis throughout the game:

```
    // set up a repeating invoke to update our race position,
    // rather than calling it every single tick or update
    InvokeRepeating("UpdateRacePosition",0, 0.5f);
}
```

UpdateRacePosition() asks the global race manager which position this player is in, and then stores it in the variable myRacePosition:

```
public void UpdateRacePosition()
{
    // grab our race position from the global race manager
    myRacePosition=GlobalRaceManager.Instance.GetPosition(racerID );
}
```

The UpdatePhysics() function is called each FixedUpdate() by the BaseVehicle script. The function here is an override to the original UpdatePhysics() in BaseVehicle.cs, but even though that original function has been overridden, it still exists and may still be called. When the script is allowed to control the vehicle, base.UpdatePhysics() is used to call the UpdatePhysics() function in that BaseVehicle.cs script:

```
public override void UpdatePhysics ()
{
        if(canControl)
        base.UpdatePhysics();
```

At low speeds, it can be difficult to turn the vehicle quickly. When the user crashes into a wall, that slow turning speed can make the game a very frustrating experience. The main aim of this overridden version of UpdatePhysics() is to add some turn helper force, to make the vehicle turn faster at lower speeds so that getting out of a crash may be easier. It also means that the vehicle can do some rather fun donuts on the track, but that's another story…

Here we check the value of mySpeed (which, of course, holds the player's current movement speed) and see whether it is below the value of TurnTorqueHelperMaxSpeed. The intention is that its value will be set in the Unity editor Inspector window. If mySpeed is greater than TurnTorqueHelperMaxSpeed, no helper force will be applied to the vehicle. If it is traveling below that threshold, rigidBody.AddTorque() is used to turn the vehicle:

```
        // if we are moving slow, apply some extra force to turn the
        // car quickly so we can do donuts (!) - note that since
        // there is no 'ground detect' it will apply it in the air,
        // too (bad!)
        if( mySpeed < TurnTorqueHelperMaxSpeed )
        {
                myBody.AddTorque( new Vector3( 0, steer *
                myBody.mass * turnTorqueHelper * motor, 0 ) );
        }
    }
```

The global race manager tracks the race state and whether or not the race is running, but it will also communicate it to each player's race controller. LateUpdate() starts by getting the state of the race from raceControl.raceRunning and storing it into a variable named isRaceRunning:

```
public override void LateUpdate()
{
        // get the state of the race from the race controller
        isRaceRunning= raceControl.raceRunning;
```

If the race is running, this function will go on to do all of the things we need to do during the race:

```
        if(isRaceRunning)
        {
```

We regularly call Check_If_Car_Is_Flipped() to check to see whether the car's rotation is at irregular angles, to see whether it has flipped and needs respawning:

```
                // check to see if we've crashed and are upside
                // down/wrong(!)
                Check_If_Car_Is_Flipped();
```

Whenever the race is running on an AI, gunControl should be able to fire, so gunControl.canControl is set to true:

```
                // make sure that gunControl has been told it can fire
                if(isAIControlled)
                        gunControl.canControl=true;
```

When this script is updating an AI player, inputs to drive the vehicle come from the GetAIInput() function. Otherwise, GetInput() will provide inputs from the default_input object:

```
                // we check for input in LateUpdate because Unity
                // recommends this
                if(isAIControlled)
                {
                        GetAIInput();
                } else {
                        GetInput();
                }
        } else {
```

When the Boolean variable isRaceRunning is false, the race is over for this player, and the LateUpdate() function needs to ignore input. Instead of getting the inputs for the vehicle, this code just disables the gun control script (gunControl) so that nobody can fire after the game ends:

```
if(isAIControlled)
{
        // since the race is not running, we'll tell
        // the AI gunControl not to fire yet
        gunControl.canControl=false;
}
}
```

The race controller always needs to track waypoints for position tracking and lap counting, regardless of whether or not the race is still running. raceControl does not call its own update function so the next part of LateUpdate() calls UpdateWaypoints() to keep it updating:

```
// tell the race controller to update
raceControl.UpdateWaypoints();
```

The code continues by calling CheckLock() to see whether or not the vehicle should be held in place, and then there is a call out to raceControl to CheckWrongWay():

```
// see if our car is supposed to be held in place
CheckLock();
// tell race control to see if we're going the wrong way
raceControl.CheckWrongWay();
```

When raceControl detects that the vehicle is traveling around the track the wrong way, the assumption is made that a non-AI-controlled player will be the user. The code below tells the game controller to update its wrong-way status, with a call to GameController_MVD.Instance.UpdateWrongWay():

```
// check to see if we're going the wrong way and act on it
if(raceControl.goingWrongWay)
{
        if (!isAIControlled)
            GameController_MVD.Instance.UpdateWrongWay(true);
```

When raceControl first detects that the vehicle is heading in the wrong direction, its timeWrongWayStarted variable acts like a timestamp as it is set to the value of the system property Time.time. This code checks against raceControl.timeWrongWayStarted and Time.time to see whether the vehicle has been going in the wrong way for longer than the time set by the variable resetTime:

```
// if going the wrong way, compare time since wrong
// way started to see if we need to respawn
if(raceControl.timeWrongWayStarted!=-1)
        timedif= Time.time -
        raceControl.timeWrongWayStarted;

if(timedif>resetTime)
```

```
                    {
```

If the vehicle has been going the wrong way for too long, the function Respawn() is called to put it back on the track facing in the right direction:

```
                    // it's been x resetTime seconds in the wrong
                    // way, let's respawn this thing!
                    Respawn();
            }
    } else if (!isAIControlled){
```

When this condition is met, the car is not going the wrong way and it is not an AI-controlled vehicle so a call is made to the game controller to UpdateWrongWay(), telling it that we are not going the wrong way so that the UI may be updated accordingly:

```
    GameController_MVD.Instance.UpdateWrongWay(false);
    }
```

In racing games, one common method for keeping the game interesting is to employ something called rubber banding. It gets its name from the type of effect that happens when the top speed of racers is increased when they fall too far behind and decreased when they get too far ahead—the players rubber band in front and behind the main player.

Done with some subtlety, rubber banding can help to provide an exciting race each time. When it is not handled well, the effect can be frustrating as the AI players gain the lead each time the player starts getting ahead, so use it with caution! This really is one of those unseen parts of the game that needs to be carefully balanced but that, despite having such a strong impact on gameplay, most players will not even notice exists.

To tell when it is time for an AI player to go faster and when it is time for that player to go slower, the code here looks at myRacePosition to see where this player stands. If my = RacePosition is greater than 3—meaning that this player is in fourth place or worse—then the maximum acceleration rate of the vehicle, in the variable accelMax, is set to catch = UpAccelMax to make it go faster. If the position of this player is first (myRacePosition<2), then accelMax is set to the original acceleration rate held by originalAccelMax multiplied by 0.25, slowing down the vehicle:

```
    accelMax= originalAccelMax;

    // do catch up if this car is falling behind in the race
    if(isRaceRunning && isAIControlled)
    {
            if(myRacePosition>3)
            {
                    // speed up
                    accelMax= catchUpAccelMax;
            } else {
                    accelMax= originalAccelMax;
            }

            // first place, let's slow you down!
            if(myRacePosition<2)
```

```
                    {
                          accelMax= originalAccelMax*0.25f;
                    }
            }
```

The last part of the function will update the pitch of the engine audio based on the current speed of the vehicle. This happens in the UpdateEngineAudio() function, which is called here:

```
            // update the audio
            UpdateEngineAudio();
      }
```

The GetInput() function overrides the original one found in the BaseVehicle script. This one works almost the same, with additions of the respawning functionality and weapon support:

```
public override void GetInput()
{
        // calculate steering amount
        steer= Mathf.Clamp( default_input.GetHorizontal() , -1, 1 );

        // how much accelerator?
    motor= Mathf.Clamp( default_input.GetVertical() , 0, 1 );

        // how much brake?
        brake= -1 * Mathf.Clamp( default_input.GetVertical() , -1, 0 );
```

The default_input object is of type Keyboard_Input, which has support for respawn. Finding out whether the user is hitting the respawn key is a call to default_input. GetRespawn(), which will return true or false. If the user hits the respawn key, the vehicle is not respawning already and canRespawn is true, the Respawn() function is called to reset the car, and the variables isRespawning and canRespawn are set to disable any further respawning. They will both be reset when the call to resetRespawn is made, as scheduled here by an Invoke() function set for 2 s time:

```
                if( default_input.GetRespawn() && !isRespawning &&
                canRespawn)
                {
                        isRespawning=true;
                        Respawn();
                        canRespawn=false;
                        Invoke ("resetRespawn",2);
                }
```

To keep the flexibility of still being able to work without a weapon controller, the firing input code starts with a null check on weaponControl. If default_input.GetFire() is true and canFire is set, weaponControl.Fire() is called to make the current weapon do its thing:

```
                // first, we make sure that a weapon controller exists
                // (otherwise no need to fire!)
                if( weaponControl != null )
```

```
            {
                    // fire if we need to
                    if( default_input.GetFire() && canFire )
                    {
                            // tell weapon controller to deal with firing
                            weaponControl.Fire();
                    }
            }
    }
```

When the respawn happens, a call to resetRespawn() resets the state of canRespawn to allow future respawning:

```
    void resetRespawn()
    {
            canRespawn=true;
    }
```

GetAIInput() is called when a car is AI controlled. The AI vehicles get their inputs from the AI controller script; steer and motor inputs simply come from the AIController object instead of the input object:

```
    public void GetAIInput ()
    {
            // calculate steering amount
            steer= Mathf.Clamp( AIController.GetHorizontal(), -1, 1 );

            // how much accelerator?
        motor= Mathf.Clamp( AIController.GetVertical() , 0, 1 );
    }
```

When the race is over, FinishedRace() will be called to stop control of the vehicle and to tell the race controller (raceControl) that this player is done:

```
    public void FinishedRace ()
    {
        // stop allowing control for the vehicle
        canControl = false;
        brake = 1;
        motor = 0;

        // set a flag so it's easy to tell when we are done
        raceControl.RaceFinished();
    }
```

SetAIInput() is used to tell this script whether the player should be controlled by AI or not:

```
    public void SetAIInput (bool aiFlag)
    {
        isAIControlled = aiFlag;
    }
```

When the function IsFinished() is called, it looks to the race controller for its (Boolean) return result:

```
public bool IsFinished ()
{
    return raceControl.GetIsFinished();
}
```

GetCurrentLap() looks to the race controller to find out what lap this player is currently racing to use as a return value:

```
public int GetCurrentLap ()
{
    return raceControl.GetCurrentLap();
}
```

The race controller can tell us which waypoint the player is currently at via Get CurrentWaypointNum():

```
public int GetCurrentWaypointNum ()
{
    return raceControl.GetCurrentWaypointNum();
}
```

The race controller tracks distance from the player to its next waypoint, available via its GetCurrentWaypointDist() function:

```
public float GetCurrentWaypointDist ()
{
    return raceControl.GetCurrentWaypointDist();
}
```

When all of the waypoints have been passed, but the player has not yet passed the start/finish line to increase the lap number, IsLapDone() will return true. Again, this is something held by the race controller:

```
public bool IsLapDone ()
{
    return raceControl.GetIsLapDone();
}
```

As a player is spawned by the game controller, it calls upon SetWayController() to tell the race controller about the instance of Waypoints_Controller it should be using:

```
public void SetWayController( Waypoints_Controller aControl )
{
        raceControl.SetWayController(aControl);
}
```

OnCollisionEnter is called when a collision occurs between the vehicle's Collider and another Collider in the game world:

```
void OnCollisionEnter(Collision collider)
{
```

If this is an AI controlled player, to register as a hit, the other collider involved in the collision needs to be on layer 9 (the layer used by user-controlled player projectiles). The hit will not register if either isRespawning or isInvulnerable is true:

```
if(isAIControlled)
{
        if(collider.gameObject.layer==9 && !isRespawning &&
        !isInvulnerable)
        {
```

See the Hit() function later in this chapter to see what it does:

```
                Hit();
        }
} else {
```

AI-controlled player's projectiles are on layer number 17:

```
        if(collider.gameObject.layer==17 && !isRespawning &&
        !isInvulnerable)
        {
                Hit();
        }
    }
}
```

The race controller will check for a trigger hit between this player's collider and the start/finish line trigger, but this script has an OnTriggerEnter function to check for triggers used to force a respawn. The respawn triggers are placed on the buildings and under the track in case the player falls off the track and into oblivion. Rather than letting the vehicle fall forever, a hit with a respawn trigger will make a call to the Respawn() function:

```
public void OnTriggerEnter( Collider other )
{
```

A respawn trigger is a collider, set to act as a trigger, on a specific layer. respawnLayerMask should be set in the Unity editor Inspector window to include the layer that the respawn object(s) is (are) on.

The code constructs its own layer mask for objLayerMask from the other Collider's layer (other.gameObject.layer). It then checks to see whether the respawnLayerMask contains the objLayerMask:

```
        int objLayerMask = (1 << other.gameObject.layer);

        if ((respawnLayerMask.value & objLayerMask) > 0)
        {
```

Respawn() will reposition the player back on the track, facing the right way:

```
                Respawn();
        }
}
```

When a projectile hits a player, its Hit() function is called to reduce the health level held by the data manager, which checks whether the player should explode and do any relevant effects like explosion particles or sound effects:

```
void Hit()
{
```

The data manager handles health, so myDataManager.ReduceHealth is called with a parameter of how much to reduce the health by, as an integer:

```
// reduce lives by one
myDataManager.ReduceHealth(1);
```

If the player's health is less than 1, the player needs to explode and respawn. First, isRespawning is set to true, to avoid duplicate respawn calls. Next, the script adds an explosion force around the player. If there are any other players (or physics rigidbodies) around when the player is hit, they will be pushed away from the impact point:

```
if(myDataManager.GetHealth()<1) // <- destroyed
{
        isRespawning=true;
```

rigidBody.AddExplosionForce() takes three or four parameters: the explosion force as a float value, a Vector3 position of the explosion, and the radius of the explosion, as a float. The final parameter is an optional one: a float to act as an upward modifier, making the explosion force upward as if it were from beneath the object.

The Unity documentation has this to say about AddExplosionForce():

Applies a force to the rigidbody that simulates explosion effects. The explosion force will fall off linearly with distance to the rigidbody.

The function also plays nicely with ragdolls.

If radius is 0, the full force will be applied no matter how far away position is from the rigidbody. upwardsModifier applies the force as if it was applied from beneath the object. This is useful since explosions that throw things up instead of pushing things to the side look cooler. A value of 2 will apply a force as if it is applied from 2 meters below while not changing the actual explosion position. explosionPosition is the position from which the explosion force is to be applied. explosionRadius is the radius of the explosion. Rigidbodies further away than explosionRadius will not be affected.

In this case, the explosion force is going to be a huge amount for dramatic effect: the mass of the player vehicle multiplied by 2000. The explosion is at the center of the vehicle, and the blast has a radius of 100:

```
// blow up!
myBody.AddExplosionForce(myBody.mass * 2000f,
myBody.position, 100);
```

To help the drama of the explosion, the next line makes the vehicle's rigidbody spin in random directions. rigidbody.angularVelocity is set to a Vector3 containing three random amounts from −100 to 100:

```
myBody.angularVelocity=new Vector3( Random.Range
(-100,100), Random.Range (-100,100), Random.Range
(-100,100) );
```

The game controller deals with making explosion particle effects, so the next line tells GameController_MVD about the hit:

```
                    // tell game controller to do a nice big explosion
          GameController_MVD.Instance.PlayerBigHit(myTransform );
```

After the explosion, the player will respawn 4 s later:

```
          // respawn
          Invoke("Respawn",4f);
```

In this game, the player will always be respawned with full health since the goal is not to win a battle but to make it to the finish line first. myDataManager contains a function to directly set health, which is used to restore its value to that of startHealthAmount:

```
          // reset health to full
          myDataManager.SetHealth(startHealthAmount);

     } else {
```

If the player's data manager health value is not yet at 0, there's much less drama in the reaction. Instead of a large explosion, we just tell the game controller to make a small particle effect via its PlayerHit() function:

```
          // tell game controller to do small scale hit
          GameController_MVD.Instance.PlayerHit( myTransform );

     }
  }
```

When the player is respawned, its position and rotation will be reset, and it is also important to reset its velocity and angular velocity so that the vehicle does not continue to flip or rotate after:

```
void Respawn()
{
     // reset the 'we are respawning' variable
     isRespawning= false;

     // reset our velocities so that we don't reposition a
     // spinning vehicle
     myBody.velocity=Vector3.zero;
     myBody.angularVelocity=Vector3.zero;
```

The race controller provides a waypoint suitable for using to respawn with from the GetRespawnWaypointTransform() function:

```
          // get the waypoint to respawn at from the race controller
          tempTR= raceControl.GetRespawnWaypointTransform();
          tempVEC= tempTR.position;
```

Waypoints are not always positioned in exactly the right position above the ground, so to make things work a little better, the script uses a raycast straight down from above the waypoint, to find the ground and try to position the vehicle in a good place:

```
          // cast a ray down from the waypoint to try to find the
          // ground
```

```
RaycastHit hit;
```

The raycast starts at the position of the waypoint (from tempVEC) with 300 units added straight up to it, to ensure that the raycast starts well above the ground. The ray direction is −Vector3.up (straight down), but in this call to Physics.Raycast, there is no distance set, and the ray should detect everything below it no matter how far away:

```
if(Physics.Raycast(tempVEC + (Vector3.up * 300),
-Vector3.up, out hit)){
        tempVEC.y=hit.point.y+15;
}
```

myTransform is ready to be set up to its new position and rotation:

```
// reposition the player at tempVEC (the waypoint position
// with a corrected y value via raycast) and also we set the
// player rotation to the waypoint's rotation so that we are
// facing in the right direction after respawning
myTransform.rotation= tempTR.rotation;
myTransform.position= tempVEC;
```

After the respawn, the player is made invulnerable (by a call to the MakeInvulnerable() function). Invoke() is used to schedule a call to MakeVulnerable in 3 s time, limiting the player invulnerability time:

```
// we need to be invulnerable for a little while
MakeInvulnerable();

Invoke ("MakeVulnerable",3);
```

Whenever a respawn happens, the weapon is reset to its default setting of using the first slot:

```
// revert to the first weapon
if( weaponControl!=null )
        weaponControl.SetWeaponSlot(0);
}
```

The MakeInvulnerable() and MakeVulnerable() functions just set the isVulnerable Boolean variable to true or false, respectively. When isInvulnerable is true, the collision function (OnCollisionEnter() from earlier in this script) will ignore collisions with the projectiles' layer:

```
void MakeInvulnerable()
{
        isInvulnerable=true;
}

void MakeVulnerable()
{
        isInvulnerable=false;
}
```

PlayerFinished() lets the player know that it is finished racing. As well as disabling firing with canFire set to false, everything that might drive or steer the player is disabled in this function, too:

```
public void PlayerFinished()
{
        // disable this vehicle
        isAIControlled= false;
        canControl= false;
        canFire= false;
        AIController.canControl= false;
        motor= 0;
        steer= 0;
}
```

To keep the car upright, the Check_If_Car_Is_Flipped() function simply checks the localEulerAngles of the car to see whether its rotations are out of the ordinary. These values are not exactly scientific; the rotation values it checks against were decided by trial and error until it felt right and detected most regular cases:

```
void Check_If_Car_Is_Flipped()
{
        if((myTransform.localEulerAngles.z > 80 &&
myTransform.localEulerAngles.z < 280) || (myTransform.localEulerAngles.x >
80 && myTransform.localEulerAngles.x < 280)){
```

As the vehicle is at a strange angle, resetTimer is incremented by Time.deltaTime. This provides a reference as to how long the vehicle has been potentially flipped:

```
                resetTimer += Time.deltaTime;
        } else {
                resetTimer = 0;
        }
```

When the resetTimer goes over resetTime, the player will be respawned:

```
        if(resetTimer > resetTime)
                Respawn();
}
```

As the race finishes, PlayerFinishedRace() is called by the race controller, with its final race position passed in as an integer:

```
void PlayerFinishedRace( int whichPositionDidFinish )
{
```

If this player is not controlled by AI, it must be the user. Here the game controller is told about the end of the game, and then the AI is told to take over control of the vehicle:

```
        if( !isAIControlled )
        {
                // tell game controller that the game is finished
        GameController_MVD.Instance.RaceComplete(whichPositionDidFinish );
```

```
                        // take over the car with AI control
                        isAIControlled=true;
                        InitAI();
                    }
                }
            }
```

12.3.5 User Interface

The user interface for this game is a collection of gameObjects with GUIText and GUITexture components attached. They are in the game scene (as gameObjects), referenced and managed by the game controller.

These are:

1. Final_Position—A gameObject with a GUIText component on it, displaying a message that will be shown at the end of the game to inform the user of his/her final race position.

2. in_1—A GUITexture containing a graphic showing the number 1, for the 3-2-1 countdown at the start of the race.

3. in_2—A GUITexture containing a graphic showing the number 2, for the 3-2-1 countdown.

4. in_3—A GUITexture containing a graphic showing the number 3, for the 3-2-1 countdown.

5. Text_Lap—A GUIText object positioned in the top left of the screen to show how many laps the user's player has completed.

6. Text_Position—A GUIText object positioned in the top right of the screen to show the current race position of the user's player.

7. WrongWay—A GUIText object positioned just up from the center of the screen. Its gameObject will be made active whenever the user's vehicle is going the wrong way around the track.

13 Dish: Making the Game *Tank Battle*

In 1974, Kee Games, a subsidiary of Atari, Inc., released an arcade game called *Tank!* It was a two-player game where players had to drive around a maze and destroy the other player's tank. Although its graphics were simplistic black and white from a fixed top-down viewpoint, the game was extremely advanced for the time. Its control system was outstanding; it used two single-axis (up and down) joysticks to steer each vehicle as if each stick were controlling an individual track on each side of the tank.

Tank! required two players to play; there was no artificial intelligence. Perhaps this was because of the complexity of AI programming and the technological limitations of the time, or perhaps it was a design decision; it had no apparent impact on its success, and the game was a huge hit. It would be quite a while before a single-player tank game would make it into the arcades.

I personally recall the privilege of playing a tank game in an arcade in the late 1970s; I played a multiplayer top-down tank game, but it was so long ago now that I can't be sure it was the original *Tank!* When I see screenshots, it looks very familiar, at least. Despite brushing with it at the arcades, the strongest memories of playing *Tank!* come from its later incarnation as a game for the Atari 2600 game console. Variations on *Tank!* came on a game cartridge called *Combat*, released in 1977, which included a collection of 27 variations on five game types, all tied together by the main theme in the title. Most of my time on the Atari 2600 was spent battling against my brother or my cousin, each of us trying to blast each other out of the games or beat each other's high scores. *Tank!* was a huge hit with us, and I'm sure that *Combat* would have ended up being the most worn cartridge we owned.

Sometime in the early 1980s, something arrived at my local arcade that would change my perspective on video games forever. It was the game that really fired up my interest in virtual reality: *Battlezone*.

Battlezone features vector 3D graphics and one of the most amazing arcade cabinets any 80s kid could encounter. Instead of having to stand and look at the screen to play, *Battlezone* had a viewing goggle that looked rather like binoculars. Since it was a goggle, the player had to place his/her head to it and vision was taken up entirely by the game.

Battlezone was a single-player game, with enemies controlled by artificial intelligence. Just as with the original game *Tank!*, its control scheme used two single-axis joysticks to simulate control of individual tracks; push both sticks forward and the tank moved forward, pull one back and one forward then the tank would turn. The viewpoint was first person, from inside the tank. When a projectile hit the player's vehicle, a vector-based screen glass cracking effect was displayed in front of the view as though the window of the tank had been hit. At that time, *Battlezone* was the closest thing possible to being inside a computer game. In the early 1980s, it was a truly mind-blowing experience; 3D vector graphics were new, and the submersion level offered by the game, its control system, and its goggle-based arcade cabinet were second to none.

The design for the example game *Tank Battle* plonks itself down somewhere between *Tank!* and *Battlezone*. The action takes place in a maze, with a number of AI-controlled tanks driving around the game world trying to blast each other into oblivion (see Figure 13.1). The camera view is third person, behind the tank, with a fixed turret firing projectiles forward.

Its overall structure differs a little from other games in this book, as seen in Figure 13.2.

This game may be found in the example games project, with its scenes in the Scenes/Tank Battle folder named menu_TB and game_TB.

Its prefabs are located in the Prefabs/Games/Tank Battle folder.

The most important thing to note about it is that there are several elements extremely close to those from the other example vehicle game in this book, *Metal Vehicle Doom*. The tanks are, in fact, the exact same car prefabs except for the fact that the tanks have invisible

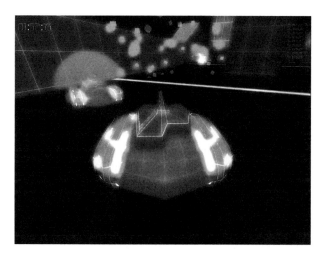

Figure 13.1 The example game, *Tank Battle*.

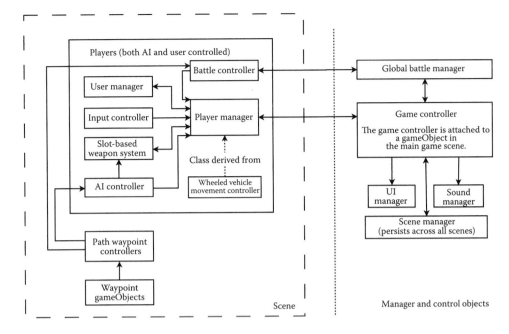

Figure 13.2 *Tank Battle* game structure.

wheels and a different body model. They work exactly the same as the cars, with a different set of parameters set to make acceleration and steering more like a tank and less like a car.

Each player has a battle controller component attached to them and a global battle manager manages the overall race state; this is the exact same format as the race controllers and global race manager scripts from *Metal Vehicle Doom*.

▇ 13.1 Main Game Scene

Tank Battle has two scenes: a main menu and the main game battle arena scene.

The main menu consists of a single gameObject, and the main menu script is shown in Chapter 10.

The main game scene Hierarchy structure contains the following:

- ARENA

  - (Models that make up the environment, including a directional light to brighten it up)

- GameController

- Main Camera

- MusicController

- Player_Startpoints
  - StartPoint_1 (1–10)
- Players
- SoundController
- UI
  - Game Over Graphic
  - Get Ready Graphic

Note that the game controller dynamically creates players and enemies, when the game starts. References to several prefabs and gameObjects are set in the Unity Inspector window:

- The game controller references these prefabs and objects:
  - Explosion prefab (a particle effect for explosions)
  - StartPoints array containing a reference to the Startpoint_X gameObjects in the scene
  - Player Prefab List array containing a reference to the Top_Down_Player prefab
- The BaseSoundController.cs script attached to the Sound Controller gameObject has an array called Game Sounds, containing references to
  - shoot1
  - explode2
  - player_explode
  - powerup
  - spawner 1
- The Spawn Controller gameObject has an instance of WaveSpawner.cs attached to it, with the following references in its Spawn Object Prefabs array:
  - Spawn_Structure1
  - Spawn_Structure2
  - Spawn_Structure3

- The UI gameObject has a script named UI_LBS.cs attached to it. It refers to

  - GAMEOVER_GRAPHIC gameObject

  - GETREADY_GRAPHIC gameObject

▌ 13.2 Prefabs

The prefabs that make up the game are as follows:

- PLAYERS

  - Tank

  - AI_Tank

- PROJECTILES

  - Tank_StandardFire

- WEAPONS

  - TankProjectileBlaster_Player

  - TankProjectileBlaster_Enemy

▌ 13.3 Ingredients

The game uses these ingredients:

1. Game Controller—The game controller script for this game derives from BaseGameController.cs

2. Battle Controller—Each player has a battle controller script attached to it, which holds information relevant to its battle stats (number of frags/number of times fragged, etc.). To be clear, a frag is a hit. When the player is destroyed, it counts as a frag.

3. Global Battle Manager—The global battle manager talks to all of the player's battle controllers and tracks global information on the state of the battle, such as player battle positions and whether or not the battle is still in progress.

4. Vehicles (tanks):

   a. Main player

   b. AI opponents

5. Scene Manager

6. User Interface—The user interface for in-game will derive from the BaseUIDataManager script from Chapter 4, which adds data management. The main menu uses the main menu system outlined in Chapter 10.

7. Sound Controller—The sound controller script from Chapter 8.

8. Music Controller

■ 13.4 Game Controller

The game controller script GameController_TB.cs looks like this:

```
using UnityEngine;
using System.Collections;

public class GameController_TB : BaseGameController
{
        public string mainMenuSceneName = "menu_TB";
    public int numberOfBattlers = 4;
        public int gameTime= 120;

    public Transform playerParent;
    public Transform [] startPoints;
    public Camera_Third_Person cameraScript;

    [System.NonSerialized]
    public GameObject playerGO1;

    private CarController_TB thePlayerScript;
    private CarController_TB focusPlayerScript;

    private ArrayList playerList;
        private ArrayList playerTransforms;

    private float aSpeed;

    public GUIText timerText;
    public GUIText posText;

        private bool isAhead;
    private CarController_TB car2;
    private int focusPlayerBattlePosition;

    public GameObject count3;
    public GameObject count2;
    public GameObject count1;

    public GUIText finalPositionText;

    public GameObject [] playerPrefabList;

    [System.NonSerialized]
    public static GameController_TB Instance;

        public Waypoints_Controller WaypointControllerForAI;
```

```
// scale time here
public float gameSpeed = 1;
    private bool didInit;

    private TimerClass theTimer;

public GameController_TB ()
{
    Instance = this;
}

void Start ()
{
    Init();
}

void Init ()
{
            SpawnController.Instance.Restart();

    // in case we need to change the timescale, it gets set here
    Time.timeScale = gameSpeed;

            // tell battle manager to prepare for the battle
            GlobalBattleManager.Instance.InitNewBattle ();

    // initialize some temporary arrays we can use to set up the
    // players
    Vector3 [] playerStarts = new Vector3 [numberOfBattlers];
    Quaternion [] playerRotations = new Quaternion [numberOfBattlers];

    // we are going to use the array full of start positions that must
    // be set in the editor, which means we always need to make sure
    // that there are enough start positions for the number of players

    for ( int i = 0; i < numberOfBattlers; i++ )
    {
        // grab position and rotation values from start position
        // transforms set in the inspector
        playerStarts [i] = (Vector3) startPoints [i].position;
        playerRotations [i] = ( Quaternion ) startPoints [i].rotation;
    }

    SpawnController.Instance.SetUpPlayers( playerPrefabList,
    playerStarts, playerRotations, playerParent, numberOfBattlers );

            playerTransforms=new ArrayList();

            // now let's grab references to each player's controller
            // script
            playerTransforms = SpawnController.Instance.
            GetAllSpawnedPlayers();

            playerList=new ArrayList();

            for ( int i = 0; i < numberOfBattlers; i++ )
    {
```

```
                    Transform tempT= (Transform)playerTransforms[i];
                    CarController_TB tempController= tempT.
                    GetComponent<CarController_TB>();

                    playerList.Add(tempController);

                    BaseAIController tempAI=tempController.GetComponent
                    <BaseAIController>();

                    tempController.Init ();

                    if( i>0 )
                    {
                            // grab a ref to the player's gameobject for
                            // later use
                    playerGO1 = SpawnController.Instance.GetPlayerGO( 0 );

                            // tell AI to get the player!
                            tempAI.SetChaseTarget( playerGO1.transform );

                            // set AI mode to chase
                            tempAI.SetAIState( AIStates.AIState.steer_to_
                            target );
                    }
            }

        // add an audio listener to the first car so that the audio
        // is based from the car rather than from the main camera
        playerGO1.AddComponent<AudioListener>();

        // look at the main camera and see if it has an audio
        // listener attached
        AudioListener tempListener= Camera.main.
        GetComponent<AudioListener>();

        // if we found a listener, let's destroy it
        if( tempListener!=null )
                Destroy(tempListener);

    // grab a reference to the focussed player's car controller script,
    // so that we can do things like access its speed variable
    thePlayerScript = ( CarController_TB ) playerGO1.
    GetComponent<CarController_TB>();

    // assign this player the id of 0 - this is important. The id
    // system is how we will know who is firing bullets!
    thePlayerScript.SetID( 0 );

    // set player control
    thePlayerScript.SetUserInput( true );

    // as this is the user, we want to focus on this for UI etc.
    focusPlayerScript = thePlayerScript;

    // tell the camera script to target this new player
    cameraScript.SetTarget( playerGO1.transform );
```

```
        // lock all the players on the spot until we're ready to go
        SetPlayerLocks( true );

        // start the game in 3 seconds from now
        Invoke( "StartGame", 4 );

                // initialize a timer, but we won't start it right away. It
                // gets started in the FinishedCount() function after the
                // count-in
                theTimer = ScriptableObject.CreateInstance<TimerClass>();

        // update positions throughout the battle, but we don't need
        // to do this every frame, so just do it every half a second instead
        InvokeRepeating( "UpdatePositions", 0f, 0.5f );

        // hide our count-in numbers
        HideCount();

        // schedule count-in messages
        Invoke( "ShowCount3", 1 );
        Invoke( "ShowCount2", 2 );
        Invoke( "ShowCount1", 3 );
        Invoke( "FinishedCount", 4 );

        // hide final position text
        finalPositionText.gameObject.SetActive( false );
        doneFinalMessage = false;

                didInit=true;
}

void StartGame ()
{
                // the SetPlayerLocks function tells all players to unlock
        SetPlayerLocks( false );

                // tell battle manager to start the battle!
                GlobalBattleManager.Instance.StartBattle();
}

    void UpdatePositions()
    {
                // update the display
                UpdateBattlePositionText();
    }

void UpdateBattlePositionText ()
{
                // get a string back from the timer to display on screen
        timerText.text = theTimer.GetFormattedTime();

                // get the current player position scoreboard from the
                // battle manager and show it via posText.text
                posText.text = GlobalBattleManager.Instance.
                GetPositionListString();
```

```
                    // check the timer to see how much time we've been playing.
                    // If it's more than gameTime, the game is over
                    if( theTimer.GetTime() > gameTime )
                    {
                            // end the game
                            BattleComplete();
                    }
        }

        void SetPlayerLocks ( bool aState )
        {
            // tell all of the players to set their locks
            for ( int i = 0; i < numberOfBattlers; i++ )
            {
                            thePlayerScript = ( CarController_TB ) playerList [i];
                thePlayerScript.SetLock( aState );
            }
        }

        private bool doneFinalMessage;

        public void BattleComplete ()
        {
                    // tell battle manager we're done
                    GlobalBattleManager.Instance.StopBattle();

                    // stop the timer!
                    theTimer.StopTimer();

                    // now display a message to tell the user the result of the
                    // battle
            if ( !doneFinalMessage )
            {
                            // get the final position for our local player
                            // (which is made first, so always has the id 1)
                            int finalPosition= GlobalBattleManager.Instance.
                            GetPosition(1);

                            if ( finalPosition == 1 )
                                    finalPositionText.text = "FINISHED 1st";

                            if ( finalPosition == 2 )
                                    finalPositionText.text = "FINISHED 2nd";

                            if ( finalPosition == 3 )
                                    finalPositionText.text = "FINISHED 3rd";

                            if ( finalPosition >= 4 )
                                    finalPositionText.text = "GAME OVER";

                            doneFinalMessage = true;

                            finalPositionText.gameObject.SetActive(true);

                            // drop out of the battle scene completely in 10
                            // seconds...
                            Invoke( "FinishGame", 10 );
            }
        }
```

```csharp
void FinishGame ()
{
    Application.LoadLevel( mainMenuSceneName );
}

void ShowCount1 ()
{
    count1.SetActive( true );
    count2.SetActive( false );
    count3.SetActive( false );
}
void ShowCount2 ()
{
    count1.SetActive( false );
    count2.SetActive( true );
    count3.SetActive( false );
}
void ShowCount3 ()
{
    count1.SetActive( false );
    count2.SetActive( false );
    count3.SetActive( true );
}

    void FinishedCount ()
    {
            HideCount ();

            // let the timer begin!
            theTimer.StartTimer();
    }
void HideCount ()
{
    count1.SetActive( false );
    count2.SetActive( false );
    count3.SetActive( false );
}

    public void PlayerHit(Transform whichPlayer)
    {
            // tell our sound controller to play an explosion sound
            BaseSoundController.Instance.PlaySoundByIndex( 1,
            whichPlayer.position );

            // call the explosion function!
            //Explode( whichPlayer.position );
    }

    public void PlayerBigHit(Transform whichPlayer)
    {
            // tell our sound controller to play an explosion sound
            BaseSoundController.Instance.PlaySoundByIndex( 2,
            whichPlayer.position );

            // call the explosion function!
            Explode( whichPlayer.position );
    }
```

```
public void Explode ( Vector3 aPosition )
{
        // instantiate an explosion at the position passed into this
        // function
        Instantiate( explosionPrefab,aPosition, Quaternion.identity );
}
}
```

13.4.1 Script Breakdown

GameController_TB.cs is very similar to the game controller used in the example game *Metal Vehicle Doom*. It derives from the BaseGameController class and uses a lot of the same logic, so rather than repeat everything here I will highlight the main differences and go through those, instead.

As per the other game control scripts in this book, it derives from BaseGameController:

```
using UnityEngine;
using System.Collections;

public class GameController_TB : BaseGameController
{
```

There are a few differences in the Init() function worth mentioning:

```
void Init ()
{
        SpawnController.Instance.Restart();

    // in case we need to change the timescale, it gets set here
    Time.timeScale = gameSpeed;
```

Unlike *Metal Vehicle Doom*, there is no lap counting in this script—the player's position, in a leaderboard-style scoring system, is tracked by the battle controller and battle manager scripts. Here in the Init() function is where GlobalBattleManager gets its call to initialize:

```
        // tell battle manager to prepare for the battle
        GlobalBattleManager.Instance.InitNewBattle ();
```

Just like *Metal Vehicle Doom*, all of the players' start positions and rotations are copied into new arrays ready to be fed to the SpawnController to set up:

```
        // initialize some temporary arrays we can use to set up the players
        Vector3 [] playerStarts = new Vector3 [numberOfBattlers];
        Quaternion [] playerRotations = new Quaternion [numberOfBattlers];

        // we are going to use the array full of start positions that must
        // be set in the editor, which means we always need to make sure
        // that there are enough start positions for the number of players

        for ( int i = 0; i < numberOfBattlers; i++ )
        {
            // grab position and rotation values from start position
            // transforms set in the inspector
```

```
        playerStarts [i] = (Vector3) startPoints [i].position;
        playerRotations [i] = ( Quaternion ) startPoints [i].rotation;
    }
```

One important thing to note is that the first player listed in the playerPrefabList (set in the Unity editor Inspector window) should always be the user's player prefab and not an AI—the script is based on the assumption that the first player will always be the one to focus on for UI, scoring, and camera following, etc.:

```
SpawnController.Instance.SetUpPlayers( playerPrefabList,
playerStarts, playerRotations, playerParent, numberOfBattlers );

    playerTransforms=new ArrayList();

    // now let's grab references to each player's controller script
    playerTransforms = SpawnController.Instance.
    GetAllSpawnedPlayers();

    playerList=new ArrayList();

    for ( int i = 0; i < numberOfBattlers; i++ )
    {
            Transform tempT= (Transform)playerTransforms[i];
            CarController_TB tempController=
            tempT.GetComponent<CarController_TB>();

            playerList.Add(tempController);

            BaseAIController tempAI=tempController.GetComponent
            <BaseAIController>();

            tempController.Init ();
```

The AI players in *Tank Battle* are going to need to know which gameObject the player is, to be able to chase and track it. We start the game with all of the tanks defaulting to look for the user. This behavior will, in fact, be overridden by the AI if it gets close enough to another AI opponent, as it will attack a close target regardless of whether or not it is the user.

Here the condition is to check to see whether the loop (i) is at a value greater than 0 so that we know this is not a user (remember that users are always the first in the playerPrefab array and will always be 0 index):

```
        if( i>0 )
        {
```

The SpawnController.Instance.GetPlayerGO() function gives back the gameObject for a specific player based on its ID passed in as a parameter:

```
            // grab a ref to the player's gameobject for
            // later use
        playerGO1 = SpawnController.Instance.GetPlayerGO( 0 );
```

Next, the user's transform is passed on to the AI player with a call to SetChaseTarget:

```
            // tell AI to get the player!
        tempAI.SetChaseTarget( playerGO1.transform );
```

In *Metal Vehicle Doom*, the default state for the AI was for it to follow waypoints in AIState.steer_to_waypoint. In this game, rather than path following, the enemy players need to go on the attack, and their first state is AIState.steer_to_target, which means that the AI provides steering inputs that should point its vehicle at its chase target:

```
                // set AI mode to chase
                tempAI.SetAIState( AIStates.AIState.steer_to_target );
                }
        }
```

The AudioListener component is removed from the camera and added to the user's tank, instead:

```
            // add an audio listener to the first car so that the audio
            // is based from the car rather than from the main camera
            playerGO1.AddComponent<AudioListener>();

            // look at the main camera and see if it has an audio
            // listener attached
            AudioListener tempListener=
            Camera.main.GetComponent<AudioListener>();

            // if we found a listener, let's destroy it
            if( tempListener!=null )
                    Destroy(tempListener);

        // grab a reference to the focussed player's car controller script,
        // so that we can do things like access its speed variable
        thePlayerScript = ( CarController_TB )
        playerGO1.GetComponent<CarController_TB>();

        // assign this player the id of 0 - this is important. The id
        // system is how we will know who is firing bullets!
        thePlayerScript.SetID( 0 );

        // set player control
        thePlayerScript.SetUserInput( true );

        // as this is the user, we want to focus on this for UI etc.
        focusPlayerScript = thePlayerScript;

        // tell the camera script to target this new player
        cameraScript.SetTarget( playerGO1.transform );

        // lock all the players on the spot until we're ready to go
        SetPlayerLocks( true );

        // start the game in 3 seconds from now
        Invoke( "StartGame", 4 );
```

The game is timed. The winner is the player who has the highest frag count when the timer finishes. A simple TimerClass script is used to manage the timing, which gets instanced here and a reference held by the variable theTimer:

```
            // initialize a timer, but we won't start it right away. It
            // gets started in the FinishedCount() function after the
            // count-in
            theTimer = ScriptableObject.CreateInstance<TimerClass>();
```

13. Dish: Making the Game *Tank Battle*

Although this is not a battle, the game follows a similar format to *Metal Vehicle Doom* in terms of its position list: a leaderboard-like scoring system. To keep this up to date, a repeating Invoke calls UpdatePositions() every half second:

```
// update positions throughout the battle, but we don't need
// to do this every frame, so just do it every half a second instead
InvokeRepeating( "UpdatePositions", 0f, 0.5f );

// hide our count-in numbers
HideCount();

// schedule count-in messages
Invoke( "ShowCount3", 1 );
Invoke( "ShowCount2", 2 );
Invoke( "ShowCount1", 3 );
```

In the *Metal Vehicle Doom* Init() function, the final Invoke call was to HideCount(), but in this function, there is something else that needs to be done before starting the game that happens in the FinishedCount() function, so the call is made to FinishedCount() instead of HideCount():

```
Invoke( "FinishedCount", 4 );

// hide final position text
finalPositionText.gameObject.SetActive( false );
doneFinalMessage = false;

        didInit=true;
}
```

Further down in the script, UpdateBattlePositionText() updates GUIText components with the current time left on the timer and a list of players and their positions on the score board:

```
void UpdateBattlePositionText ()
{
```

The TimerClass script has a function called GetFormattedTime(), which returns a string containing the time formatted as mm:ss:ms. The timer GUIText component's text is set to the function's return value here:

```
// get a string back from the timer to display on screen
timerText.text = theTimer.GetFormattedTime();
```

There is a function in the global battle manager called GetPositionListString() that will not only return a sorted score list but also return it as a formatted string with line breaks in it, ready to put right into a GUIText component:

```
// get the current player position scoreboard from the
// battle manager and show it via posText.text
posText.text = GlobalBattleManager.Instance.
GetPositionListString();
```

In all honesty, this may not be the best place for this to happen (since it's supposed to be a UI-specific function), but it does serve to keep all of the timer logic in one function. Here the timer is checked to see whether it is time to end the game.

TimerClass.GetTime() returns an integer, which is compared to the variable game-Time here. gameTime is an integer representing the game length in seconds. When the timer hits gameTime, the BattleComplete() function shuts down the game:

```
            // check the timer to see how much time we've been playing.
            // If it's more than gameTime, the game is over
            if ( theTimer.GetTime() > gameTime )
            {
                    // end the game
                    BattleComplete();
            }
    }
```

The BattleComplete() function of the *Tank Battle*'s game controller is the equivalent to *Metal Vehicle Doom*'s RaceComplete(). It tells the GlobalBattleManager to stop the battle, stops the timer, and composes a message to display via the GUIText component referenced in the variable finalPositionText:

```
public void BattleComplete ()
{
            // tell battle manager we're done
            GlobalBattleManager.Instance.StopBattle();

            // stop the timer!
            theTimer.StopTimer();

            // now display a message to tell the user the result of the
            // battle
    if ( !doneFinalMessage )
    {
                    // get the final position for our local player
                    // (which is made first, so always has the id 1)
                    int finalPosition= GlobalBattleManager.Instance.
                    GetPosition(1);

                    if ( finalPosition == 1 )
                            finalPositionText.text = "FINISHED 1st";

                    if ( finalPosition == 2 )
                            finalPositionText.text = "FINISHED 2nd";

                    if ( finalPosition == 3 )
                            finalPositionText.text = "FINISHED 3rd";

                    if ( finalPosition >= 4 )
                            finalPositionText.text = "GAME OVER";

                    doneFinalMessage = true;

                    finalPositionText.gameObject.SetActive(true);
```

Now that the final position message is on the screen, a call to FinishGame will load the main menu scene:

```
            // drop out of the scene completely in 10 seconds...
            Invoke( "FinishGame", 10 );
```

```
        }
}

void FinishGame ()
{
    Application.LoadLevel( mainMenuSceneName );
}
```

The timer is started at the end of the countdown, with a call to StartTimer():

```
void FinishedCount ()
{
        HideCount ();

        // let the timer begin!
        theTimer.StartTimer();
}
```

∎ 13.5 Battle Controller

The battle controller is *Tank Battle*'s equivalent to *Metal Vehicle Doom*'s race controller. It is applied to all players to be tracked as members of the battle, and the global battle manager will talk to these script components to keep an overall picture of the battle (managing the score board, etc.). The full script looks like this:

```
using UnityEngine;
using System.Collections;

public class BattleController : MonoBehavior
{
    private bool isFinished;

        private Vector3 myPosition;

        private Transform myTransform;
        public int howmany_frags;
        public int howMany_fraggedOthers;

        public bool battleRunning;

        private bool doneInit;

        // we default myID to -1 so that we will know if the script hasn't
        // finished initializing when another script tries to GetID
        private int myID =-1;

        public BattleController ()
        {
                myID= GlobalBattleManager.Instance.GetUniqueID( this );

                Debug.Log ("ID assigned is "+myID);
        }

        public void Init()
```

```
            {
                    myTransform= transform;
                    doneInit= true;
            }

            public int GetID ()
            {
                    return myID;
            }

            public void Fragged ()
            {
                    howmany_frags++;
            }

            public void FraggedOther ()
            {
                    howMany_fraggedOthers++;
            }

            public void GameFinished ()
            {
                    isFinished=true;
                    battleRunning=false;

                    // find out which position we finished in
                    int finalBattlePosition=
                    GlobalBattleManager.Instance.GetPosition( myID );

                    // tell our car controller about the battle ending
                    gameObject.SendMessageUpwards("PlayerFinishedBattle",
                    finalBattlePosition, SendMessageOptions.
                    DontRequireReceiver);
            }

            public void BattleStart ()
            {
                    isFinished=false;
                    battleRunning=true;
            }

            public bool GetIsFinished ()
            {
                    return isFinished;
            }

            public void UpdateBattleState( bool aState )
            {
                    battleRunning= aState;
            }

            public void OnTriggerEnter( Collider other )
            {
            }
    }
```

13.5.1 Script Breakdown

BattleController is very similar in format to the RaceController class from *Metal Vehicle Doom*. This script derives from MonoBehavior so that it can tap into the system functions called automatically by Unity:

```
using UnityEngine;
using System.Collections;

public class BattleController : MonoBehavior
{
```

When the player is hit by another player's projectile, it is deemed as a frag, and the function Fragged() is called to register it:

```
        public void Fragged ()
        {
                howmany_frags++;
        }
```

When the player's projectile hits another player, it is a frag, and the function FraggedOther() is called on the player with the projectile's battle controller:

```
        public void FraggedOther ()
        {
                howMany_fraggedOthers++;
        }
```

Just as the RaceController from *Metal Vehicle Doom* had the RaceFinished() function, the battle controller has its equivalent that will be called by the game controller when the timer reaches its limit:

```
        public void GameFinished ()
        {
                isFinished=true;
                battleRunning=false;

                // find out which position we finished in
                int finalBattlePosition= GlobalBattleManager.Instance.
                GetPosition( myID );

                // tell our car controller about the battle ending
                gameObject.SendMessageUpwards("PlayerFinishedBattle",
                finalBattlePosition, SendMessageOptions.
                DontRequireReceiver);
        }
```

The Boolean variable battleRunning is used to tell whether or not the battle is still active. When BattleStart() is called, it is set to true and isFinished set to false:

```
        public void BattleStart ()
        {
                isFinished=false;
                battleRunning=true;
        }
```

UpdateBattleState() is this script's equivalent to UpdateRaceState() in the *Metal Vehicle Doom* game. It sets battleRunning to whatever Boolean value is passed in as a parameter:

```
public void UpdateBattleState( bool aState )
{
        battleRunning= aState;
}
```

▌ 13.6 Global Battle Manager

The battle controller script manages data for each player and registers itself with the global battle manager as it instantiates. The global battle manager takes care of managing the bigger picture, dealing with comparing players to calculate score board positions and keeping tabs on the global race state.

The GlobalBattleManager.cs script in full:

```
using UnityEngine;
using System.Collections;

public class GlobalBattleManager : ScriptableObject
{
        private int currentID;

        private Hashtable battleControllers;
        private Hashtable battlePositions;
        private Hashtable battleFinished;
        private Hashtable sortedPositions;

        private int numberOfBattlers;

        private int myPos;
        private bool isAhead;
        private BattleController tempRC;
        private BattleController focusPlayerScript;
        private bool battleRunning;

        private static GlobalBattleManager instance;

        public static GlobalBattleManager Instance
        {
                get
                {
                        if (instance == null)
                        {
                                instance =
                                ScriptableObject.CreateInstance
                                <GlobalBattleManager>();
                        }
                        return instance;
                }
        }

        public void OnApplicationQuit ()
        {
                instance = null;
        }
```

```
public void InitNewBattle()
{
        // initialize our hashtables ready for putting objects into
        battlePositions= new Hashtable();
        battleFinished= new Hashtable();
        battleControllers= new Hashtable();
        sortedPositions= new Hashtable();

        currentID=0;
        numberOfBattlers=0;
}

public int GetUniqueID(BattleController theBattleController)
{
        // whenever an id is requested, we increment the ID counter.
        // this value never gets reset, so it should always
        // return a unique id (NOTE: these are unique to each battle)
        currentID++;

        // now set up some default data for this new player
        if(battlePositions==null)
                InitNewBattle();

        // this player will be in last position
        battlePositions.Add(currentID, battlePositions.Count + 1);

        // store a reference to the battle controller, to talk to later
        battleControllers.Add ( currentID, theBattleController );

        // default finished state
        battleFinished[currentID]=false;

        // increment our battler counter so that we don't have to do
        // any counting or lookup whenever we need it
        numberOfBattlers++;

        // pass this id back out for the battle controller to use
        return currentID;
}

public void SetBattlePosition(int anID, int aPos)
{
        if(battlePositions.ContainsKey(anID))
        {
                // we already have an entry in the battle positions
                // table, so let's modify it
                battlePositions[anID]=aPos;
        } else {
                // we have no data for this player yet, so let's add
                // it to the battlePositions hashtable
                battlePositions.Add(anID,aPos);
        }
}

public int GetBattlePosition(int anID)
{
        // just returns the entry for this ID in the battlePositions
        // hashtable
```

```
                return (int)battlePositions[anID];
        }

        private string posList;
        private int whichPos;

        public string GetPositionListString()
        {
                // this function builds a string containing a list of
                // players in order of their scoring positions
                // we step through each battler and check its
                // positions and build a hash table that can be
                // accessed by using the position as an index
                for ( int b = 1; b <= numberOfBattlers; b++ )
                {
                        whichPos= GetPosition( b );

                        tempRC = (BattleController) battleControllers [b];

                        sortedPositions[whichPos]= tempRC.GetID();
                }

                if(sortedPositions.Count<numberOfBattlers)
                        return "";

                posList="";

                // now we have a populated sortedPositions hash table, let's
                // iterate through it and build the string
                for ( int b = 1; b <= numberOfBattlers; b++ )
                {
                        whichPos= (int)sortedPositions[b];
                        posList=posList+b.ToString()+". PLAYER
                        "+whichPos+"\n";
                }

                return posList;
        }

        public int GetPosition ( int ofWhichID )
        {
                // first, let's make sure that we are ready to go (the
                // hashtables may not have been set up yet, so it's
                // best to be safe and check this first)
                if(battleControllers==null)
                {
                        Debug.Log ("GetPosition battleControllers is
                        NULL!");
                        return -1;
                }

                if(battleControllers.ContainsKey(ofWhichID)==false)
                {
                        Debug.Log ("GetPosition says no battle controller
                        found for id "+ofWhichID);
                        return -1;
                }
```

```
        // first, we need to find the player that we're trying to
        // calculate the position of
        focusPlayerScript= (BattleController)
        battleControllers[ofWhichID];

        // start with the assumption that the player is in last
        // place and work up
myPos = numberOfBattlers;
        for ( int b = 1; b <= numberOfBattlers; b++ )
{
    // assume that we are behind this player
    isAhead = false;

                // grab a temporary reference to the 'other' player
                // we want to check against
        tempRC = (BattleController) battleControllers [b];

                // if car 2 happens to be null (deleted for example)
                // here's a little safety to skip this iteration in
                // the loop
                if(tempRC==null)
                        continue;

        if ( focusPlayerScript.GetID() != tempRC.GetID() )
        { // <-- make sure we're not trying to compare same objects!

                        // check to see if this player has fragged
                        // more
                        // if( focusPlayerScript.howMany_fraggedOthers
                        // > tempRC.howMany_fraggedOthers )
                                // isAhead=true;
                        // we check here to see if the frag count is
                        // the same and if so we use the id to sort
                        // them instead
                        if( focusPlayerScript.howMany_fraggedOthers
                        == tempRC.howMany_fraggedOthers &&
                        focusPlayerScript.GetID() > tempRC.GetID() )
                                isAhead=true;

                        // alternative version just for fun... counts
                        // fragged times too
                        // check to see if this player has fragged more
                        if( ( focusPlayerScript.howMany_fraggedOthers
                        - focusPlayerScript.howmany_frags ) >
                        ( tempRC.howMany_fraggedOthers -
                        focusPlayerScript.howmany_frags ) )
                                isAhead=true;

                        if ( isAhead )
            {
                                myPos--;
            }
                }
        }
}

        return myPos;
}
```

```
public void StartBattle()
{
        battleRunning=true;
        UpdateBattleStates();
}

public void StopBattle()
{
        // we don't want to keep calling everyone to tell them about
        // the battle being over if we've already done it once, so
        // check first battleRunning is true
        if(battleRunning==true)
        {
                // set a flag to stop repeat calls etc.
                battleRunning=false;

                // tell everyone about the update to the state of
                // battleRunning
                UpdateBattleStates();

                // tell all players that we're done, by sending a
                // message to each gameObject with a battle
                // controller attached to it
                // to call the PlayerFinishedBattle() function in
                // the car control script
                for ( int b = 1; b <= numberOfBattlers; b++ )
                {
                        tempRC = (BattleController) battleControllers
                        [b];
                        tempRC.gameObject.SendMessage("PlayerFinished
                        Battle",SendMessageOptions.DontRequireReceiver);
                }
        }
}

public void RegisterFrag( int whichID )
{
        focusPlayerScript= (BattleController)
        battleControllers[whichID];
        focusPlayerScript.FraggedOther();
}

void UpdateBattleStates()
{
        for ( int b = 1; b <= numberOfBattlers; b++ )
        {
                tempRC = (BattleController) battleControllers [b];
                tempRC.UpdateBattleState(battleRunning);
        }
}
}
```

13.6.1 Script Breakdown

This global battle manager is, again, very similar to the global race manager from the *Metal Vehicle Doom* game we looked at in Chapter 12. For that reason, I will highlight and run through the main differences rather than repeat everything. If the reasoning or workings of anything in this script are unclear, take a look back at Chapter 12 to the global race manager.

GlobalBattleManager derives from ScriptableObject:

```
using UnityEngine;
using System.Collections;

public class GlobalBattleManager : ScriptableObject
{
```

The global battle manager starts with the code to make sure that only one instance of it exists:

```
        public static GlobalBattleManager Instance
        {
                get
                {
                        if (instance == null)
                        {
                                instance =  ScriptableObject.CreateInstance
                                <GlobalBattleManager>();
                        }
                        return instance;
                }
        }
```

InitNewBattle() initializes the Hashtables (and a couple of other variables) ready for the game. These are almost the same Hashtables as those found in the global race manager from Chapter 12, except that the word race has been replaced with battle. They do serve the same function: battlePositions refers to positions on the score board, the battleFinished table holds each player's game state, battleControllers is used to store the player's battle controller components and a new Hashtable, sortedPositions, is used to provide a formatted and sorted score board for the UI:

```
        public void InitNewBattle()
        {
                // initialize our hashtables ready for putting objects into
                battlePositions= new Hashtable();
                battleFinished= new Hashtable();
                battleControllers= new Hashtable();
                sortedPositions= new Hashtable();

                currentID=0;
                numberOfBattlers=0;
        }
```

Skipping down past a few functions in the original script now, we can see that the function GetPositionListString() provides the formatted, sorted list of players in order of their race positions, for the game controller to display as a text object.

GetPositionListString() will return a string:

```
        public string GetPositionListString()
        {
```

The sortedPositions Hashtable is constructed here by looping through all of the players. Each player's score board position is used as a key in sortedPositions, adding the value of the player's battleController:

```
// this function builds a string containing a list of
// players in order of their scoring positions
// now we step through each battler and check their
// positions to determine whether or not
for ( int b = 1; b <= numberOfBattlers; b++ )
{
        whichPos= GetPosition( b );

        tempRC = (BattleController) battleControllers [b];

        sortedPositions[whichPos]= tempRC.GetID();
}
```

In case something has gone wrong with building the sortedPositions Hashtable, a quick count check ensures that some kind of string will get returned regardless. If there has been a problem (which, in theory, should not happen), an empty string is returned:

```
if(sortedPositions.Count<numberOfBattlers)
        return "";

posList="";
```

We can now access the sortedPositions Hashtable by its score board position key. To build out the sorted string, the loop b goes through to the value of numberOfBattlers, each time adding the value of sortedPositions[b] (the player number as per the original playerPrefabs array on game controller) to posList, as a string with a little extra formatting:

```
// now we have a populated sortedPositions hash table, let's
// iterate through it and build the string
for ( int b = 1; b <= numberOfBattlers; b++ )
{
        whichPos= (int)sortedPositions[b];
        posList=posList+b.ToString()+". PLAYER
        "+whichPos+"\n";
}

return posList;
}
```

GetPosition() will look at all of the players and compare scores to find the score board position of the player identified by the ID passed in as a parameter:

```
public int GetPosition ( int ofWhichID )
{
```

The function starts out with a few safety checks to make sure everything is set up correctly and that the ID passed in is a valid one:

```
// first, let's make sure that we are ready to go (the
// hashtables may not have been set up yet, so it's
// best to be safe and check this first)
```

```
if(battleControllers==null)
{
        Debug.Log ("GetPosition battleControllers is
        NULL!");
        return -1;
}

if(battleControllers.ContainsKey(ofWhichID)==false)
{
        Debug.Log ("GetPosition says no battle controller
        found for id "+ofWhichID);
        return -1;
}
```

Next, the code grabs a reference to the BattleController component attached to the player we want to find out about and keeps it in focusPlayerScript:

```
// first, we need to find the player that we're trying to
// calculate the position of
focusPlayerScript= (BattleController)
battleControllers[ofWhichID];
```

This code is very similar to the race position checking from the global race manager, except there is no waypoint, lap, or distance checking; instead, it is all based on frag numbers. The script begins with the assumption that the player is in last place, as the logic works backward in terms of calculating the score rank:

```
myPos = numberOfBattlers;
for ( int b = 1; b <= numberOfBattlers; b++ )
{
// assume that we are behind this player
isAhead = false;
```

Step 1 is to get a reference to the current battleController instance we need to talk to, which is stored in the variable tempRC:

```
// grab a temporary reference to the 'other' player
// we want to check against
tempRC = (BattleController) battleControllers [b];
```

A quick null check is made to make sure the game does not crash if a player were to get prematurely deleted during play or as the game ends:

```
// if player 2 happens to be null (deleted for
// example) here's a little safety to skip this
// iteration in the loop
if(tempRC==null)
        continue;
```

Comparing the player we want to look at with its own battleController would be pointless, so the script compares the IDs of each battleController before any sort of score checking takes place:

```
if ( focusPlayerScript.GetID() != tempRC.GetID() )
{
```

focusPlayerScript.howMany_fraggedOthers contains a count of how many other players this player has fragged.

There is code in this script for three different systems of a player moving up in rank. The first one only takes into account the number of frags. Whichever player has fragged the most others gets higher in the ranking. This is commented out in the example game, as it uses the second ranking system further on in the script:

```
// if ( focusPlayerScript.howMany_fraggedOthers >
// tempRC.howMany_fraggedOthers )
   // isAhead=true;
```

When both players have fragged the same amount, ranking will be based on ID. Higher ID will come first on the score board:

```
// we check here to see if the frag count is
// the same and if so we use the id to sort
// them instead
if ( focusPlayerScript.howMany_fraggedOthers
== tempRC.howMany_fraggedOthers &&
focusPlayerScript.GetID() > tempRC.GetID() )
         isAhead=true;
```

The third and final condition both takes the number of frags and subtracts it from the number of times this player has been fragged:

```
if ( ( focusPlayerScript.howMany_fraggedOthers - focusPlayerScript.
howmany_frags ) > ( tempRC.howMany_fraggedOthers -
focusPlayerScript.howmany_frags ) )
        isAhead=true;
```

If one of the conditions has set isAhead to true, the myPos variable is decremented, which moves the player up one in the rankings. The loop then either completes or goes through this process again:

```
             if ( isAhead )
   {
                  myPos--;
   }
         }
}

      return myPos;
}
```

The game controller will call StopBattle() when the game is over. StopBattle() sets battleRunning to false, then calls out UpdateBattleStates() to tell all of the battle controllers about the change:

```
public void StopBattle()
{
      // we don't want to keep calling everyone to tell them about
      // the battle being over if we've already done it once, so
      // check first battleRunning is true
      if(battleRunning==true)
      {
```

```
                        // set a flag to stop repeat calls etc.
                        battleRunning=false;

                        // tell everyone about the update to the state of
                        // battleRunning
                        UpdateBattleStates();
```

Next, PlayerFinishedBattle() is called for all of the battle controllers, telling them to shut down their battle:

```
                        // tell all players that we're done, by sending a
                        // message to each gameObject with a battle controller
                        // attached to it to call the PlayerFinishedBattle()
                        // function in the car control script
                        for ( int b = 1; b <= numberOfBattlers; b++ )
            {
                                tempRC = (BattleController) battleControllers
                                [b];
                                tempRC.gameObject.SendMessage("PlayerFinished
                                Battle",SendMessageOptions.DontRequireReceiver);
                        }
                }
        }
```

When the player script (CarController_TB.cs) detects a collision with a projectile, it calls GlobalBattleManager.Instance.RegisterFrag() to tell this script about the hit. When this script gets the call, it uses the BattleController for the ID passed in, to tell the other player (who sent the projectile) about the hit:

```
        public void RegisterFrag( int whichID )
        {
                focusPlayerScript= (BattleController)
                battleControllers[whichID];
                focusPlayerScript.FraggedOther();
        }
```

▌ 13.7 Players

The CarController_TB.cs script is attached to all tanks. It derives from BaseVehicle and bears more than a passing resemblance to the controller script from the example game *Metal Vehicle Doom* in Chapter 12. The full player script looks like this:

```
using UnityEngine;
using System.Collections;

public class CarController_TB : BaseVehicle
{
        public BaseWeaponController weaponControl; // note that we don't
                                                   // use the standard slot
                                                   // system here!

        public bool canFire;
        public bool isRespawning;
        public bool isAIControlled;
        public bool isInvulnerable;
```

```
public BaseAIController AIController;

public int startHealthAmount= 50;

public BasePlayerManager myPlayerManager;
public BaseUserManager myDataManager;

public float turnTorqueHelper= 90;
public float TurnTorqueHelperMaxSpeed= 30;

public float catchUpAccelMax= 8000;
public float originalAccelMax= 5000;
public float resetTime= 4;

public LayerMask respawnLayerMask;

private BaseArmedEnemy gunControl;
private BattleController battleControl;

private int racerID;
private int myBattlePosition;
private bool isGameRunning;
private float resetTimer;
private bool canRespawn;
private bool canPlayFireSound;
public float timeBetweenFireSounds= 0.25f;
private bool isFinished;

private Vector3 respawnPoint;
private Vector3 respawnRotation;

public Material treadMaterial;
public GameObject shieldMesh;
public float respawnInvunerabilityTime= 5;

public override void Start ()
{
        // we are overriding the Start function of BaseVehicle
        // because we do not want to initialize from here!
        // Game controller will call Init when it is ready

        myBody= rigidbody;
        myGO= gameObject;
        myTransform= transform;
}
public override void Init ()
{
        Debug.Log ("CarController_TB Init called.");

        // cache the usual suspects
        myBody= rigidbody;
        myGO= gameObject;
        myTransform= transform;

        // allow respawning from the start
        canRespawn=true;
```

```
// save our accelMax value for later use, in case we need to
// change it to do AI catch up
originalAccelMax= accelMax;

// add default keyboard input if we don't already have one
default_input= myGO.GetComponent<Keyboard_Input>();

if( default_input==null )
        default_input= myGO.AddComponent<Keyboard_Input>();

// cache a reference to the player controller
myPlayerController= myGO.GetComponent<BasePlayerManager>();

// call base class init
myPlayerController.Init();

// with this simple vehicle code, we set the center of mass
// low to try to keep the car from toppling over
myBody.centerOfMass= new Vector3(0,-6.5f,0);

// see if we can find an engine sound source, if we need to
if( engineSoundSource==null )
{
        engineSoundSource= myGO.GetComponent<AudioSource>();
}

AddBattleController();

// get a ref to the weapon controller
weaponControl= myGO.GetComponent<BaseWeaponController>();

// if a player manager is not set in the editor, let's try
// to find one
if(myPlayerManager==null)
        myPlayerManager=
        myGO.GetComponent<BasePlayerManager>();

// cache ref to data manager
myDataManager= myPlayerManager.DataManager;

// set default data
myDataManager.SetName("Player");
myDataManager.SetHealth(startHealthAmount);

if(isAIControlled)
{
        // set our name to an AI player
        myDataManager.SetName("AIPlayer");

        // set up AI
        InitAI();
}

isGameRunning= true;

// store respawn point
respawnPoint= myTransform.position;
respawnRotation= myTransform.eulerAngles;
```

```
                MakeVulnerable();

                // grab volume from sound controller for our engine sound
                audio.volume= BaseSoundController.Instance.volume;
        }

        void InitAI()
        {
                // cache a reference to the AI controller
                AIController= myGO.GetComponent<BaseAIController>();

                // check to see if we found an AI controller component, if
                // not we add one here
                if(AIController==null)
                        AIController= myGO.AddComponent<BaseAIController>();

                // initialize the AI controller
                AIController.Init();

                // tell the AI controller to go into waypoint steering mode
                AIController.SetAIState( AIStates.AIState.steer_to_waypoint );

                // disable our default input method
                default_input.enabled=false;

                // add an AI weapon controller
                gunControl= myGO.GetComponent<BaseArmedEnemy>();

                // if we don't already have a gun controller, let's add one to
                // stop things breaking but warn about it so that it may be fixed
                if( gunControl==null )
                {
                        gunControl= myGO.AddComponent<BaseArmedEnemy>();
                        Debug.LogWarning("WARNING! Trying to initialize car
                        without a BaseArmedEnemy component attached. Player
                        cannot fire!");
                }

                // tell gun controller to do 'look and destroy'
                gunControl.currentState=
                AIAttackStates.AIAttackState.look_and_destroy;
        }


        void AddBattleController()
        {
                if(myGO==null)
                        myGO=gameObject;

                // add a battle controller script to our object
                battleControl= myGO.AddComponent<BattleController>();

                // grab an ID from the battle control script, so we don't
                // have to look it up whenever we communicate with
                // the global battle controller
                racerID= battleControl.GetID();
```

```
        // we are going to use the same id for this player and
        // its weapons
        id=racerID;

        // tell weapon controller this id so we can add it to
        // projectiles. This way, when a projectile hits something
        // we can look up its id and trace it back to this player
        weaponControl.SetOwner(id);

        // set up a repeating invoke to update our position, rather
        // than calling it every single tick or update
        InvokeRepeating("UpdateBattlePosition",0, 0.5f);
}

public void UpdateBattlePosition()
{
        // grab our score board position from the global battle
        // manager
        myBattlePosition=
        GlobalBattleManager.Instance.GetPosition( racerID );
}
public override void UpdatePhysics ()
{
        if( canControl )
        base.UpdatePhysics();

        if( isFinished )
                myBody.velocity *= 0.99f;

        // if we are moving slow, apply some extra force to turn the
        // car quickly so we can do donuts (!) - note that since there
        // is no 'ground detect' it will apply it in the air, too (bad!)
        if( mySpeed < TurnTorqueHelperMaxSpeed )
        {
                myBody.AddTorque( new Vector3( 0, steer * myBody.
                mass * turnTorqueHelper * motor, 0 ) );
        }
}

private float timedif;

public override void LateUpdate()
{
        // get the state of the battle from the battle controller
        isGameRunning= battleControl.battleRunning;

        if( isGameRunning )
        {
                // check to see if we've crashed and are upside
                // down/wrong(!)
                Check_If_Car_Is_Flipped();

                // make sure that gunControl has been told it can fire
                if( isAIControlled )
                        gunControl.canControl=true;

                // we check for input in LateUpdate because Unity
                // recommends this
```

```
                        if( isAIControlled )
                        {
                                GetAIInput();
                        } else {
                                GetInput();
                        }
                } else {
                        if( isAIControlled )
                        {
                                // since the battle is not running, we'll
                                // tell the AI gunControl not to fire yet
                                gunControl.canControl=false;
                        }
                }

                // see if our car is supposed to be held in place
                CheckLock();

                // update the audio
                UpdateEngineAudio();

                // finally, update the tread scrolling texture
                if(treadMaterial!=null)
                        treadMaterial.SetTextureOffset ( "_MainTex", new
                        Vector2(0, treadMaterial.mainTextureOffset.y +
                        (mySpeed * -0.005f) ) );
        }

        public override void GetInput()
        {
                // calculate steering amount
                steer= Mathf.Clamp( default_input.GetHorizontal() , -1, 1 );

                // how much accelerator?
                motor= Mathf.Clamp( default_input.GetVertical() , 0, 1 );

                // how much brake?
                brake= -1 * Mathf.Clamp( default_input.GetVertical() , -1, 0
                );

                if( default_input.GetRespawn() && !isRespawning &&
                canRespawn)
                {
                        isRespawning=true;
                        Respawn();
                        canRespawn=false;
                        Invoke ("resetRespawn",2);
                }

                // fire if we need to
                if( default_input.GetFire() && canFire )
                {
                        // tell weapon controller to deal with firing
                        weaponControl.Fire();

                        if(canPlayFireSound)
                        {
                                canPlayFireSound=false;
```

```
                              Invoke ("ResetFireSoundDelay",
                              timeBetweenFireSounds);
                    }
            }
    }

    void ResetFireSoundDelay()
    {
            canPlayFireSound=true;
    }

    void resetRespawn()
    {
            canRespawn=true;
    }

    public void GetAIInput ()
    {
            // calculate steering amount
            steer= Mathf.Clamp( AIController.GetHorizontal(), -1, 1 );

            // how much accelerator?
    motor= Mathf.Clamp( AIController.GetVertical() , -1, 1 );
    }


public void SetAIInput (bool aiFlag)

{

    isAIControlled = aiFlag;

}


    private ProjectileController aProj;
    private GameObject tempGO;

    void OnCollisionEnter(Collision collider)
    {
            // when something collides with our ship, we check its layer
            // to see if it is a projectile (Note: remember when you add
            // projectiles, set the layers correctly!) by default, we're
            // using layer 17 for projectiles fired by enemies and layer
            // 9 for projectiles fired by the main player but all we
            // need to know here is that it *is* a projectile of any type

            if(!isRespawning && !isInvulnerable) // make sure no
                                                 // respawning or
                                                 // invulnerability is
                                                 // happening
            {
                    // temp ref to this collider's gameobject so that we
                    // don't need to keep looking it up
                    tempGO= collider.gameObject;

                    // do a quick layer check to make sure that these
                    // are in fact projectiles
```

```
                                if(tempGO.layer==17 || tempGO.layer==9)
                                {
                                        // grab a ref to the projectile's controller
                                        aProj= tempGO.GetComponent<ProjectileControl
                                        ler>();

                                        // quick check to make sure that this
                                        // projectile was not launched by this player
                                        if( aProj.ownerType_id != id )
                                        {
                                                // tell the hit function about this
                                                // collision, passing in the
                                                // gameobject so that we can
                                                // get to its projectile controller
                                                // script and find out more about
                                                // where it came from
                                                Hit();
                                                // tell our battle controller that we
                                                // got hit
                                                battleControl.Fragged();

                                                // tell the global battle controller
                                                // who fragged us
                                GlobalBattleManager.Instance.RegisterFrag
                                ( aProj.ownerType_id );
                                        }
                                }
                        }

                }

        public void OnTriggerEnter( Collider other )
        {

                // check to see if the trigger uses any of the layers where
                // we want to automatically respawn the player on impact
                int objLayerMask = (1 << other.gameObject.layer);

                if ((respawnLayerMask.value & objLayerMask) > 0)
                {
                        Respawn();
                }
        }

        void Hit()
        {
                // reduce lives by one
                myDataManager.ReduceHealth(1);

                if(myDataManager.GetHealth()<1) // <- destroyed
                {
                        isRespawning=true;

                        // blow up! (apply a force to affect everything in
                        // the vicinity and let's get the model spinning
                        // too, with angular velocity)
                        myBody.AddExplosionForce(myBody.mass * 2000f,
                        myBody.position, 100);
```

```
            myBody.angularVelocity=new Vector3( Random.Range
            (-100,100), Random.Range (-100,100), Random.Range
            (-100,100) );

            // tell game controller to do a nice big explosion
            GameController_TB.Instance.PlayerBigHit( myTransform
            );

            // respawn
            Invoke("Respawn",4f);

            // reset health to full
            myDataManager.SetHealth(startHealthAmount);

        } else {

            // tell game controller to do small scale hit if we
            // still have some health left
            GameController_TB.Instance.PlayerHit( myTransform );
        }
    }
    void Respawn()
    {
        // reset the 'we are respawning' variable
        isRespawning= false;

        // reset our velocities so that we don't reposition a
        // spinning vehicle
        myBody.velocity=Vector3.zero;
        myBody.angularVelocity=Vector3.zero;

        // get the waypoint to respawn at from the battle controller
        tempVEC= respawnPoint;

        // cast a ray down from the waypoint to try to find the ground
        RaycastHit hit;
        if(Physics.Raycast(tempVEC + (Vector3.up * 300),
        -Vector3.up, out hit)){
            tempVEC.y=hit.point.y+15;
        }

        // reposition the player at tempVEC (the waypoint position
        // with a corrected y value via raycast) and also we set
        // the player rotation to the waypoint's rotation so that we
        // are facing in the right direction after respawning
        myTransform.eulerAngles= respawnRotation;
        myTransform.position= tempVEC;

        // we need to be invulnerable for a little while
        MakeInvulnerable();

        Invoke ("MakeVulnerable", respawnInvunerabilityTime);

        // revert to the first weapon
        weaponControl.SetWeaponSlot(0);

        // show the current weapon (since it was hidden when the
        // ship explosion was shown)
```

```
                weaponControl.EnableCurrentWeapon();
        }

        void MakeInvulnerable()
        {
                isInvulnerable=true;
                shieldMesh.SetActive(true);
        }

        void MakeVulnerable()
        {
                isInvulnerable=false;
                shieldMesh.SetActive(false);
        }
        public void PlayerFinishedBattle()
        {
                Debug.Log ("PlayerFinished() called!");

                // disable this vehicle
                isAIControlled= false;
                canControl= false;
                canFire= false;
                // if we have an AI controller, let's take away its control
                // now that the battle is over
                if(AIController!=null)
                        AIController.canControl= false;
                motor= 0;
                steer= 0;
                isFinished=true;
        }

        void Check_If_Car_Is_Flipped()
        {
                if((myTransform.localEulerAngles.z > 80 &&
                myTransform.localEulerAngles.z < 280) ||
                (myTransform.localEulerAngles.x > 80 &&
                myTransform.localEulerAngles.x < 280)){
                        resetTimer += Time.deltaTime;
                } else {
                        resetTimer = 0;
                }

                if(resetTimer > resetTime)
                        Respawn();
        }
}
```

13.7.1 Script Breakdown

The CarController_TB.cs script is similar in format to the CarController_MVD.cs script from *Metal Vehicle Doom*. There are several main differences between the two scripts:

1. The way that respawning is dealt with.

2. This version has a battle controller not a race controller.

3. WeaponControl for this script is a BaseWeapon class type, rather than the slot weapon system. This decision was made so that *Metal Vehicle Doom* is open to receive switchable weapons in a slot system, whereas this game only requires a single turret with no switching.

4. There is no waypoint or wrong-way direction checking.

5. When the player is respawned, it uses the position and rotation of its original start point.

6. A shield mesh is displayed, a sphere that wraps around the player, when it is invulnerable.

Besides the differences highlighted at the start of this section, it is extremely similar to the car controller script from Chapter 12.

Note that the steering for this game is dealt with by the BaseAIController script's TurnTowardTarget() function to patrol and find targets. It does not use any horizontal inputs. As it uses the TurnTowardTarget() function to turn, the turning speed of the tanks is set by the value of the variable modelRotateSpeed on the AIController.

■ 13.8 AI Chasing with SetAIChaseTargetBasedOnTag.cs

The AI system is programmed to patrol and then chase a specific target object around. The tanks in this game require this behavior to be more dynamic, with some kind of target-finding system that can pick out targets for itself. The script SetAIChaseTargetBasedOnTag acts as a component to be added to an AI object, which will use Unity's tag system to find all objects of a specified tag to check their distance and pick the nearest one as a target for the AIController component to use.

The script:

```
using UnityEngine;
using System.Collections;
using AIStates;

public class SetAIChaseTargetBasedOnTag : MonoBehavior
{
        public BaseAIController AIControlComponent;
        public string defaultTagFilter= "enemy";
        public bool checkForWalls;
        public LayerMask raycastWallLayerMask;
        public float chaseDistance;
        private GameObject myGO;
        private Transform myTransform;
        private GameObject tempGO;
        private RaycastHit hit;
        private Vector3 tempDirVec;
        private bool foundTarget;
        public float visionHeightOffset= 1f;
        void Start ()
        {
                // first, let's try to get the AI control script
                // automatically
```

```
                    AIControlComponent= GetComponent<BaseAIController>();

                    myGO= gameObject;
                    myTransform= transform;

                    // quick null check, to warn us if something goes wrong
                    if( AIControlComponent == null )
                    {
                            Debug.LogWarning("SetAIChaseTargetBasedOnTag cannot
                            find BaseAIController");
                    }
                    InvokeRepeating( "LookForChaseTarget", 1.5f, 1.5f );
            }

            void LookForChaseTarget ()
            {
                    // null check
                    if( AIControlComponent == null )
                            return;

                    GameObject[] gos = GameObject.FindGameObjectsWithTag
                    ( defaultTagFilter );

                // Iterate through them
                foreach ( GameObject go in gos )
                {
                            if( go!= myGO ) // make sure we're not comparing
                                            // ourselves to ourselves
                            {
                                    float aDist =
                                    Vector3.Distance( myGO.transform.position,
                                    go.transform.position );
                                    if(checkForWalls)
                                    {
                                            // wall check required
                                            if( CanSee( go.transform )==true )
                                            {
                                    AIControlComponent.SetChaseTarget( go.transform );
                                                    foundTarget= true;
                                            }
                                    } else {
                                            // no wall check required! go ahead
                                            // and find something to chase!
                                            if( aDist< chaseDistance )
                                            {
                                                    // tell our AI controller to
                                                    // chase this target
                                    AIControlComponent.SetChaseTarget( go.transform );
                                                    foundTarget= true;
                                            }
                                    }
                            }
                }

                    if( foundTarget==false )
```

```
        {
                // clear target
                AIControlComponent.SetChaseTarget( null );

                // change AI state
                AIControlComponent.SetAIState( AIState.moving_looking_
                for_target );
        }
    }

    public bool CanSee( Transform aTarget )
    {
            // first, let's get a vector to use for raycasting by
            // subtracting the target position from our AI position
            tempDirVec= Vector3.Normalize( aTarget.position -
            myTransform.position );

            // let's have a debug line to check the distance between the
            // two manually, in case you run into trouble!
            Debug.DrawLine( myTransform.position, aTarget.position );

            // cast a ray from our AI, out toward the target passed in
            // (use the tempDirVec magnitude as the distance to cast)
            if( Physics.Raycast( myTransform.position +
            ( visionHeightOffset * myTransform.up ), tempDirVec, out hit,
            chaseDistance ))
            {
                    // check to see if we hit the target
                    if( hit.transform.gameObject == aTarget.gameObject )
                    {
                            return true;
                    }
            }

            // nothing found, so return false
            return false;
    }
}
```

13.8.1 Script Breakdown

This script will utilize some of the functionality provided by MonoBehavior, which is where it derives from:

```
using UnityEngine;
using System.Collections;
```

The AIStates namespace is used by this script to make accessing the AIStates enumeration list easier:

```
using AIStates;

public class SetAIChaseTargetBasedOnTag : MonoBehavior
{
```

Start() begins by getting a reference to the AI controller component. It does this with Unity's GetComponent() function, employed here as a keyword, meaning that it will look for the component on the gameObject this script is attached to:

```
void Start ()
{
        // first, let's try to get the AI control script
        // automatically
        AIControlComponent= GetComponent<BaseAIController>();
```

Next, the regular gameObject and transform references are cached, and a quick null check is made to make sure that we have an AI controller:

```
        myGO= gameObject;
        myTransform= transform;

        // quick null check, to warn us if something goes wrong
        if( AIControlComponent == null )
        {
                Debug.LogWarning("SetAIChaseTargetBasedOnTag cannot
                find BaseAIController");
        }
```

The main part of this script is within LookForChaseTarget(), but it is not something we need to do every step or frame of the game running. Instead, InvokeRepeating schedules a repeated call to it every 1.5 s:

```
        InvokeRepeating( "LookForChaseTarget", 1.5f, 1.5f );
}
```

This script will not work if it has not been able to find an AI controller script (BaseAIController.cs) attached to the same gameObject. LookForChaseTarget() does a quick null check to get started:

```
void LookForChaseTarget ()
{
        // null check
        if( AIControlComponent == null )
                return;
```

To find another chase target, references to all of the potential gameObjects need to be retrieved and put into an array. GameObject.FindGameObjectsWithTag() returns an array of all gameObjects in the scene whose tag matches the one passed in as a parameter. The defaultTagFilter variable is actually just a string containing the word "enemy," which corresponds to the tag with the same name set in the Unity editor:

```
        GameObject[] gos = GameObject.FindGameObjectsWithTag
        ( defaultTagFilter );
```

A foreach loop now steps through each gameObject in the array named gos, which holds all of the tagged objects returned by the call to FindGameObjectsWithTag():

```
// Iterate through them
foreach ( GameObject go in gos )
{
```

Of course, it makes no sense for this gameObject to ever chase itself, and to avoid this, there is a quick check to see whether go!=myGO:

```
if( go!= myGO )  // make sure we're not comparing
                 // ourselves to ourselves
{
```

To see whether this is a viable target, the process is a simple distance check with Vector3.Distance() between myGO's transform position (this player) and go's transform. position (the most recent gameObject picked up by the foreach loop):

```
float aDist =
Vector3.Distance( myGO.transform.position,
go.transform.position );
if(checkForWalls)
{
        // wall check required
        if( CanSee( go.transform )==true )
        {
                AIControlComponent.
                SetChaseTarget( go.transform );
                foundTarget= true;
        }
} else {
```

When no wall check is required, aDist is compared to chaseDistance to see whether the target set by the loop is close enough to be chased:

```
// no wall check required! go ahead
// and find something to chase!
if( aDist< chaseDistance )
{
```

The AI controller now needs to target the current gameObject from the foreach loop, which is passed to it via BaseAIController.SetChaseTarget():

```
// tell our AI controller to
// chase this target
AIControlComponent.
SetChaseTarget( go.transform );
```

We need to track whether or not a target has been found, so that if no suitable target turns up, we can adapt the AI behavior:

```
foundTarget= true;
                        }
                }
        }
}
```

Here, if the variable foundTarget is false, we know that no target was found by the previous distance checks. If a target has not been found, the current chase target needs to be cleared out and the AI controller state switched back to its moving_looking_for_target stage:

```
if( foundTarget==false )
{
        // clear target
        AIControlComponent.SetChaseTarget( null );
```

With the chase target set to null, we set the AIState to AIState.moving_looking_for_target to make sure that the AI will be moving even though the target has been set to null:

```
        // change AI state
        AIControlComponent.SetAIState( AIState.moving_looking_
        for_target );
}
}
```

CanSee() is almost the exact same code as the CanSee() function built into the BaseAIController.cs script. Take a look at the breakdown in Chapter 9 for a full description on how this function works:

```
public bool CanSee( Transform aTarget )
{
        // first, let's get a vector to use for raycasting by
        // subtracting the target position from our AI position
        tempDirVec= Vector3.Normalize( aTarget.position -
        myTransform.position );

        // let's have a debug line to check the distance between the
        // two manually, in case you run into trouble!
        Debug.DrawLine( myTransform.position, aTarget.position );

        // cast a ray from our AI, out toward the target passed in
        // (use the tempDirVec magnitude as the distance to cast)
        if( Physics.Raycast( myTransform.position +
        ( visionHeightOffset * myTransform.up ), tempDirVec, out hit,
        chaseDistance ))
        {
                // check to see if we hit the target
                if( hit.transform.gameObject == aTarget.gameObject )
                {
                        return true;
                }
        }

        // nothing found, so return false
        return false;
}
}
```

14 Dish: Making the Game *Interstellar Paranoids*

In 1978, a game came along from a company named Taito that would change the face of video gaming forever. Designer Tomohiro Nishikado said that his inspiration came from Atari's arcade game, *Breakout*, and his concept was so advanced that Nishikado, a solo developer, had to develop the necessary hardware himself. He named it *Space Monsters*, but a superior of his changed the name before it was released, to *Space Invaders*.

By the end of 1978, Taito had installed over 100,000 arcade machines and grossed over $600 million in Japan alone.* The game was soon a hit right across the world, and now, 35 years on, players still get to enjoy numerous remakes, clones, and arcade-style games that pay homage to it.

A year on, in 1979, a new video game named *Galaxian* was launched by Namco. It was designed by Kazunori Sawano; unlike Nishikado, Sawano had a small team to work with, and they were able to accomplish much more technically that would help them to build on the original *Space Invaders* concepts. This time around, the enemy sprites had bright colored graphics, animations, and a scrolling starfield. Audio was much improved now, too, with the addition of background music and a theme. *Galaxian* saw the alien invaders swooping down at the player, attacking much more aggressively than *Space Invaders*, making for a faster-paced, more visceral experience.

---

* "Can Asteroids Conquer Space Invaders?" *Electronic Games*, Winter 1981, 30–33 (http://www.digitpress. com/library/magazines/electronic_games/electronic_games_winter81.pdf).

The overall style of *Galaxian* should not be underestimated. Its look and feel became iconic throughout the 1980s and something that may have influenced the design style of other popular games around the time and for a while after.

Besides the advancement in technology, another feature of *Galaxian* was the addition of a two-player mode. Players could alternate, playing until a life was lost, to see who could get the highest score. Although not a feature unique to this game, introducing competitive play to *Galaxian* no doubt went a long way in helping its success in arcades across the world.

In 1980, Taito distributed another shooter in a similar style to *Galaxian*, called *Phoenix* and developed by a company named Amstar Electronics. Featuring color graphics and distinctive shooting sounds, the game's main enemies were birds that would swoop down at the player's spaceship. Most notably, *Phoenix* featured a limited implementation of power-up, as the projectile firing rate was varied based on the difficulty of the level. At the end of a level, the player had to battle a huge mothership—one of the earliest implementations of the end-of-level boss in video gaming.

In video gaming, the rules were just starting to be written; some of the most prominent features from today's games began to evolve. Somewhere between *Galaxian* in 1981 and *Xevious* in 1983, someone got the idea to take the scrolling starfield backdrops (sometimes plain black backdrops) and turn them into actual maps and game environments. A missing link may be the 1982 game *Zaxxon*, which was an isometric view shooter game featuring a rich, scrolling environment filled with both ground targets and flying targets such as missiles and alien ships.

Perhaps the next revolution in arcade gaming came in the form of *Xevious*, Atari's first vertical scrolling shooter launched in 1983 and published by Namco. Instead of simple starfield backdrops set in an abstract universe, *Xevious* brought with it a detailed view of the Earth's surface. Alien forces both in the air and, for the first time, on the ground act as enemies as the game world makes its way down the screen toward the player. Although not the first game to feature them, *Xevious* was certainly one of the most popular games to

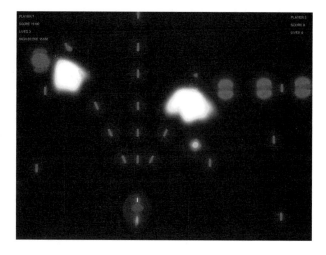

Figure 14.1 The example game *Interstellar Paranoids*.

14. Dish: Making the Game *Interstellar Paranoids*

feature early boss battles. At the end of levels, tougher, stronger enemies were required to be destroyed before advancing to the next stage.

The game *Interstellar Paranoids* (shown in Figure 14.1) pays homage to these classic games. It features a spaceship that moves left, right, up, and down around the screen, and it can fire to destroy enemies. The enemies swoop in from the top and left and right sides of the screen, flying around along paths as they shoot projectiles at the player. At the end of each stage will be a boss enemy that requires a lot more hits to take down.

The sound effects are old fashioned, arcade style, and there is a scrolling starfield in the background with explosions lighting up the screen as collisions happen. Its overall structure differs a little from other games in this book, as seen in Figure 14.2.

This game may be found in the example games project, its scenes in the Scenes/ Interstellar Paranoids folder named level_1, level_2, and menu_IP.

Its prefabs are located in the Prefabs/Games/Interstellar Paranoids folder.

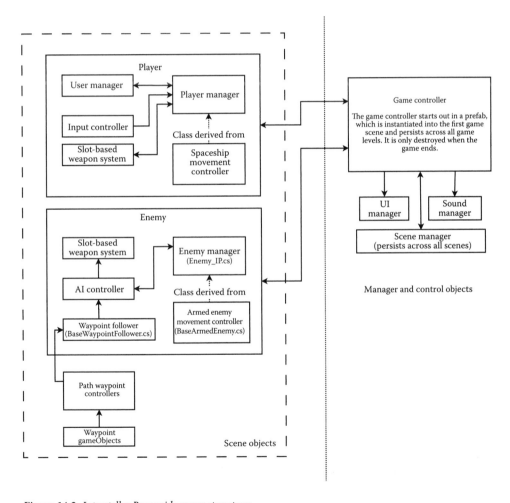

Figure 14.2 *Interstellar Paranoids* game structure.

▐▌ 14.1 Main Menu

Interstellar Paranoids has a main menu scene and two game levels. The main menu is contained in a single scene that uses the scene manager component (as discussed in Chapter 4, Section 4.10) to load the first game scene. From there, the scene manager is used to manage level count and level loading.

The main menu scene has a single camera named Main Camera. The main menu script is attached to it as a component, rendering the menu and dealing with its interaction. This is the same script that is used in all of the example games menu screens, but it is the only one that adds a two-player mode and displays an extra button on the menu to start it.

On the script component MainMenuController, when the string variable coopGameStartScene has something in it (entered in through the Unity editor Inspector window), an extra button is displayed on the menu with the label START CO-OP.

The MainMenuController.cs script is outlined in full in Chapter 10 of this book, but to add some context, here is the code that adds the extra button to the menu:

```
if(coopGameStartScene!="")
{
        if(GUI.Button(new Rect(0, 250, 300, 40 ),"START CO-OP"))
        {
                PlayerPrefs.SetInt( "totalPlayers", 2 );
                LoadLevel( coopGameStartScene );
        }
}
```

When the button is clicked, the totalPlayers prefs key is set to 2. The game will pick up on this and add the extra player when it is required to. The game is loaded in the same way as the single-player game, through the LoadLevel() function of the menu script.

▐▌ 14.2 Game Scenes

Each game level's environment and enemy objects are contained in single scenes, although some core game elements persist throughout the game such as the game controller, player, and camera. This means that the game only needs to run its main setup functions once to create the player and arrange the core elements. They persist until the game ends, when they are destroyed before the main menu scene reloads.

There are two levels in the example game, but they have the exact same Hierarchy structure in both scenes. The Hierarchy contains

- Directional light

- Level

    - Models that make up the environment—in this game, this is mostly instances of attack pattern prefabs (containing waypoints and spawners for enemies)

- LevelSetup

- ScrollStopper

- SoundController

The game controller for this game is created dynamically by the LevelSetup script component attached to the empty gameObject named LevelSetup. The actual script will be broken down later in this chapter, but the basic function of the script is to check to see whether a game controller exists in the scene and, if not, to instantiate one. It references two prefabs, one called GameController and one SceneManager.

By creating the game controller and scene manager objects dynamically, these objects can exist across different game levels. The level setup script first checks to see whether they exist, and if the game scene is a level other than the first one, the objects will not be duplicated accidentally.

When the game controller prefab is instantiated, its gameObject looks like this, in the Hierarchy window of the Unity editor:

- GameController
  - GameCamera
    - BulletDestroyer
    - BulletDestroyer
    - Player_Parent_Object
    - StarsLayer1
      - StarsLayer2
  - UI
    - GAMEOVER_GRAPHIC
    - GETREADY_GRAPHIC

It can be seen that the GameController prefab contains everything required for the game controller to function, create a player, and have a camera and UI available to use during the game. The prefab contains the minimum amount required to run the game, the most important elements. With the exception of the LevelSetup gameObject in each game scene, everything else in the level scenes is specific to the level.

14.3 Prefabs

The prefabs used for this game are

- ENEMIES
  - EnemyShip_1
  - EnemyShip_2
  - EnemyShip_3
  - Gameboss

- LEVEL CONTROL
  - GameController
- PLAYERS
  - PlayerShip_1
  - PlayerShip_2
- POWERUPS
  - Powerup
- PROJECTILES
  - Double_Projectile
  - Projectile_1
- SPAWNERS
  - AttackPattern_1
  - AttackPattern_2
  - AttackPattern_3
  - AttackPattern_4
  - AttackPattern_5
- WEAPONS
  - 3WayBlaster_Boss

14.3.1 Ingredients

The game uses these ingredients:

1. Game Controller—The game controller script for this game derives from BaseGameController.cs

2. Player:

   a. PlayerSpaceShip_IP

   b. Standard slot weapon controller

   c. Base player manager

   d. Keyboard input and mouse input

3. Enemies:

    a. BaseWaypointFollower

    b. BaseAIController

4. Scene Manager

5. User Interface—The user interface for in-game will derive from the BaseUIDataManager script from Chapter 4, which adds data management. The main menu uses the main menu system outlined in Chapter 10.

6. Sound Controller—The sound controller script from Chapter 8.

7. Music Controller

14.3.2 Game Controller

The GameController_IP script:

```
using UnityEngine;
using System.Collections;

public class GameController_IP : BaseGameController
{
        public string mainMenuSceneName = "menu_IP";
        public bool didInit;
        public Transform playerParent;
        public GameObject[] playerPrefabList;

        public GameObject powerUpPrefab;

        public float levelForwardSpeed =1f;
        public Transform CameraTransform;

        [System.NonSerialized]
        public GameObject playerGO1;
        public GameObject playerGO2;

        private Player_SpaceShip_IP playerScript1;
        private Player_SpaceShip_IP playerScript2;

        public BaseUserManager mainPlayerDataManager1;
        public BaseUserManager mainPlayerDataManager2;

        private int powerupExplosionCounter =0;
        public int numberOfExplosionsToMakePowerup =10;

        public UI_IP UIControl;
        public UI_GameOver gameOverUIScript;

        public BaseCameraController cameraControl;

        private int tempINT;
        private Vector3 tempVec3;
        private Quaternion tempQuat;
```

```
private bool isStopped;

[System.NonSerialized]
public static GameController_IP Instance;

public float gameSpeed=8;

public bool BossWinToNextLevel= true;

// there should always be one player
public int totalPlayers= 1;

public SceneManager;

public float CameraStartPositionZ= -11;

public GameController_IP()
{
        Instance=this;
}

public void Start()
{
        // we want to keep the game controller alive right through
        // the game, so we use DontDestroyOnLoad to keep it alive
        DontDestroyOnLoad (this.gameObject);
}

public void LevelLoadingComplete()
{
        Init();
        UIControl.Init();
}

public void Init()
{
        // tell the player that it can move, in 4 seconds
        Invoke ("StartPlayer",4);

        // in case we need to change the time scale, it gets set here
        Time.timeScale=gameSpeed;

        // we store the current game's number of players in a pref
        // so it may be set elsewhere (the main menu for example) and
        // carried into every level of the game.
        if(PlayerPrefs.HasKey( "totalPlayers" )) // does this pref exist?
        {
                totalPlayers= PlayerPrefs.GetInt( "totalPlayers" );
                // then use the value it holds
        } else {
                totalPlayers= 1; // default to single player
        }

        // find player parent transform
        playerParent=
        GameObject.Find("Player_Parent_Object").transform;

        Vector3[] playerStarts= new Vector3[totalPlayers];
        Quaternion[] playerRotations= new Quaternion[totalPlayers];
```

```
                  // this may be a little over-the-top, but hard coding it
                  // just wouldn't fit in with the overall theme of re-use
                  for(int i=0; i<totalPlayers; i++)
                  {
                          tempQuat= Quaternion.identity;

                          if(i==0)
                          {
                                  // place player 1 at the default start
                                  // position of -5,0,0
                                  tempVec3= new Vector3( -5, 0, 0 );
                          } else {
                                  // we'll make player 2 a start position 5
                                  // units to the right of the start position
                                  // of player 1
                                  tempVec3= new Vector3( -5 + (i*5), 0, 0 );
                          }
                          playerStarts[i]=tempVec3;
                          playerRotations[i]=tempQuat;
                  }

                  // if we haven't already got players set up, didInit will
                  // still be false... otherwise we skip creating the players
                  if(!didInit)

                          SpawnController.Instance.SetUpPlayers
                          ( playerPrefabList, playerStarts, playerRotations,
                          playerParent, totalPlayers );

                  // grab a ref to the player's gameobject for later use
                  playerGO1= SpawnController.Instance.GetPlayerGO( 0 );

                  // if we have a two-player game, let's grab that second
                  // player's gameobject too
                  if( totalPlayers>1 )
                          playerGO2= SpawnController.Instance.GetPlayerGO( 1 );

                  // find the game camera
                  CameraTransform = GameObject.Find("GameCamera").transform;

                  // position the camera at the specified start position
                  // (set in the Unity editor Inspector window on this
                  // component)
                  tempVec3 = CameraTransform.localPosition;
                  tempVec3.z = CameraStartPositionZ;
                  CameraTransform.localPosition = tempVec3;

                  // if we don't have a camera control script object set by
                  // the editor, try to find one
          cameraControl= CameraTransform.GetComponent<BaseCameraController>();

                  isStopped=false;

                  // make sure we have a scene manager to talk to
                  GetSceneManager ();

                  didInit=true;
          }
```

```
public void LateUpdate ()
{
        if(!isStopped)
        {
                // do fly movement through the level
                CameraTransform.Translate( Vector3.up *
                Time.deltaTime * levelForwardSpeed );
        }
}

public void StartPlayer ()
{
        Debug.Log ("StartPlayer!!!");
        // find the player's control script and hold it in
        // playerScript
        playerScript1= playerGO1.GetComponent<Player_SpaceShip_IP>();

        mainPlayerDataManager1=
        playerGO1.GetComponent<BasePlayerManager>().DataManager;

        // all ready to play, let's go!
        playerGO1.SendMessage( "GameStart" );

        // now, if there *is* a player 2, let's tell it to get going
        if(totalPlayers>1)
        {
                // find the player's control script and hold it in
                // playerScript
                playerScript2=
                playerGO2.GetComponent<Player_SpaceShip_IP>();

                mainPlayerDataManager2=
         playerGO2.GetComponent<BasePlayerManager>().DataManager;

                playerGO2.SendMessage( "GameStart" );
        }
}

public void StopMovingForward ()
{
        isStopped=true;
}

public void ContinueForward()
{
        isStopped=false;
}

public void BossDestroyed()
{
        ContinueForward();

        if( BossWinToNextLevel )
        {
                // go to next level
                Invoke("FinishedLevel", 3f);
        }
}
```

```
public void FinishedLevel ()
{
        // make sure we have a scene manager to talk to
        GetSceneManager ();

        // tell scene manager to load the next level
        if( sceneManager != null )
        {
                sceneManager.GoNextLevel();
        } else {
                Debug.LogError("SCENE MANAGER DOES NOT EXIST. CAN'T
                MOVE TO NEXT LEVEL!");
        }
}

void GetSceneManager ()
{
        // find level loader object
        GameObject sceneManagerGO = GameObject.Find ( "SceneManager" );

        // check to see if we managed to find a manager object
        // before trying to get at its script
        if( sceneManagerGO!=null )
                sceneManager=
                sceneManagerGO.GetComponent<SceneManager>();
}

public override void EnemyDestroyed ( Vector3 aPosition,
int pointsValue, int hitByID )
{
        // tell our sound controller to play an explosion sound
                BaseSoundController.Instance.PlaySoundByIndex( 1,
                aPosition );

                // play an explosion effect at the enemy position
                Explode ( aPosition );

                if(hitByID==1)
                {
                // tell main data manager to add score
                mainPlayerDataManager1.AddScore( pointsValue );

                // update the score on the UI

UpdateScoreP1( mainPlayerDataManager1.GetScore() );
        } else {
                // tell main data manager to add score
                mainPlayerDataManager2.AddScore( pointsValue );

                // update the score on the UI

UpdateScoreP2( mainPlayerDataManager2.GetScore() );
        }

        // count how many have been destroyed and if necessary spawn
        // a powerup here instead
        powerupExplosionCounter++;
if( powerupExplosionCounter>numberOfExplosionsToMakePowerup )
```

```
                {
        Instantiate( powerUpPrefab,aPosition,Quaternion.identity );
                powerupExplosionCounter=0;
                }
        }

        public void Explode ( Vector3 aPosition )
        {
                // instantiate an explosion at the position passed into this
                // function
                Instantiate( explosionPrefab,aPosition, Quaternion.identity );
        }

        public void PlayerHit(Transform whichPlayer)
        {
                // tell our sound controller to play an explosion sound
                BaseSoundController.Instance.PlaySoundByIndex( 2,
                whichPlayer.position );

                // call the explosion function!
                Explode( whichPlayer.position );
        }

        // UI update calls
        public void UpdateScoreP1( int aScore )
        {
                if( UIControl != null )
                        UIControl.UpdateScoreP1( aScore );
        }

        public void UpdateLivesP1( int aScore )
        {
                if( UIControl != null )
                        UIControl.UpdateLivesP1( aScore );
        }

        public void UpdateScoreP2( int aScore )
        {
                if( UIControl != null )
                        UIControl.UpdateScoreP2( aScore );
        }

        public void UpdateLivesP2( int aScore )
        {
                if( UIControl != null )
                        UIControl.UpdateLivesP2( aScore );
        }

        private void StopPlayers()
        {
                playerScript.GameFinished();
        }

        private bool player1Dead;
        private bool player2Dead;
```

```
        public void PlayerDied(int whichID)
        {
                if(whichID==1)
                        player1Dead=true;

                if(whichID==2)
                        player2Dead=true;

                if(player1Dead && player2Dead && totalPlayers>1)
                {
                        // both players are dead, so end the game
                        UIControl.ShowGameOver();
                        Invoke ("Exit",5);
                } else if(totalPlayers==1)
                {
                        // this is a single-player game, so just end the
                        // game now both players are dead, so end the game
                        UIControl.ShowGameOver();
                        Invoke ("Exit",5);
                }
        }

        void Exit()
        {
                SpawnController.Instance.Restart();
                Destroy( this.gameObject );

                // make sure we have a scene manager to talk to
                GetSceneManager ();

                sceneManager.LoadLevel( mainMenuSceneName );
        }
}
```

14.3.2.1 Script Breakdown

The GameController_IP script is based on BaseGameController:

```
using UnityEngine;
using System.Collections;

public class GameController_IP : BaseGameController
{
```

When GameController_IP is instantiated, the static variable Instance is populated with a reference to this script, so that it can be accessed from other scripts in the scene:

```
        public GameController_IP()
        {
                Instance=this;
        }
```

To keep the game controller alive between scenes, the Start() function makes a call to DontDestroyOnLoad():

```
public void Start()
{
        // we want to keep the game controller alive right through
        // the game, so we use DontDestroyOnLoad to keep it alive
        DontDestroyOnLoad (this.gameObject);
}
```

When a new scene is loaded, the LevelLoadingComplete() function gets called by an instance of the LevelSetup.cs script. The script here can then reinitialize itself and the user interface so that the game can continue in the new scene:

```
public void LevelLoadingComplete()
{
        Init();
        UIControl.Init();
}
```

The Init() function is composed in such a way as to be reusable and will be called at the start of each level:

```
public void Init()
{
```

The player starts out held in place. An Invoke call to StartPlayer schedules the player to be released 4 s after this function is called:

```
        // tell the player that it can move, in 4 seconds
        Invoke ("StartPlayer",4);
```

The Time.timeScale value can affect the whole feel of the game. Some shooters demand more enemies and slower movement, and some have faster movement and fewer enemies; the movement and update speeds of the game are determined by the type of game you are building (including artistic style, world type, and any other game elements that may affect the overall pace). The gameSpeed variable can be set to change time scale, and the code here changes the physics engine time setting to suit:

```
        // in case we need to change the time scale, it gets set here
        Time.timeScale=gameSpeed;
```

This game allows for one or two players. The main menu scene displays an extra button for cooperative play. By starting the game through this additional button, a preferences key is written called totalPlayers. The first main game scene is then loaded in the same way.

At this stage in the Init() function, the PlayerPrefs value is retrieved, stored in the integer type variable totalPlayers, and used to setup the game differently:

```
        // we store the current game's number of players in a pref so it
        // may be set elsewhere (the main menu for example) and
        // carried into every level of the game.
        if(PlayerPrefs.HasKey( "totalPlayers" )) // does this pref exist?
        {
                totalPlayers= PlayerPrefs.GetInt( "totalPlayers" );
                // then use the value it holds
        } else {
                        totalPlayers= 1; // default to single player
        }
```

Spawning works the same here as with the other games, although instead of using an array full of start positions, it only uses a single transform for the spawn position. Unity's GameObject.Find() function is used to look for a gameObject named Player_Parent_Object. Its transform information will be used on all game levels as the starting point for the players:

```
// find player parent transform
playerParent= GameObject.Find("Player_Parent_Object").transform;

Vector3[] playerStarts= new Vector3[totalPlayers];
Quaternion[] playerRotations= new Quaternion[totalPlayers];
```

As with the other example games, the SpawnController SetUpPlayers() function is used to instantiate players into the game. It requires an array of positions and an array of rotations, which are made here. This game only has a single start point and not an array of start points as other games might have, but it uses the same system purely for the sake of consistency throughout the book. Of course, if you are the reader who is going to take this game and add 50 players to it, then this is, no doubt, going to be useful to have:

```
for(int i=0; i<totalPlayers; i++)
{
        tempQuat= Quaternion.identity;

        if(i==0)
        {
                // place player 1 at the default start position of
                // -5,0,0
                tempVec3= new Vector3( -5, 0, 0 );
        } else {
                // we'll make player 2 a start position 5 units to
                // the right of the start position of player 1
                tempVec3= new Vector3( -5 + (i*5), 0, 0 );
        }
        playerStarts[i]=tempVec3;
        playerRotations[i]=tempQuat;
}
```

The players are only spawned when didInit is still false. In this game, the players persist throughout the whole game, so we need to make sure that players only spawn once to avoid chaos in the scene:

```
                // if we haven't already got players set up, didInit will
                // still be false... otherwise we skip creating the players
                if(!didInit)

SpawnController.Instance.SetUpPlayers( playerPrefabList,
playerStarts, playerRotations, playerParent, totalPlayers );
```

The reference held by the variable playerGO1 will be used later. SpawnController will return a gameObject from its GetPlayerGO() function based on the index passed in as a parameter to it:

```
                // grab a ref to the player's gameobject for later
                playerGO1= SpawnController.Instance.GetPlayerGO( 0 );
```

playerGO2 will hold a reference to the second player when a cooperative game is selected from the main menu and totalPlayers is greater than 1:

```
// if we have a two-player game, let's grab that second
// player's gameobject too
if( totalPlayers>1 )
        playerGO2= SpawnController.Instance.GetPlayerGO( 1 );
```

When a level begins, a game controller prefab is instantiated. Within the child objects of the game controller prefab are several objects central to the game, one of which is a camera named GameCamera. Until the game controller prefab is added to the scene, the in-game levels have no camera. As the Init() function runs on the game controller script, it grabs a reference to the camera here and repositions it at the correct point for starting the level. CameraTransform is used to hold the main reference:

```
// find the game camera
CameraTransform = GameObject.Find("GameCamera").transform;

// position the camera at the specified start position
// (set in the Unity editor Inspector window on this
// component)
tempVec3 = CameraTransform.localPosition;
tempVec3.z = CameraStartPositionZ;
CameraTransform.localPosition = tempVec3;
```

The variable cameraControl holds a reference to the camera controller script:

```
// if we don't have a camera control script object set by
// the editor, try to find one
cameraControl=
CameraTransform.GetComponent<BaseCameraController>();
```

As a top-down scrolling shoot 'em up game, the scrolling of the level is continuous until isStopped is true. The isStopped Boolean variable will be used to stop scrolling when the player reaches the boss battle:

```
isStopped=false;
```

To be able to change game scenes, this script needs to have a reference to the scene manager. It looks for the scene manager in the GetSceneManager() function:

```
// make sure we have a scene manager to talk to
GetSceneManager ();

didInit=true;
}
```

After all of the main updates are done, the camera is moved forward through the level a little more in LateUpdate(). During the game, there are several really important objects parented to the camera that will be moved along with it. These are

BulletDestroyer	A large invisible object with a box collider on. There are two of these objects, located just off camera, blocking the path across the width of the play area for projectiles. One is at the top of the play area, one at the bottom. When a projectile hits the collider, it is destroyed. This stops projectiles from firing off into infinity.

Player_Parent_Object	When the player is spawned by the game controller, it will be parented to this object. In turn, as this object is parented to the camera, the player will always move along with the camera.
StarsLayer1	Particle effects used to simulate stars in the background. This effect moves along with the camera, and the particles move down to look as though it is a constant movement through space.

If the Boolean variable isStopped is set to true, the camera will not be moved further through the level. This is used at the end of the level during the boss battle. The Translate function only requires a movement vector, which is multiplied by Time.deltaTime, in this case, to make sure that the movement is time based:

```
public void LateUpdate ()
{
        if(!isStopped)
        {
                // do fly movement through the level
                CameraTransform.Translate( Vector3.up *
                Time.deltaTime * levelForwardSpeed );
        }
}
```

StartPlayer() is scheduled by the Init() function to be called several seconds after the level first loads. Until this point, the player (or players) will be held in place. This function starts out by grabbing references to the Player_SpaceShip_IP component with Unity's GameObject.GetComponent(), followed by another GetComponent() call to find the DataManager component (the BasePlayerManager and DataManager scripts were discussed back in Chapter 3):

```
public void StartPlayer ()
{
        Debug.Log ("StartPlayer!!!");
        // find the player's control script and hold it in
        // playerScript
        playerScript1= playerGO1.GetComponent<Player_SpaceShip_IP>();

        mainPlayerDataManager1=
        playerGO1.GetComponent<BasePlayerManager>().DataManager;
```

Now that references have been stored for playerScript1 and mainPlayerDataManager1, a message is sent to the player's control script component to call its GameStart() function. GameObject.SendMessage() is used to send it:

```
        // all ready to play, let's go!
        playerGO1.SendMessage( "GameStart" );
```

If there is more than one player, the game controller is going to need to know how and where to talk to the second player. This part of the script grabs the same component references as it just did for the first player but this time for the second player and placed into variables suffixed with a 2 instead of a 1:

```
// now, if there *is* a player 2, let's tell it to get going
if(totalPlayers>1)
{
        // find the player's control script and hold it in
        // playerScript
        playerScript2=
        playerGO2.GetComponent<Player_SpaceShip_IP>();
        mainPlayerDataManager2=
playerGO2.GetComponent<BasePlayerManager>().DataManager;
```

Just as with the first player, a message is sent to the player's Player_SpaceShip_IP component to prepare the player by calling upon its GameStart() function:

```
        playerGO2.SendMessage( "GameStart" );
}
}
```

StopMovingForward() and ContinueForward() will be called from another script component when movement through the level is required to stop.

```
public void StopMovingForward ()
{
        isStopped=true;
}

public void ContinueForward()
{
        isStopped=false;
}
```

In this game, when the player reaches the boss at the end of the level, Stop MovingForward() is called, then ContinueForward() will be called once the boss has been defeated just before the next level loading is started by FinishedLevel() 3 s later:

```
public void BossDestroyed()
{
        ContinueForward();

        if( BossWinToNextLevel )
        {
                // go to next level
                Invoke("FinishedLevel", 3f);
        }
}
```

After the big boss battle at the end of the game levels, when the boss is defeated, FinishedLevel() is called upon to move on to the next level:

```
public void FinishedLevel ()
{
```

The SceneManager variable contains a reference to the SceneManager component that will be responsible for figuring out which level to load in next. First, GetSceneManager() is called to make sure we have a working reference to it:

```
// make sure we have a scene manager to talk to
GetSceneManager ();
```

As long as SceneManager exists (and is not null), the call to GoNextLevel() will have the scene manager load the next game scene and increment its current level counter:

```
// tell scene manager to load the next level
if( sceneManager != null )
{
        sceneManager.GoNextLevel();
} else {
        Debug.LogError("SCENE MANAGER DOES NOT EXIST. CAN'T
        MOVE TO NEXT LEVEL!");
}
}
```

To find the SceneManager.cs script component, the GetSceneManager() function first needs to find its gameObject. The gameObject has been named SceneManager in the Unity editor, so a call to GameObject.Find() should return it without any trouble:

```
void GetSceneManager ()
{
        // find level loader object
        GameObject sceneManagerGO =
        GameObject.Find ( "SceneManager" );
```

Assuming that the gameObject has been found and a reference stored in scene ManagerGO, which we do a quick null check on here, we can go ahead and grab another reference, this time to the SceneManager component itself. GameObject.GetComponent() finds the SceneManager:

```
        // check to see if we managed to find a manager object
        // before trying to get at its script
        if( sceneManagerGO!=null )
                sceneManager=
                sceneManagerGO.GetComponent<SceneManager>();
}
```

EnemyDestroyed() is an overridden version of the function, which can be found in the original base class (BaseGameController.cs). We need to add some extra functionality to it:

```
public override void EnemyDestroyed ( Vector3 aPosition,
int pointsValue, int hitByID )
{
```

When an enemy is destroyed, the scene would not be complete without a sound effect. BaseSoundController provides a nice explosion sound:

```
// tell our sound controller to play an explosion sound
BaseSoundController.Instance.PlaySoundByIndex( 1, aPosition );
```

Along with the audio, this exploded enemy needs a nice explosion particle effect. Rather than duplicate code whenever we need an explosion, the function Explode() provides exactly that:

```
// play an explosion effect at the enemy position
Explode ( aPosition );
```

The hitByID variable (integer) tells where the projectile came from. In this game, when there is more than one player, it is used to tell which player to award the score to.

If hitByID is 1, this is the main user. The score for this hit goes to mainPlayerDataManager1, player 1's data manager:

```
if(hitByID==1)
{
        // tell main data manager to add score
        mainPlayerDataManager1.AddScore( pointsValue );
```

The user interface code will display info for one player by default, or for two players when totalPlayers is more than 1. Here the UpdateScoreP1() function is passed player 1's score:

```
        // update the score on the UI
        UpdateScoreP1( mainPlayerDataManager1.GetScore() );
} else {
```

As there are only two potential players in this game, the check to see whether player 2 caused this hit does not check against a specific ID. If the ID of this hit is not 1 (as per the hitByID variable), we assume that this is the second player. The score will be added to the data manager of player 2, and the user interface update goes out to the UpdateScoreP2() function:

```
        // tell main data manager to add score
        mainPlayerDataManager2.AddScore( pointsValue );

        // update the score on the UI
        UpdateScoreP2( mainPlayerDataManager2.GetScore() );
}
```

The power-ups will appear after a certain number of hits by the player(s). In this line, a counter variable named powerupExplosionCounter, to track explosions, is incremented:

```
// count how many have been destroyed and if necessary spawn a
// powerup here instead
powerupExplosionCounter++;
```

When powerupExplosionCounter passes the value of the variable numberOfExplosionsToMakePowerup, a power-up is instantiated into the game scene. It is assumed that numberOfExplosionsToMakePowerup is set or modified in the Unity editor Inspector window. The Instantiate call uses a prefab referenced in the variable powerUpPrefab, and it is spawned wherever the enemy hit happened. powerupExplosionCounter is reset to 0 after the Instantiate call:

```
if( powerupExplosionCounter>numberOfExplosionsToMakePowerup )
```

14. Dish: Making the Game *Interstellar Paranoids*

```
        {
                Instantiate( powerUpPrefab,aPosition,Quaternion.identity );
                        powerupExplosionCounter=0;
        }
}
```

Explode() is a simple function to instantiate an explosion special effect as required. Its only parameter is a position for the explosion to happen at:

```
public void Explode ( Vector3 aPosition )
{
        // instantiate an explosion at the position passed into this
        // function
        Instantiate( explosionPrefab,aPosition, Quaternion.identity );
}
```

When a player is hit by a projectile, its Player_SpaceShip_IP script component has its LostLife() function called. It takes care of most of the logic behind the respawning and UI update, but the instantiation of an explosion effect is dealt with by this PlayerHit() function, which will also be called by the player controller script:

```
public void PlayerHit(Transform whichPlayer)
{
```

BaseSoundController is called to play an explosion sound effect:

```
        // tell our sound controller to play an explosion sound
        BaseSoundController.Instance.PlaySoundByIndex( 2,
        whichPlayer.position );
```

The Explode() function takes care of the particle effect:

```
        // call the explosion function!
        Explode( whichPlayer.position );
}
```

In contrast to the other example games in this book, *Interstellar Paranoids* has its own UI control script that uses Unity's OnGUI() system to render text to the screen. This script holds a reference to the UI script in the variable UIControl. Rather than affecting GUIText components directly, as the other example games do, the update calls to the UI simply pass on the details to UIControl:

```
// UI update calls
public void UpdateScoreP1( int aScore )
{
        if( UIControl != null )
                UIControl.UpdateScoreP1( aScore );
}

public void UpdateLivesP1( int aScore )
{
        if( UIControl != null )
                UIControl.UpdateLivesP1( aScore );
}

public void UpdateScoreP2( int aScore )
```

```
        {
                if( UIControl != null )
                        UIControl.UpdateScoreP2( aScore );
        }

        public void UpdateLivesP2( int aScore )
        {
                if( UIControl != null )
                        UIControl.UpdateLivesP2( aScore );

        }
```

Player_SpaceShip_IP.cs will deal with the player's health/lives management, but when a player runs out of lives, it calls the PlayerDied() function here so that the game controller can decide whether or not the game is actually over. If this is a single-player game, the game can end right after this function call, but if it is a two-player game, we need to make sure that both players have lost all their lives before ending the game completely:

```
        public void PlayerDied(int whichID)
        {
```

The ID of the player with no lives left is passed in as a parameter named whichID. This is used to set player1Dead or player2Dead to true, depending on the ID number:

```
        if(whichID==1)
                player1Dead=true;

        if(whichID==2)
                player2Dead=true;
```

This part of the code checks to see whether this is a two-player game and, if so, tells the UIControl script to show the game-over message. A call to Exit() is scheduled by an Invoke call 5 s later:

```
        if(player1Dead && player2Dead && totalPlayers>1)
        {
                // both players are dead, so end the game
                UIControl.ShowGameOver();
                Invoke ("Exit",5);
```

When totalPlayers is 1, this must be a single-player game, so there is only a need for one call to happen to this function for it to show the game-over message and end the game:

```
        } else if(totalPlayers==1)
        {
                // this is a single-player game, so just end the game now
                // both players are dead, so end the game
                UIControl.ShowGameOver();
                Invoke ("Exit",5);
        }
}
```

Once the PlayerDied() function has established that the game is over for all players, the Exit() function is called to shut things down and leave the game, loading the menu scene:

```
void Exit()
{
```

Any references held by the spawn controller are wiped out at the end of the game, with SpawnController.Restart(), and this game control script is destroyed:

```
SpawnController.Instance.Restart();
Destroy( this.gameObject );
```

SceneManager will be used to load the menu scene. GetSceneManager() makes sure that we have a reference to it, then a call to its LoadLevel() function passes the name of the menu scene to be loaded:

```
// make sure we have a scene manager to talk to
GetSceneManager ();

sceneManager.LoadLevel( mainMenuSceneName );
    }
}
```

14.3.3 Player Spaceship

BaseTopDownSpaceShip is a movement control class discussed in Chapter 5 of this book.

```
using UnityEngine;
using System.Collections;

public class Player_SpaceShip_IP : BaseTopDownSpaceShip
{
        private Standard_SlotWeaponController weaponControl;

        private bool isInvulnerable;
        private bool isRespawning;

        public bool isMouseControlled;
        private bool fire_input;

        // alternative control method
        private Mouse_Input mouse_input;

        public GameObject theMeshGO;
        public GameObject shieldMesh;

        public BasePlayerManager myPlayerManager;
        public BaseUserManager myDataManager;

        public bool godMode =true;
        public int ownerID =-1;

        public override void Start()
        {
```

```
        // we want to keep the player object alive right through the
        // game, so we use DontDestroyOnLoad to keep it alive
        DontDestroyOnLoad (this.transform);

        didInit=false;

        // tell our base class to initialize
        base.Init ();

        // now do our own init
        this.Init();
}

public override void Init ()
{
        // hide the invulnerability shield(!)
        if(!godMode)
        {
                MakeVulnerable();
        } else {
                MakeInvulnerable();
        }

        // get a ref to the weapon controller
        weaponControl=
        myGO.GetComponent<Standard_SlotWeaponController>();

        // tell weapon control who we are (so all weapon control can
        // tell projectiles who sent them)
        weaponControl.SetOwner(ownerID);

        // if a player manager is not set in the editor, let's try
        // to find one
        if(myPlayerManager==null)
                myPlayerManager=
                myGO.GetComponent<BasePlayerManager>();

        myDataManager= myPlayerManager.DataManager;
        myDataManager.SetName("Player");
        myDataManager.SetHealth(3);

        // update UI lives
        if(ownerID==1)
        {
                // if our owner ID is 1, we must be player 1
GameController_IP.Instance.UpdateLivesP1(myDataManager.GetHealth());
        } else {
                // we are player 2, so set that UI instead
GameController_IP.Instance.UpdateLivesP2(myDataManager.GetHealth());
        }

        if(isMouseControlled)
        {
                // if we are going to use mouse controls, add a
                // mouse input controller
```

```
                mouse_input= gameObject.AddComponent<Mouse_Input>();
        }

        didInit=true;
    }

    public override void Update ()
    {
        // don't do anything until Init() has been run
        if(!didInit)
            return;

        // do the update in our base
        UpdateShip ();

        // check to see if we're supposed to be controlling the
        // player before checking for firing
        if(!canControl)
            return;

        // fire if we need to
        if(fire_input)
        {
            // tell weapon controller to deal with firing
            weaponControl.Fire();
        }
    }

    public override void GetInput ()
    {
        if(isMouseControlled)
        {
            // we're overriding the default input function to
            // add in the ability to fire
            horizontal_input= mouse_input.GetHorizontal();
            vertical_input= mouse_input.GetVertical();

            // firing isn't in the default spaceship
            // (BaseTopDownSpaceShip.cs) behavior, so we
            // add it here
            fire_input= mouse_input.GetFire();
        } else {
            // we're overriding the default input function to
            // add in the ability to fire
            horizontal_input= default_input.GetHorizontal();
            vertical_input= default_input.GetVertical();

            // firing isn't in the default spaceship
            // (BaseTopDownSpaceShip.cs) behavior, so we
            // add it here
            fire_input= default_input.GetFire();
        }
    }

    void OnCollisionEnter(Collision collider)
    {
        if(collider.gameObject.layer==17 && !isRespawning &&
           !isInvulnerable)
```

```
                       {
                               LostLife();
                       }
               }

       void OnTriggerEnter(Collider other)
       {
               if( other.gameObject.layer==12 )
               {
                       // tell our sound controller to play a powerup sound
                       BaseSoundController.Instance.PlaySoundByIndex( 3,
                       myTransform.position );

                       // hit a powerup trigger
                       Destroy ( other.gameObject );

                       // advance to the next weapon
                       weaponControl.NextWeaponSlot( false );
               }
       }


       void LostLife()
       {
               isRespawning=true;

               // blow us up!
               GameController_IP.Instance.PlayerHit( myTransform );

               // reduce lives by one
               myDataManager.ReduceHealth(1);

               // update UI lives
               if( ownerID==1 )
               {
                       // as our ID is 1, we must be player 1

GameController_IP.Instance.UpdateLivesP1( myDataManager.GetHealth() );
               } else {
                       // as our ID is 2, we must be player 2

GameController_IP.Instance.UpdateLivesP2( myDataManager.GetHealth() );
               }

               if(myDataManager.GetHealth()<1) // <- game over
               {
                       // hide ship body
                       theMeshGO.SetActive(false);

                       // disable and hide weapon
                       weaponControl.DisableCurrentWeapon();

                       // do anything we need to do at game finished
                       PlayerFinished();
               } else {
                       // hide ship body
                       theMeshGO.SetActive(false);
```

```
                         // disable and hide weapon
                         weaponControl.DisableCurrentWeapon();

                         // respawn
                         Invoke("Respawn",2f);
             }
       }

       void Respawn()
       {
                  // reset the 'we are respawning' variable
                  isRespawning= false;

                  // we need to be invulnerable for a little while
                  MakeInvulnerable();

                  Invoke ("MakeVulnerable",3);
                  // show ship body again
                  theMeshGO.SetActive(true);

                  // revert to the first weapon
                  weaponControl.SetWeaponSlot(0);

                  // show the current weapon (since it was hidden when the
                  // ship explosion was shown)
                  weaponControl.EnableCurrentWeapon();
       }

       void MakeInvulnerable()
       {
                  isInvulnerable=true;
                  shieldMesh.SetActive(true);
       }

       void MakeVulnerable()
       {
                  isInvulnerable=false;
                  shieldMesh.SetActive(false);
       }

       public void PlayerFinished()
       {
                  // tell the player controller that we have finished
                  GameController_IP.Instance.PlayerDied( ownerID );
       }
}
```

14.3.3.1   Script Breakdown

Player_SpaceShip_IP derives from its movement controller, as do all of the player scripts:

```
using UnityEngine;
using System.Collections;

public class Player_SpaceShip_IP : BaseTopDownSpaceShip
{
```

The player spaceships persist across levels, keeping the same gameObjects and components from the start of the game right through to the end. In the Start() function, DontDestroyOnLoad tells Unity to keep this gameObject's transform alive throughout:

```
public override void Start()
{
        // we want to keep the player object alive right through the
        // game, so we use DontDestroyOnLoad to keep it alive
        DontDestroyOnLoad (this.transform);
```

There are some variables that need to be set up by the base class (BaseTopDownSpaceShip), and rather than duplicating the code in this derived class, we call base.Init() to run the original script's Init() function before calling Init() on this class:

```
didInit=false;

        // tell our base class to initialize
        base.Init ();

        // now do our own init
        this.Init();
}
```

The Boolean variable godMode is used to make the player invulnerable. The intention is that godMode will be set in the Unity editor Inspector window and only used during testing to get through a level easily. When Init() starts up, the first thing that happens is that the default state for vulnerability/invulnerability is set. The functions MakeVulnerable() and MakeInvulnerable() will deal, respectively, with showing or hiding a shield mesh around the player, as well as with setting the right variable to make it work:

```
public override void Init ()
{
        // hide the invulnerability shield(!)
        if(!godMode)
        {
                MakeVulnerable();
        } else {
                MakeInvulnerable();
        }
```

The weapon control system needs to know what this player's ID is, so that it can tell all of the projectiles it spawns which ID to carry with them (making the projectiles traceable back to either player 1 or player 2). The Standard_SlotWeaponController reference gets found and stored into the variable weaponControl, then its SetOwner() function is called to set the owner ID to the ID of the player:

```
// get a ref to the weapon controller
weaponControl= myGO.GetComponent<Standard_SlotWeaponController>();

// tell weapon control who we are (so all weapon control can tell
// projectiles who sent them)
weaponControl.SetOwner(ownerID);
```

14. Dish: Making the Game *Interstellar Paranoids*

The default values for the player manager's data manager are set up here:

```
// if a player manager is not set in the editor, let's try to find one
if(myPlayerManager==null)
        myPlayerManager= myGO.GetComponent<BasePlayerManager>();

        myDataManager= myPlayerManager.DataManager;
        myDataManager.SetName("Player");
        myDataManager.SetHealth(3);
```

The health system of the data manager is used, but instead of health points, it is used as a store for the number of lives. ownerID is used again here to tell the game controller which part of the UI (either player 1 or player 2) to update with this player's default number of lives:

```
// update UI lives
if(ownerID==1)
{
        // if our owner ID is 1, we must be player 1
GameController_IP.Instance.UpdateLivesP1(myDataManager.GetHealth());
} else {
        // we are player 2, so set that UI instead
GameController_IP.Instance.UpdateLivesP2(myDataManager.GetHealth());
}
```

Setting the isMouseControlled variable to true will add a new script component from the script Mouse_Input.cs to be used as input for this player:

```
if(isMouseControlled)
{
        // if we are going to use mouse controls, add a mouse input
        // controller
        mouse_input= gameObject.AddComponent<Mouse_Input>();
}
```

With Init() all done, the didInit Boolean variable is set to true. Other functions will refer to this to check that the player has been set up successfully before trying to manipulate it in ways that might otherwise cause errors or problems:

```
        didInit=true;
}
```

The Update() function is used for all of the main player updates. It overrides the Update() function from the base class (BaseTopDownSpaceShip.cs):

```
public override void Update ()
{
```

Before doing anything to the player, such as updating its position or talking to the weapon controller, the Init() function needs to have been called and completed. If it has, didInit will be true. If not, didInit will be false, and this part of the code will drop out of the function before anything untoward happens:

```
// don't do anything until Init() has been run
if(!didInit)
        return;
```

The base class provides a function called UpdateShip(). It deals with moving the ship around, so all we need to do for the spaceship to behave as expected is to call UpdateShip() and the BaseTopDownSpaceShip class will do the rest:

```
// do the update in our base
UpdateShip ();
```

When canControl is false, the function will drop out before it gets to check the input from the fire button:

```
// check to see if we're supposed to be controlling the
// player before checking for firing
if(!canControl)
        return;
```

fire_input is a Boolean set by the GetInput() function. When the fire button is down, fire_input will be true, and the call is made to weaponControl.Fire() to launch a projectile:

```
// fire if we need to
if(fire_input)
{
        // tell weapon controller to deal with firing
        weaponControl.Fire();
}
}
```

To keep the script flexible, the GetInput() function talks to the input controller. If we were to use a different input system, the GetInput() function in the base class may be overridden to include whatever is needed. That is exactly what happens here, as the GetInput() function is overridden:

```
public override void GetInput ()
{
```

Mouse input is used for the second player during a two-player cooperative game. The default system is either a game controller or the keyboard (as used by the Keyboard_Input.cs script), but when isMouseControlled is true, it will use mouse_input object for input, instead. The variables:

```
if(isMouseControlled)
{
        // we're overriding the default input function to add in the
        // ability to fire
        horizontal_input= mouse_input.GetHorizontal();
        vertical_input= mouse_input.GetVertical();
```

```
        // firing isn't in the default spaceship
        // (BaseTopDownSpaceShip.cs) behavior, so we add it here
        fire_input= mouse_input.GetFire();
    } else {
        // we're overriding the default input function to add in the
        // ability to fire
        horizontal_input= default_input.GetHorizontal();
        vertical_input= default_input.GetVertical();
```

The BaseTopDownSpaceShip controller script only includes code to move the spaceship around and not to fire, so we need to add some code here to detect the fire button from the default_input input controller and to set the variable fire_input:

```
                    fire_input= default_input.GetFire();
        }
    }
```

The enemy projectiles are on layer 17—named enemy_projectile—which is set by the enemy weapon's mounting point. Whichever layer the mounting point is set at will be used for its projectiles. Here OnCollisionEnter() looks for collisions between the player and the enemy projectiles to see whether or not the player should lose a life:

```
    void OnCollisionEnter(Collision collider)
    {
```

The collider belonging to the other object involved in a collision is passed in by the engine, as a parameter, to this function. The collider's gameObject layer is checked to see whether it matches the enemy projectile layer 17. If the player is not respawning and is not set to be invulnerable, we can go ahead and call the LostLife() function:

```
    if(collider.gameObject.layer==17 && !isRespawning &&
    !isInvulnerable)
        {
                LostLife();
        }
    }
```

Power-ups, which upgrade the weapon, are gameObjects with box colliders on that are set to be triggers (the IsTrigger property of the collider set to true via the Unity editor Inspector window). When the player hits the trigger, a sound is played and the power-up is destroyed. To upgrade the weapon, the weapon controller is told to advance on to the next weapon slot.

What this means is that the weapon system should be set up so that the lowest-powered weapon is in the first slot and, progressively, more powerful weapons set in each slot up from there. Adding and setting up weapons are simply a case of using the Unity editor Inspector window (with the player gameObject selected) and dragging in the pre-fabs for each weapon into the Weapons array of the Standard_Slot Weapon Controller component (see Figure 14.3).

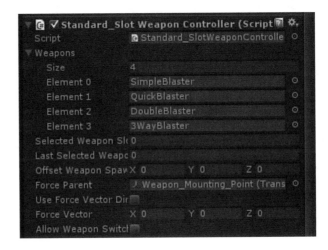

Figure 14.3 The Standard_Slot Weapon Controller weapons slots with prefabs setup.

weaponControl.NextWeaponSlot() tells the weapon controller to move on to the next slot:

```
void OnTriggerEnter(Collider other)
{
        if( other.gameObject.layer==12 )
        {
                // tell our sound controller to play a powerup sound
                BaseSoundController.Instance.PlaySoundByIndex( 3,
                myTransform.position );

                // hit a powerup trigger
                Destroy ( other.gameObject );

                // advance to the next weapon
                weaponControl.NextWeaponSlot( false );
        }
}
```

LostLife() is called when the player is hit by an enemy projectile:

```
void LostLife()
{
```

The respawning process takes a little time, so isRespawning is a Boolean set to ensure that it does not try to respawn more than once at the same time:

```
isRespawning=true;
```

The game controller's PlayerHit() function will make a nice explosion effect at the position of the transform passed into it:

```
// blow us up!
GameController_IP.Instance.PlayerHit( myTransform );
```

This player's data manager tracks health levels. myDataManager.ReduceHealth() takes a single integer parameter of how much health should be reduced. In this game, the health level is treated as lives, so it is called to take away one life here:

```
// reduce lives by one
myDataManager.ReduceHealth(1);
```

The game controller is called on to update the UI, either UpdateLivesP1() or UpdateLivesP2(), depending on the ownerID for this player:

```
// update UI lives
if( ownerID==1 )
{
    // as our ID is 1, we must be player 1

GameController_IP.Instance.UpdateLivesP1( myDataManager.GetHealth() );
} else {
    // as our ID is 2, we must be player 2
GameController_IP.Instance.UpdateLivesP2( myDataManager.GetHealth() );
}
```

When this player's health level is less than 1, it is game over for this player:

```
if(myDataManager.GetHealth()<1) // <- game over
{
```

The player spaceship model is hidden by GameObject.SetActive():

```
// hide ship body
theMeshGO.SetActive(false);
```

The weapon needs to be disabled when the player is not active, which is the job of the DisableCurrentWeapon() function on the weapon controller script (a reference to Standard_SlotWeapon_Controller held in the variable weaponControl):

```
// disable and hide weapon
weaponControl.DisableCurrentWeapon();
```

The PlayerFinished() function is called now to close down this player:

```
        // do anything we need to do at game finished
        PlayerFinished();
} else {
```

Reaching the else of this condition means that the player just needs to be respawned and that it has more than 1 life remaining. The player model is hidden with GameObject. SetActive():

```
// hide ship body
theMeshGO.SetActive(false);
```

The weapon is disabled (it will be re-enabled when the player is respawned):

```
// disable and hide weapon
weaponControl.DisableCurrentWeapon();
```

Finally, a call to the Respawn() function of this class is scheduled to happen 2 s from now via Unity's Invoke() function:

```
        // respawn
        Invoke("Respawn",2f);
    }
}
```

After the player has been destroyed by an enemy projectile, it is hidden from view and its collisions ignored. The Respawn() function resets the player state back to operational:

```
    void Respawn()
    {
```

By the end of this function call, the player will have respawned, which means isRespawning is now to be set to false:

```
        // reset the 'we are respawning' variable
        isRespawning= false;
```

To prevent respawning the player into a dangerous place on screen (such as right into the path of a projectile) and causing instant death upon respawn, the player is made invulnerable for a few seconds:

```
        // we need to be invulnerable for a little while
        MakeInvulnerable();
```

The player regains its susceptibility to explode upon projectile impact in 3 s time, which is done with an Invoke call to MakeVulnerable():

```
        Invoke ("MakeVulnerable",3);
```

The player's spaceship model is set active, effectively displaying it again, here:

```
        // show ship body again
        theMeshGO.SetActive(true);
```

Any power-ups are lost on respawn by setting the weapon slot back to the beginning. If you wanted to keep power-ups even after a life is lost, you could comment this line out or perhaps replace it with weaponControl.PrevWeaponSlot() to downgrade the weapon to the previous slot rather than reset it all the way back to the beginning:

```
        // revert to the first weapon
        weaponControl.SetWeaponSlot(0);
```

The EnableCurrentWeapon() function on weaponControl will make sure that the weapon is displayed correctly after it is re-enabled:

```
        // show the current weapon (since it was hidden when the ship
        // explosion was shown)
        weaponControl.EnableCurrentWeapon();
    }
```

MakeInvulnerable() and MakeVulnerable() set the isInvulnerable Boolean variable accordingly and show or hide the shield mesh referenced in shieldMesh, using GameObject.SetActive:

```
void MakeInvulnerable()
{
        isInvulnerable=true;
        shieldMesh.SetActive(true);
}

void MakeVulnerable()
{
        isInvulnerable=false;
        shieldMesh.SetActive(false);
}
```

The only thing left to do when this player has run out of lives (health) is to tell the game controller script about it. That way, the game controller can decide whether or not to end the game completely:

```
public void PlayerFinished()
{
        // tell the player controller that we have finished
        GameController_IP.Instance.PlayerDied( ownerID );
}
}
```

14.3.4 Enemies

The Enemy_IP.cs script:

```
using UnityEngine;
using System.Collections;

public class Enemy_IP : BaseArmedEnemy
{
        private bool isRespawning;

        // here we add collision and respawning to the base armed enemy
        // behavior

        public void OnCollisionEnter(Collision collider)
        {
                // when something collides with us, we check its layer to
                // see if it is on 9 which is our projectiles
                // (Note: remember when you add projectiles, set the layer
                // of the weapon parent correctly!)
                if( collider.gameObject.layer==9 && !isRespawning )
                {
                        myDataManager.ReduceHealth(1);

                        if( myDataManager.GetHealth()==0 )
                        {
                        tempINT= int.Parse( collider.gameObject.name );

                        // tell game controller to make an explosion at our
                        // position and to award the player points for
                        // hitting us
```

```
                             TellGCEnemyDestroyed();

                    // if this is a boss enemy, tell the game controller
                    // when we get destroyed so it can end the level
                    if( isBoss )
                             TellGCBossDestroyed();

                    // destroy this
                    Destroy(gameObject);
            }
        }
    }
    // game controller specifics (which will be overridden for
    // different game controller scripts)
    // ------------------------------------------------------------

    public virtual void TellGCEnemyDestroyed()
    {

    GameController_IP.Instance.EnemyDestroyed( myTransform.position,
    pointsValue, tempINT );
    }

    public virtual void TellGCBossDestroyed()
    {
            GameController_IP.Instance.BossDestroyed();
    }

    // ------------------------------------------------------------

}
```

14.3.4.1 Script Breakdown

The enemy behavior is based on path following provided by the BaseAIController.cs script. It derives from the BaseArmedEnemy class, discussed in Chapter 9:

```
public class Enemy_IP : BaseArmedEnemy
{
```

The BaseArmedEnemy class adds a data manager and support for the weapon system to our enemy script, but it does not deal with anything more than that. This script starts out by adding collision checking and will deduct health from the data manager when hit:

```
        public void OnCollisionEnter(Collision collider)
        {
```

In this game, the player projectiles are set to use layer 9 (named player_projectile). When a collision occurs with this enemy, the colliding collider is passed in as a parameter and its layer compared. If it matches with the player projectile and this enemy is not respawning, a call to the data manager stored in myDataManager is made to reduce health by 1:

```
            if( collider.gameObject.layer==9 && !isRespawning )
            {
                    myDataManager.ReduceHealth(1);
```

When this enemy's health is at 0, it is time to explode:

```
if( myDataManager.GetHealth()==0 )
{
```

Now, as I write this, I can almost hear the collective mutter of hundreds of programmers tutting at how the ID is retrieved from the projectile. It is not the most efficient or the tidiest way of doing it, but it works. Each projectile is named by its owner ID, meaning that the quickest way to find out where the projectile came from is to get its name via collider. gameObject.name. In this line of code, the ID is retrieved from the name of the projectile hitting the enemy, converted into an integer by int.Parse() and stored in the variable tempINT for use later in the script.

Perhaps a cleaner method would have been to store a reference to the collider's gameObject and use gameObject.GetComponent to find its ProjectileController.cs script component. From there, we could have gotten the ID from ProjectileController; however, without doing some extensive tests, it is hard to say which method would end up more or less efficient. In this code, the gameObject's name is converted to an integer, and I would expect the difference in CPU hit to be negligible between converting the string to an integer and having to look up the ProjectileController component with GetComponent():

```
tempINT= int.Parse( collider.gameObject.name );
```

The way that this script tells the game controller about the destruction of this enemy may seem a little odd, as it is contained in another function named TellGCEnemyDestroyed(). By splitting it out into its own function, any script that were to derive from this one could easily override the TellGCEnemyDestroyed() function to easily swap out the game controller for one of another type or name:

```
// tell game controller to make an explosion at our position
// and to award the player points for hitting us
TellGCEnemyDestroyed();
```

Boss enemy types will use this script, too, so we have the Boolean variable isBoss to tell whether or not this is a regular enemy or an end-of-level boss. If it is a boss, TellGCBossDestroyed() is called, which tells the game controller about the hit so that it can act differently to this enemy's destruction. In this game, the game controller will start to end the level when the boss has been destroyed, and this function is called:

```
// if this is a boss enemy, tell the game controller when we
// get destroyed so it can end the level
if( isBoss )
        TellGCBossDestroyed();
```

Regardless of the type of enemy, it was a hit, and its health is at 0, so it needs destroying. The Destroy command removes this enemy's gameObject from memory:

```
                // destroy this
                Destroy(gameObject);
        }
    }
}
```

As mentioned early in this section, the TellGCEnemyDestroyed() function (and also the TellGCBossDestroyed() function) is designed to be overridden if a new type of game controller is used. These functions call EnemyDestroyed() or BossDestroyed() on it.

GameController_IP.EnemyDestroyed() takes three parameters: the position of the enemy destroyed, how much score the player should be awarded for blasting it, and, finally, the owner ID of the projectile so that the player may be identified. Without the ID, the game controller would not know which player to award the score to:

```
public virtual void TellGCEnemyDestroyed()
{

GameController_IP.Instance.EnemyDestroyed( myTransform.position,
pointsValue, tempINT );
}

public virtual void TellGCBossDestroyed()
{
        GameController_IP.Instance.BossDestroyed();
}
```

14.3.5 Waypoint Follower

Enemy spaceships move along waypoint paths as they fire at the player at the bottom of the screen. The BaseArmedEnemy script controls weapon firing, and the AI controller deals with path following (through its translate_along_waypoint_path state). For the AI controller to do this, it needs to know which waypoint controller to use and needs to have its AIState set (its default state is to patrol, not follow, waypoints) and the BaseWaypointFollower.cs script serves this purpose.

The BaseWaypointFollower.cs script:

```
// uses the translate_along_waypoint_path function of the AIController to
// follow along a path

public class BaseWaypointFollower : ExtendedCustomMonoBehavior
{
        public BaseAIController AIController;

        public virtual void Start ()
        {
                if(!didInit)
                        Init ();
        }

        public virtual void Init ()
        {
                // cache our transform
                myTransform= transform;

                // cache our gameObject
                myGO= gameObject;

                // cache a reference to the AI controller
                AIController= myGO.GetComponent<BaseAIController>();
```

```
                    if(AIController==null)
                            AIController= myGO.AddComponent<BaseAIController>();

                    // run the Init function from our base class
                    // (BaseAIController.cs)
                    AIController.Init();

                    // tell AI controller that we want it to control this object
                    AIController.SetAIControl(true);

                    // tell our AI to follow waypoints
AIController.SetAIState( AIStates.AIState.translate_along_waypoint_path );

                    // set a flag to tell us that init has happened
                    didInit= true;
            }

        public virtual void SetWayController( Waypoints_Controller
        aWaypointControl )
        {
                    if(AIController==null)
                            Init ();

                    // pass this on to our waypoint controller, so that it can
                    // follow the waypoints
                    AIController.SetWayController(aWaypointControl);
            }
}
```

14.3.5.1 Script Breakdown

The BaseWaypointFollower class derives from ExtendedCustomMonoBehavior, which adds some extra functionality and common variables:

```
public class BaseWaypointFollower : ExtendedCustomMonoBehavior
{
```

As per most of the scripts in this book, Start() calls Init():

```
        public virtual void Start ()
        {
                    if(!didInit)
                            Init();
            }
```

Init() creates references to the transform and gameObjects, and the variable AIController is set (GameObject.GetComponent() looks for BaseAIController):

```
        public virtual void Init ()
        {
                    // cache our transform
                    myTransform= transform;

                    // cache our gameObject
                    myGO= gameObject;

                    // cache a reference to the AI controller
                    AIController= myGO.GetComponent<BaseAIController>();
```

In this game, as there are properties we need to set through the Unity editor Inspector window, there will always be a BaseAIController component attached to the enemy prefabs, but in the event that no BaseAIController component has been attached to this object, this script uses GameObject.AddComponent() to make a new one. This is mainly so that the script can be reused in other games:

```
if(AIController==null)
        AIController= myGO.AddComponent<BaseAIController>();
```

The AIController needs to be initialized:

```
// run the Init function from our base class
// (BaseAIController.cs)
AIController.Init();
```

AIController.SetAIControl() tells the AI controller that it can control this enemy. Its SetAIState() function is called next, setting the state to translate_along_waypoint_path (see Chapter 9 of this book for a full breakdown of AIStates and the BaseAIController.cs script):

```
// tell AI controller that we want it to control this object
AIController.SetAIControl(true);

// tell our AI to follow waypoints
AIController.SetAIState( AIStates.AIState.translate_along_waypoint_path );

// set a flag to tell us that init has happened
didInit= true;
}
```

SetWayController() will be called by the game controller to tell this script which Waypoints_Controller instance to use. Once this function has it, a call to AIController. SetWayController() passes on the reference:

```
public virtual void SetWayController( Waypoints_Controller
aWaypointControl )
{
        if(AIController==null)
                Init ();

        // pass this on to our waypoint controller, so that it can
        // follow the waypoints
        AIController.SetWayController(aWaypointControl);
}
}
```

Final Note

It's the end of the book, but I hope it's only the beginning of how you make use of what's in it. There is a lot of code here that, at the very least, should be a good starting point for just about any type of game. I encourage you to use the code, use the assets—make your games and tell your stories.

As you do, remember that this book presents just one way to do things. After over a decade of game making, I still see every new game as an adventure filled with new lessons to be learned and new problems to solve. Programmers constantly evolve; not just to keep up with the latest technologies, hardware or trends but to find better ways of doing things. Better ways for all the environmental variables such as the platform, input methods or tech limitations, and also better ways for the individual developer.

Engineering knowledge can take you to the road, but it's up to you to cross it and the path may not always be as you expect it to be. Find what works for you and try to enjoy the journey of making games.

Thank you for reading this book and for choosing to do something as wonderful and creative as making games. Let me know what you create, via Twitter @psychicparrot or drop by my website and send me a message when you're done. I look forward to playing your game.

All the best,
Jeff

Index